Matthew Henry Peacock

History of the Free Grammar School of Queen Elizabeth at Wakefield

Founded A.D. 1591...

Matthew Henry Peacock

History of the Free Grammar School of Queen Elizabeth at Wakefield
Founded A.D. 1591...

ISBN/EAN: 9783337276720

Printed in Europe, USA, Canada, Australia, Japan

Cover: Foto ©ninafisch / pixelio.de

More available books at **www.hansebooks.com**

History

of

The Free Grammar School

of

Queen Elizabeth at Wakefield.

FOUNDED A.D. 1591.

*Written in commemoration of the 300th Anniversary
of its Foundation*

by

Matthew Henry Peacock, M.A., B.Mus.,

Twenty-first Head Master.

Wakefield:
W. H. MILNES, THE RADCLIFFE PRINTING WORKS.
1892.

In · Alumnorum

Qui · Fuerunt · Honorem,

Qui · Sunt · Incitamentum,

Qui · Futuri · Sint · Augurium.

PREFACE.

THE following pages represent an attempt to give a plain and unadorned record of what may be considered to be of greatest interest and importance in the History of this School. They have been put together at spasmodic intervals, when a busy Schoolmaster, in these exacting years at the close of the bustling nineteenth century, has found a few available leisure hours after his School duties have been accomplished.

About six years ago my attention was drawn to the Kennett MSS. in the British Museum, where may be found much of the early history of the School, and a copy of its Statutes, all carefully transcribed from the books of the Governors by Bishop White Kennett during a visit to Wakefield in July, 1724.

From this foundation the superstructure has been raised, by the assistance of the Governors of the School, and the kind help of many friends and acquaintances, some of whom would have executed the work in a far more efficient manner, as they would have been able to draw from a much greater store of antiquarian knowledge, and have employed a much abler pen.

Foremost amongst these must be mentioned the Rev. J. H. Lupton, M.A., Sur-Master of S. Paul's School, and author of "Wakefield Worthies," without whose encouragement this book would hardly have been attempted, and upon whose aid I have always been able to count. I have also to acknowledge the stimulus given to all my efforts by Mr. J. W. Walker, F.S.A., the author of "The Cathedral Church of Wakefield," who has carefully read over the proof-sheets, and supplied me with many useful details. Mr. J. H. Wice, lately Spokesman of the Governors, has also put me and my readers under an obligation by undertaking a similar task of revision. The Principals of Clare and Emmanuel Colleges, Cambridge, have sent me much information; the Provost of Queen's College, Oxford, has done me a similar service: the Bursar of S. John's College, Cambridge, has generously allowed me to consult the College Registers, and to see proofs of a forthcoming work upon the subject: the Librarians of Clare and Corpus Christi Colleges, Cambridge, and of Exeter College, Oxford, have done their best to ensure correctness of detail, as far as they have been applied to: and Mr. H. M. Taylor, M.A., Fellow of Trinity College, Cambridge, has given me extracts from the College Books and other information.

The Vicar of Wakefield (Ven. Archdeacon Straton, M.A.), has accorded me the privilege of reading through the old Parish Registers: the Rev. S. Hailstone has allowed me to reproduce the Portrait of Archbishop Potter from "Portraits of Yorkshire Worthies," by the late E. Hailstone, Esq.: the late Canon Falloon, Rector of Ackworth, and Canon Kemp, Vicar of Birstal, have shown me their Parish Registers: and the Rev. Canon Prescott, of Carlisle, the Rev. J. H. Carter, of Manchester, the Rev. Dr. Hiley, of Tadcaster, the Rev. T. H. Shaw, of Everton, the Rev. H. Heap, Head Master of Rotherham School, Dr. John Sykes, F.S.A., of Doncaster, Mr. Wm. Fennell, of Wakefield, Mr. John Batty, of East Ardsley, Dr. Wright, of Wakefield, and my predecessors, Dr. Taylor, and Mr. Leighton, Head Master of Bristol Grammar School, have rendered me help in various ways: the assistance of others is acknowledged in the text.

In the last place, the Governors of the School have placed all their records at my disposal for consultation, and their Clerk, Mr. Wm. Walker, has given me all the information in his power.

I have constantly had before me the following well known works of local interest :— Banks' " Walks about Wakefield," Lupton's "Wakefield Worthies," Taylor's " Rectory Manor of Wakefield," and Walker's " Cathedral Church of Wakefield;" and I have so frequently referred to them that they are generally quoted by their authors' names alone. Two other works must be mentioned, as containing an almost inexhaustible store of interesting matter in connexion with School education, viz. :—Carlisle's " Endowed Grammar Schools," and the Report of the Schools Inquiry Commissioners in 1868.

Notwithstanding all these advantages which I have enjoyed, it is inevitable that many names of men, educated at this School, have never been mentioned at all; whilst others, whose names I have merely given, may deserve some fuller record of their career. I can only hope that the deficiency of my knowledge may be to some degree supplied by details sent to me by friends who may read the book, for I can assure every reader that anything known to them about Wakefield Grammar School, which has escaped my notice, will be heartily welcomed and treasured up for some future use.

MATTHEW H. PEACOCK.

SCHOOL HOUSE, WAKEFIELD,
December, 1891.

CONTENTS.

		PAGE
Chap. I.	The Foundation and Charter	1
II.	The School Buildings	18
III.	The Benefactors	33
IV.	The Statutes	53
V.	The Governors and their Spokesmen	86
VI.	The Head Masters, Ushers, and Assistants	113
VII.	The Library	166
VIII.	Scholarships and other Endowments	173
IX.	Register of Pupils	201
X.	Miscellaneous	226
	Indexes	243

ILLUSTRATIONS.

1.	New Building in 1886	(*Frontispiece*).
2.	Old Building in 1860	*to face page* 18
3.	Inscription on Old Building	,, 22
4.	Interior of Old Building	,, 65
5.	Old Master's House in Almshouse Lane	,, 83
6.	Dr. Bentley, Master of Trinity College, Cambridge	,, 128
7.	Head Masters from 1814 to 1891	,, 149
8.	Old Building and Library Room in 1820	,, 166
9.	Dr. John Radcliffe	,, 205
10.	Dr. Potter, Archbishop of Canterbury	,, 208
11.	Dr. Edmund Cartwright, Inventor of the Power Loom	,, 215
12.	Present Master's House	,, 226

The Illustrations are Collotypes prepared under the supervision of Messrs. J. & G. HALL, of Wakefield, from their own Photographs.

Chapter 1.

THE FOUNDATION AND CHARTER.

THE "Free Grammar School of Queen Elizabeth at Wakefield" was established by Royal Charter, dated at Westminster "the nineteenth day of November in the four and thirtieth year of our reign," *i.e.*, November 19th, 1591 [1], at the request of the Inhabitants of the Town and Parish of Wakefield. But it must not be supposed that the people of Wakefield had previously been without any means of education for their sons: that would have been a remarkable state of affairs for a place of such importance as it was, in comparison with other West Riding towns, during the 15th and 16th centuries [2]: as a matter of fact, there is clear evidence of the existence of at least one school in Wakefield both before and after the religious and educational changes of the reign of Henry VIII.

The education of the young was carried on in various ways, as might be expected, during the middle ages. In some cases private tutors were engaged, who not only prepared their pupils for the Universities, but even accompanied them thither, and superintended their work—a fact which partly accounts for the very early age at which some students entered in former days [3]. But in the vast majority of cases boys were educated in schools, as at the present time. These were of various kinds. There were a few very ancient Grammar Schools of independent position [4], others in connexion

---

(1) The date of the Charter is erroneously given in many books as Nov. 19, 1592 (or even as Sept. 19, 1592): and the mistake has arisen from the fact that Eliz. 34 was not commensurate with A.D. 1592, but lasted from Nov. 17, 1591, to Nov. 16, 1592. The Charter was therefore obtained on the third day of Eliz. 34. The Rev. J. H. Lupton kindly supplies the following confirmation of this statement:—"1591. Nov. 19. Westminster. Grant of a Free Grammar School for the town of Wakefield, Yorkshire," (from State Papers—domestic series—of the Reign of Elizabeth, ed. by M. A E. Green, 1867, p. 122).

(2) Thus Mr. Lupton (W. W. p. 44) shews that in 1540 Wakefield probably had about 3,000 inhabitants, while Leeds, Bradford, and Halifax had about 2,000 each.

(3) Thus between 1567 and 1621 one student entered Oxford University at the a e of *five*, six at the age of *seven*, 14 at the age of *eight*, 12 at the age of *nine*, 57 at the age of *ten*, and so on (Register of the University of Oxford, A. Clark, 1887).

(4) Such appear to have been the Grammar Schools at Oswestry and Sevenoaks, both founded in the 15th century (S.I.C Report, 1868).

with monasteries, others attached to cathedrals and parish churches, and others supported by various Trade Guilds. The monastic schools appear to have been of two different kinds : on the one hand we hear of schools within the monasteries for the training of such boys as were intended for the service of the church, as choristers and the like, or destined to take orders when they had come to the proper age : and in many cases there were also schools held in buildings near the monasteries, in which boys intended for secular pursuits might obtain the best available education ; and these often seem to have been most important establishments [1]. Schools were also maintained in connexion with the various cathedrals in the country for the purpose of training the young, not only for the office of chorister, but also for business occupations [2]. The cathedral authorities often established other schools in the most important towns of the diocese : and these still remained under their control, though they were, of course, affiliated to the parish churches of the various towns [3]; they were generally put under the charge of óne of the chantry priests attached to the church. And, lastly, the influential trade guilds helped on the cause of education in the busiest towns of the country, chiefly by calling in the aid of preaching friars and secular priests, to impart such instruction as was thought desirable for the sons of their members [4].

There is but little evidence to show what were the educational advantages possessed by the town and neighbourhood of Wakefield before the dissolution of the monasteries in the reign of Henry VIII. [5] It may be supposed, however, that a school of some sort existed in connexion with the Priory at Nostell, and perhaps another in connexion with the branch established at Woodkirk. But there certainly was a school in charge of one of the chantry priests at Wakefield Parish

---

(1) Carlisle Grammar School was established by William Rufus, it is said, to be taught by one of the monks of the convent founded by him there (*ibid*).

(2) This was the origin of the famous College at Winchester, intended for 16 choristers and 70 scholars (*ibid*).

(3) Such was Penrith Grammar School originally (*ibid*).

(4) So the Goldsmiths' Company maintained schools at Stockport and Cromer as early as 1487 and 1505 respectively: and the Mercers provided education at St. Paul's School, London, from 1510 (*ibid*).

(5) 27 Hen. VIII., c. 28, and 31 Hen. VIII., c. 13, are the Acts under which this was done : by the former, monasteries, priories, and other religious houses not possessed of a clear yearly income of £200 were suppressed and given to the King : and by the latter all over the yearly value of £200 were surrendered.

Church, doubtless under the authority of the Archbishop of York [1]. For when the Act for the dissolution of chantries was passed in the year 1547, Commissioners were appointed to report upon the claims of the chantry priests to pensions, and with regard to Wakefield the following report, amongst others, was made:—

> "Wakefield Parish.—The Chauntry called Thurstone Chauntry in the seid paryshe churche—Edward Woode, Incombent, lii. yeres of age, well learned and teacheth youth there, hath none other lyving than the profitts of the said Chauntrie."

It is quite clear from this statement that boys were taught in connexion with Wakefield Parish Church, but it is impossible to say whether only such boys were taught as were required to assist in the daily services, or whether a larger circle of pupils was admitted. The probability is that Edward Woode conducted a public school, similar to many others which existed in various large towns, and which subsequently became Grammar Schools [2].

Nothing is known of the existence of any Trade Guild School in Wakefield: but the existence of the Trade Guilds themselves is proved from references made to them in the Towneley Mysteries, which were acted at Woodkirk under the superintendence of the monastic establishment there. In the text of the plays we find the following Guilds mentioned as each undertaking the expense of representing one of the series of plays, viz.:—The Barkers (or Tanners), the Glovers, and the Fishers; and the centre of these guilds would doubtless be at Wakefield. It is perhaps therefore possible that some school was provided in the town for the benefit of the members.

But whatever were the educational advantages of Wakefield before the dissolution of the monasteries and chantries, it is quite certain that the town and neighbourhood sent out into the world in the 15th and 16th centuries a great number of well-educated men, who afterwards distinguished themselves in no ordinary manner. Particulars about them may be found in "Wakefield Worthies," by the Rev. J. H. Lupton, M.A., a book well known to local readers. It will suffice here merely to mention some of their names. Among them were Dr. Richard Fleming, Bishop of Lincoln and founder of Lincoln College, Oxford; John Forman, founder of Royston School;

---

(1) I do not forget that the church was appropriated to the Dean and Chapter of St. Stephen's College, Westminster (Walker, p. 14); but the Archbishop's rights were always preserved, and when the Grammar School was founded he had great control over its management.

(2) In addition to the instance of Penrith already quoted, we may give the Grammar Schools of Launceston, Blackburn, and Liverpool (S.I.C. Report, 1868).

Robert Wakefield, a great Orientalist; Dr. Thomas Knolles, Vicar of Wakefield and President of Magdalen College, Oxford; Sir Richard Lister, Lord Chief Justice of England; Dr. Thomas Robertson, Vicar of Wakefield and one of the twelve compilers of the Prayer Book of Edward VI.; John Field, a most famous astronomer; Christopher Saxton, a distinguished geographer and publisher of maps; and Sir Martin Frobisher, the renowned explorer and admiral.

There can be no doubt that the sweeping reforms in religion, introduced in the reign of Henry VIII., created for many years very serious difficulties in the matter of education. In all but the most favoured districts—districts, that is to say, where there was some old established Grammar School or Trade Guild School of independent position—the monastic and chantry schools must have been the only means of preserving the little learning that existed during the long middle ages of intellectual darkness. And when these were of necessity abolished with the rest of the monastic system, there arose at once a pressing need of other permanent establishments to take their place [1]. But these were not provided without considerable delay, and much liberality and self-sacrifice on the part of the inhabitants of populous districts: indeed a century may almost be said to have elapsed before the needs of the country were even tolerably well satisfied in this respect: and even then enormous damage was done by the Civil War in the middle of the seventeenth century. The list of Grammar Schools published by the Schools Inquiry Commissioners in 1868 shows that in the 38 years of the reign of Henry VIII. sixty-three such schools were founded to supply the place of the monastic schools: in the six years of Edward VI. the number was 51: in the five years of Mary there were 19: in the 45 years of Elizabeth there were 117: in the 22 years of James I. there were 63: in the 24 years of Charles I. there were 59: and the numbers still continue large in each reign until the end of the 17th century.

Turning to Wakefield, we find that seven years after the Act was passed for the dissolution of chantries, *i.e.*, in 1553, the Chantry Priests at Wakefield were dismissed and pensioned: Edward Woode, the Priest in charge of the Parish Church School, was awarded a

---

[1] "Thus 1 Edw. vi., c. 14, speaks of "the alteration, change, and amendment of the same (*i.e.*, monasteries and chantries), and converting to good and godly uses, as in erecting of Grammar Schools to the education of youth in virtue and godliness." This was the Act for the dissolution of Chantries Collegiate.

yearly pension of four guineas. But before this, in 1548, two curates had been appointed to take their places in the service of the Church [1], and we may well suppose that the educational duties previously executed by the Thurstone Chantry Priest were now entrusted to one of them, perhaps under the superintendence of the Vicar. There is, however, no doubt that such teaching was being provided a few years later, for a document, which will be found printed in full two pages below [2], speaks of one who probably was a Curate of the Church, and of his scholars, in a manner which makes it almost certain that a systematic attempt had been made for many years before that time (*i.e.*, 1590) to provide instruction at a school in connexion with the Parish Church.

There are many other facts, in addition to the above, which lead to the almost inevitable conclusion that not only did a school exist in connexion with the Parish Church at Wakefield before the dissolution of the chantries, but that when the Chantry Priests were discharged, the educational work devolved on one of the Curates, and that this school ultimately became the Grammar School. For, in the first place, this is known to have been the origin of many other town schools in different parts of the country [3]. Then the first Head Master of the Grammar School was also Vicar of Wakefield, and he would hardly have held both offices unless there had been a close connexion between the School and the Church: probably he had previously had charge of the school as curate, and when it became the Grammar School still continued to conduct it, not even resigning his educational duties when he was appointed Vicar. [4] The Vicar of Wakefield also, by virtue of his office, had very important rights in the school, such as that of selecting the boys for the University Scholarships, and sometimes has claimed to be an *ex officio* Governor. [5] There are also other facts, of less importance when considered singly, but not unimportant when taken together. Thus, the Governors of the Grammar School originally used to hold their

---

(1) Walker; p. 195.   (2) See p. 7.

(3) "Before the Reformation, Chantries were frequently founded for a priest to say mass for the repose of the founder's soul, and the priest was often required, in virtue of his endowment, to keep a grammar school also. The choirs in training to sing the Latin offices appear to have been the nucleus of many early grammar schools: and when the chantries and monasteries were dissolved at the Reformation, the schoolmaster was restored with the Latin Grammar in his hand." (S.I.C. Report, 1868, vol. i., p. 117.)

(4) The S.I.C. Report of 1868 (i., 231) quotes instances of this double responsibility in other places in the North of England.   (5) See below, Ch. v.

meetings in the room over the South Porch of the Parish Church, and this was especially devoted to their use, and regarded as belonging to them. Further, the Head Master of the Grammar School was always to be a member of the Church of England, and was bound to teach the principles of its religion. The boys of the school were also assigned fixed places in the church, and were expected to attend regularly in charge of their Master. Finally, it may be remarked that many of these points of connexion between Parish Church and Grammar School are also observed in the case of many other town schools which are known to have had their origin in Church schools. It will, therefore, be allowed that there is very good ground for believing that the Wakefield Grammar School had a similar origin, and that before its formal establishment by Royal Charter it existed as a Church school, at which, doubtless, some of the eminent men referred to above received part of their education.

It is now time to trace the steps taken in Wakefield to provide a Grammar School, similar to those which were being founded in large numbers in other towns, in the period immediately following the dissolution of monasteries and chantries. A beginning was made in the year 1563-4, when, by his will (dated February 20th, 1563-4, and proved July 31st, 1566), one FRANCIS GRANT, mercer, of Wakefield, bequeathed "the yearlie rents and proffetts of one little house or cottage, now in the occupacion of Richard Mercer, adjoyninge to the tenement where I now dwell in, of the yearlie value of ten shillings, to the use of a fre schole, yf any such fortune to be within the towne of Wakefeild, for ever and for so longe time as the same shall contynewe, and in defalt of such fre schole then the same yearlie rents to remayne and be to the use of the poore people within the towne of Wakefeild aforesaid."

There is no record known of any further effort being made to raise sufficient funds to endow a Grammar School until some twenty-five years after this date. But the Governors have in their possession a most interesting document, in which are recorded the promises of lands and money which were made up to the year 1590. The paper may either be the record of the result of a public meeting held about this time for the purpose of obtaining help, or may have been kept by Mr. Mawde, the Schoolmaster, and added to from time to time, as he secured promises. It runs as follows :—

A bouke of the names of all those persons which promise yearely mantenaunce (to Mr. Mawde and his successors, for teaching the poorer sorte of children at Wakefield) so longe as thay live, and what every one will give at ther death, If God make them able, under their owne hands.

I do promise (by the grace of God) to give yearly xx*s*. towards the mantenaunce of pore Children as above to be payd quarterly after the graunt obtayned and ten pounds for a stocke to the said use at my death, if God make me able, and the xx*s*. to cease.   by me Henry Arthington.

Item, I do promes to geve xx*s*. yearly rent furthe of my lands or xx*li*. in money in forme aforesaid.   Thomas Cave.

I do promes to geve x*li*. in money towards the premisses.
 by me Henrye Watkinson.

I doe promise to give as longe as I live thirtie shillings yearlie and at my death as much as it shal please God to mack me able and put me in minde to give.   Mrs. Elizabeth X Savile of Standley.

I do promise to give presently as above ten pounds in money or ten shillings by the yeare, in lands.   by me Richard Wyttonn.

I do promise to geve x*s*. yearly so long as Mr. Henry Arthington dothe pay xx*s*. yearly to the use above said | and further as god shall move me.
 Wm. Pollard /—/ marke.

I do promise to geve vi*li*. xiii*s*. iv*d*. to be imployed to the use of the said Scoule.   by me John Battye.

I do promyse to give tene pounds in money or tenn shillings per annum out of my Lands at my dyscression or choyse upon the obtayninge of a foundatyon of the sayd fre scole.   by me Robt. ———.

I do promis to give ether fyve shillings in Lands or fyve pounds in money upon the obtayninge of the said foundation.
 By me John Mawde.

I do promise to give foure pounds in money upon the obtayninge of the said foundation.   By me Thomas Robinson.

I do promise to give ten shillings in landes upon the obtayninge of the foundation of the free schoole at Wakefeild, to the use of the same scoole for ever.   By me Henrye Burton.

I do promise to geve iiii*li*. yerly for ever to the use above sayde.
 By me Oswald Laburn.

I do promise by the grace of God to geve yerlye to the free schoole of Wakefeild upon the obtayninge of the foundation thereof the some of tenne shillings.   By me Richard Sproxton.

1590. A bouke of the names of those persons........................ lands or a stocke of money to the Scole................................. Wakefeild for ever, when the foundation........................ /............ with the severall summes under every donors hand.

I do promes by the grace of god to assure to the fre schole in Wakefeld in perpetuytie lands to the yearly value of iiii*li* by yeare, and the assurance to be made and assured to the use of the Schole and payable halfe yearly ymmediatly after the foundacion shalbe optayned | or else somuche yearly rent with clause of distresse fourthe of all my lands in the parisshe of Wakefeild.   By me George Savil.

Having obtained these promises of support [1], we may suppose that Mr. Mawde and his friends took immediate steps to obtain the charter for the proposed Grammar School: and there can be practically no

---

[1] A reference to Chap. III. will show how they were carried out.

doubt that the Saviles took the lead in this worthy undertaking, for they are mentioned in the places of honour in the charter, and they made handsome gifts of money, land, and materials for the benefit of the new school. The late Mr. W. H. Leatham, in his "Lectures on the History of Wakefield and its Antiquities," says, doubtless with good authority for the statement, "it is probable that mainly through the instigation" of Sir Henry Savile [1], Tutor of the Greek language to Queen Elizabeth, "that royal personage was induced to grant a charter for the foundation of the Grammar School at Wakefield." It may also be taken for granted that the other gentlemen who were appointed first Governors of the School, in conjunction with the Saviles, were those who were likely to give the chief support to the movement: indeed many of them appear on the document just quoted. The names of the first Governors are thus given in the charter:—"Our welbeloved Syr George Savile Knyghte, John Savile Esquier our Stewarde of Wakefilde, Thomas Savile Esquier our Surveyour in those partes, Robarte Bradforde Esquyer, George Savile Gentleman, Henrie Arthington Gent, Richarde Sproxton Gent, Roger Pollarde yoman, Richarde Cleton yoman, William Savile yoman, Thomas Cave yoman, Henrie Watkynson yoman, John Battye yoman, and Thomas Robinson yoman, fouretene Inhabitants of the Towne and parisshe of Wakefilde or within two miles thereof."

A few particulars about these first Governors may fitly be given in this place.

1. "Our welbeloved SYR GEORGE SAVILE Knyghte" was a member of the Thornhill branch of the Savile family, born in 1550, created baronet in 1611, appointed High Sheriff of Yorkshire in 1614, and died in 1622 [2].

2. "JOHN SAVILE Esquier, our Stewarde of Wakefilde," was one of the Saviles of Howley Hall, born in 1556, appointed "custos rotulorum" and Steward of Wakefield, Pontefract, and Bradford, six times elected Member of Parliament for the County, created Baron Savile of Pontefract by Charles I., and appointed first Alderman or Mayor of Leeds in 1626, giving to the arms of that borough the owls of the Savile crest as supporters: he died August 31, 1630, and is buried in Batley Parish Church [3].

---

(1) Born at Bradley Hall, November 30, 1549, and educated at Merton College, Oxford; of which society he was elected a Fellow in 1577, and died its Warden in 1621. He was also Provost of Eton College.

(2) Whitaker, p. 313.   (3) Whitaker, p. 235; Banks, pp. 53, 526.

3. "THOMAS SAVILE Esquier, our Surveyour in those partes"[1] perhaps was a younger son of the Thornhill family[2].

4. "ROBARTE BRADFORDE Esquyer" was of Bradford Hall, afterwards Clarke Hall, in Stanley[3].

5. "GEORGE SAVILE gentleman" may be considered the real founder of the school. He lived in Hasleden Hall, in Northgate, Wakefield, which he apparently purchased from the Pegge (or Peck) family in 1584. He is described by Dodsworth[4] and Anthony-à-Wood[5] as a Blackwall Hall man, by which is meant that he was a merchant selling woollen cloth in the Hall of that name in Basinghall-street, near the Guildhall, in London. He was the younger son of Thomas Savile, of Wakefield, and grandson of Thomas Savile, of Lupset, and died October 24, 1593, leaving two sons, George and Thomas, whose names appear with his upon the walls of the old school.

6. "HENRIE ARTHINGTON Gent" was the owner of Milnethorpe, in Sandal[7].

7. "RICHARDE SPROXTON Gent" was connected with the Saviles by marriage with Dorothy[8], daughter of Henry Savile of Bradley, and sister of Sir John Savile of Methley, and Sir Henry Savile of Merton College, Oxford, already mentioned.

8. "ROGER POLLARDE yoman" resided in Westgate, Wakefield, and was probably the father of the William Pollard, chapman, of Westgate, whose name appears amongst the benefactors of the school.

9. "RICHARDE CLETON yoman" was a Westgate draper: his daughter married Thomas, son of George Savile of Haselden Hall[9].

10. "WILLIAM SAVILE yoman" was Deputy Steward of the Manor of Wakefield and Steward of the Manor of Newland[10]. He performed valuable service in a legal capacity by executing free of charge the necessary formalities for enrolling the charter and other deeds, and was the first Spokesman of the Governors of the School.

11. "THOMAS CAVE yoman" was another Westgate chapman, or draper: he subsequently became one of the chief

---

(1) *i.e.*, Surveyor of Crown Lands in the North of England. (2) Whitaker, p. 313. (3) Banks, pp. 53, 180. (4) see Chap. II. (5) see Chap. III. (6) see Clay's Yorkshire Wills, p. 60; Taylor, p. 42. (7) see Banks, pp. 53, 399. (8) see Whitaker, p. 274. (9) see Taylor, p. 58. (10) see Banks, p. 54.

benefactors of the School by establishing the Scholarships which bear his name at Clare College, Cambridge. He also founded the Grammar School at Otley. He died in 1603.

12. "HENRIE WATKYNSON yoman" lived in Westgate, Wakefield, and was probably a mercer, like his son Edward, who is so described at a later time.

13. "JOHN BATTYE yoman" was another Westgate chapman.

14. "THOMAS ROBINSON yoman" lived in Northgate, which then only contained a very few houses close to the Church, and Haselden Hall at its extreme end, called "Northgate Head." The bulk of the houses were in and near Westgate, Kirkgate and Warrengate.

The original Charter of the School is still in existence, and in a very good state of preservation, only a few words being illegible. It has been for some time kept in an iron case provided for its safety by some previous generation of Governors. The seal was however destroyed by the soldiers who broke into the Governors' Room over the South Porch of the Parish Church during the Civil War in 1643, but a portion of the cord by which it was attached still remains. A full text of the Charter is appended :—

> Elizabeth, By the grace of god Quene of Englund | Fraunce and Irelande defender of the faithe etc To all men to whom thies present letters shall comme sendith greting Bee it knowen unto you that wee att the humble sute made | unto us by the Inhabitants of the Towne and parisshe of Wakefilde in our countie of Yorke for a free Grammer Scoole there to be erected and establisshed for euer for the contynuall teachinge instructinge | and bringinge up of children and youthe in good lernynge, namlie those belonginge to the said parisshe of Wakefilde, Of our especiall grace certen knowledge and meere motion Wee doe will | graunte and ordayne for us our heires and successors that hereafter there be and shalbe one Grammer Scoole in the saide Towne of Wakefilde whiche shalbe called the free Grammer Scoole of Queene | Elizabeth att Wakefilde for the teachinge instructinge and bringinge up of children and youthe in Grammer and other good learnynge to contynue to that use forever. And wee by these presents doe erecte | ordeyne create founde and establisshe the saide free scoole of one master or teacher and one ussher and ₁ underteacher for ever to contynue. And that our saide purpose and foundation maye haue and take the | better effecte · and the landes tenements · rentes · stockes · reuercions · and reuenewes · withe suche like grauntes assigned and appoynted · or hereafter to be graunted assigned and appoynted for the contynuall | mayntenaunce of the saide scoole maie be trulie conuerted and ymploied to the use and maintenaunce of the saide free Grammer Scoole forever Wee will and ordeyne and for us our heyres and successors doe | graunte by these

---

(¹) This is apparently a mistake of the copyist for "or."

GRAMMAR SCHOOL.

presents, that hereafter there be and shalbe forever within the parishe of Wakefilde or dwellinge within two myles thereof fouretene honest men of the moste wise discreete and religeous persons | who shalbe called Governers of the said free Grammer Scoole att Wakefilde and of all the possessions reuercions and goodes thereunto belonginge . And therefore and to that ende wee have assigned nomynated | chosen and appointed, And by these presents doe assign nomynate and appointe our welbeloved Syr George Savile Knyghte John Savile Esquier our Stewarde of Wakefilde Thomas Savile Esquier our Surveyour | in those partes Robarte Bradforde Esquyer George Savile Gentleman Henrie Arthington Gent Richarde Sproxton Gent Roger Pollarde yoman Richarde Cleton yoman William, Savile yoman Thomas Cave yoman | Henric Watkynson yoman John Battye yoman and Thomas Robinson yoman fouretene Inhabitants of the Towne and parisshe of Wakefilde or within two miles thereof, to be the firste Governers of the saide free | Grammer Scoole att Wakefilde , and nowe to beare the names of the present Governers of the saide free scoole and of all the possessions revenewes and goodes belonginge or whiche hereafter shall belonge thereunto 𝔗𝔬 | 𝔥𝔞𝔳𝔢 𝔥𝔬𝔲𝔩𝔡𝔢 occupie exercise and faithfullie to execute the saide office of Governors from the date of thies presents duringe theire lives usinge them selves well and uprightlie towardes the sayde | Scoole And that the saide Governers in deade facte and name be and shalbe one bodie corporate and politique of them selves forever to be contynued by the name of Governers of the saide free Grammer | Scoole of Queene Elizabeth att Wakefilde in the Countie of Yorke. And wee doe incorporate them by these presents to be Governers of the saide free Grammer Scoole of Quene Elizabeth att Wakefilde and of | all the possessions revenues and goodes belonginge or which shall hereafter belonge thereunto. 𝔄𝔫𝔡 𝔴𝔢𝔢 𝔡𝔬𝔢 𝔠𝔯𝔢𝔞𝔱𝔢 erecte ordeyne make appointe and establisshe them by these presents reallye | and fullie to be a bodye corporate and politique by the saide name to contynue forever.   𝔄𝔫𝔡 𝔣𝔲𝔯𝔱𝔥𝔢𝔯 𝔴𝔢𝔢 𝔴𝔦𝔩𝔩 ordeyne and graunte by these presents for us our heires and successors that the aforenamed present Governers of the free Grammer Scoole | of Queene Elizabeth att Wakefilde shall and maie by the saide name haue a contynuall succession forever. And by the saide name be and shalbe able persons by the lawe and by these presents be made able and capeable from tyme to tyme to purchase gett receive | possesse and enioie to them selves and theire successors Governers of the saide free Grammer Scoole att Wakefilde forever mannors lands tenements tithes and other possessions hereditaments revenues rents goodes and chattells whatsoever of us our heyres and successours | or of any other person or persons within our domynyons. And also wee ordeyne graunte and decree by these presents for us our heires and successors . that so often and whensoeuer anie one or moe of the aforenamed fouretene Governers for the tyme beinge or anye | that shalbe chosen hereafter for to departe this liffe or to dwell withe theire famylies above two myles owt of the saide parisshe of Wakefilde for the space of one whole yere together (Excepte the saide Sir George Savile Knighte . and the saide John Savile Esquier our Stewarde | of Wakefilde[1]) that then and soe often it shalbe lawfull for the

---

([1]) It will be observed on referring back to p. 8 that these gentlemen lived in the parishes of Thornhill and Mirfield respectively.

reste of the Governers dwellynge withe theire famylies in the said paryshe of Wakefilde or within two myles thereof to take unto them the Scoolemaster of the saide free Scoole for the tyme beinge and to | nomynate chose and appointe one or moe meete person or persons of the Inhabitants of the saide parishe of Wakefilde or dwellinge within two myles thereof into the roome and place or roomes and places of everie such person or persons soe dead and departed this liffe . | or withe his or theire famylie or famylies removed to dwell owt of the saide parisshe of Wakefeilde more than two myles distant thereunto. Whiche person or persons so chosen and agreed uppon by the more parte of the Governers then livynge with the consente and likynge | of the saide Scoolemaster shalbe reputed and taken from the daie of their eleccion to be from thensfourthe Governor or Governors of the saide free Grammer Schole of Queene Elizabeth att Wakefeilde and after this maner soe often to procende as neede shall requyre within | syxe weekes nexte after anie place of a Governer voide by death or otherwise as aforesaide. And if the saide election of a Governer be differred att any tyme aboue sixe weekes nexte after suche place of a Governer voide as aforesaid Then and soe often it shalbe lawfull | for the lorde President of the Northe Partes or the Archbushoppe of Yorke for the tyme being withe the knowledge and consente of sixe of the Governors then livinge at the leaste to name and appointe [a person or p¹]ersons in the place or roome of everye suche | person or persons soe deade or removed to dwell as aforesaide . whiche person or persons soe named and appoynted shalbe [taken and reputed]¹ from thensfurthe for a Governor or Governors of the saide free Grammer Scoole amongeste the reste of the Governors thereof. And | furthermore we will and graunte for us our heires and successors by these presents unto the aforenamed Governors and theire successors, that theye foreuer hereafter shall have a Common Seale to serve for the cawses and busynes abowt the saide Scoole | And that the saide Governors and theire successors hereafter shall and maie by the aforesaide name of Governors of the free Grammer Scoole of Queene Elizabeth att Wakefeilde pleade and be impleaded defende and be defended answeare and be answered in all | manner of Cowrtes plees and demaundes of what kynde nature or condition soever they be or for anie transgression offence thinges cawses or matter by anie person or persons made or donne or to be made or donne by any personne or persons in uppon or | abowt the premysses or anie parcell thereof or towchinge or concerninge anie thinge specified within these presents after the saide manner and forme , as other our leige people of this our realme of Englaunde beinge able persons and in lawe capeable maie | pleade or be impleaded answere and be answered defende and be defended. And furthermore of our abundant favoure [sure] knowledge and meere motion wee haue geoven and graunted and by these presents for us our heires and successors doe geve and graunte unto the afore named Governors and their successors forever that whensoveuer the place of Scoolemaster of the saide free Grammer Scoole att Wakefeilde is or shalbe voide and destitute of a Scoolemaster That then and soe often the Governers for the tyme beynge | or the more parte of them forever shall haue full power and aucthoritie by warraunt of this our graunte from tyme

---

(¹) These letters are inserted to fill a gap in the original where the writing is worn away.

to tyme to chose and nomynate and under theire common seale within threscore daies nexte after the place be voide by what occasion soever to | present a meete man for knowledge religion and liffe att theire discretion so the partye be well reported of and hathe taken the degree of a master of the artes unto the Archebusshoppe of Yorke yf there be anie att the tyme of the election who shall alowe him to be | Scoolemaster there accordynglie. And the partie so presented shall from thenceforthe be taken to be Scoolemaster of the said free Grammer Scoole att Wakefilde soe longe as he be founde by the governers of the saide schole or the more parte of them to be | diligent and faithfull in his saide office and fitt for the same bothe for his religion and conuersation and no longer , but uppon one quarters warninge to remove hym and to proceade unto a newe election for another Scoolemaster as aboue. 𝔅nt if t𝔥e | aforesaide Governors or theire successors hereafter shall nott present a fitt Scoolemaster within threscore daies nexte after the place be voide by what occasion soever, Then it shalbe lawfull for the master and fellowes of Emanuell Colledge[1] in Cambridge havynge | intelligence of the place voide to nomynate chuse and electe a fytt master of arte to be Scoolemaster of the saide free Grammer Scoole att Wakefilde withe the consent of sixe of the Governors at the leaste who shalbe then admytted under the common seale of the saide | Scoole accordinglie who shall from thenceforthe be reputed and taken for the Scoolemaster of the saide free Grammer Scoole of Queene Elizabeth att Wakefeilde · so longe as he be dilligent and faithfull in his saide office , Butt otherwise to be removed uppon one quarters | warnynge as above. 𝔚e 𝔥a𝔟e also geven and graunted and by these presents for us our heires and successors doe geve and graunte to the aforenamed Governers and theire successors forever or the more parte of them withe the helpe and assistaunce of the | Scoolemaster then beinge to chuse nomynate and appointe from tyme to tyme a fytt Ussher or underteacher in the saide Scoole within one moneth nexte after the place be voide and that the saide Governors withe the consent of the Scoolemaster shall haue like power to | displace everie suche Ussher or under teacher agayne uppon one quarters warnynge if he be founde necligent in his office or unfytt for his place either in religion lerninge or behaviour, whiche orders for chusinge the said master and Ussher , 𝔚ee 𝔚ill an𝔡 | comman𝔡e to be contynuallie kepte and observed from tyme to tyme hereafter . 𝔄n𝔡 𝔴ee ge𝔟e furt𝔥er po𝔴er and aucthoritie unto the afore named Governors of the saide free grammer scoole att Wakefilde and theire successors forever or | the more parte of them withe the Scoolemasters advice and consent for the tyme beinge to make good and necessarie Statutes and Ordynaunces in writinge under the common seale for the better orderynge rulinge and governinge of the saide free Scoole and Scoolemasters | and of the landes possessions revenues and goodes of the saide Scoole from tyme to tyme hereafter withe all other thinges whatsoever unto the saide scoole belonginge, So they be nott repugnant to the lawes and Statutes of this our Realme , All whiche Statutes and ordynaunces | made or to be made hereafter for the better gouernment of the saide Scoole we will and commaunde by these presents

---

(1) Probably this College was chosen because it had been founded by Queen Elizabeth's orders in 1584.

be safelie kepte for the use and benefitt of posterities under two lockes whereof the Scoolemaster for the tyme beynge to have thone keye, and one of the | Governers by consent of the reste to haue the other keye for the better and more faithfull dealinge in all cawses and matters belonginge or apperteyninge to the said schoole from tyme to tyme forever. 𝔄lso we will and require by these presents that the | Governors masters and usshers of the saide free Grammar Schoole hereafter to be made shall take their corporall othe before the Governers assembled for their electyon the daye of theire entrie, into the saide office to be faithfull and carefull for the good of the sayde | Scoole in all things apperteyninge to theire office and chardge accordynge to the truste reposed in them. 𝔉urthermore for the better mayntenaunce of the saide Schoole and Scoolemasters att Wakefeilde from tyme to tyme hereafter · wee doe of our | speciall favour and love unto lernynge for us our heires and successors by these presents geue and graunte to the aforenamed Governors of the free Grammar Scoole of Queene Elizabeth att Wakefeilde, and their succesors for ever our speciall licence withe free and | lawfull libertie power and aucthoritie to gett purchase receive and take to them and theire successors for ever to the use of the saide Scoole aswell of us our heires and successors as of any other person or persons whosoever mannors mesuages lands tenements and other | hereditaments whatsoever to the cleare yerelie value of one hundrethe markes in rente or under. So that the saide landes be nott holden of us our heires and successors in capite nor by Knyghtes service nor of anye other person or persons by Knyghtes service, the statute of | mortmayne or anye other acte heretofore made to the contrarie notwithstandinge, And also wee do geve and graunte like licence power and aucthoritie unto all and everie other person or persons whatsoever to geve graunte or assure unto the saide Governors and theire | successors mannors mesuages lands tenements rentes reuercions and other hereditaments whatsoever to the full value of one hundrethe marks or under, So that the same be nott houlden of us our heires and successors in capite nor by Knightes service nor of any other | person or persons by Knyghtes service the saide statute of mortmaine or any other acte or statute heretofore made to the contrarie notwithstandinge. 𝔄nd further wee will and graunte that the aforenamed Governors of the saide Scoole att Wakefeild maie and shall have these our letters patents under our great seale of Englaunde in due fowrme to be made and sealed without fyne or fee greate or smale to us in our hanoper₁ or otherwise to be geven or paide. 𝔄lthoughe expresse mention of the true | yerelie value or certentie of the premysses or anie of them or anie other giftes or grauntes by us or by anie our progenitors to the aforesaide Governors of the saide free Grammar Scoole of Queene Elizabeth att Wakefeilde heretofore made in these presents is nott made | or any statute acte ordynaunce prouiso or restrainte thereof to the contrarie made ordeyned or provided, or anie other thinge cawse or matter whatsoever in any wise notwithstandinge. 𝔍n witnes whereof wee have cawsed these our letters to be | made patents. 𝔚itnes our selfe att Westmynster the nynetenthe daie of November in the fower and therthethe yere of our raigne.

          (per breue de priuato sigillo, &c.)   . S . GERRARDE

(¹) *i.e.,* Treasury or Exchequer.

The Charter is endorsed twice, the original hand having written—

"A graunte to the Inhabitants of the towne and parishe of Wakefilde in the Countie of Yorke for a free Grammar Scoole there for ever. Glendower."

The second endorsement is by a later hand—

"No. 5. Queen Elizabeth Grant to the Inhabitants of Wakefield of a free Grammar School. Dated Nov. 19 in the 34 year of her Reign. A."

As far as can be gathered from a comparison of the above document with others of a similar nature, it does not seem that any extraordinary powers were granted to the Governors of this School, or any special favours allowed to them, if we except the trifling concession as to the residence of Sir George Savile and John Savile, Esq., more than two miles beyond the limits of the parish of Wakefield.

It may be interesting in this place to add a few words about the meaning of the title of this School and others of a similar character, for there has been much difference of opinion upon one point in this connexion.

We need not waste words in commenting upon the curious fact that the Greek word for "leisure time" has become the English name for a place of education [1]. The name "grammar school," according to Dr. Johnson, was given to establishments where the learned languages were taught grammatically; and a famous decision of Lord Eldon, in the case of Leeds Grammar School, laid down the principle, which was afterwards only too strictly acted upon in many cases, that nothing but Greek and Latin was intended to be taught in such schools.[2] Many Grammar Schools, however, made no pretence of teaching anything but Latin: for the study of Greek was not introduced into England until the beginning of the 16th century; and, on the other hand, until the end of the 17th century, Latin was the language in which learned books were written, the means of communication between scholars in different countries, and the official language of Church and State: even a country Parish Clerk had to keep his Registers in Latin. Latin grammar was therefore the first and most important subject to be learned by boys three hundred years ago, and a reference to the Statutes of this School, in a subsequent chapter, will show how it was taught.

The meaning of the word "free" in the designation of some grammar schools is a question on which there is by no means an

---

(1) Gk. scholó, leisure time = leisure for mental instruction.
(2) See Chap. II.

agreement amongst those best qualified to speak on the subject [1].

The most natural interpretation of the word, in view of modern usage, is to take it as denoting a school where the education given to the boys, or at least to the great majority, is to be gratuitous or without payment of any sort.

But mature consideration has led many to adopt the opinion that this is an erroneous view, and for the following reasons. The Latin words, of which "free school" is a translation, are "libera schola;" and it is urged that "libera" cannot mean gratuitous, however much allowance is made for unclassical usage: thus, "libera villa" means a town free from the jurisdiction of the sheriff, and "libera capella" a chapel free from the authority of the bishop. Moreover, the charters of many of these "Free Grammar Schools" will be searched in vain for any indication that the teaching was to be gratuitous: in some cases, however, it is plainly ordered that the boys shall be "freely taught." In the case of Wakefield School there is a clear distinction made by the statutes between "scholars free and foreigners [2]," showing that many of the boys in this "Free Grammar School" were not to be taught gratuitously. In many schools, also, where no regular fees were charged, some payment was required from all, either as admission money, or as quarterages, Shrovetide, Easter, or Christmas dues; and yet they are called free schools. Again, the use of the English word in such common terms as "freeman" and "freehold" indicates that it frequently meant the same as the Latin "libera," *i.e.*, exempt from external control. The weight of evidence, therefore, seems to compel the adoption of the view that though a "free scholar" is one who is taught gratuitously, yet a "free school" is one that is exempt from such control as was once exercised over places of education by cathedrals, colleges, monasteries, or trade-guilds.

A third view is represented by those who hold that a "free school" is one where the teaching is public and open to all comers. This was certainly a characteristic of most of these establishments, but hardly appears to have been a sufficiently striking one to justify the view now referred to: and in some "Free Grammar Schools"

([1]) The question is discussed in the Schools Inquiry Commissioners' Report, 1868, vol. i., pp. 122-3: and the substance of the following remarks is taken partly from this source.

([2]) Scholars from the town who pay no fees, and scholars from outside who pay for their education.

the number of pupils was limited, and their selection confined to a particular district[1].

And, finally, it is asserted by some that a "free school" is one where the education is of a "liberal" character, *i.e.*, includes instruction in subjects which are regarded as necessary for a gentleman of birth and position, or what we now call "Literæ humaniores." But here again it may be objected that although Grammar School education in 1600 may have seemed "liberal" in this sense, there is not sufficient evidence that from this fact the name "Free" was given to Grammar Schools.

It seems therefore preferable to accept the second view mentioned above, and to consider that by a "Free Grammar School" is meant a place of education for the young in which instruction in Latin Grammar is provided, and which is possessed of the right of self-government, conferred upon it by Royal Charter, and therefore exempt from external control.

(1) Thus Wotton-under-Edge, in Gloucestershire, had a Free Grammar School for "a master and two poor scholars": many others were open only to boys from a particular place. (S.I.C. Report, 1868.)

Chapter 2.

THE SCHOOL BUILDINGS.

IF the remarks in the previous chapter have been well founded, the Wakefield Parish Church School became legally and theoretically the "Free Grammar School of Queen Elizabeth at Wakefield" on and from the date of the Charter, November 19, 1591; and the curate then in charge of the School became the first Head Master. In any case it is certain that a Head Master was at once appointed in the person of the Rev. Edward Mawde, M.A., probably Fellow of St. John's College, Cambridge; for in a letter [1] from the Master of Emmanuel College he is said to have "enjoyed the place of the Scoole Master" from the time of the foundation of the School.

But it is not easy to understand what actual changes were made in the School. For there was as yet only an income of ten pounds a year available, from the bequest of Francis Grant and the donations mentioned in the previous chapter: there was no School building erected, nor even any land as yet given for the purpose of erecting one: the Governors did not commence to transact their business, if there was any to transact, in a regular and formal manner until the year 1606, when the first Spokesman or President Governor was elected: and there were no Statutes passed for the management of the School until the year after the first election of a Spokesman.

Yet there seems to be no reason to doubt the accuracy of the statement just quoted: it must therefore be supposed that for the present the teaching of the new School was given in the premises previously occupied, (perhaps some building adjacent and belonging to the Parish Church), and that the existing arrangements in other respects were not disturbed to any considerable degree.

After the Charter of Foundation had been obtained, the people of Wakefield had next to provide funds to carry on the School—for the great majority of the pupils were to pay no fees—and to procure a building suitable for the purpose. In this effort a noble

(1) See below, Chap. VI.

example was set by the Saviles of Haselden Hall, and it was followed by a display of remarkable liberality on the part of the inhabitants of the town and district, as the long list of benefactors, which will be found in the next chapter, amply proves. Yet the fact that the work of providing the building and endowment seems to have lasted over a period of some fifteen years (1591-1605) is a sign that the necessary funds were not procured without much energy and labour on the part of the Governors and Masters, and much self-sacrifice on the part of the donors.

As has been said, the Saviles set a noble example. In the year 1593 GEORGE SAVILE the elder, of Haselden Hall, gave by will, dated October 6, "four score pounds of current money of England to the Governors of the Free Schole of Wakefield to the use of the said Schole," to be paid within two years after his decease, if there should be "any house builded for kepinge of the said schole within the said two years." He also gave to the Governors "a small close with the buildings thereupon erected lying near the Goodybower between Goodybower Lane on the east and a certain croft of Henry Grice Esquire on the west." This field, as we are told by Roger Dodsworth [1], had been specially purchased by him to present to the Governors as a site for the School, but was not actually surrendered. This was done on October 3, 1594, by GEORGE SAVILE the younger, who thus confirmed his father's gift. The right of obtaining stone out of such parts of the close as should not be built upon, in the course of the next ten years after the date of surrender, was reserved by the donor for himself and his heirs. In the same year, 1594, by will dated December 16, the same GEORGE SAVILE the younger gave a hundred pounds "to the Governors of the Free School of Wakefield to be employed for the purchasing of so much freehold land to the use of the said School as the same will extend unto": an income of £6 a year was the result of the purchase. By the same will he also gave one-third of the tithes of Hooton Pagnell to the School, if his daughter should die without heirs; and as this event actually happened, the Governors came into possession both of the tithes and right of presentation to the living, but not until after some tedious disputes, in the year 1679.[2] In the year 1596 THOMAS SAVILE, who inherited Haselden Hall on the death of his brother, George Savile the younger (Jan. 3, 1595-6)

---

(1) See below, p. 21.

(2) See Hunter's "South Yorkshire," ii. 145. The advowson of this living was sold in 1855 to enable the Governors to purchase the new School Buildings.

confirmed by deed, dated Oct. 24 in that year, his father's and brother's gift of the close near the Goodybower, reserving to himself the right of getting stone for ten years. And in 1599 he also gave a rent charge of "three pounds six shillings and eightpence to be paid annually from and in all that rectory of Thorparch," as well as certain lands and houses in Gawthorpe and Alverthorpe.

Thus the father and sons had given, within ten years of the foundation of the School, a sum of £180 in money, perhaps equivalent to £1500 now, a site for the future School Buildings, abundance of stone upon the spot ready for quarrying, and a considerable income in lands, houses and tithes. Fitly, therefore, may we call them the founders of the School, and rightly were their names recorded upon the walls of the original building [1].

The Governors entered into possession of the Goodybower close by Attorney—Hugh Sewell, chapman, of Wakefield, being appointed by them—on the day of its surrender by George Savile the younger, October 3, 1594: but the fact of the subsequent confirmation of the gift by Thomas Savile in 1596 seems to show that the building operations were not commenced until the latter year. But, when the work was once begun, numerous friends came forward to contribute their share towards the erection. Thus we are told that WILLIAM SAVILE, the Deputy Steward, not only gave £10 in money, but also "procured twentie trees to build the Schole, the seats and flores thereof, and also he repaired the Churche Porche for the Scholes use." Besides this, he "did give the great desk in the middle of the School, and the plate dyall which standith in the courte, and the queen's arms in a frame which be in the upper end there." We are also told of other gifts, as follows :—

"RICHARD BUNNYE, Esquire [2], glased one window with his arms in it.
WILLIAM SAVILE, Gentleman, glased one window with his arms in it.
WILLIAM ELLIOTT [3], glased one other window with his name in it.
THOMAS ROBINSON and JOHN MAWDE, glased one other window between them with their names in it.
WILLIAM RODES, glased one other window with his name in it.
GEORGE TYNDALL, gentleman, clarke of the Peace, glased one other window.
MR. RICHARD CLAYTON, draper, glased one window."

[1] It may be added that their name is also preserved in "The Savilian, or Wakefield Grammar School Magazine," which was started in 1889.
[2] Of Newland; died in 1608; (Banks pp. 72, 249). [3] Buried Oct. 24, 1604 (Walker, p. 298).

GRAMMAR SCHOOL.

The erection of the School therefore took place under very favourable conditions. The site and the stone were already the property of the Governors, the wood was given by one friend, and several windows, then a costly item, glazed by others; and it must also be remembered that about the year 1600 an average workman did not receive more than 5d. or 6d. per day in wages, as may be seen from some accounts two pages below.

The building itself is thus described by Roger Dodsworth, the well-known Yorkshire antiquary [1]:

"EBOR. FREE SCHOOL OF WAKEFIELD. Was founded by George Sayvill, a Blackwall Hall man [2], and George Sayvill, and Thomas Sayvill. It is a very beautyfull house and pleasantly seated on a piece of ground distant a bow shoot of the north from the Church, which was purchased purposely for that end by George Sayvill the father, who besides gave £6 a year [3] for ever towards the maynetenaunce thereof, both his sonnes being benefactors, and a laye was gathered in the towne [4] for the sufficient supply thereof. The Queene granted them lycence to purchase lands to the value of an hundred marks per annum thereto. On the doore is this inscription :—

Schola Elizabethæ Reginæ
Builded by George Sayvill and George Sayvill Esquire and Thomas Sayvill his sonnes."

The "very beautyfull house" still exists, but can no longer be justly so called, and much less be said to be "pleasantly seated." At the time when it was built and for at least two centuries afterwards the situation was one of the most attractive. The Goodybower was in the midst of fields and gardens, and the School Building, when first erected, would probably be the most northerly one in the town, except Haselden Hall, the home of George Savile at Northgate Head. Even so late as 1818 it is described by Carlisle, in his "Endowed Grammar Schools," as being in "a retired and silent quarter of the town." There is now, however, no retirement and silence there, and instead of green fields and trees to hem it in, there are on every side buildings entirely without attractive features.

The School itself is still in a very good state of repair, which testifies to the substantial manner in which it was erected, but is unfortunately now put to a very unromantic use. Compared, however, with the original buildings of other town schools, it can hardly be denied that it was once "very beautyfull [5]." The building at first

---

(1) Dodsworth MSS., Vol. CXXV., p. 149, in the Bodleian Library, Oxford; he visited Wakefield about 1640. (2) This term is explained in the previous chapter, p. 9.
(3) This is probably a mistake, and should be assigned to George Savile the younger. (4) This is explained in the following chapter. (5) Those who wish to make comparisons are referred to Buckler's "Sixty Endowed Grammar Schools," from which work one of our illustrations is taken.

consisted of two rooms, the School itself being about 80 feet in length and 25 feet in breadth, with a lofty roof; while on the south side, where the Library was afterwards built, there was also a "Master's Chamber."

The entrance was originally on the east side of the School, from the playground, and the doorway had over it the inscription quoted, though not quite correctly, by Dodsworth. It may still be traced, but the illustration, from a photograph taken 20 years ago, shows it in a more legible form. It ran as follows:—

Schola Reginæ Elizabethæ.

Owl	Builded by	Royal	George Savile	Owl
—	George Savile	Arms	and	—
Savile	Esquire		Thomas Savile	Savile
Arms			His Sonnes	Arms

The words "builded by" have long since disappeared, and the coats of arms are also very much worn away.

There was a spacious playground on the east side of the School, which went by the name of the "School Croft," and near it there was a quarry, which was not filled up until very recent times, having been the scene of many a boyish prank.

According to a statement which may be found in Chapter VII., and which was made by the Governors themselves, no alterations or repairs of any serious extent were needed in the School Building during the first hundred years of its existence. But in the year 1717 the Head Master of that time, Mr. Thomas Clark, wisely made an effort to have a Library built in close proximity to the School; and it was erected, and now exists, on the south side of the building, the "Master's Chamber," being at the same time demolished to make room for it. The cost was borne out of a fund raised by public subscription, and the language of the appeal, together with the names of the subscribers and the amounts of their subscriptions, will be found in a subsequent chapter dealing with the Library. But while this fund of £69 19s. 6d. (probably worth £400 now) was spent on raising a new building, the Governors spent a considerable sum at the same time in making the necessary alterations in the School, the most unfortunate of which were the building up of the main entrance which faced eastwards, and making a new one on the South side of

---

(1) This seems to have existed from very early times. See the passage in the Towneley Mysteries, Mactatio Abel (Surtees Society Ed., p. 16)—
When I am dede,
Bery me in Gudeboure at the Quarelle-hede—
and Banks, pp. 49-50, where it is said that this quarry probably supplied stone both for the Parish Church and the Rectory House, as well as for the School.

INSCRIPTION ON OLD BUILDING.
(From a Photograph by Messrs. G. & J. Hall.)

GRAMMAR SCHOOL. 23

the building. The accounts for this year still exist, and contain a list of the alterations and their cost, which will interest those who have had similar duties to execute in the latter part of the nineteenth century: they are as follows :—

For Roofcasting the School, prolonging the seats, removing the door, and a new door frame	16	0 0
Plastring the low part, mending the old, dressing the stone windows, whitening the whole School	02	0 0
For mending the Floor and seats from top to bottom, 10 days work, and finding all materials	00	16 0
Wainscotting each side of the chimney up to the seats, and finding wainscott, etc.	00	14 0
For fixing and finding wood for 2 round windows at each end of the School above the roof	00	7 0
A trap door with ferm Landing and strong joyce to go to the dales above the roof	00	6 0
For fixing those dales from end to end	00	3 6
7 foot of square wood, nails used *in removing usher*[1]	00	3 6
A new desk and hinges with Lock and key for Mr. Clark desk ..	00	5 9
Pointing inside of the slate and finding lime	00	3 6
Lime used in making up the old door place chimney chamber and other breaches in taking down the chamber	00	5 0
Lead to fix the iron Stanches at bottom oth School	00 00	6
Box pulley and screw to fix at the top of the School	00	01 2
10 yds. board and 5 yds of Role for pins to hang hats on ..	00	06 3
Lime Jos: Field used for slating	00	01 2
16 yds plastring against the pan of the roof	00	07 0
To Jos: Field for Flaggs and Flagging the School	03	7 1
To do for Slates blown off	00	7 2
Wm Heald for leading flaggs to the Schoole	00	3 6
For dales above the roof casting from Tho: Pitts	1	5 6
Robt Lee's note for windows mending	1	19 1
For cleaning all the School windows	0	6 0
Pd Mathew Robinson for pointing the winds	0	4 6
To the old woman twice or thrice cleaning the Schoole	00	1 6
To Henry Sharp 3 load of Coal to thaw the flaggs	00	1 6
To Captain Burton 9¼ 100 of Bricks	00	0 6
To Carr of Horbury for making 2 round holes at the ends of the School and mending a window at the end	00	5 4
Ob. Readhead for paving the Goodibour	00	1 6
To Do. and 2 more labourers 2 days clearing rubbish[2]	00	2 6
Wm Bullock for steps and Flagging to the School door	03	05 10
Loss in paying 38 guineas 6d per guinea[3]	00	19 0

(1) I hope this means removing *the usher's desk*.
(2) This is at the rate of 5d. a day per man, the ordinary wages of that time.
(3) In the year 1717 the guinea was reduced in value by royal proclamation from 21s. 6d. to 21s.: see Notes and Queries, 7th S. xi. 335.

Considerable repairs were made in the School in 1758, on the appointment of John Clarke to the Head Mastership, and on other occasions; but the buildings remained substantially the same until they were abandoned in the year 1855 in favour of the present premises.

The most constant source of expense and trouble seems to have been the School windows. After the year 1671 the Head Masters no longer lived on the premises, and there is no trace of a resident Porter or Beadle, as he was called in those days; therefore it was only to be expected, that as the building was apparently only occupied during school hours, windows would be broken both by the boys in their play in the School yard, and by others of a more wantonly destructive spirit. A set of rules framed June 11, 1695, and transcribed in our last chapter, contains a regulation making it part of the monitor's duty on Sundays "to goe out (of Church) once or oftener in Sermon time to see if there be no idle persons about the Schole breaking the windows." The Governors also invoked the assistance of the Town Crier in this matter, as the following oft-repeated record shows:—

Paid for crying the School Windows being broke   00   00   4

The Statutes of 1607 had provided that "if the glasse windowes of the Schole shalbe broken by anye scholler or outcomer then the maister or usher under whose teachinge the said scholler at that time was shalbe answerable for the damage and it make good." But notwithstanding this order, it seems from a volume of accounts from the year 1698 that the Governors at that time paid for the cost of repairing them, and what that cost was is apparent from the following extracts:—

Year	Description	£	s.	d.
1698—9	Robt Lee for Charge of Windows for a year	00	12	0
1699—1700	Robt Lee the Glazier	01	00	0
1700—1	To Widow Lee the remainder by Agreement for Glazing the Schole	00	10	0
1701—2	To Robt Lee the Glazier	00	12	10
1702—3	Paid Robt Lee for new glass and for leading the old glass new as per bill	05	00	0
1704—5	For glazing the School, new doors and repairing the walls, &c.	01	17	11
1705—6	To Robt Lee for mending the School Windows	00	11	6
1706—7	To Robt Lee for mending the School Windows	00	09	0
1707—8	To Robt Lee for mending the School Windows	00	16	0
1708—9	Pd Goodison the Glazier for mending the Windows	00	12	0
1709—10	To Benj. Goodison Glazier his Bill	00	12	0
1710—1	Pd Benj. Goodison his Bill	00	14	8
1711—2	To Goodison for Glazing	00	12	0
1712—3	Pd Goodison for Glazing	00	17	0

GRAMMAR SCHOOL. 25

1713—4	Rob_t Leigh for repairing the windows	..	..	..	02	08	0
1714—5	Pd Robt Leigh for repairing the windows		..	..	01	06	8
1716—7	To Robt Leigh his note for repairing windows			..	01	09	1
1717—8	Robt Lee's note for windows mending	..		..	01	19	1

After this time the Governors seem to have insisted upon the Master and Usher being responsible for the repair of the windows as the Statutes directed, but the trouble was not thereby stopped; for on Nov. 11, 1811 the Governors ordered :—

> "That the windows of the Free Grammar School be immediately repaired at the expense of the Governors, but that in Future they be kept in Repair by the Master and Usher of the School, agreeably to the Statutes."

And as late as Oct. 19, 1837, the following notice was issued :—

> "Whereas the premises and windows of the Free Grammar School have frequently been very much damaged and broken by stones and other missiles, Notice is hereby given that all persons found committing such offences will be severely punished, and a Reward will be paid to any person giving such Information at the Office of the Governors as shall lead to the conviction of the offenders."

Under these circumstances, it will indeed be only expected that all trace of the painted windows given by Richard Bunny, William Savile, and others mentioned above, has long since disappeared.

Grammar School education originally consisted of training in the Latin and Greek languages only, and these were the only subjects which the Masters and Ushers were expected to teach, and the only ones which privileged pupils could claim to be taught without payment of extra fees. This fact was clearly stated in a famous decision by Lord Eldon in the Court of Chancery in connexion with Leeds Grammar School; in the year 1805 the trustees of that School desired to extend the education beyond the Greek and Latin languages, but the schoolmaster opposed them, and the Lord Chancellor decided in his favour, when appealed to, in these words[1] :—

> "The question is not what are the qualifications most suitable to the rising generation of the place where the charitable foundation subsists, but what are the qualifications intended. If upon the instruments of donation the charity intended was for the purpose of carrying on free teaching in what is called a free grammar school, I am not aware, nor can I recollect from any case, what authority this Court has to say the conversion of that institution by filling a school intended for that mode of education with scholars learning the German and French languages, mathematics, and anything but Greek and Latin, is within the power of the Court."

(1) See S.I.C. Report 1868. Vol. I. p. 452.

This being the case, writing and mathematics, when introduced into the curriculum, were usually taught by an extra master at an extra charge, either in the schools themselves or in a contiguous building.

In the case of Wakefield Grammar School, these subjects were added at a very early time [1], and in the year 1758 the pupils in the School were so numerous that the writing master asked the Governors to provide him another building :—

> Nov. 4, 1758. "And upon the petition of Mr. Gargrave to the Governors of the School, to build him a Room apart from the School wherein to teach the Boys writing and mathematics, &c. : It is also ordered to be minuted that the Governors do approve of the Scheme he has laid down in his petition for that purpose."
>
> Mar. 22, 1759. "That a Writing School shall be built for Mr. Gargrave in the Free School Croft according to the plan delivered in by him to the Governors."

The Writing School was accordingly built to the north of the Grammar School, the master paying rent and making his own terms with the boys as to their payments to him. The building still exists, having been purchased from the Governors by the Borough Market Company under their compulsory powers.

The Head Master was originally expected to reside in the School Building, and his "chamber" was on the south side, as has already been pointed out. There is an inventory still extant of some of the furniture of this apartment, which runs as follows :—

> "Item, one faire long joyned table with a forome or bench in the Mr his chamber, made of the schoole charges.
>
> Item, one bedstead, of waynscott carved and wrought, made at the charges of the Governors, standing in the Master's Chamber.
>
> Item, one Study [2] made of waynscott in the Master's Chamber at the charges likewise of the Governors."

The provision of one room could, however, be adequate only in exceptional cases, and a master who was married would have to provide himself with a house elsewhere. It is, therefore, only natural that such accommodation would soon be condemned by the Governors themselves, and this was actually done in the year 1626, at which

---

(1) In many Grammar Schools the Latin and Greek languages actually remained the sole subjects of education until the Endowed Schools' Act of 1869, after which new schemes of instruction were everywhere introduced.

(2) We should now call this a writing-desk or 'escritoire.'

time Mr. Doughty, who was then Master, and the father of a large family, was living in a house provided at his own expense.

> Dec. 26, 1626. "This day William Paulden, spokesman, moved before the present Governors that for the better encouragement of Mr. Doughtye his industrious and diligent instructing of his scollers wee doe allow him iiii. *li.* per annum for his house rent till such tyme as wee did provide him of a fitt house."

Nothing, however, was done in the direction of providing a "fitt house" during Mr. Doughty's tenure of office, which lasted until the year 1663. But in 1671 the Head Master at that time, Mr. Jeremy Boulton, was occupying a house which was subsequently the residence of most of his successors. The "Master's Chamber" was ultimately demolished, as has been already said, to make room for the new Library in 1717.

As to Mr. Boulton's place of residence, it is recorded:—

> Sep. 30, 1671. "The scoole is debtor to the present Governors thirty pounds, deposited towards the paying Thomas Savell Esquire of Lupset for the dwelling house wherein Mr. Boulton now dwelleth."

The house referred to is that in Almshouse Lane, now the residence of W. A. Statter, Esq. An illustration of it, from a photograph by Messrs. G. & J. Hall, of Wakefield, will be found elsewhere.

The inconvenience of having the Master's residence so far from the School was often felt, both by the Governors and the Head Masters, and many proposals appear to have followed the suggestion of providing a "fitt house," which was brought forward in 1626, as the subject is frequently mentioned in the records of the School. But, notwithstanding this conviction, no better arrangement was thought possible by the Governors, and the house remained the Master's residence until 1751, when the Rev. John Clarke was appointed to the Headmastership of the School, at a time when its reputation was attracting a large number of pupils, not only from the County of Yorkshire, but from other counties and countries as well. In this year the house was leased to William Marsden for 21 years on condition of his quitting the premises on a year's notice given by the Governors "for the sake of providing a habitation for the Schoolmaster only, but in no other case." Mr. Clarke, therefore, must have lived elsewhere, probably nearer to the School, as he doubtless felt that the residence placed at his disposal was too far away from his duties.

After the resignation of Mr. Clarke, his successor, Mr. Atkinson, again occupied the usual residence in Almshouse Lane, which is thus described in the advertisement [1] for a successor to Mr. Atkinson:—"Dwelling house in a good state of Repair, and large enough for the Accommodation of Boarders, with suitable out-offices, Stable, Garden, Orchard, and other Conveniences adjoining." The next Master, however—the Rev. Thomas Rogers—in the year 1811 found it necessary to ask the consent of the Governors to enlarge the house by the addition of "a room 20 ft. by 18 ft., with a chamber above it, to be erected contiguous or adjoining to the west end of his present dwelling," and this additional accommodation was provided in 1812.

Dr. Naylor, the successor of Mr. Rogers, lived in a house at Eastmoor, near the present Chapel of the West Riding Asylum; but his successor, Dr. Carter, occupied the usual residence in Almshouse Lane, as did Dr. Taylor, until the erection of the present one in the School Grounds.

The idea of removing the Grammar School from what had become a busy part of the town into a more healthy and convenient situation seems to have occurred as early as the year 1839, when Mr. Carter, who was then Head Master, presented a memorial to the Governors "for the removal of the Grammar School to a more desirable site;" and to this the Governors promised by resolution (dated Nov. 25, 1839) to accede "in the most efficient manner in their power." The resolution then passed was ordered to be inserted in "The Wakefield Journal," and subscriptions were invited in aid of the work.

The scheme, however, came to nothing, partly, no doubt, owing to the fact that the West Riding Proprietary School, founded in 1834, had not been so successful as it at one time promised to be, and in consequence there was a prospect that the fine buildings erected for its accommodation might at some time be acquired by the Governors for the Grammar School.

The West Riding Proprietary School was opened on August 6, 1834, by Earl Fitzwilliam, the president of the institution, with a nominal capital of £15,000, represented by 240 shares. The architect of the building was Mr. Richard Lane, of Manchester, and the foundation stone was laid by the Earl of Mexborough on February 6, 1833.

(1) *Leeds Intelligencer*, Jan. 17, 1795.

GRAMMAR SCHOOL.

For a few years it had a very successful career, the maximum number of boys in attendance being 215, and the teaching provided in it has been very highly spoken of. But from various causes its success was only short-lived, and after about 10 years of existence it became clear that the support which was given to it would not enable the proprietors to carry on the work so auspiciously begun and so useful in its character.

In the year 1847 a Committee was appointed by the Governors of the Grammar School to "confer with the Directors of the Proprietary School towards effecting an union of the Grammar and Proprietary Schools," and at the same time the opinion of counsel was sought for as to the legality of such union. The opinion being adverse, the project was abandoned.

On the very day of the last-mentioned decision—viz., July 30, 1847—the Rev. James Taylor was appointed to the Head Mastership, and he took up the question of removing the Grammar School with resolution and enthusiasm [1]; for on March 3, 1848, he sent an appeal for subscriptions to the *Wakefield Journal*, and on September 30, 1848, he informed the Governors that amongst other promises John Maude, Esq., of Moor House, had undertaken to give £200 for the purpose, provided the removal was effected before the end of 1850. Accordingly the Governors gave their consent to the scheme, and also allotted a piece of land for the purpose, as the following advertisement from the *Wakefield Journal* will shew:—

GRAMMAR SCHOOL OF QUEEN ELIZABETH, WAKEFIELD.

The Grammar School of Queen Elizabeth, in Wakefield, which has been built about 250 years, was once situated in an open and healthy locality. Now, however, it is surrounded by slaughter-houses, dung-heaps, and the most disreputable and offensive lanes and alleys of the town. Owing to the prevalence of the cholera all round, the medical men of the district ordered the School to be closed [2]. But though the cholera added one more objection to the situation of the School, it was a small, because passing one, compared with the physical and moral nuisances of a permanent character. Danger to the health is not greater than the moral risks of the Youth; the vilest of the vile of both sexes being necessarily seen and heard in passing to and from the School. The only remedy which presents itself is to erect a New School, but the endowment is so scanty that it scarcely suffices to secure the services of a Head Master and Usher at £160 and £80 per annum respectively. The Governors, therefore, have no funds wherewith to build, in consequence

(1) Dr. Taylor contributed full particulars of his share in the transactions to the *Wakefield Journal* in December, 1857. (2) The School was for some time conducted in a room in the Corn Exchange during this visitation in the year 1849.

of which and the pressing nature of the case they have unanimously passed the following resolution :—

"Resolved—That the Field belonging to the Governors, in the occupation of Mr. Senior (on Cliffe Hill) and numbered 28 on the Plan Book, page 3, be granted for the purpose of the Erection of a New Grammar School, on the express condition that an adequate sum of money be first raised by subscription for that purpose, and such a plan be also submitted to the Governors as may meet with their approbation."

The site above referred to, on Cliffe Hill, is very eligibly situated for a New School. The expense is estimated at about £1000, and the Committee earnestly hope that you will be kind enough favourably to consider this statement, and be led to assist them in furthering what is on all hands allowed to be a most necessary undertaking.

Subscriptions will be thankfully received at either of the Wakefield Banks, or by any Member of the Building Committee.

BUILDING COMMITTEE.

John Maude, Esq., Chairman, Governor of the Grammar School.
Rev. J. Pullein, M.A., Governor.
Rev. J. P. Simpson, M.A., Governor.
E. Tomlinson, Esq., Governor.
Samuel Stocks, Esq.
D. B. Kendall, M.B., Cantab.
Rev. J. Taylor, M.A., Head Master, Secretary.

Subscriptions Already Promised.

	£	s.	d.
John Maude, Moor House, Esq.	200	0	0
W. H. Leatham, Esq., Heath	50	0	0
A Governor	50	0	0
Rev. J. Taylor, Head Master	50	0	0
S. Stocks, Esq., South Parade	20	0	0

Nothing was, however, done towards erecting a School on Cliffe Hill, as intended, and for two reasons. The subscriptions—though amounting to £700—were not thought sufficient, and there was every year a greater probability that the premises of the Proprietary School would soon be offered for sale. Accordingly the project of building was abandoned, and subscriptions were not called in Mr. John Maude, however, presented the Governors with his promised £200, although the original condition of his donation had not been fulfilled.

On December 7, 1853, the Directors of the Proprietary School at a Special General Meeting were empowered to offer the premises for sale, and the Governors entered into negotiations with them, which at the time proved fruitless. But when the property was advertised for sale by auction, the Governors resolved that it should

GRAMMAR SCHOOL.　　31

be purchased if possible. The School was accordingly sold by auction in December, 1854, and purchased by the Governors, and on the 12th of that month they passed the following interesting vote of thanks :—

> "That the cordial thanks of the Governors are due to the Hon. and Rev. Philip Yorke Savile for his valuable exertions in effecting a purchase of the West Riding Proprietary School on behalf of the Governors of the Free Grammar School, who wish also to express their satisfaction that it has fallen within the Spokesmanship of the Hon. and Rev. Philip Yorke Savile to add that valuable property to an institution so largely indebted to Mr. Savile's family for its foundation and endowments."

The nominal amount of the purchase money was £4050, but the real cost to the Governors, part of which was met by the sale of the advowson of Hooton Pagnell, was much less, owing to the fact that a great number of the Proprietors had given their shares as a present, and many others had sold theirs to the Head Master and the late Wm. Stewart, Esq., who purchased them on behalf of the Governors. In consequence of these facts the Governors passed a vote of thanks to these gentlemen, and sent out the following circular :—

> "The Governors of the Wakefield Grammar School request me to inform you that a vote of thanks has been entered on their minutes to yourself and other Shareholders of the late Proprietary School, for the gift of your share, and to express their hope that the future progress of the Institution may realize the expectations of its Founders.
> "Believe me, yours truly,
> "PHILIP YORKE SAVILE,
> "Spokesman.

"Governors' Offices,
"Wakefield, Aug. 8, 1855."

The present buildings are both commodious and well situated. They consist of a central Hall, which is also used as a Library, measuring about 60 feet by 30 feet, with a small gallery at the west end ; four lofty class-rooms about 40 feet long by 18 feet wide, and eight smaller rooms, the average measurements of which are 16 feet by 20 feet. The School is built upon arches, under which is a convenient playground for wet weather, and two or three rooms available at any time for workshops or other purposes. There is also an excellent cricket and football field behind the buildings, and a green for lawn tennis in the front.

At the present time (1891) it is intended to erect a new Laboratory, Art Room, and Gymnasium at the south end of the School, in commemoration of the 300th anniversary of its foundation ;

and the addition will doubtless be made in the course of the year, from the plans of a former pupil of the School, Mr. George Vialls, of London.

The residence for the Head Master was commenced very soon after the acquisition of the new School building, from the plans of Mr. Richard Lane, of Manchester. Land was procured for the purpose adjoining the playground from Mr. Burnley by the Head Master, who presented it to the Governors; about £500 was raised in subscriptions, and an equal amount resulted from a bazaar which was held in the School: besides this, Colonel J. C. D. Charlesworth presented a similar sum to the Governors for this object in the form of a remission of a tithe rent charge on certain lands of which he was the lay impropriator. The house was finished and occupied in the year 1858 and a wing for the accommodation of boarders was added, from the plans of Messrs. Lockwood and Mawson, of Bradford, in 1878.

Chapter 3.

THE BENEFACTORS.

THERE are many lists in the possession of the Governors recording the names of the numerous benefactors to the School, and the nature and conditions of their gifts: one of them also appears painted on a board in the Cathedral under the title of "A List of the Pious and Worthy Benefactors to this Town and Parish": but this is by no means complete. Mr. Banks, in his "Walks about Wakefield," has also given a number of names not to be found recorded in the Cathedral. This place, however, seems to be the fitting one for doing a well-deserved honour to the memory of all the benefactors whose names are known, by giving short particulars of their gifts, in chronological order; the addition, in the case of donations of land or rents, of some particulars as to various personal and place-names will doubtless be of interest to local readers. It should also be explained that many of the deeds have been translated from the Latin.

1563-4. Feb. 20. FRAUNCYS GRAUNT, of Wakefield, mercer, made his will as follows :—"In the name of the Father and of the Sonne and of the Holye Ghost: Amen. The xxth day of Februarye Anno Domini 1563, and also in the eight yeare of the reigne of our sovereigne Ladye Elizabeth by the grace of God Queene of England, France and Ireland, defender of the faith, &c. I, Frauncys Graunt of Wakefield in the Countye of Yorke, mercer . . . . give and bequeath the yearlie rents and proffettsof one little house or cottage, now in the occupacion of Richard Mercer, adjoyninge to the tenement where I now dwell in [1] of the yearlie value of *ten shillings*, to the use of a fre schole, yf any such fortune to be within the towne of Wakefeild for ever and for so longe tyme as the same shall contynewe, and in defalt of such fre schole then the same yearlie rents to remayne and be to the use of the poore people within the towne of Wakefeild aforesaid." (Prob. July 31, 1566 by the Dean of Pontefract to Henry Grice and Richard Watkinson.)

[1] Elsewhere described as being in the market.

1592. Sep. 12. JOHN FREESTON, of Altofts, Esquire, gave by deed to the Master and Fellows of University College, Oxford, his estate called The Trinities in Pontefract, under trust to make the following payments, amongst others, viz. :—To the Schoolmaster at Wakefield *four pounds* a year, and to two Scholars at University College *ten pounds* a year each. Such Scholars to be chosen out of Normanton Grammar School, or else out of the Free School at Wakefield, or else out of the free Schools of Pontefract and Swillington, or else out of the free Schools in the County of York.[1]

1592-3. March 23. ALLICIA GRAUNTE, widow of Francis Grant above-mentioned, gave "*one rood and a half of land* and all the buildings thereon erected, with the appurtenances thereof, situate lying and being in the Town of Alverthorpe in the Graveship of Alverthorpe aforesaid, and now or lately in the occupation of Christopher Smythe or his assigns." (Surrendered by William Savile; fine for admission 4d).

1593. Oct. 6. GEORGE SAVILE (the elder) of Wakefield, gentleman, gave by will as follows :—" Also I will and appointe that *fourescore pounds* of currant money of England shalbe given out of the goods which I have conveyed to my brother Robert Savile John Battie and George Spivye, to the governors of the free schole of Wakefield to the use of the said schole, to be paid within two years after my decease, if there be any howse builded for kepinge of the said schole within the said two yeares, and if there be not a house builded there for that use within the said tyme, then I will and appoint that the said somme shalbe given to George Savile and Thomas Savile my sonnes, Richard Sproxton, Richard Clayton, William Savile, John Battie, Thomas Robinson and Thomas Cave [2], to be ymployed and bestowed att the discrecion and appointment of them or any foure of them, whereof the one of my said sonnes to be one, to the best use proffitt and commoditie for the poore of the toune of Wakefield." (Prob. Nov. 2, 1593, by the Dean of Pontefract to George Savile and Thomas Savile his sons.)

1594. Oct. 3. GEORGE SAVILE (the younger), of Wakefield [3], gentleman, gave by deed as follows :—" To all faithful Christian

---

([1]) From Reports of University Commissioners, 1873 : there are now three Scholarships of £50 a year each.

([2]) With the exception ot the two sons of George Savile, all these were Governors of the School, a fact which seems to suggest that the first Governors were all friends of George Savile, the founder of the School.

([3]) He was a barrister of the Inns of Court, and died in London Jan. 3, 1595-6. This deed formally carried out the gift of the close by his father, as has been pointed out in the previous chapter, p. 19.

people to whom this present writing may come, George Savile of Wakefield in the County of York, gentleman, greeting in the Lord for ever. Know ye that I the aforesaid George for divers good causes and considerations specially moving me thereto, Have given granted enfeoffed and by this my present writing confirmed to the Governors of the free School of Queen Elizabeth at Wakefield in the County of York and their successors *one small close*, with the buildings thereon erected, lying near the Goodyboure between the Goodybower Lane on the east and a certain croft of Henry Grice, Esquire, on the west. To have and hold the aforesaid close with the buildings thereon erected with their appurtenances by the said governors of the said free school and their successors, For the use and benefit of the said governors and their successors for ever. To be held of the chief lords of the fee by the services previously due and of right accustomed for ever. And I the said George Savile and my heirs will warrant and for ever defend by these presents the said close with the buildings thereon erected with their appurtenances to the said governors and their successors, For the use and benefit above specified against me and my heirs. Provided always that it shall be lawful for me the said George Savile and my heirs during the space of ten years next following to dig up the land and foundation of the said close or any part thereof not built upon, and to make quarries for the purpose of obtaining stones, for my own use and not otherwise."

1594. Nov. 26. JOHN FREESTON, of Altofts, Esquire, gave by will *five hundred pounds* to be laid out in the purchase of twenty-five pounds a year: for a Fellowship of ten pounds a year, and two Scholarships of five pounds a year each, in Emmanuel College 2, Cambridge, the remainder to be for the maintenance and benefit of the said College; boys from Normanton, Wakefield, Pontefract and Rotherham Schools were to have the preference for the Fellowship and Scholarships in the order named.

1594. Dec. 16. GEORGE SAVILE (the younger) of Wakefield, gentleman, gave by will "*an hundreth pounds* of currant englishe money of my parte of the money which is owinge to my brother and me out of my father's detts or other detts which are or may be due joyntlye to us both, whome, I doubt not, will (accordinge to his faithfull promise) performe the truste I have in him, with a good conscience towards

(1) Elsewhere said to be in the tenure of Leonard Cookson.
(2) Subsequently transferred to Sidney Sussex College, see Chapter VIII. The date of the gift is stated in the S.I.C. Report, 1868, p. 190, as being March 26, 1594.

my executors" . . . . "to be ymployed for the purchasinge of so much frehould land to the use of the said schole, As the same will extend unto, And to be no otherwise ymployed uppon payne and condicion of makinge the said legacie and bequest void. And if there want of the said some to be dewe unto me as aforesaid, because of ill detts and the detts which are owinge to Mr Crompton, then I will that the want thereof shalbe supplyed out of the profitts and rents which I have out of the tiethes of Otley and Calverley, and for the further surer payment of the said supply out of the said tiethes, (If it be not paid within thre yeares next after my decease) then I will that the governors aforesaid shall enter to and receive so much of the rentes and profitts of the said tythes as shall make upp the said payment. Also whereas I haue the tiethes of Hooton Pannell to me and to my heires in fee farme, with the advowson of the vickaredge there, (If it happen that I dye without any other yssue besides my daughter aforesaid) Then I give and bequeath the said tiethes with the said Advowson to my said daughter and the heires of her bodye lawfullie begotten, and for defalt of such heires Then I give and bequeath *the third parte of the said tiethes* in three parts to be divided and also *the said advowson* wholy unto Edward Mawde Pastor att Wakefeild, Robert Cooke Pastor at Ledes, Robert Dickson Pastor at Birstall, Edward Whittakers Pastor at Thornehill, gentlemen, Hughe Suell and George Spivye and their heires, To the intent and uppon condicion, that they the said Edward Robert Robert Edward Hughe and George, or the survivor [1] or survivors of them and their heires, shall convey the same to the Governors of the fre Schole of Queene Elizabeth att Wakefeild, payinge the third parte of the rent and other duties due for the same."

1596. Oct. 24. THOMAS SAVILE, of Wakefield, Esquire [2], confirmed by deed his brother's (and father's) gift of the close near the Goodybower, likewise reserving to himself the right of getting stone for ten years from the parts unbuilt on.

1599. April 23. THOMAS SAVILE, of Wakefield, Esquire, gave by deed "to Sir George Savile, Knight, Sir John Savile, Knight, William Savile, gentleman, Richard Clayton and Thomas Cave and their heirs, one annual rent of *three pounds and six shillings*, to be paid annually from and in all that rectory of Thorparch in the said

---

([1]) Hugh Sewell, the surviving trustee, executed a Deed of Sale of Hooton Pagnell Tithes and Vicarage to the Governors of the School as here directed, in default of heirs to George Savile's daughter.

([2]) Second son of George Savile the elder, of Haselden Hall : he became heir on his brother's death, Jan. 1595-6.

County . . . . after the lease thereof now in being, for the use of the master and scholars in the Free Schole of Wakefield."

1599. April 25. EDWARD MAWDE, Clerk, late Vicar of Wakefield [1], gave "one annuity or annual rent of *ten shillings*, to be paid yearly at the feasts of Pentecost and Saint Martin the Bishop in the winter by equal portions, from and in one messuage and all the buildings thereon erected and one garden adjoining the same, in Wrengate in Wakefeild aforesaid near a certain stream called Skittericke Brooke [2], and now in the occupation of Richard Arundell or his assigns." Commutable for the sum of *ten pounds*. (Surrendered by Thomas Cave and Oswald Layborne, fine for admission 8d.)

1599. June 1. THOMAS SAVILE, of Wakefield, Esquire, gave "*one house* or tenement with all the houses thereon built and one close of land belonging to the same tenement . . . . . in Gawkethorpp in the Graveship of Ossett, containing by estimation eight acres, now or lately in the tenure or occupation of Richard Oldroyd. Also *one rood and a half of land* and pasture lying near Flansawe Lane, and adjoining a close called Wheateroyde on the north, and the King's highway on the south, in the Graveship of Alverthorpe, now or lately in the tenure or occupation of Thomas Harrison or his assigns. . . . . . . for the support and maintenance of the master and scholars of the Free Schole of Wakefeild." (Surrendered by Richard Clayton and John Batty, fine for admission 4s. 4d.)

1602. Oct. 22. SARAH SAVILE, widow [3], gave "*one cottage* with all the buildings thereon erected, in Horbury, and now or lately in the tenure or occupation of Joan Sunderland and Joan Haldesworthe widows." (Surrendered by John Battie, fine for admission 4d.)

1602. Oct. 22. JOHN BATTIE, of Westgate, Wakefield, yeoman, surrendered "*one messuage* or tenement builded on the Lord's waste near the Church-sceele [4] of Wakefield, adjoining the high street called Northgate on the east, another street called Bredebothes [5] on the south, a house lately belonging to Richard Flemynge, Gentleman, on the north, and a house once belonging to Francis Graunte on the west, and now in the tenure or occupation of John Marsden."

(1) Also first Head Master of the School.
(2) This started from the neighbourhood of Eastmoor, traversed Wrengate, and ran down Kirkgate, joining the Calder near the bridge: it appears to have been part drain and part brook: the marshy ground near its junction with the river was called the Softs, the name often occurring in the Governors' books.
(3) Widow of Thomas Savile, who died in 1599, afterwards wife of Sir Robert Mounson, Knight: she died in August, 1640.
(4) *i.e.*, common land near the church steps.
(5) The stalls for sellers of bread originated both this and the present name of Bread Street.

1602. Oct. 22. JOHN MOWBRAY, of Wakefield, gentleman, gave "one annuity or annual rent of *twenty shillings*, to be paid by equal portions at the feasts of Pentecost and St. Martin the Bishop in the winter, from and out of the messuage or cottage and all the buildings thereon erected . . . . . in Wakefield, in a certain street there called Northgate, in a certain place called the Bitchehill [1], now in the tenure or occupation of Gervase Brooke or his assigns, the first payment to be made on that feast of the feasts aforesaid next after my decease, [2] for the need and use of the Governors of the Free Grammar School of Queen Elizabeth at Wakefield and their successors for ever, for the stipend and salary of the Schoolmaster and Usher of the said School, also for the repair of the School-house, for the increase of the library of the same, and other needs of the said School. Provided always that if the aforesaid School shall not be fully and perfectly established consummated and finished with one Schoolmaster and one Usher [3] for the teaching of children freely there, according to the true intent of the Letters Patent of the said Queen Elizabeth made for the same, within the space of three years next following after the date of this Court, that then at once the aforesaid yearly rent shall be repaid for the need and use of the poor of the hospital of the late Leonard Bate, Esquire, in the western end [4] of the aforesaid town of Wakefield." (Surrendered by William Savile : fine for admission 20d.)

1602-3. THOMAS CAVE, of Westgate, Wakefield, chapman, one of the Governors of the School, gave " one annuity or annual rent of *forty shillings* [5] from and in one capital messuage or tenement with its appurtenances, situate in Normanton, and in all the buildings thereon erected, lands, tenements, meadows, pastures thereunto belonging, now in the tenure or occupation of Walter Clarke or his assigns." Commutable at £40 within five years.

1602-3. Feb. 6. THOMAS CAVE, of Westgate, Wakefield, chapman, gave by will [6] "to the Fellowes and Schollers of Clarehall in Cambridge and to their successors for ever, all that *half Rectory or Parsonage* of Warmefield . . . . . to the intent and purpose that two of

---

([1]) Elsewhere called Birchehill. Mr. Lumb says it is near the Bull Ring. (Banks, p. 60).

([2]) "He died after Martynmas anno 1609," and the first payment was made at Pentecost 1610.

([3]) Mr. Banks (p. 60) argues that this proviso implies that there was yet no School building erected, whereas such a building is expressly mentioned in the gift. The more likely and natural supposition is that no Usher had hitherto been employed, as the charter had provided : the first mention of an Usher is in 1621.

([4]) *i.e.* at Brooksbank, at the bottom of Westgate.

([5]) This deed was never executed, but the gift was superseded by the subsequent legacy of six pounds a year, mentioned in the next paragraph.

([6]) The will may be found in greater detail in Chapter VIII.

the poorest schollers of the fre gramer schole of Wakefield ..... may be contynuallye for ever maynteyned and kept att learninge within Clarehall aforesaid." He also gave to the governors a yearly rent of *six pounds* out of all his "glebe lands with theire appurtenances belonging to the said Rectory or Parsonage of Warmefield or being part or parcel thereof." (Prob. at York June 7, 1603, by John Bennett, Doctor of Laws, and William Goodwyn, Doctor of Divinity, commissioners for Matthew Archbishop of York, to Robert Cooke [1], Clerk, William Lyster [2], Clerk, Christopher Cave, and Thomas Scoley.)

1602-3. WILLIAM BROMHEADE, of Northgate, Wakefield, clothier, gave by deed "all that *cottage* or tenement with all and singular its appurtenances, situate in Wakefield aforesaid, in a certain street there called Kirkegate, lying between the King's highway on the west and a certain lane called the Owtlane on the south.

1602-3. RICHARD CLAITON, of Westgate, Wakefield, draper, one of the Governors of the School, gave by deed "all that *tenement* situate in Northgate in Wakefield aforesaid, in a certain place there called The Butcher Rawe, between a tenement in the occupation of Peter Alderson on the east, and a tenement in which Elizabeth Lecke widow now lives on the west, now in the tenure or occupation of Elizabeth Snawden or her assigns."

1602-3. GEORGE WHARTON, of Westgate, Wakefield, draper, gave by deed "one annuity or annual rent of *six shillings and eight pence* from and in all that tenement or cottage and all the buildings thereon erected, in Wakefield aforesaid [3], now or lately in the tenure or occupation of Thomas Hawkesworthe or his assigns."

1603. April 21. JOHN ALLOTT, of Bentley [4] in the county of York, yeoman, gave by deed "one annuity or annual rent of *ten shillings* from and in one cottage or tenement with its appurtenances lying in Northgate in Wakefield, now in the tenure or occupation of Katherine Birkdall widow."

1603. July 13. THOMAS BRAMLEY, of London, "citizen and haberdasher," gave by deed "to John Bradley of Wakefield, clothier, and Leonard Wilson of Wakefield, clothier," in reversion for the use of the School after his death, "*one burgage* with a garden thereto belonging, and *three cottages* or tenements with their appurtenances, situate in a street there called Kirkegate, now in the separate tenures or occupations of Thomas Lomme, Robert Gibson and Edmond Bradford, or their assigns": by the same deed he appointed Christopher

---

(1) Vicar of Leeds.   (2) Vicar of Wakefield.   (3) This was in Kirkgate.
(4) Of Bentley Grange, who died March 1, 1655-6.

Naylor of Wakefield, gentleman, and John Wilborc of Wakefield yeoman, his attornies to enter into the said burgage and cottages.

1603. July 13. THOMAS BRAMLEY, of London, "citizen and haberdasher," gave by deed *a cottage* "in a certain place called the Eastmore near Windehill, and *one little close* in Stanley, lying on Windehill near Wakefield aforesaid, and *one other close* lying in Stanley aforesaid, containing by estimation six roods of pasture with their appurtenances, and now in the occupation of Elizabeth Hamshier widow or her assigns": Christopher Naylor and John Wilbore of Wakefield were appointed his attornies in this matter, as in the preceding.

1603. Oct. 7. THOMAS ROBINSON, of Northgate, Wakefield, one of the Governors of the School, gave by deed, "one annuity or annual rent of *six shillings and eight pence* from and in four selions and one other selion called a Headland of meadow and pasture with their appurtenances, lying in or near Wakefield aforesaid, in one close called Allyson rawe in the Cliffeild, between land lately belonging to Thomas Savile, gentleman, deceased, on the south, north, and west, and the Swan lane on the east, now in the occupation of me the aforesaid Thomas or my assigns."

1603. Oct. 16. EDWARD WATKINSON [1], of Westgate, Wakefield, mercer, one of the Governors of the School, gave by deed "one annuity or annual rent of *sixteen shillings and eight pence* from and in one messuage or tenement with the appurtenances, situate in Wakefield, in a certain street there called Westgate, in the market there, between one burgage or tenement called The Black Swan in the occupation of Christopher Sym, and one burgage or tenement called The Crosse Keyes in the occupation of John Richardson, and lately in the tenure or occupation of Nicholas Hoile or his assigns."

1603. Nov. 17. GEORGE SPIVYE, of Northgate, Wakefield, chapman [2], gave by deed "one annuity or annual rent of *five shillings* out of and in all that messuage or tenement and all the buildings houses and structures thereon erected, commonly called or known by the name of The Horshed [3], with all its appurtenances, situate in Wakefeild aforesaid in a street there called Westgate, and a court called a foldstead, one garden and one croft adjoining the same messuage or

---

[1] In some places this gift is put to the credit of "Henry Watkinson mercer and Edward Watkinson his son." Perhaps the son carried out the father's intention.

[2] George Savile the elder married Elizabeth, daughter of George Spivy, and perhaps sister of this George Spivy.

[3] This place seems afterwards to have been called The Golden Cock.

tenement, with their appurtenances, now in the several tenures or occupations of Thomas Patton and Robert Smalfoot or their assigns."

1603. Nov 17. WILFRID ARMITAGE, of Westgate, Wakefield, yeoman, gave by deed "one annuity or annual rent of *three shillings and four pence* from and in one cottage or tenement with its appurtenances, situate in Heckmondwike in the parish of Birstall, now in the tenure or occupation of Richard Chadburne or his assigns."

1603. Nov. 17. WILLIAM POLLARDE, of Westgate, Wakefield, chapman, gave by deed "one annuity or annual rent of *six shillings and eight pence* out of all that messuage or tenement and garden thereto belonging with all and singular their appurtenances, situate in Wakefield in a certain street there called Westgate, and now or lately in the tenure or occupation of Christopher Hollings or his assigns."

1603. Dec. 16. JOHN JACKSON, of Westgate, Wakefield, gentleman, gave "*eleven roods of meadow land* or pasture with the appurtenances, lying in Thornes, within the Graveship of Thornes, now in the occupation of William Shepley or his assigns": (surrendered by John Batty, fine for admission 16*d*.)

1603. Dec. 16. ROBERT WATERHOUSE, of Northgate, Wakefield, mercer, gave "one annuity or annual rent of *five shillings* from and out of five acres and one rood of land with their appurtenances in Thornes, and from and out of a moiety of three acres of land abutting upon Thornes More, and from and out of one rood of land and meadow in Thornes Holme, and also from and out of a moiety of a certain close called Morecrofte with its appurtenances, within the Graveship of Thornes, containing by estimation two acres, now in the tenure or occupation of the aforesaid Robert or his assigns": (surrendered by John Battye; fine for admission 5*d*.)

1603. Dec. 16. ROBERT PIGHILLS, of Westgate, Wakefield, gentleman, gave "one annuity or annual rent of *ten shillings* out of one parcel or close of meadow land or pasture, containing by estimation five roods, with all and singular its appurtenances, lying in the Cliffeild within the Graveship of Alverthorpe, and now in the tenure or occupation of William Smyth or his assigns." (Surrendered by himself, fine for admission 10*d*.)

1603. Dec. 31. ROGER FEILD, of Westgate, Wakefield, chapman, gave by deed "one annuity or annual rent of *four shillings* from and in all that messuage tenement or burgage situate in Wakefield, and in a certain street there called Westgate, and from and in one garden, one croft, and one stable, with the appurtenances to the same belonging, lying between land lately belonging to Henry Waterhouse on the east, and land lately belonging to Roger Pollard, gentleman, on the west, and abutting on the Cliffeild on the north, and now in the tenure or occupation of me the said Roger Feild."

1603-4. Jan. 20. ROLAND BURROWE, of Kirkgate, Wakefield, clothier, gave by deed "one annuity or annual rent of *four shillings* from and in all that messuage or burgage, with the garden and croft thereto adjoining, situate in Wakefeild aforesaid, in a street there called Kirkgate, between land of Robert Dolliffe both on the north side and on the west, and land of George Nailor on the south side, and now in the tenure of me the aforesaid Roland Burrowe or my assigns."

1603-4. Jan. 20. JOHN MAWDE, of Northgate, Wakefield, chapman, one of the Governors of the School, gave by deed "one annuity or annual rent of *twenty shillings* from and in all that messuage tenement or half-burgage, and all the buildings and structures thereon erected, with a garden thereto adjoining, with all and singular the appurtenances thereof, lying in Wakefield in a certain street there called Northgate, between land of Francis Hardye on each side, and now in the tenure of John Hewett or his assigns."

1604. April 4. ROBERT SMYTH, of Westgate, Wakefield, junior, surrendered "*half an acre of land* lying in divers fields in Horburye, namely:—one rood lying in a field called Milnefeild, and another rood lying in the Westefeild of Horbury aforesaid." (Fine for admission 3*d.*)

1604. April 6. JOHN DIGHTON, of Staincliffe, gentleman, gave "*six roods of land* with its appurtenances, lying in divers places in a field there called the Netherfield of Thornes, *two roods of land* or meadow lying as follows, namely:—one rood in the Narholme of Thornes, and another rood in the Farholme: also *one rood of land* or meadow in a place there called Rishie lands, with all and singular their appurtenances, in the Graveship of Thornes [1], and now in the tenure or occupation of John Stable or his assigns:" (surrendered by Robert Pighells: fine for admission 12*d.*)

1604. July 20. MILES BRIGGES, Inhoulder, of Westgate, Wakefield, gave "one annuity or annual rent of *six shillings and eight pence* from and in one rood of meadow land or pasture with the buildings thereon erected, lying in Newton, near one close there called Parson Flatt, with the appurtenances thereof, in the Graveship of Alverthorpe, now in the occupation of Miles Grenewood or his assigns:" (surrendered by John Battye: fine for admission 6*d.*)

([1]) Elsewhere described as being in the Lawe Field, which is perhaps only another name for Netherfield.

1604. July 20. OSWALD LAYBURNE, of Westgate, Wakefield, mercer, gave "one annuity or annual rent of *four shillings* from and in one messuage, one croft, and one garden thereto adjoining, lying in Thornes, now in the tenure or occupation of Jenette Bestwicke or her assigns :" (surrendered by John Battye : fine for admission 4*d*.) This annuity was to be commutable for £4.

1604. July 20. ROBERT KAY, of Westgate, Wakefield, gave "one annuity or annual rent of *fifteen shillings* from and in one messuage or tenement, with all the houses shoppes and buildings thereon erected, with their appurtenances, in the Graveship of Wakefield, situate in a certain place there called Breadboothes [1], and now in the occupation of Richard Askewe and Humfer Cowper or their assigns :" (surrendered by John Battye: fine for admission 15*d*.)

1605. Sept. 5. FRAUNCES ROBINSON, of Westgate, Wakefield, gave "one annuity or annual rent of *six shillings and eight pence* from and in one messuage or cottage, and all the buildings thereon erected, with an orchard and garden thereto adjoining, with their appurtenances, within the Rectory of Wakefield, now in the tenure of George Hill or his assigns " : (surrendered by himself : fine for admission 4*d*.)

1605. Dec 20. RICHARD LISTER, of Milnethorpe, Clerk, gave by deed " one annuity or yearly rent of *twenty shillings* from and in all that messuage or tenement lying in Woodthorpe, and from and in all meadow lands and pastures lying near Woodthorpe, or within the fields of Sandall called Carre and Carrflatts, lately in the tenure of Richard Wilcocke, containing by estimation thirty six acres of land to the said messuage or tenement belonging, with their appurtenances, in Woodthorpe aforesaid and Sandall, now in the tenure or occupation of me the aforesaid Richard Lister or my assigns."

1605. Dec 21. GERVASE HATFEILD, of Stanley, gentleman, gave by deed "*one messuage* or tenement, and *one gardenstead* to the said messuage or tenement belonging, situate in Wakefield in a street there called Wrengate, with their appurtenances, now in the tenure or occupation of William Richardson."

1606. Nov. 25. ANDREW SCATCHERD, of Northgate, Wakefield, chapman, gave by deed "one annuity or annual rent of *thirteen shillings and four pence* from and in all that messuage or tenement, with its appurtenances, situate in Northegate in Wakefield aforesaid, now in the tenure or occupation of Ralph Robson or his assigns."

---

[1] Elsewhere called "a messuage in bredbothes at the bull rynge."

1607. May 8. THOMAS HARRISON, of Westgate, Wakefield, yeoman, gave "*one cottage* in Alverthorpe, with one croft to the same belonging, with their appurtenances, within the Graveship of Alverthorpe aforesaid:" (surrendered by John Battye.)

1608. Nov. 21. WILLIAM ROODES, of Crofton, chapman, gave by deed "one annuity or annual rent of *twenty shillings* from and in one close of meadow or pasture, called Lister close, containing by estimation ten acres, lying in Crofton aforesaid, between one close of me the said William Roodes on the north, and lands of Sir Richard Gargrave, Knight, on the south, and now in the tenure of me the said William Roodes or my assigns."

1609. June 9. JOHN BATTYE, and ELIZABETH BATTYE his wife, gave "all that *tenement or cottage* with all the buildings thereon erected, with their appurtenances, in Northgate in Wakefield, and *one garden* to the same belonging, situate in a certain street there called Wrengate, with its appurtenances, within the Graveship of Wakefield aforesaid, now in the tenure of Thomas Sonyer or his assigns: (surrendered by themselves.)

1611. Sept 24. SIR RICHARD GARGRAVE, Knight, of Nostell, gave by deed "*one close of pasture* containing by estimation two acres, situate in the township of Stanley of the parish of Wakefield, adjoining the Easte moore at the southern boundary, and lying between the Easte moore lane on the west, and lands of John Cudworth, gentleman, on the east, and now in the tenure or occupation of Robert Swifte or his assigns. And also the reversion and reversions, remainder and remainders, of the said close with its appurtenances, and all the estate, right, title, interest and demand of me the said Richard Gargrave whatsoever in and to the said close or parcel thereof, also the rents and annual profits whatsoever, under whatever demises or grants of the premises in any manner reserved."

The above gifts are those which were made up to the year 1611, of which the detailed records have been preserved: but there are many other benefactions which must have been made during the first 20 years of the School's history, and are mentioned in various documents in the possession of the Governors, though their dates are lost. A list of these is now given, as complete as it is possible to make it.

GRAMMAR SCHOOL. 45

"ROBERT COCKILL, mercer, gave by yeare xx*s.* for ever for one Close in the Cliffield in the occupacion of Thomas Hawkesworth.

HENRY GRYCE, of Sandall, Esquier, did give one little parke in the Swallinge Stones, in the tenure of William Savile, gentleman, worth by yeare for ever x*s.*

MRS. MARYE BIRKHEADE and NATHANIEL BIRKHEADE, Esquier, her sonne, gave x*s.* by yeare for ever.

MRS. MARYE BIRKHEADE gave an Annuitie duringe her liffe per annum vi*s.* viii*d.*

MR. EDWARD ROBARTS, of Kirkgate, Wakefield, merchant, gave by yeare v*s.* for ever out of halfe an acre of lande in Faireburne near Brotherton [1].

MR. WILLIAM SAVILE, of Kirkgate, Wakefield, gentleman, gave by yeare in lands x*s.* for ever: he hathe drawen, ingrossed, and inrolled all the evidence for the poore, repaired the Churche Porche for the use of the Governors to kepe their evidence and sitt in for good orders for the Schole: he hathe bestowed costes sundry waies on the Schole, and hathe given by will to it ten pounds, and provided twenty tymber trees which builded, floured, and seated the Schole: and other things he gave to the Schole.

CHRISTOPHER NAYLOR, gentleman, gave ten pounds in money.

GREGORY PAULDEN, of Kirkgate, Wakefield, gave by year for ever vi*s.* viii*d.*

MR. ROBERT SAVILE, gentleman, of Ouchthorpe, gave in lands x*s.* for ever. He died and never made assurance, and

MISTRESS ALICE SAVILE, daughter to Robert Savile, deceased, gave xl*s.* in money.

MR. HENRY ARTHINGTON, gentleman, gave xx*s.* yearly in money durante vita.

MR. WILLIAM LISTER, Vicar of Wakefield, gave xx*s.* yearly in money durante vita.

MR. JOHN FLEMING, gave out of a house in Wrengate, x*s.* yearly during his father's life.

HUGHE CRESSYE Esquier, gave xx*s.* yearly durante vita sua from the 14th April, An. Dni. 1609, sub conditione to have the placing of two scholars [2], though hereafter he remove his Dwelling out of the towne and parishe.

THOMAS PILKINGTON, Esquire, of Horbury, gave twenty pounds in money for the purchase of lands.

(1) In the parish of Fryston.
(2) One of his sons afterwards became one of the most distinguished men ever educated at the School.

Mr. JOHN DIGHTON gave ten pounds in money.
MICHAELL BENTLAY and MARTIN LISTER gave ten pounds in money.
MR. SAVILE of Milnethorpe gave ten pounds in money, which was paid by Mrs. Elizabeth Savile, his widow.
MR. WATKINSON gave six pounds thirteen shillings and fourpence in money.
JOHN JENKINSON gave xl$s$. in money.
THOMAS SONYER gave xl$s$. in money.

In Kirkgate in landes given :—

Thomas Burrowe,	vi$s$. viii$d$.
John Bradley	vi$s$. viii$d$., out of his house.
Gregory Paulden	vi$s$. viii$d$.
Robert Dymonde	vii$s$.
Robert Lumme	iv$s$., out of his house.

In Stanley in landes given :—

Mrs. Woodrove	xx$s$.
Thomas Dinisoun	vi$s$. viii$d$.
Mr. Francis Savile	xs.
Mr. Bradforth	....
John Stockes	....

In Horbury in landes given :—

Mr. Lister	xx$s$.
John Longley	xs.
Roger Awdesley	vi$s$. viii$d$.

Given in money to the fre Schole at Wakefield by the inhabitants of Westgate :—

Mr. Robert Kay	xli.
Mr. Somestar	vili.
William Elliott	vli.
Roger Fielde	iiiili.
Robert Warriner	iiili.
Robarte Beeston	iiili.
Thomas Grene, mercer	iiili.
Richard Poile	iiili.
Thomas Browne, chapman	iiili
William Smithe	xl$s$.
Robart Smithe	xl$s$.
Wilfray Armitage	xl$s$.

GRAMMAR SCHOOL. 47

John Woffenden	xxx$s$.
William Morehouse	xxx$s$.
Mathew Browne	xxx$s$.
William Riddlesden	xx$s$.
John Benson	xx$s$.
John Tomson	xx$s$.

Such in Norgate as giveth money :—

George Spivie	vli.
James Rawsonn	vli.
Robart Patten	iiili. vi$s$. viii$d$.
Thomas Senior	xl$s$.
John Walker	xx$s$.
Thomas Tomsonn	xx$s$.
Brian Garnet	xx$s$.
Roger Elmsall	xx$s$.
Leonard Willsonn	xl$s$.
Francis Tailer	xx$s$.

Such in Kirkgate as giveth money :—

Thomas Burrow	vili. xiii$s$. iiii$d$.
Gregorie Paulden	vili. xiii$s$. iiii$d$.
John Newbie	vili. xiii$s$. iiii$d$.
Robert Lumme	iiili. vi$s$. viii$d$.
Robart Swifte	iiili.
John Tottie, clothier	iiili.
Robart Cooke	xl$s$.
Widdowe Browne	xxx$s$.
John Bromehead	xx$s$.
John Siddall, clothier	xx$s$.
John Thornes	xx$s$.
Henry Casson, dier	xs.

The above list of benefactors is, without doubt, a very imposing one; it would indeed seem from it that almost every inhabitant of importance in the town and neighbourhood had given something to the School, so as to endow it with a satisfactory sum. The words of Roger Dodsworth, quoted in the previous chapter, "and a laye was gathered in the town for a sufficient supply thereof," seem to indicate that in the end, in order to complete the endowment, all the wealthier inhabitants, who had hitherto given nothing, agreed to contribute a sum towards the foundation proportionate to their income: and some colour is given to this supposition by the fact that in one or two cases the gift of money which was expected was never actually paid. It is also worthy of remark that if all the promised gifts had been received, the annual income of one hundred marks (£66 13s. 4d.) would apparently have been obtained as authorized in the Charter: as a matter of fact, the endowment did not quite reach that sum. This can hardly be a mere coincidence, but seems to show that the "laye" was intended to produce 100 marks.

A careful calculation shows that in or about the year 1611, the gifts which had been made to the School, included—

(1) about £350 in money, chiefly used to purchase lands and to build the School, say £2,500 in present value.

(2) rents and annual gifts of about £50 a year, say £350 of our money [1].

(3) a Freeston Fellowship of £10 a year (worth £52 in 1850) and two Freeston Scholarships of £5 a year each (worth £26 in 1850) at Emmanuel (afterwards at Sidney Sussex) College, Cambridge, open to boys from Normanton, Wakefield, Pontefract, and Rotherham Schools [2].

(4) two Cave Scholarships of £6 a year each (worth £50 now) at Clare Hall, Cambridge, open to Wakefield boys only.

(5) two Freeston Scholarships of £10 a year each (now three of £50 each) at University College, Oxford, open to boys from Normanton, Wakefield, Pontefract, and Swillington Schools.

Anthony à Wood, the famous Oxford antiquary, visited Wakefield in 1618, and gives the following account [3] of the state of the School

---

[1] The careful management of the Governors of the School for 300 years could hardly receive better testimony than the fact that the amount now coming in from this source, notwithstanding the losses during the Civil War and at other times, is just about £480 per annum.

[2] These are now lost to the School: see Chap. VIII.

[3] The MS. is in the Bodleian Library at Oxford.

at that time, which agrees tolerably well with the records possessed by the Governors :—

> WAKEFELD IN YORSH.
> The free School there founded by Qu. Elizabeth about the 30 yeare of her raigne endowed with lands and houses in and about the towne to the value of 50 *ll* p. an. by the benevolence of the parishioners. Note that the said Queen granted a mortmain to the parishioners to purchase lands to the value of 100 marks p. an. which is brought alreadie to the value of 50 *ll* almost by the care of the governors chosen for that purpose—George Savile a Blackwell Hall man and his sons Georg of the Inns of Court and Thom. 2d son gave the scite thereof—George Savill the father gave besides the site 6 *ll* p. an. ¹ and a legacy of 100 *ll* toward the building of the house.
> (This relation was from Mr. Isaack Schoolmaster an. 1618.)

The imperfections of this account, and the omission of all mention of the Scholarships already belonging to the School, may easily be explained by supposing that Anthony à Wood was content with verbal information of a general character from the Head Master of that time, and did not consult the books of the Governors.

The endowment of the School with such a considerable estate in lands and money so early in its history was a great achievement, and one for which subsequent generations owe both admiration and gratitude. Yet there is reason to believe that many benefactions have never been recorded at all. For it appears that, although the School was intended to provide education without payment for the poorer boys of the town and parish, yet parents in prosperous circumstances, though residing in Wakefield, were expected to give some equivalent for the education of their sons. There is sufficient evidence in the Governors' books to this effect :—

> April 13, 1624. " This day it is agreed that Mr Doughty shall cause divers of the Scollers whose parents are thought to be able to be benefactors to the Schole to give notice to their parents to come before the Governors on Wednesday after Whitsunday next to show cause why they should not be benefactors to the Schole or els their children not to be taught."

> Jan. 12, 1624-5. " The Governors, aided by Sir John Savile, this day enquired into the reason of parents being veric backward and unwilling to geve : and it is ordered by all the said Governors present that there shalbe a note made of all such as being fitt to geve have refused or offered so verie little that it is not thought fitting to accept of such small gifts : and that it shalbe sett upon the Spokesman's order to Mr Doughty that he shall not teache any of their children frely in the Scole, but if any of their children come to be taught that he shall take at the least one third part more of wages for them than he doth for strangers."

(¹) Anthony à Wood seems to fall into the same mistake, of confusing father and son, which has been referred to above.

Oct. 8, 1627. "This day it is further ordered that all such persons within the towne and parishe who now have their children taught at the schole whose names are hereunder written, being thought men of ability and such as have not bene benefactors to the said schole, that except they do paye to Mr Doughty and Mr Wilcocke 26 shillings and 8 pence per annum for every of such children as they still have taught, the said children shalbe returned from the said schole and not taught there, according to a former order made the xii th day of January 1624 by the consent of the Rt. Hon. Sir John Savile of Haighe Knt, and the governors then present, viz:—the children of Mr Cotton Horne, Edward Copleye, John Sunderland, Tymothie Denisone. It is also this day ordered that the aforesaid Scholemaisters shall every year the day after Michs day, being the day whereon there is a new Spokesman to be chosen, bring in to the Governors a perfecte note of all such scollers as shall be taught by them, with notice how many be forreners and strangers, and how many are taught within the town and parish of Wackfeilde."

These records will not only help to explain the large number of benefactions apparently given in the first twenty years of the School's history, but will also naturally lead to the supposition that there are many others of a smaller amount which have not been recorded. However, in 1627 it seems that parents of position were no longer expected to give land or houses or yearly sums of money, but to pay regular School fees for their sons, like those who lived outside the parish.

It now only remains to add the benefactions which are known to have been made at a later time, some of them very important and valuable.

1672. Dec. 7. RICHARD WILSON, of Wakefield, gentleman, gave "*a close of land* commonly called and known by the name of Ingholme with the appurtenances lying and being at or near Thornes," the rents of which were to be divided into five equal portions, to be given to the Vicar and Curate of Wakefield, the Head Master and Usher of the Free Grammar School at Wakefield, and the poor of Wakefield.

1674. April 29. JOHN STORIE, merchant, of Hasleborrow, in the parish of Norton, in the County of Derby, gave by will *all his lands*, copyhold and freehold, in the County of York, to his sister, Margaret Wingfield, for her life, and after her decease to maintain three poor boys at Cambridge or Oxford for three years. These boys were to be chosen from those who had passed into Wakefield Grammar

School from the Petty School [1] which he founded there [2]. He also gave *a thousand pounds* to his niece, Margaret Wingfield, if she married with her mother's consent and approbation: otherwise the money was to be used to educate three more poor boys at Cambridge or Oxford for three years [3].

1684. Oct. 14. WILLIAM DENISON, of Wakefield, gentleman, gave one moiety of his tithes called *Cliffield Tithe* to the Vicar of Wakefield, two-thirds of the other moiety to the poor of Wakefield, and the third part of the second moiety to the Governors of the School, to be divided into three parts, two for the Master, and one for the Usher [4].

1722-3. Jan. 3. JOHN BROMLEY, of Wakefield, gentleman, gave "*twenty pounds a year* to the two teaching masters of the Grammar School of Wakefield, share and share alike, at the feast of the Nativity of our Lord God, commonly called Christmas day. Item, I give *five pounds* to be bestowed in Books for the use of the Library in the Free Grammar School in Wakefield aforesaid, to be bought with the approbation of the Head Master there."

1725-6. Feb. 20. JAMES SILL, of Wakefield, mercer, gave as follows :—" I give and bequeath to the Governors and Trustees of the free Grammar School of Wakefield the summe of *thirty pounds* to be imployed by them for the benefit of the said school in such manner as they shall think most advantageous for the same."

1733. Dec. 26. "*A gentleman unknown*," according to the Governors' books, "has by the hands of Mr. Newstead [5] given *Sixty Pounds* to be appropriated to the same use as Mr. Storie's Gift to the University, and likewise desired the same may be laid out in the purchase of lands for that purpose."

1734. Feb. 3. "*An unknown hand*" is said to have paid *Sixty Pounds* to Mr. Rey. Newstead for the same purpose as the preceding gift; and this sum "with sixty pounds formerly paid by the said Mr. Newstead" is also to be laid out in lands.

(1) This School was never fully established. See Ch. viii.

(2) The value of this gift was about £25 a year in 1700, and £35 in 1750: now it produces about £400 a year, having been augmented by subsequent gifts for the same purpose.

(3) Nothing was received under this head, see Ch. viii.

(4) The University Commissioners in 1827 reported this as being not worth collecting. Reports Vol. 17, p. 684.

(5) Mr. Reynold Newstead was Deputy-Registrar of Deeds for the West Riding (Taylor p. 315).

1747. Oct. 21. THE MOST REV. DR. JOHN POTTER, Archbishop of Canterbury, gave as follows :—" Also I give the sum of *One Hundred Pounds* to the Governors of the Free School at or near Wakefield in Yorkshire, to be by them applied according to their discretion [1] for the benefit of the said School the Place of my Education."

1765. THE REV. JAMES WOOLLEN, Rector of Emley, in the West Riding of the county of York, gave as follows :—"At the expiration of my wife's natural life, I bequeath the sum of *Sixty Pounds* to the Governors and Trustees of the Free Grammar School of Wakefield, as a grateful acknowledgment of the Exhibition of Twenty Pounds per annum I received from them in the needful part of my Education, beseeching the Governors to realize the said sum (as soon as they conveniently can [2]) and so incorporate it with the Exhibition of Twenty Pounds per annum as to be annually conferred upon one and the same person that shall be thought duly qualified for the other."

1851. Oct. 28. JOHN MAUDE, of Moor House, Stanley, Esquire, gave *two hundred pounds* towards the removal of the School from the Market Place to its present situation.

1856. Nov. 4. JOHN CHARLESWORTH DODGSON CHARLESWORTH, of Chapelthorpe Hall, Esquire, gave the *tithe rent charges* on the property belonging to the Governors of which he was Lay Impropriator, in the townships of Wakefield, Alverthorpe and Stanley, in trust for the benefit of the Head Master of the Grammar School for ever, if a house were built for the Head Master.

([1]) This legacy was first appropriated to the School account, but in 1750 it was transferred to the Storie University Gift account, as the three previous legacies had been.

([2]) The sum was paid to the Governors on Jan. 30, 1792, with 5 years' interest which had accrued since the death of the donor's wife.

Chapter 4.

THE STATUTES.

IT has been already pointed out that in the first twenty years of the History of the School the endowment was practically completed and the School buildings erected; a supply of scholars also was regularly being sent to the Universities, and the other duties of the School satisfactorily discharged. But it was not until November 25, 1606, fifteen years from the foundation of the School, that the first Spokesman, or Chairman of the Governors, was elected; and one of the first duties undertaken by the Governors after this necessary step was to frame proper statutes for the management of the School. The Charter of Queen Elizabeth had empowered them to do this, and the power remained theirs until removed by "The Endowed Schools Acts" of 1869, 1873, and 1874, when it passed into the hands of the Charity Commissioners, who framed a scheme in 1875 for the first time, and have just completed another in 1891. Within eight months of the appointment of the first Spokesman the "Statutes of the Free Grammar School of Queen Elizabeth at Wakefield" were prepared and signed, and everything requisite thus provided for the efficient working of the School in the future.

From the elaborate nature of the Statutes it would seem that they were the work of experienced hands; certainly they are the work of men of education and University training. It should be noted that the day of their approval is also the day of the resignation of the Schoolmaster of that time, Mr. Jeremy Gibson; that his appointment was from the commencement intended to be temporary; that he only held office for seven weeks, nearly two of which fell in the holidays; and that he signed the Statutes, although his successor was appointed on the same day. These facts seem to make it probable that he was appointed almost for the purpose of drawing up the Statutes, a work in which he may have had experience elsewhere, though almost nothing has been discovered about his previous or subsequent history. It is quite certain that there is some resemblance shown by some of the Wakefield Statutes to those of other Schools, as may be seen by a reference to "Carlisle's Endowed Grammar Schools," in which several School Statutes are quoted *in extenso*: but there is no ground at present known to the writer for supposing that the Wakefield ones are mere copies of any others.

It is therefore probable, under all the circumstances mentioned above, that the credit for the drawing up of the Statutes of this School should be given to the first Spokesman—Mr. William Savile, deputy steward of the Manor of Wakefield – the Rev. William Lister, M.A., who was then Vicar of Wakefield, and the Rev. Jeremy Gibson, M.A., who was then Schoolmaster.

The original copy of the Statutes still remains in very good condition: the handwriting is probably that of the Schoolmaster. The book contains not only the first Statutes, but also other additions made from time to time, and the autograph signatures of the various Governors and Schoolmasters who gave their approval to them. A full transcription of them is here appended, with the curious vagaries of spelling carefully preserved: the abbreviations are, however, not kept, but the words written in full.

The Preface to the Statutes of the Free Grammer Schole of Quene Elizabethe att Wakefelde.

The Preface. THERE is nothinge that can more advaunce the florishinge and constant happines of any Kingdome or common welth, then in them the advancement of divine and humane knowledge, the undoubted mother of all good pollicie in the magistrate, and of all right obedience in the people. And thus not onelie the Jewes had theire Scholes in Siloh, Ramoth Gilead, Hiericho, Bethel, and Mount Carmel, and their eighte and fortie dispersed scholes, the cities of the Levites, with theire synagogues in after tyme of their decayed churche and state, but heathen princes in theire severall countreies were carefull for the erectinge and contynuance of scholes and howses of good learninge. Answerable to whiche examples, it pleased the high and mightie prince Quene Elizabeth, Quene of Englande, France and Irelande, &c., a prince of blessed memory in hir other princelie care of the Universities and scholes of this land, to erect and found a free grammer schole at Wakefeld, by the name of the free gramer schole of Quene Elizabeth at Wakefeld. By which hir foundacion amongst other things, power and aucthoritie was geven to the governours and to theire successours for ever, or to the more part of them, with the scholemaisters advice and consent for the tyme beinge, to make good and necessarie statutes and ordinances in writinge under theire common seale, for the better orderinge rulinge and governinge of the saide free schole, and scholemaister, and of the landes, possessions revenues and goodes of the saide schole from tyme to tyme, with all other things whatsoever unto the saide schole belonging : So that the saide Statutes and ordinances were not repugnant to the Lawes and statutes of the realme. We therefore the present governours dulie consideringe the necessitie of statutes to be made, without which we adjudge the schole maymed and imperfect in it selfe, and also consideratly weighinge the trust reposed in us, for the generall welfare of the schole, and for the framinge of fitt statutes for the same, with the advice and consent of the Scholemaister for the tyme beinge: Doe (with the present scholemasters advice and consent) ordaine and decree as statutes of this schole, theise followinge (which we have subscribed with oure handes, and ratifyed by the putting to of oure common seale) to be observed and kept as the Statutes of the free grammer Schole of Quene Elizabeth att Wakefeld.

Of the Spokesman or President Governour.

CAP. I.
To chuse the Spokesman on the morowe after Micha's daye.

The daie next after the feast of St. Michael tharchangell, if it be not the Sabbaothe daie, and then the next daye immediatlye followinge, all the governours shall yearlie frome time to tyme meet together att eighte of the clocke in the morninge, in the litle chamber over Wakefeld Church porche, if no other place hereafter be appointed as the ordynarie place of the Governours generall meetinge for schole causes : and then we will they shall meet att the ordinary place so appointed, att the same hower and same daie, there amongst themselves out of theire owne number to make choice of a Spokesman or President governour for the yeare followinge. Att which assemblie we will that the President governour for the yeare last past or in his constrained absence the deputie governour be present : where we will that the Governours beinge come together, the Spokesman if present, or in his absence the

The Spokesman to deliver up the keys, accounts, and money to the most ancient Governor.

deputie shall delyver up the keyes of his office and second booke of Statutes and Indenture of accompte to the governour there present most auncyent by election, which donne he shall take his owne place of senioritie as it falls amonge the rest. And then the seniour govenour shall exhort the govenours assembled everie one to nominate a Spokesman for the yeare followinge, and him whom the greater part shall name for Spokesman, the senior

Every one to nomynate a Spokesman and chuse him.

Governour shall pronounce to be elect Spokesman or President governour for the yeare followinge, who so chosen, if he be present, shall then, or if absent, att the next meetinge, take a corporall othe ministred unto him by the seniour governour in this forme—

The Spokesman's othe.   I, *A.B.* chosen Spokesman of the free Grammar Schole of Quene Elizabethe att Wakefeld, will to the uttermoste of my power studie, devise, forsee and take care for all such things as touch the commodities and good order of this schole. The Statutes of the schole made and established I will diligentlie see kept so far as in me lyes. And when I shall knowe any thinge by my selfe, or by informacion of others that ys doubtfull, or necessarie, and toucheth the welth or good order of this schole, I will call my fellowe governours together, and quietly debate the matter with them, and that that shalbe agreed upon by the moste part, I will diligently putt in execution to my power, so farr as it concernes me, So helpe me God in Christe Jesus.

To enter to his place and have the keyes delivered to hym. So soone as the Spokesman elect haithe thus taken his othe, the keys of office and second booke of statutes and Indenture of accounte shalbe delivered him, and thenceforwarde he shall take the place and execute the office of Spokesman for that yeare, unles in the meane tyme he die, or through the litle care of his othe and place, be by the governours deposed from *The deputie execute.* his place of Spokesman and governour, as unworthie. In both which cases we will, that the deputie Spokesman shall execute the whole office of the Spokesman or President Governour for the remainder of the yeare unexpired. Otherwise the Spokesman elect shall execute the office without deputie by himselfe, if he be att home *Eleccion of a deputie Spokesman* and in healthe. The election of a deputie Spokesman shall be made in the same sorte and order, as was the election of the Spokesman, and imediatly followinge upon it. Att this dyet also shall in the third place be elect by consent of the greater part of governours present, a keper of the seconde keye of the greate *The kepeing of the keyes.* chest. Of which as of the litle chest, the Spokesman shall alwaies keep the one key, and of the litle chest the Scholemaster for the tyme beinge shall alwaies kepe the other. These elections made, the Spokesman shall propounde (as the tyme and occasion shall require) the matters of the Schole, For it appertaineth to the Spokesman, in all meetings of the Governours to declare the cause of the meetinge, to moderate theire conferences, to take the voices of the other governours, to geve the answeres agreed upon by the greater part, to sucche as are suters for Leasses, or have occasion with the governours, to see that all things needful to be regestred, be truelie inrolled in the bookes appointed for these purposes, to give the othe to all suche as in his yeare by statute are to be sworne, to gather carefullie the whole rentes, providentlie to lay out for the schole wants, and ffaithfullie to account for his whole yeare of Presidentshipp with the governours. The indenture of accounte signed by the governours he shall keep for his yeare, and in the gevinge up of his office he shall with his keyes and second booke of Statutes it delyver up, to the governour present most aunctent by election. In consideracion of all which his paines, we order and decree, that in all meetings when the voices of the governours (in which number we account him one) shalbe equal, that then and not els, the voice of the President governour shall be a castinge voice, and the consent shalbe as of the greater part. And we will further that all the Governours (savinge unto everye man his higher place of worshipp and degree) shall respect and regard the Spokesman, as theire moderatour and chiefe for that yeare, both willinglie yieldinge unto him the right of his place, and undergoinge the censure of his reprehension att theire meetings, yf any such happen to be drawen from him, by the to much forwardnes of mens provokinge and provoked speaches. Yet shall it not be lawfull for the Spokesman or the deputie Spokesman, secretly and by stelth to procure any meetinge of a few governours without sufficient and lawfull warninge geven to the whole companie of governours att home, so they dwell in Wakefelde or with in two myles thereof, of tyme and place to passe any leasse or grant, or make any acte touchinge any thinge that concerns the schole. But whatsoever shalbe so enacted we adjudge utterly voide to all purposes. Now sufficient and lawfull warninge we interpret, when the President governour or he that for that tyme executes that place, doth either in the disolvinge of a present meeting give warninge by himselfe of the tyme of the next dyet, or doth by the bedle of the scole for the tyme beinge, send word particularlye to all the Governours being at home, as ys afforesaide, of the appointed tmye of meetinge, and leaves word thereof att their howses in theire beinge abrode. And lastly we will have it taken for sufficient warninge, when the statute appoints in particuler the tyme of meetinge, although no other warninge thereof be given. The governours thus warned, we ordaine and decree shall come together and contynue att the place of appointed meeting unles they be hinderred by mightie and urgent occasion, to be allowed by the greater part of governours if exception be taken to the absence. And upon such warninge, notwithstandinge the absence of divers the governours, we will and ordaine that the greater part of the governours shall and may lawfullie order any cause concerninge the schole in as good and ample sorte, as yf the whole number of governors had the same decreed, and that, and every such acte this statute doth ratyfie, as good and lawfull. But it shall not be lawfull to enact, order, decree, graunt or confirme anye thinge concerninge schole affaires, when as there are not assembled the greater part of the whole number of Governours, no not though all present should consent in the decree or graunt. The displacinge of the Spokesman shall not be but upon great cause, as perjurie, murther, theft, fornication, adulterie, incest, forgerie of evidence, notorious neglect of his place and office, and faults of the like kinde, to be adjudged by the governors. In all which cases it shall be lawfull for the Governoure most auncient by election of all those that dwell in Wakefield or two miles thereof by election most auncyent, to call together the rest of the Governors, and upon the notoriousnes of the fact of misdemeanour by the Spokesman committed, to displace him frome the office of Spokesman or Governour, with the consent of the greater part of Governors, never after to be chosen governour of the saide schole.

Of meteinge appointed by statute.

All Governors to mete uppon warnying

The greater parte to order any cause.

Displaceing of the Spokesman uppon great cause of defaut.

Of the Governors, theire Quallitie, Election and Othe.

CAP. 2. **Because** the cheife well doinge of the schole can not but consist in the vigilancie and godlie care of the Governours thereof. We will therefore and ordaine that no man shalbe chosen governour of this schole, which ys not able to governe himselfe, or that lyves inordinatlie or fraudulouslie with his neighbours, as either beinge a negligent or a frutles hearer of Gods worde, or is free of notorious crime, yet under the age of xxxtie yeares, or not able to lyve well or competentlie of himselfe. But suche a one we would have chosen governour as is a frequent and attentive hearer of Gods holy truth, and an expressour of the same in his practice, and that

What manner of person a Governor shalbe.

GRAMMAR SCHOOL.   59

lyvinge within Wakefeld or within two miles thereof, is discreet, moderate, peacable, not too much given to the world, or to his owne ease, but such a one as for the scholes good will willinglie be imployed, though it be with some losse and hinderance to himselfe. As often therefore as it shall happen the place of one Governour or more to be voide we will that within foure daies of the vacancie knowen the Spokesman for the yeare shall call together his fellowe Governours and havinge declared the said vacancie to them, he shall desire them, by themselves and with others diligentlye to consider of some meet person or persons dwellinge in Wakefeld or within two miles thereof, to be chosen into the place or places vacant, whose election we will shalbe the fourth daie after the present meetinge if it be not the Sabbaoth, and then the daie immediatlie followinge. Att which tyme the Governors beinge assembled, and calling unto them the Scholemaister for the time beinge, it shalbe lawfull for anie of the saide Governours to nominate to the vacant place of Governour whom he shall judge meet to be chosen. And he or they whome the greater part of Governours shall agree upon, with the consent or likinge of the Scholemaster for the tyme beinge shall thenceforward be reputed and taken as governour or governours of the free grammer schole of Quene Elizabeth att Wakefeld. Provided alwaies that if the Scholemaster for the time beinge have lawfull warninge of the daye of the election two daies before the appointed election, and yet wilfullie doe absent himselfe, or otherwise be not present by anye his owne default, this default to be iudged by the greater part of governours, then the election made by the greater part of Governours shalbe reputed as made with the consent and likinge of the Scholemaistre. And furthermore we charge the Spokesman, Governours and Scholemaister in the Lord that all forstowinge of tyme and partialitie sett apart, everie one of them as muche as in him lieth, does his beste and uttermoste indevour, that the election of governours and scholemaister alwaies reside and remayne with themselves, and be not devolved upon others by anie theire untowardnes or other default. And yf it happen (which we would not) that the vacant place of a governour be not supplied within six weekes, after the vacancie, by ordinary election of the Governours themselves, then we will that six or more of the governours delay not to nominate unto the Lord President of the North or the Archbyshop of Yorke for the tyme beinge. some one or more fitt person or persons into the place or places vacant, and the partie or parties by one of the saide Lordes, President or Archbyshop

To chuse Governours.

The Scholemaster to be present at the election of Governours.

Nott to forstow their eleccion or deferre it.

allowed, we will shalbe reputed as lawfull elect governour of the saide schole. Nevertheles we will and ordaine, that no person reputed as Governour by the Lord President of the North or the Archbyshop, or by free election of the governours themselves, shall intermeddle as governour in anye action belonginge to the schole, till he have solemly in the presence of the greater part of Governors, and att the ordinary place of their meetinge for schole causes, taken his corporall othe, in this forme.

<small>The othe of the Governours.</small>
I. *A.B.* chosen Governour of the free grammer schole of Quene Elizabeth at Wakefeld, doe call God a witness unto any soule that I wilbe faithfull and carefull for the good of the saide schole in all thinges appertaininge to my office and charge, accordinge to the trust reposed in me, so help me God in Christe Jesus.

<small>Refusing of the othe.</small>
This othe if anye Governour elect refuse to take, or take not in manner aforesaide, within one quarter of a yeare of his election beinge thereunto requested by the Spokesman and warned of the daye of the Governours meetinge for that purpose, we will and by this statute ordaine that his former election be reputed as voide, and a newe governour be chosen, into his place as tho he were naturallie deade.

Of the office of a Governour of this Schole.

CAP. 3. **And** least a Governour thus chosen and sworne be ignorant of the office and charge wherewith he is trusted, We there-
<small>To se to the duties of the Mr Ussher and Schollers.</small>
fore by this statute declare and make knowne, That it ys the office of a Governour, advisedly to regard the generall course of Religion and good nurture in the scollers of this schole, but principallie he shall have an eye to the profession and carriadge of the maister and usher, that it be accordinge to the truthe of Christe, and that not onelie in theire course of life with others of theire owne sorte and condycion, but in the course of theire industrious and painfull instructinge of the schollers of this schole, whome by callinge, othe and maintenance they are in speciall sorte bound to applye and promote, which thynge yf accordinglie they shall doe, we will that the governours shall take yt as no smale parte of theire dutye therein to incoradge them, by the
<small>Causes of augmenting or rewarding the Mr and Ussher.</small>
increase of theire love and kindnes to them ward, and the augmentation of theire sett stipends by some good meanes of increase, if conveniently it may be without

GRAMMAR SCHOOL. 61

hurt to the schole. Contrariwise when the Governours shall perceive in either maister or usher a popish disposition, or loose behaviour, cruell correction, or negligence in teachinge arisinge <small>Abuses in the Mr and Ussher.</small> frome what cause soever, either muche companie keepinge or often gamminge, or much beinge frome home, or when they are at home late commynge to theire schollers, or litle stay with them, or in their stay followinge of theire owne studies, and neglect of the schollers teachinge, then we will and ordaine, that it shall by this statute, and so by other appertaine to the Governours, privatly to admonish the maister or usher so offendinge : which if it take no good effect, it is the office of the Spokesman upon the <small>To be reformed by the Spokesmen and Governours.</small> notoriousnes of the fault, to call together the Governours, and by their advice and consent to send for the maister or usher so offendinge, and him or them gravely to reprove and exhort to amendment of his or theire misdemeanour. Upon which so moderate and grave admonition yf there followe no amendment, it ys the dutie of the Spokesman againe to call together the Governours and by theire advice and consent, or with the advice and consent of the greater part present, the maister or usher the second tyme to call before them, and him or them by vertue of this Statute to admonishe, within one quarter of a yeare next followinge to amend the unsoundnes of his or theire religion, or the loosnes of their life, cruell correctinge, or negligence in teachinge, in such sort that he or they approve themselves to the governours, att that tyme to be reformed, or els we will, order and decree, that he the maister or usher shall for ever loose his place of beinge Schoolmaister or usher in this schole, and the Governours shall proceed to the election of other more fitt in theire place or places. It shall ffurther <small>To se that the lands houses annuities sele and books all safely kepte.</small> appertaine to the dutie of a governour to see that the landes, howses, goods, annuities, muniments and bookes to the schole beloninge be safelie kept, defended, repayred, and preserved as the nature and qualitie of them requireth without recovere from the schole, losse impairinge, or convertinge to other use than was the will of the donour or donours thereof. And <small>Not to sell alien or graunt anything but for better.</small> therefore it shall not be lawfull for the Governours of this schole, to sell give or putt away, anye part of the landes, revenewes, howses, buyldings or annuities to the schole belonginge, but for the procuringe of as good or better, and upon as good or better assurance and of the same yearlie value att the least, to be bestowed upon the schole, and this they shall see done, before anye bargaine or puttinge away of any suche landes, rentes, annuities, or goodes, be made, written, sealed and delyvered. And as often as any lease of the schole landes, howses or cottages shalbe expired forfeited surrendered or by any meanes become voide, it shalbe lawfull for the governours for the tyme beinge, to make a newe graunt or demise thereof, att the ould rent, and not under, if it be so worth, and can be had. Now, yf the benefitt to the lessee shalbe such, that conveniently with reason a fyne may be taken, we will that answerablie to the benefitt, the governours shall take fine, not to be converted by the name of sealinge money or otherwise, to theire owne use and benefitt, but to the benefit and use of the schole only. Yet it shall not be lawfull to make lease of any of the schole lands howses or cottages, till either the former lease be expired, given up, forfeited, or be within two yeares of the expiration, and that not for above the tearme of one and twentie yeares, the interest of these yeares, or any part of them not to be sett over by the tenant, without consent of the greater part of governours under their common seale, and further clause of re-entre for non payment of rent and bond for performance of covenantes. Att all which grauntes we will that for the seale shalbe paied three shillings and ffower pence to the governours, for theire owne use and meeting. We will further that the governours for the tyme beinge shall accordinge to their election to any office, made by the greater part of governours, both willinglie undertake it, and faithfullie discharge it to theire will power and knowledge. Lastly in all causes, that shall or may concerne the scholes good, we will that every governour shall by this statute repute himselfe as bound to imploy his uttermost care for the good welfare, credit and estimation of the saide schole. And if anye governour shall live irreligiouslie, an atheist, a prophane person, a murderer, a theife, incestuous, perjured or in like crime, or be notorious negligent in the execution of the office of a Governour, we will that therefore upon admonition he be deposed frome his place by the Spokesman with the consent of the greater part of governours, and another chosen into his place of government.

The maner of letting and graunting of leases.

Sealling money.

Governours chosen to any office, willingly to undertake it.

Of the Scholemaister his qualities, election, and othe.

CAP. 4. ℱor as much as this schole is principallie ordained a seminarie for bringinge up of christian children, to become in time ambassidours of reconciliation from God to his Church; and generally is intended a schole of christian instruction for vertue and maners,

GRAMMAR SCHOOL. 63

therein to be learned of all the schollers thereof. Therefore we will that especiall care be had in the placeinge of a fitt teacher frome whome as the roote the schollers are to drawe the sapp and iuice of religion, _{What maner of} learninge and good nurture. We ordaine therefore _{person the Scholemr ought} and decree that none shalbe chosen Scholemaister of this _{to be.} Schole hereafter, but such a one as havinge taken the degree of a Maistre of Arts in the Universitie of Cambridge or Oxford is withall well reported of for his knowledge, religion and life, and knowne to be an enemie to popish superstition, a lover and forward imbracer of Gods truth, a man formarlie diligent and painefull in his owne studies, of a sober and amiable cariadge towardes all men, able to maintaine the place of a Scholemaister with dignitie and gravitie, given to the diligent readinge of God's worde, but not called either to a pastorall charge, or hired to serve as a preacher minister or curate in the churche, ffor in all these cases we will that he forthwith cease to be a maister of this schole. And it shalbe lawfull for the governours to chuse an other scholemaister into his roome, yet will we have none to be elect Scholemaster but suche a one as is able to teache his scollers the truthe of religion, out of Gods booke, and who also is as it were a minister and preacher of the same _{The place being} truthe to his schollers under him. When therefore the _{void the Spokes-man within thre} place of a Scholemaister shalbe voide, we will that _{daies to call the Governours to} within three daies of the vacancie, known to the Spokes-_{chuse another.} man, he shall call together the rest of the governors, and the same vacancie he shall declare to them, withall exhortinge them to make diligent inquirie within one month next imediatlie followinge, of such a one or more, by them, or any of them to be nominated unto the place vacant, as they in theire owne consciences shall iudge the statute of the schole directlye to ayme att. The same daie month of which meetinge, we will shalbe the daie of election. Att which time the Governours beinge assembled into the place of theire ordinarye meetinge by eight a clocke in the morninge, the spokesman if he be present or in his absence the deputed Spokesman, or if he be absent himselfe the senior governour present shall reade or cause to be read this Statute, which donne himself in his owne person first, and consequentlie all the Governours present in the order of theire admittance to be Governours shall take his corporall othe—

_{The othe for chusing of a Scholemr.} I *A.B.* one of the Governors of the free grammer Schole of Quene Elizabeth att Wakefeld, call God a witnes unto my soule, that I will nominate and chuse him maister of the said schole, whome in my

conscience I doe judge the Statutes of this Schole directly and principallie to aime att, all partialitie and sinister affection whatsoever sett apart, so help me God and his holy worde.

<small>All the Governours to come to the election of the Mr and Ussher.</small> 𝔄𝔫𝔡 we straitly charge all the Governours in the Lord God theire righteous Judge, that upon all elections of maister and ussher of this Schole they carefullie come as electours att the place and time appointed, to give an affirmative voice in the election of maister and ussher, and that they doe not willinglie absent themselves upon any occasion att suche a necessarie meetinge. The Spokesman and Governours having taken theire othe, the Spokesman first, and in the order of theire senioritie all the rest, shall nominate and give voice with him whome they would have maister elect in that choice. Neither shall anye absent give his voice by a proxie to some present, neither shall anye presente comprimitt his voice to another, but upon whome the greater parte of voices of <small>The most voices to prevaile.</small> the governours (the Spokesman to have a castinge voice, when the voices are in number equall) shall agree, him we will shalbe reputed as scholemaster elect and to the Lord Archbuyshop of Yorke presented, which scholemaister upon his presentment passed shalbe sent for before the governours, and <small>The Scholemr to read the statutes.</small> havinge first read the statutes of this schole in the original statute booke (which we will shalbe graunted to him for this purpose) he shall take this corporall othe—

<small>The Scholemr his othe.</small> I. *A. B.* chosen scholemaister of the free grammer schole of Quene Elizabeth att Wakefield, doe call God a righteous witnes to my soule, that I doe in hart abhor all popishe superstition, and renounce all forraine Jurisdiction of the church of Rome and the now Pope. And I doe receive and reverence as the undoubted word of God the bookes of canonicall scripture comprised in the ould and newe testaments and the truthe in them contained I shall by the grace of God constantly professe and willinglie practice. The youth of this schole I shall diligentlie instruct in religion, learninge and good manners. And I shall further be faithfull and carefull for the good of the saide schole, in all thinges appertaininge to my office and charge, according to the truste reposed in me, so help me God through Jesus Christ.

INTERIOR OF OLD BUILDING.

GRAMMAR SCHOOL. 65

This othe if (upon time overslipped) the election of the Scholemaister shall be in the Maister and Fellowes of Emanuel Colledge in Cambridge, we will shalbe administered unto the partie by them chosen, and the same he shall solemly take before he intermeddle as scholemaister in this schole or receive wages for teachinge.

Of the office of the Scholemaister elect, his sett stipend, and the increase thereof.

CAP. 5.
His dutie and charge.

The scholemaisters office and charge is diligently to instruct and informe his schollers in the groundes of religion, for which purpose we will that upon the Saturdaies frome one of the clocke till two in the afternoone, he shall teache and examine his schollers in the principles of christian religion. Upon the Sabbaoth daies he shall cause them diligently to repaire to churche where his carefull eye shall overview their cariadge and behaviour, their attention, also and diligence in notinge the heads of instruction delyvered by the preacher: for we will have him to geve order to all his schollers (which by theire capacitie and skill in writinge are able) in writinge to note the sermons for the helpe of their memories and theire more profitable learninge. Of which their profittinge the maister shall take further knowledge by examyninge upon Munday morninge either all his schollers, or such as in his discretion he shall thinke for the tyme most meet to be apposed: and theire severall absences, negligencies, and misbehaviours at church, either noted by himself or given up by the monitours in their bille, he shall at his like discretion correct either by word or by the rodd, as the qualitie of the offence deserveth. For the instructinge of
How to teache and what and in what order.
his schollers in good literature, we will that he shall in the plainest and most familiar sorte teach them grammer, and the Latin and greeke tongues, reading unto them the most classick authors, as in Latin these or some of them, Terence, Tully, Cæsars comentaryes, Titus Livius, Ovid, Virgil, Horace: in Greeke Isocrates, Demosthenes, Hesiode or Homer. For the Latin tongue he shall follow and teach Lylyes Grammar: ffor the greeke, that Grammar which in the universitie of Cambridge ys most usually read in the greater number of Colledges, by their chosen readers of the greek tongue. In which Grammars oure cheife care is, that the maister and usher labour to make their schollers for their yeares and capacitie perfect Gramarians, as able both to repeat the rule by hart, and rightly to apply theire readinge and exercises to their rule with

5.

understandinge. And we do straitly in the lord charge the Scholemaister and Usher of this Schole for ever, that they do not so much hasten their schollers in the to soone clyminge of their formes especially in the too haistye goinge frome prose unto verse, and from latin to greek, or from greek to hebrew or logicke. And therefore we will that the Schollers be not sett to verse till they be able to write in Latin an epistle and theame of good force and congruitie, neither shall they from verse be sett to greeke, before they both well knowe the rules of versifyinge, and are able of a theme in reasonable time to make halfe a score or a dozen of tollerable, if not of good verses, the like wishe we to be done in their goinge from Greek to higher learninge. And in all this learning we will that the maister shall take diligent examination of the exercises of his schollers, for the Orthography, phrase, inversion, elocution and disposition of the whole matter, herein playnelie showinge them what they have well donne, and what in all these they ought to have amended and how, and that not onelie by speache in the daylie examynation of theire exercises but by his often writeinge exercises of the same matter with his schollers to be shewed unto them as paterns of imitation. And thus the displeasinge hardnes of learninge, shalbe made easie in the welpleasinge mannor of teachinge. Theis duties by the maister thus performed, yet lyes there upon him a last dutie of informing his youth in good nurture and maners which are of themselves an ornament to religion and good learninge. We adjudge it therefore a part of the maister and ushers dutie, respectively to instruct theire schollers to reverence their betters in all places, to be curteous in speach to all men, and in theire apparrell alwaies clenly in theire whole cariadge ioyninge decencie with modestie, and good manners with good learninge. Ffor the which contynual care and paynes of the Scholemaister, we will that quarterlie shall be paide unto him out of the revenues of the Schole by the handes of the Spokesman fforty markes that ys to saie att Easter or within one fortnight thereof vi*li*. xiii*s*. iiii*d*, att midsomer or within one fortnight thereof vi*li*. xiii*s*. iiii*d*., att michaelmas or within one fortnight thereof vi*li*. xiii*s*. iiii*d*., and att Christenmas or within one fortnight thereof vi*li*. xiii*s*. iiii*d*., which wages, in the good deservinge of the Scholemaister, we would that the Governours should increase and augment by assigninge unto him the whole ingress money of all such as shall be entred schollers under him, or the givinge unto him the fyne of some lease or leases, yf the state and condicion of the Schole will beare it. Yet this augmentation we

His wages to be paid to him by he Spokesman Quarterlie.

His reward upon well deservinge.

would shalbe arbitrarie, and not setled upon scholemaister, but to be continued accordinge as the necessities of the schole and diligence of the maister shall requier.

Of the Usher or underteacher, his qualitie, election, othe, office, stipend and remove, if need be.

CAP. 6. *This* schole we would never should longer be without usher, then in the vacancie there can a fitt man be provided for the place, him by this statute we adjudge fitt, who is a man *Whatmaner of person he ought to be.* truelie fearinge God, learned in good sorte, formerly knowne to have bene painefull in teachinge of youth, att the least painfull and industrious in his owne studies, moderate in his cariadge, no minister with pastorall charge nor stipendarie preacher, nor reader in the church, save in the church at Wakefeld and that not without expresse licence therto obtained of the greater part of governours under there common seale and that onely durante bene placito. In the vacancie therefore of the ushers place, *The place void how to elect another.* by what occasion soever, the Spokesman shall within one weeke of the place knowne voide, call the Governours and scholemaister together, and exhort them to harken after a fitt underteacher or usher to be chosen that daie three week, unless in the mean tyme upon sufficient knowledge of a fitt man to be had for the place, a sooner daie of meetinge be appointed by the Spokesman for the election. Att which appointed daie, whomsoever the greater part of governours present, with the help and assistance of the scholemaister for the tyme beinge shall chose, him we will thenceforward shall be reputed and taken as Usher elect. The election by the greater part of governours to be good, notwithstandinge the maister's consent to the election not had, or any his absence from the election, yf he have bene thereunto lawfully called by warninge given unto him of the tyme of election, by the space of two daies forgoeinge the election. The same *His othe to be the same as of the Mr.* othe which the scholemaister toke upon his election sett downe in the ffowerth chapter of theise statutes in the same wordes shall the usher elect take his othe to the schole, onely the word usher shalbe changed for the word scholemaister. The usher sworne, shall knowe that yt apperteineth to his office and charge in like sorte to teache the principles of Religion to his schollers, to see to their behaviour at church, and to frame them to good manners for the capacitie of their yeares, as the scholemaister *The Usshers dutie.* was charged in the former chapter of these statutes. It shall further appertaine to the office and dutye of the usher to instruct the yonger sorte of schollers in the rudiments of the Latine tongue, and in the latin grammar—and namelie, he shall teach them perfectly to declyne a noune and to conjugate a verb, to ioyne the substantive and adiective in all cases genders and numbers, the antecedent and the relative in gender and number, the nominative case and the verb in number and person, Which till they can do in some good sort aptly, readielie and with understandinge, he shall neither post hast them in gramer, nor dull them with exercises of writinge latine, but after suche tyme as by muche practice they have attained this steill, he shall with grammer read to them Cato, or some like booke, teachinge them rightly to referr theire readinge to the grammer rule, and their lecture some thinge altered in English translation, to turn againe into Latin construction. Which while they are learninge to doe, the Usher shall att his best leasure, sett them copies or gett them copies sett by some of the schollers, and appointe them one hower for wrytynge every teachinge daie after the midest after noone, in which theire writinge, he shall oversee and instruct them. And thus practised in writing and often makinge of translations or Latins, taught also the grammer with all care and diligence, both by hart to repeate and in the example rightlie to understande the rule, so that in legible hand they are able to write their owne translations and latins, performed with some pretie understandinge, and withall informed both rightlie to pronounce and write their short exercises, we will that from the Usher they be promoted to the maisters teachinge, for theise groundes and beginnings of good learninge, as they are most unpleasant for the Schollers to learn, so are they most troublesome for the scholmaister to teache, and require a long and unpleasant tyme of carefull instruction. Wherefore we will that the Usher shall never be charge with above halfe of the whole number of schollers, as belonginge to his teachinge neither att anye tyme with such as are fitt for the maister's instruction. But all those that are under his teachinge, we will and charge him in the Lord, carefullie with all diligence to instruct, for this is a maine trust which we repose in him, and which God shall require of him att the last daie of fearful judgment in his accounts if it be not answerablie discharged by him.

Examples or copies to write.

The Ussher to be charged with halfe number of Schollers.

The causes of displaceinge of the Ussher.

The same shalbe the causes and maner of the ushers remove which was of the maisters, savinge that the usher being convented by the Governours and admonished, his removeall and displaceinge shall not be without consent of the maister for the tyme beinge. Which consent if in the opinion of the greater part of governours it ought to be graunted by the maister, but yet he refuse so to doe, we order and decree that it shalbe lawfull for the Governours by consent and agrement of the greater part of themselves to subtract so much of the Ushers wages and for such tyme, as in theire discretions shalbe thought meet. Of all which damages to the Usher, as also of his whole dutie least he should be ignorant, we will that before he take his othe to the Schole, he shall have graunted to him the originall booke of Statutes to read over, that advisedly and with good conscience he maie take his appointed othe. And for the discharge of this trust which by this statute we have reposed in him, we will that quarterly shalbe payed unto him by the hands of the Spokesman fiftie shillings that is to say at the daies and tymes in the which the Scholemaisters wages is by statute appointed to be paide unto him, he shall also in equall porcion of his named stipend receive his whole and entire wages. An augmentation of the Ushers wages in his care and paines over his Schollers augmented, we would should be made by the like meanes, and in like sorte as we have spoken of the increase of the Scholemaister's stipend, in the end of the former chapter.

To read over the Statute.

His wages and augmentacion.

Of the schollers free and fforrenours.

CAP. 7. **None** shalbe admitted to be taught as Schollers in this Schole, upon what pretext soever, unles he be able in tollerable sorte to read Englishe and be promoted to the accidence, and be also thereunto fitt, of which his fitnes if question be made, we will the resolution shalbe from the greater parte of Governours. Everie scholler entered into the Schole to be taught grammer beinge of the Towne or parish or freed by graunt of the governors under theire common seale for some liberall contribution given to the schole shall the daie of his admittance paye to the hands of the maister or usher under whose teaching he is to be entered Twelve pence as his admission money. Unles he be the sonne of a daytaile man or one of like povertie: and then his admission shalbe free. And everie forrenour admitted whatsoever be the state or condicion of his father shall paye Two shillings. The which some shalbe answered quarterlie to the Spokesman by the maister or Usher for everie Scholler so entred, before the receivinge of his or their quarters stipend. And because the graunt of Quene Elizabeth of

None to be admytted but suche as learne the accidence.

All free to pay xiid. at their admyttance to the Mr. or Usher use.

All fforeyners to pay iis. to the Spokesman for the scholes use.

famous memory foundres of this Schole principallie and in a manner solie respecteth the foundacion off a free Schole for the schollers of the towne and parish Wakefeld, we therefore will and ordaine that this schole shall not be burthened with too great a number of forrenours.

<small>How many forreyners the Mr. and Usher may take to teache.</small> And therefore it shall not be lawfull for the Scholemaister at anye time to receive into his teachinge above the number of twentie schollers beinge not priveledged as free schollers by her majesties foundacion or graunt of the governours under theire common seale, for some forepassed liberall contribution to the schole, neither shall it be lawfull for the Usher to receive into his teachinge of forrenours alike unpriveledged above the number of Tenn successivelie which number notwithstandinge we will frome time to time may be lessened or inlarged by graunt in writinge or decree of the greater part of present governours for the time. The wages which is payed by the parents or frends of those forrenours for their teachinge we will and ordaine shall entierlie come and belonge to him as his proper right under whose teachinge they are, whether it be

<small>Order for the bookes, wyndows and other things in the schole.</small> maister or Usher. Provided alwaies that if the glasse windowes of the schole shalbe broken or the bookes to the schole belonginge shalbe purloined or torne by any scholler or outcommer then the maister or usher under whose teachinge the saide scholler at that time was shalbe answerable for the damage and it make good. All these schollers free or forrenours we will shall carefullie learne to knowe and love God and therefore none shall contynue scholler in this schole which either att all comes not to churche or upon admonition and correction can not

<small>Order for the unrulye scollers in the scole and Churche.</small> be drawn to frequent it with reverence or is notoriously negligent in his learninge and cannot by the word and rodd of his maister be reformed or which continues and braves a contempt against his maister or offereth him violence the attempt and violence to be adjudged by the greater part of governours and the remove of everye such unfittinge scholler to be made by and with the consent of the greater part of governours att some theire appointed meetinge. For our desire and care ys that the Scholemaister and Usher should teach their schollers with that care dilligence and love, as if they were theire owne naturall children, and we would likewise that everie scholler should reverence his maister as his naturall father, applyinge theire tyme in good learninge, all swearinge, brawlinge, raylinge, lasciviousnes and vices of the like

<small>Prayer.</small> qualitie abandoned. The which that they maie more carefullie and with god's greater blessinge performe, we will

that the scholemaister shall daylie openlie and audiblely in the schole morninge and eveninge, with the schollers, call upon God by prayer, to forgive them theire sinnes, to accept their persons in Christ, to direct them by his holie spirite into his holie feare and obedience, to illuminate their understandings, to inlarge their capacities, to confirme their memories, rectifie their iudgementes, that so they maie daylie better increase in the knowledge of good literature. He shall also with his schollers thanke God for all his mercies unto them, and namelie for Quene Elizabeth, the founder of this schole, and the good benefactours thereof. And the prayer beinge concluded, with petition for the church and state, in the morninge there shall in order a Chapter be read, and att night a psalme songe before theire departure home, for which purpose everie scholler shall have a psalme Booke in meeter of his owne. And because this schole is not ordained for petties but for grammarians, we will that all the schollers under the maisters teachinge shall be tyed to the speakinge of latin, a fitt meanes (as we take it) both to restraine noise and wonder in the schole, and

<u>Times and libertie to playe.</u> to better their latin tongue. In all which their courses that they may be incouradged, we will that upon everie Thursdaie (there beinge no halliday in the same weeke) it shalbe lawfull for the maister to give them leave to play at Eleven a Clocke of the same daie and upon no other daye he shall have power to give leave to them to recreate themselves by play, savinge for two after noones in one quarter, or by consent of three Governours att other times. The Usher also shall have power to give all the schollers leave to play one after noone in one quarter when he shall thinke it fittest.

<u>Tymes of comyng to schole and going frome thence.</u> But therefore we will that the Maister Usher and Schollers shall att due howers come to schole and there contynue till a fitt time of departure. That is to saie, they shall all repaire to schole and the Scholemaister and Usher shall begin to teach att or upon sixe a clocke in the morninge and so contynue till six or upon six a clocke at night (saving betwixt eleven a clocke and one) from the monthe of Marche till the tenth of october. And frome thence till the tenth of Marche they shall beginne to teache frome or soone after the sunne rysinge till or near to the sunne settinge

<u>Breaking up of the schole.</u> (savinge betwixt eleven a clocke and one.) The schole shall not be broken upp but att Midsomer and att the feast of the Nativitie. At Midsomer foure daies before the feast of St. John Baptist shalbe the breakinge up and the returne to schole the tenth daye after the breakinge up thereof unles the tenth daye happen to be the Sabbaoth or the preperation to the Sabbaothe, and then the daie

of begynninge schole againe shalbe the Monday followinge. At the Natyvitie they shall breake up schole upon St. Thomas even and return the next working daie after the twelfthe daie unles it be Satturday then the daie of returne shalbe Monday.   Other breakinge up in the yeare they shall have none nor play dayes save upon the seavententh daie of November yearlie when they shall play the whole daye and those which are able shall upon that daye sett upp verses in honour and commendacion of Quene Elizabeth the blessed founder of this schole, the next daie they shall returne to schole to learne as before.

Of the time and daies of absence frome schole graunted to the Maister and Usher.

CAP. 8.   **Because** the occasions of the maister and usher may be such that their tymes of being abrode necessarilie may be drawne to other times of the yeare then the appointed tymes of breaking up and we would not have them abridged of their reasonable recreations, or hindred in their necessarie occasions of absence. We will that it shalbe lawfull for the maister to have twenty fower daies in one yeare of absence frome Schole, and the Usher sixetene daies to be taken att their discretions, either wholie together or devided so that they be not both absent att once. The daies of goinge abrode and comynge home to be accounted as daies of absence att what hower of the daie soever the goinge oute or the returne be. Att all which times of theire goinge abrode and returne home we will and charge them that they acquaint the Spokesman or in his absence the deputie Spokesman thereof trulie either the same or the next daie before or followinge their goinge abrode and cominge home who shall faithfullie sett downe in a booke appointed for that purpose the daie of the goinge out and the daie of the returne of the maister and usher, and if theire absence be for more daies then two together he that is so absent shall procure an able man to supplie his place of teachinge att his owne cost and charges. In like sort if either maister or usher shalbe sicke and not able to come to schole or for his sicknes not comminge att schole of three daies then upon the three daies expired he shall hire an able man as before till he be able himself to follow his charge and execute his place of teachinge. If the maister shalbe absent frome schole upon schole daies above the said 24 daies in one yeare or the usher above the said 16 daies unles they be held by sicknes or violent detention or have licence of more daies of absence by the graunt of the greater part of governours under their common seale he shall upon

GRAMMAR SCHOOL. 73

<small>Defaults to be noted.</small> the conviction thereof lose his place for ever or if he goe frome home without knowledge given of his beinge from home to the Spokesman or in his absence to the deputie either the daie before or else the next daie after his returne that it may be registred he shall for everie suche defaulte have abated in his wages tenn shillinges and in his often faultinge in that kinde he shalbe admonished to the losse of his place without amendment as by statute it is provided in other cases.

Of the safe Keepinge of such thinges as appertaine to the Schole, of sutes arisinge, and accounts makinge.

CAP. 9. <small>Things to be kept in the great and the lesser chestes.</small> That the graunt of Foundacion, the common seale, the evidence of Landes belonginge to the schole and the schole stocke may be safelie kept, there shall two chests be provided a bigger and a lesse, with either of them two severall locks and keyes, sett in safe place and keepinge, att the best discretion of the Governours. In the lesse chest shalbe kept the Register the Indenture of accounts passed by the Spokesman, the <small>The Keyes to be kept.</small> Rentable and the originall Booke of theise statutes. Of this the Spokesman for the tyme shall keepe the one key and the scholemaister shall keep the other. In the great chest shalbe kept the common seale, the schole evidences, the schole stocke, and what els the Governours shall thinke meet to be there placed and kept, whereof the Spokesman shall keep one keye, and in his absence the deputie, and a Governour chosen shall kepe the other key. Theise two chistes shall halfe yearly be vewed by the Governours, and the graunt of Foundacion then read, and the schole stocke <small>The morrowe after Mich. day and the first teachinge day after Easter, the days of half years accompt.</small> counted. For we will that the Governours upon the daie appointed by the First statute for the election of the Spokesman, and upon the first teachinge daie after Easter (which daies we ordaine to be the daies of the halfe yeares account to be made for schole causes) shall together vewe the two chestes, the scholehouse and bookes therto <small>The accounts to be made halfe yearlie.</small> belonginge and the houses in Wakefeild given to the schole. Or if these appointed daies shalbe spent in such other busynes that then a survey of theise things cannot conveniently be had, yet we will that what herein can not be donne these daies shalbe effected in the daies next imediatly followinge. Upon which vewe the Spokesman with the Governors shall take order, that nothinge be done or suffered to be donne to the hurt and preiudice of the schole. And if att anye tyme there shall sute arise, in the which the Governours shalbe either plantifes or defendants, or if great occasion shall be for the surveyinge of the whole or the greatest part of the howses or landes to the schole belonginge, or for the repaire of the scholehouse, or other schole buildings, then there shalbe chosen by the consent of the greater part of Governours one fitt man or more, to manage and take charge of those causes by the order and direction of the governors. And what money they shall lay out in their imployment, they shall receive it att the handes of the Spokesman, who shall account halfe yearlie, that ys to say, att the daies in this statute above named with the governors, for all things that he haith received or laid out, for the schole. These recknings cast and summed up, Indentures shall be drawen contayninge the summe of the receipts the summe of the expenses (if it so fall out) Exceedinge the receipts, and lastlie the remainder in stocke with the foote of the account. To the one part of these Indentures the Spokesman beinge the accountant, shall sett to his hand and seale, and deliver it to the Governours with all the remainder of money in his hand if any happen to be remaininge to be both laid up: the Indenture in the lesse and the monye in the greater chest. To the other part of Indentures the Governours shall setto theire handes, and delyver yt to the keepinge of the Spokesman. Yf there shall after the accounts be occasion of necessarie disbursments for the scholes use: at what tyme anye money shalbe taken out of the great chist, the keper of the key chosen by the Governours, shall see that a true note of the summe thereof signed with the hande of the Spokesman shalbe putt into the bagge, purse, or chest out of which the money was taken, there to remayne till the accounts followinge.

Sutes building repaires and suche like to be effected by one or two to be chosen.

And they to account to the Spokesmanandhe totheGovernours.

Howe the money in stocke shalbe kepte.

Of the altering of these Statutes, and the interpretation of ambiguities arisinge out of them.

CAP. 10. 𝕹𝖔𝖙𝖜𝖎𝖙𝖍𝖘𝖙𝖆𝖓𝖉𝖎𝖓𝖌𝖊 theise Statutes sett downe to be observed for the better orderinge of this Schole, yet because after time may prove some of them not to be necessarie, as att the firste they were deemed, Or that others more necessarie might well have been framed. We therefore order

GRAMMAR SCHOOL.

<small>To alter or amend the Statutes at any tyme within seaven yeares.</small>
and decree that it shalbe lawfull for the Governours of this Schole, or for the greater part of them, with the advice and assistance of the Scholemaister for the tyme beinge, to add to these Statutes, to detract frome them, to putt out or to make newe at anie time, within Seaven yeares next followinge the publication of them the saide statutes, but after the time of Seaven yeares expired, it shall not be lawfull, to add to, or detract from, or putt out, or make new or alter any Statute then standinge in force and confirmed. And like power we give unto the Governours or to the greater part of them, att all times hereafter, to expound interprett, and explayne any ambiguitie, whatsoever shall arise frome the obscuritie or doubtfulnes of anye worde or wordes, sentence or sentences in these statutes comprehended. And the interpretation by them the Governours or the greater part of them, made for the explayninge of any ambiguitie in statute, we will have all whom it may concerne shall rest in, as if the interpretation were the direct wordes of the Statute. So that the interpretation be entred into the Booke of Statutes, under the handes of the interpretours, within tenn daies of the interpretation made and agreed upon, or be offered by the interpretours to the Spokesman or senior Governour elect as readie to be entred within that time 𝕴𝖓 𝖜𝖎𝖙𝖓𝖊𝖘 𝖜𝖍𝖊𝖗𝖊𝖔𝖋 hereunto we have affixed our Common seale the Twentithe day of Julye in the yeare of our Lord God 1607.

Wm. Lister
Rychard Wytton
Willm. Savile
John Battye
Thomas Robinson
John Jackson
John Mawde
Edward Watkinson
Rich: Lister
John Flemynge
George Wharton
William Rodes
Andrew Skatcherd

JEREMY GIBSONNE, Scholemaistre.

End of Original Statutes.

A repeale of so much of the Tenth Chapter of the former Statutes as doth concerne the restrainte of altering the saide Statutes therein mentioned to have been made, and within seaven years after to be made.

Whereas by one Statute amongst others heretofore made That ys to say the Twentieth day of Julie Anno Dni 1607 yt is enacted as followeth, vidz:—(here follow the first 14 lines of Statute 10 "Notwithstandinge . . . . and confirmed") WE THE Governors whose names are hereunder subscribed with the advice and consent of Mr. Phillip Isaac the present Scholem, upon good consideracion had of the saide Statute, fynding that yf such restraint should perpetually contynue, the same in tyme to come might be very dangerous unto the Schole and good government thereof yf the inconvenience hereafter to arise might not be redressed by good and wholesome ordynaunce in such cases to be provyded, do therefore hereby utterly Repeale revoke and make voide so much of the saide Statute as before herein is recyted: and do ordeine declare and appoint, that the libertie unto us and our Successors given by the Letters Patents of the late moste worthie Quene Elizabeth be duly and carefully observed and put in practise the said Statute so repealed as aforesaide or in anything therein contrary, to the contrary notwithstanding. IN WITNESSE whereof we the saide Governours have hereunto putt our common seale the seaventeenth daie of Marche Anno Dni 1613 (1613-4) Annoque dni regis Jacobi Angliæ &c. undecimo.

George Spivie, Spokesman	PHILLIP ISACKE Ludima.
Willm Savile	
John Battye	
John Jackson	
Wm Lister	
John Mawde	
Thomas Robinson	
Andrewe Skatcherd	
Chr. Nailer	
Willm Rodes	
Hu: Cressy	

Undecimo die Januarij Anno Regni Regis Jacobi xij.º

For as much as we the present Governours whose names are hereunder wrytten have found that the former Statutes concerninge the office of the Scholemaister and Usher of the saide Schole are in some things defective, as not giveing that power unto the Scholem^r as to his place is fitting. WE THEREFORE the Governors aforesaide together with the full consent and agreement of Mr. Phillip Isacke the present Scholem^r do hereby ordeine decree and appoint That the Scholem^r of the saide Schole and his successors for ever shall have the cheife and principall oversight, care, direction, rule, government of the saide Schollers as well as in theire teaching as in the manners and behaviours. And that the Usher of the saide Schole be in place and office subordinate unto him, and subiect to his judgement and direction in the manner of his teaching of such Schollers as are or shalbe under the said Ushers government and teaching AND FURTHER we ordeine that the Scholem^r have power to admonish the saide Usher of his defects and errors and in default of reformacion upon such admonitions then diligently to inform the Governours thereof to the end they may take such further course therein as shalbe fitting. And yf any differences do happen betwene the saide Maister and Usher concerning either teaching or government, then the said differences to be reconsiled and reformed by the Governours in such sorte as to theire wisdomes shalbe thought fitting and it is hereby declared that this Act be not construed in any sorte to restreine or alter the power of the Governours of the saide schole in any thing concerning the saide Schole. And for that we the Governours aforesaide do finde that the principall ground and cause of the first foundacion and erection of the saide Schole was for the advancement and propagacion of Gods truth and Religion now professed in this Realme of England and that the same shoulde in no sorte be used as a Nursery or Seminary for Papistes or any other hereticks, which gratious and godly intentions we houlde our selves bounde in conscyence faithfully and carefully to advance, WE THEREFORE the saide Governors together with the saide Phillip Isack now Scholem^r do ordeine decree and appoint that no scholler whatsoever he be, be att any tyme hereafter admitted or contynued in the saide Schole, or under the goverment or teaching of the Scholem^r or Usher of the saide Schole who shall not ordynarilie resort upon the Saboth day unto the Parish Church of Wakefeild to the publique and Common prayers and sermons and then and there reverently and Religiously attend and abide till the same be fully ended. AND farther that no Scholler shalbe admitted unto or contynued in the saide Schole or under the teaching or goverment of the saide Scholem^r or Usher who shall by waie of Disputacion or Conference with any other Scholler or others uphould or mantayne any notorious points of Popery, or that shall endevor to move or perswade any other unto the Popish Religion or that shall keep or use any Popish Books or wryteings. AND yf any such be now already admitted into the saide Schole we do hereby ordeine declare and appoint that every such scholler shall forthwith within Twenty daies now next following be putt away from the saide Schole. Except he or they do in the meane tyme reforme such theire opynions, and conforme themselves to the Religion now established and to the publique exercises thereof as aforesaide. IN WYTTNES of all which we the saide Governors and Scholem^r have hereunto subscrybed our names and putt our Common seale thereto the daye and yeare first above wrytten.

   Hu : Cressy   PHILLIP ISACKE.
   Willm Savile
   Wm. Lister
   John Battye
   Thomas Robinson
   Andrew Skatcherd
   Chr Nailer
   William Pollard
   Robarte Waterhous

A Statute for the alteracion of so much of the Statute for eleccion of Governors of this Schole as restraineth the eleccion to persons of thertie yeares of age.

WHEREAS by a former Statute made concerninge the Eleccion of the Governors of this Schole amongst other things it is provided that no man under the age of Thirtie yeares shalbe chosen Governor of this Schole It is nowe that is to say the seaven and twentieth of July in the first yeare of the Reign of our Sovereine Lord Kinge Charles of England Scotland France and Irelande agreed and enacted by the Governors whose names are hereunder written with the consent of Mr. Robert Doughty Scholemaster of the said Schole that the same shall in no sorte be taken or construed to extend to restrayne or disable the choice of any Gentleman or of any other person brought up in learnynge either at the Universities or Inns of Courte if such person be of the age of five and twentie yeares and otherwise qualified and inhabitant accordinge to the purporte and true meanynge of the said former Statute the said former acte or Statute or any other matter or thinge whatsoever to the contrary notwithstandinge. It witnes whereof we the said Governors and Scholemaister have hereunto subscribed our names and putt our common Seale the day and yeare above written, 1625.

John Battie
Chr. Nailer
Richard Taylor
John Storye
Andrewe Skatcherd
William Pollard
John Greenewood
Tho. Somester

A Statute for the alteracion and explication of soe much of the statute for election of a schoolmaster for this schole as restraineth the day of election to bee that day month after the meeting wherein notice is given of the Vacancy.

WHEREAS by a former Statute concerning the election of the Schoolmaster of this Schole amongst other things it is enacted That the day of election of a Schoolmaster must be precisely the same day month after wherein the meetinge of the Governors is to give notice of the Vacancy wee the Governors whose names are under subscribed upon good consideracion had of the said statute finding That if the Governors should be constrained to keep the school voyd of a Master for soe long a time great inconvenience might happen and itt might prove much to the detriment of the school Wee therefore the Governors aforesaid doe hereby decree this explanatory adicion to bee added to the aforesaid statute imediately after the words (The same day month of which meeting we will shall be the day of election) viz :—unlesse in the meane time upon sufficient knowledge of a fitt man to bee had for the place, a sooner day of meeting be appointed by the spokesman for the election. And wee doe declare this to be the meaning and intent of the aforesaid statute any thing therein contained to the contrary notwithstanding. IN WITNES whereof wee the said Governors have hereunto subscribed our names and put our Common seal the twenty fourth day of January Anno Dni 1679 Annoque Regni Regis Caroli secundi Angliæ &c tricesimo primo.

    R. Witton
    O. Lee
    John Robinson
    Richard Birkhead
    Chas. Naylor
    Wm. Denison
    Daniel Mawde
    Tho. Chieriholme
    Toby Sill
    Thomas Bargh
    Tho. Horsfield
    Richard Ellis

A Statute for the Alteration and Explanation of so much of the seaventh chapter of the former Statutes as concerns the breaking up of the Schole and days of Liberty allowed for Midsomer fair with a Clause to restrain the Schollers from excluding or barring out the Master.

WHEREAS in the seaventh Chapter of the former Statutes amongst other things it is enacted that the School shall not be broken in but at Midsomer and at the Feast of the Nativity   Att Midsomer four dayes before the Feast of St John Baptist shall the breaking up and the Returne to Schole the Tenth day after the breaking up thereof unless the Tenth day happen to be the Sabboth or the preparation to the Sabboth and then the day of beginning Schole again shall bee the Monday following   We the Governors whose names are hereunto subscribed with the consent of Mr. Edmund Farrer present Schole Master upon good consideration had of the said Statute   And observing that Midsomer Fair constantly happens soon after Whitsontide do thinke Ten dayes too much to be allowed the Schollers, having usualy Ten Dayes allowed at Whitsontide which often falls to be in the same month   And there being no Liberty allowed the Schollers the other Fair which is att All Hallowtide Yearly, do think it convenient to order and enact and it is hereby ordained and enacted that the breaking up of the Schole for Midsomer Fair be

GRAMMAR SCHOOL.

allwayes on the Twenty Second Day of June in every Year and the Day of Returne of the Schollers to the Schole again on the Twenty Seaventh Day of the said Month unless the said Day shall happen to bee on a Saturday or Sunday and then the day of begining schole again shall be the Munday following and the breaking up of the Schole for the Fair at Allhallow tide shall be on the Thirtyeth day of October in every Year and the Returne of the Schollers to Schole shall be allwayes on the sixth day of November following unless the said Day shall happen to be Saturday or Sunday and then the day of begining to teach again shall bee the Munday following.

AND Wee do also further ordain and enact that the Schollers of this Schole shall not for the future exclude or barr out their Master before they have showne him their Orders and that they shall not shew their Orders to him before the Sixth day of November in any Year and in case the Orders they shall then show contain nothing that is contrary to the Statutes of this Schole nor any thing but which hath been usually granted by former Masters Wee would have the Master to grant them to the Schollers and likewise give them Liberty to play all that day that the Orders are shewne and granted. And wee further enact and ordain that in Case any Scholler or Schollers shall dare or presume to exclude the Master before they have shewne him their Orders as aforesaid that he or they so acting contrary to this Statute shall bee severely corrected by the Master and afterwards expelled the Schole and not to be admitted again but by the consent of the Governours or the Major Part of them and then upon giving very good caution not to offend again in the like manner.

IN WITNESSE whereof Wee the said Governours and Master have hereunto subscribed our names and put our Common Seal the Fifteenth Day of May 1694.

<table>
<tr><td>Ni. Fenay</td><td>EDMUND FARRER,</td></tr>
<tr><td>Chas. Naylor</td><td>Scholemr</td></tr>
<tr><td>Ri. Ellis</td><td></td></tr>
<tr><td>Jo. Scott</td><td></td></tr>
<tr><td>Jos. Watkinson</td><td></td></tr>
<tr><td>Ri. Witton</td><td></td></tr>
<tr><td>Jno. Smijth</td><td></td></tr>
<tr><td>Tho. Wilson</td><td></td></tr>
<tr><td>Ben. Watkinson</td><td></td></tr>
<tr><td>Tho. Brooke</td><td></td></tr>
</table>

WHEREAS the Schollers born in the Parish of Wakefield and Forrainers now in our Free Schole amount to about an hundred and sixty and much exceed the Numbers, which we presume the former Governors had in view, when they divided the Revenues and Government of the said Schole betwixt a Master and an Usher, who seem unequal to the Burden and Duty of overlooking and instructing so many Schollers which we judge to be a full Employment for three: We the Spokesman and Governors in Concert with Mr. Thomas Clarke our present Scholemaster taking the same into our consideracion. and the said Mr. Clarke having proposed to us, that in case we would consent, that he may receive the Salary and other profits formerly due and paid to the Usher of the said Schole, He will pay to an Usher and an Assistant elected and approved of by us the Stipend or Salary of Thirty Pounds a year to each : We the said Spokesman and Governours Deem this proposal conducive to the Good of our Schole and do hereby accept of and assent to it and accordingly Do alter and repeal all such parts of former Statutes whereby the Ushers have heretofore been entitled to a certain Share of the Rents of the said Schole and other perquisites, which have belonged to them: and order that the Spokesman for the time being shall pay unto the said Mr. Clarke all the Salary formerly paid to the Usher of the said Schole, And do authorize likewise the said Mr. Clarke to receive all such Sums of money, as the Usher of the said Schole was wont to receive for admission money or teaching : he paying to the Usher and Assistant for the time being the said yearly Stipend or Salary of Thirty pounds each. IN WITNESS whereof we the said Governours and Master have hereunto subscribed our names and put our Comon seal the Thirtieth day of September Anno Dni. 1717.

    Ben : Watkinson, spoksman   THO. CLARKE Scholemr.
    A : Bever
    Ja : Sill
    Tho : Wilson
    Wm Spinke
    Fra : Pitt
    Jos. Watkinson
    Tho. Scott

OLD MASTER'S HOUSE IN ALMSHOUSE LANE.
(From a Photograph by Messrs. G. & J. Hall.)

GRAMMAR SCHOOL.

The Statute Book contains two other entries, the first of which is dated Mar. 7. 1848, and consists of a provision to allow the Head Master to hold the post of Preacher in the Parish Church of Wakefield only, "and that not without express licence thereto obtained of the greater part of the Governors under their common seal, and that only *durante bene placito.*" This is signed by Jer. Glover (Spokesman), Samuel Sharp, William Thomas, Ldw. Tew, Jno. Hardcastle, John Pullein, John Pemberton Simpson, Edwd. Tomlinson, John Barff, and James Taylor, M.A. Schoolmaster."

The second entry is dated Feb. 6. 1855, and is of so sweeping a character that it may be said to form a new Scheme for the whole management of the School. It expressly annuls "Chapters Five Six and Seven of the Statutes now in force and as at present carried out" as being "repugnant and totally inadequate to meet the Educational requirements of the present times." After providing for the election of Head Master, Usher and Assistants, it proceeds to state that the "course of Instruction shall comprise Religious instruction in the principles of the Church of England, Scripture and Gospel History, the Latin Greek and French languages, Mathematics Algebra and Arithmetic, Writing, Geography with the use of the globes, Ancient and Modern History and English Literature with such other subjects as German, Drawing, and Music, as the Head Master with the consent of the Governors shall find expedient." Natives of the Parish of Wakefield are to pay School fees of Six guineas a year, if under 10 years of age, otherwise Eight guineas: Non-natives, or foreigners, under 10 years of age Eight guineas, otherwise Ten guineas: German and Drawing to be extras: Town-boys to be able to claim free teaching in Writing, Religious instruction, Latin and Greek. The School hours to be:—in the winter, from 9-0 a.m. to 12-0 noon, and 2-0 p.m. to 4-30 p.m.; and in the summer, from 7-0 a.m. to 8-0 a.m., 9-0 a.m. to 12-0 noon, and 2-0 p.m. to 5-0 p.m. The Vacations to consist of six weeks at Midsummer, four at Christmas, one at Easter, and one or two days at Michaelmas. Wednesday and Saturday to be half-holidays. A half-yearly examination to be held for the whole School, at Christmas by the Masters of the School, and at Midsummer by an Examiner appointed by the Governors. Donors of shares in the late Proprietary School to have the same privileges as residents in the Parish of Wakefield with regard to School-fees. The statute was signed by James Taylor, M.A. Head Master, and William Walker, agent to the Governors, on behalf of those present, who were "Philip Yorke

Savile, Clerk, Spokesman, Samuel Sharp, Clerk, Jeremiah Glover, William Thomas, Edward Tew, Esquires, John Pemberton Simpson, Clerk, Edward Tomlinson and Henry Wormald, Esquires, being a greater part of the Governors of the said School, assembled in our usual place of meeting."

As stated at the commencement of this Chapter, "The Endowed Schools Acts" gave the power of framing Statutes to the Charity Commissioners, and their first Scheme came into force on May 13, 1875; it established the Wakefield Grammar School as a First Grade School, and has been in operation until the present year, 1891. Under its provisions the constitution of the Governing Body was altered, as will be explained in the next Chapter; the Rev. Dr. Taylor, the Head Master of the School, received a pension of £200 a year, and the office of Usher was abolished; the School was divided into Junior and Senior Departments, the fees for the Junior to be between £5 and £10 a year, those for the Senior between £10 and £20, no difference being made between any scholars on account of place of birth or residence. An entrance examination was provided for, and instruction ordered to be given in Religion (according to the doctrines of the Church of England), Reading, Writing, Arithmetic, History, Geography, English Grammar, Composition and Literature, one or more Modern European languages, Latin, Greek, one branch at least of Natural Science, Mathematics, Vocal Music and Drawing. There was to be an annual Examination by an Examiner appointed by the Governors and unconnected with the School. Foundation Scholarships, exempting from payment of the whole or any part of School fees, were to be given not above the proportion of one to every ten boys in the School : £10 a year might also be allowed to deserving scholars towards the cost of books, stationery and other expenses: and £240 a year was to be devoted in providing Exhibitions to the Universities out of Storie's University Gift. At the same time a Trade School and a Girls' School were also provided for, but the former of these was, by the consent of the Charity Commissioners, abandoned.

An amended Scheme has recently been prepared by the Commissioners, and came into force on June 23, 1891, this being the day on which it received the approval of Her Majesty in Privy Council. In place of the Trade School previously contemplated, it provides for the payment of £250 a year towards Technical Instruction in various places. The Grammar School is to be a First Grade School with Classical and Modern sides, and the Girls' School

GRAMMAR SCHOOL.

is to continue as before. An additional Governor is to be appointed by the Yorkshire College. The division of the Grammar School into Senior and Junior Departments is abolished: the fees are to be between £5 and £20, but not less than £10 for boys over 15 years of age: no difference to be made on account of place of birth or residence. The entrance examination and subjects of instruction remain virtually the same as before. There are to be at least 24 Storie Scholarships in the School for boys who have been educated 3 years at any Public Elementary School in the school district of Wakefield, exempting from all payment of school fees, and carrying also a claim for £5 each boy per year towards other school expenses. The Foundation Scholarships remain unaltered, but the Storie Exhibitions to the Universities are, in cases of equal merit, to be awarded preferentially to boys who have been three years at any Wakefield Public Elementary School. The chief object of the new provisions of the Scheme may therefore be said to be the encouragement of elementary education.

Chapter 5.

THE GOVERNORS AND THEIR SPOKESMEN.

THE Charter of Foundation provided that there should be "forever within the parishe of Wakefilde or dwellinge within two myles thereof fouretene honest men of the moste wise discreete and religeous persons who shalbe called Governers of the said free Grammer Scoole att Wakefilde and of all the possessions reuercions and goodes thereunto belonginge": they were to be "a bodye corporate and politique to contynue forever" to be able to "purchase gett receive possesse and enioie" lands and other properties, "to pleade and be impleaded, defende and be defended, answeare and be answered in all manner of Cowrtes," to have power to present a Schoolmaster to the Archbishop of York for appointment by him, to hold property of the "cleare yerelie value of one hundrethe markes," and to make Statutes for the management of the School in general. All this may be found more fully stated in Chapter I.

The School Statutes also are full of details regarding the appointment and duties of the Governors, and provide for the election of a President Governor or Spokesman.

The Governors of the Grammar School, since the foundation of the School, have had many other charities entrusted to their management, and are therefore generally described as Governors of the Wakefield Charities. The consequent importance of their duties has made them for centuries perhaps the most influential body of men in Wakefield and the neighbourhood: and the long list of their names, carefully recorded and preserved, which will be found at the end of this chapter, shows that the most worthy and distinguished residents in the town and immediate district have thought it an honour to hold the office.

The first fourteen Governors were named by the Charter, and the first election to fill vacancies was held at some time in the year 1601, when the following five were appointed :—"Mr. William Lister, Vicar of Wakefield, Mr. Richard Lister, Master of Artes, John Flemynge, gent, John Jackson, and John Mawde." Two more

GRAMMAR SCHOOL. 87

were appointed on Nov. 5, 1605—Edward Watkinson and Andrew Scatcherd—and the above seven, together with Sir George Savile, Sir John Savile (John Savile, Esq., at the time of the Charter), Henry Arthington, Richard Clayton, William Savile, John Batty and Thomas Robinson, all original Governors, were in office until the Statutes were framed in 1607. From that time forward elections have been regularly made to fill vacancies caused by death, resignation, neglect of duties, removal from the district, and other reasons.

The following extracts from various books in the possession of the Governors, and in the British Museum, give interesting information concerning the mode of procedure :—

"*The daies of the deathe and avoydance of Governours and the eleccion of others in their places.*

HENRY ARTHINGTON, gentleman, resigned and surrendered up his place of Governour to the Governours, to proceed to a new election, the 20th of February 1608, as by his letter under his hand it appeareth, which is in the litle chest.

MR. WILLIAM RODES was elected Governour of this School in place of Mr. Arthington according to the Statutes, and was sworn by the Spokesman in presence of vii other Governours the 3rd of April 1609."

* * * * *

"Memo that *A.B.* being chosen a governor of this Schole and sworne for the execucion of the place accordynge to the Statutes, afterwards became negligent in dischardgeinge of his dutie, and being this present day chosen Spokesman for this yeare to come, and desired to take upon him that office and to contynue governor, did absolutely refuse to take the same upon him, or to contynue governor : alledginge for his reasons, first that he hath noe children to be taught at the Schole, Secondly that he will not be trobled with Collection of Rentes, and cheifly that he will not have the evill will of any for sueing for thinges belonginge to the Schole. Whereupon *C.D.* beinge present Spokesman together with the consent of those Governors whose names are subscribed, thinkinge a man of such disposition unworthy of his place, have this present day absolutely deposed the said *A.B.* from the said plaice."

* * * * *

July 27, 1625. This day JOHN SAVILE of Lupsett, Esq., is elected Governor in place of Mr. Mawde, Vicar, deceased.

"Memo that the Clause of the Statutes which requires that Governors of this Schole shall be 30 years old is to be altered and explained in this way, that gentlemen or men of education either in the Universities or Inns of Court may be elected Governors at the age of one and twentye yeares and that an order be made and entered into the booke of statutes for that purpose before the saide Mr Savile be sworne Governor.

April 11, 1626. This day it is agreed that the Spokesman shall write a letter to the Archbishoppe of Yorke to allowe John Savile Esq. to be a Governor though not elected accordinge to the Statutes.

Sep. 30, 1626. John Savile, of Lupset, Esq., by the consent of the Archbishoppe of Yorke, took his oathe as Governor."

* * * * *

Oct. 13, 1625. The Spokesman handed in his accounts, "deferred from the day after Michs day, for the visitation of the sickness and other occasions "₁.

* * * * *

June 17, 1633. "Mr Robarte Kay formerlie chosen a governor of the Schole in place of Mr Hugh Cressie, who is gone into Irelande as Judge, came to the tabell and uppon his comeinge semed unwillinge to take uppon him the saide place, whereuppon the governors present was not willinge to pres him further then his owne likeing, dischardged him, and proceded to a newe election."

* * * * *

The Statutes gave the Head Master of the School the right of objecting to the election of a Governor, if he did not think the choice a good one: this power of veto was often exercised, and sometimes led to complications and appeals to the Archbishop of York, as will be seen from the following extracts:—

Mar. 23, 1634-5. Mr. John Keyser is chosen Governor in place of Mr. John Mawde: but Mr. Doughty, the Schoolmaster, did not agree.

Oct. 11, 1637.—"This day the vacancie of Mr. Francis Heye being made known to the company by the spokesman, It was thought fitting by the greater parte of the governors present that he should be suspended and a newe Governor chosen in his place."

Oct. 18, 1637. "Mo. that Sir John Savile, Mr. Stansfeild, Mr. John Storye, & Leonard Willson being here present, and the Spokesman having expounded to the company to make choice of another Governor in place of Mr. Francis Hey, they departed and left the Company alledging that they wold not proceed to the election of any in place of Mr. Hey untill the roome of Mr. John Mawde, who dyed in March, 1634, was supplyed, after whose death Mr. John Keyser was chosen by the greater parte of the Governors then present in the place of the said Mr. Mawde, Mr. Doughty the Scholemaister contradicting it, whereuppon the residue of the Governors present thought fitting to stay proceeding this present to an election, and have appointed to mete on Wednesday next at one of the Clocke."

Oct. 25, 1637. "This day it is agreed by all the said Governors present that for the decyding of the controversie between the Governors and Mr. Doughty about the election of Mr. Keyser to be a Governor of this Schole, the letters patent of Queene Elizabeth under the great seale of England and the Statutes of the Schole under the common scale of the schole shalbe delivered to Mr. Stansfeld, Mr. Lyon, and John Storie, the deputy Spokesman, to attend the Archbisshop of York his [Secretarie] as is signified under a petition delivered to him by Mr. Doughty the 21 Aug., 1635, now showed to the company, to the end that his Grace may decide that controversie."

(₁) 131 persons died of the plague between August 7, 1625, and the following January 16 (Walker, p. 306).

GRAMMAR SCHOOL.

It is likewise agreed that a Governor shalbe chosen in the room of Mr. Francis Hey, on November the 1st.

Nov. 1, 1637. The Archbishop of York confirms Mr. Keyser's election, and he takes his oath as Governor.

It is agreed that "a special entrie of this matter shalbe made in the Register Book."

It is likewise agreed that "forty shillings shalbe allowed to the deputation to the Archbishop, five shillings to the Secretarie, and twelve pence to the Porter: they did go on the Thursday and came not home till Saturday at night."

Thomas Burrowe was then elected Governor in the room of Mr. Francis Hey, and took his oath.

* * * * *

May 2, 1654. JOSIAS ROOE resigns "by reason of some weaknes it hath pleased God to lay upon me." Richard Norfolke is chosen in his stead, but vetoed by Mr. Doughty.

Oct. 17. 1654. JOHN POTTER is chosen Governor, vice Josias Rooe, but vetoed by Mr. Doughty.

Nov. 14, 1654. "JOHN POTTER beinge elected the 17th of October, 1654, according to the Statutes, was excepted against by Mr. Doughtie, and this daye ther was five more named to witt Rowland Borrowe, Abraham Hagge, Richard Shutlworth, Robert Tompson, and John Robinson, and Mr. Doughtie exprest him self that unlesse wee make Choyse of Abraham Hagge or Robert Tompson wee should not have his voice."

June 12, 1655. JOHN ROBINSON was this day chosen Governor in the room of Josias Rooe.

* * * * *

April 19, 1675. "MR. OBADIA LEE is this day elected Governor in the room of Mr. Francis Somester, deceased, having before heard such exceptions as the Master did object against him, and did not find them sufficient to disapprove of him"

* * * * *

It will be seen, from the list of Governors which is printed further on in this Chapter, that the Vicars of Wakefield have nearly always been elected Governors of the School: but in two cases at least the post to which they have been elected would seem to have been claimed as an "ex-officio" one, although nothing in the Statutes can be found to support such a claim: the following extracts illustrate this point:—

Sep. 13. 1805. "The REV. RICHARD MUNKHOUSE, D.D. was this day elected Governor in the room of Dr. Bacon, deceased, late Vicar of Wakefield.

Nov. 2. 1805. The Rev. Dr. Munkhouse took the oath of Governor.

MEMORANDUM. Dr. Munkhouse was elected a Governor on the 13th September last, independent of any Claim to the office of Governor in virtue of his Vicarage of Wakefield, but it appears by a Grant or Letters Patent made in the Time of the Commonwealth, and in the name of Oliver Lord Protector, bearing date at Westminster, the 18th day of December, 1656, that the Vicar of Wakefield for the time being is ordained to be a perpetual Governor. The following words are contained in the grant :—

"It is further ordered, adjudged, and decreed by us, the Commissioners aforesaid, that the Survivors of the said Committees, by us aforesaid elected and named, and the Survivors of their Successors who in Times to come shall be chosen and appointed to succeed them or the greater number of them, and in their default, by the space of forty days, the Vicar of the said Parish of Wakefield for the time being continually resident and not beneficed elsewhere with any other benefice having cure of souls, shall himself, alone, after the Death of all or any of the said Persons Committees aforesaid or of their successors, have full power and authority from time to time to elect other like honest and fitting persons in their Rooms, to fill and make up the said number of Fifteen Persons to be joined unto the Vicar of the said Parish, who always, if he be resident and such as aforesaid, is to be one, and so to make up the number of Sixteen Persons to be Committees as aforesaid for the charitable Uses within the said Town and Parish."

Qy. Whether these Letters Patent are now in force or are repealed or annulled by subsequent Letters or Decree in Chancery."

Feb. 16. 1810. "The REV. SAMUEL SHARPE, M.A., Vicar of Wakefield, is elected a Governor in the room of Dr. Munkhouse, late Vicar of Wakefield, deceased; but by Grant or Letters Patent in the Time of the Commonwealth, it appears that the Vicar of Wakefield as such is to be a Governor as to some of the Trusts."

* * * * *

The Governors' Books give many interesting facts about the condition of Wakefield during the Civil War between Charles I. and his Parliament. The minutes suddenly break off with a record of the election of a Spokesman for the year commencing Sep. 30, 1641, and there is a gap of eight years without record, the next minute being dated Oct. 1, 1649. It is clear, however, from scattered details that the business of the School was carried on by the Governors until about Easter, 1643; for it appears that the Spokesman or some other Governor collected the School rents and paid the Master's salary until that date. But it will be remembered that Wakefield, very soon after this, was the scene of an important engagement. On Whitsunday, May 21, 1643, the Royalist force in possession of the town was driven out by Sir Thomas Fairfax, the Parliamentarian general.[1] The Head Master of that time—the Rev. Robert Doughty—remained at his post and proved himself worthy of his name, notwithstanding these troubles, and ultimately obtained the authority of Fairfax to collect the School rents in the absence of the Governors, who had been scattered about

(1) 35 soldiers who fell in the battle were buried in the graveyard of Wakefield Parish Church on the two following days.

the country, or had died or fallen in battle. When comparative quiet was restored, and the Governors were again called together, he presented accounts of sums received from Dec. 10, 1644 to Sep. 29, 1649; from which it would appear that nothing was obtained from tenants between Easter, 1643, and December, 1644, a fact which will not be considered strange when it is remembered that, during this period, Yorkshire was the scene of many recorded and unrecorded disturbances, which culminated in the battle of Marston Moor, fought on July 2, 1644.

And not only did Mr. Doughty execute the duties of Governors in looking after the School property, but he also kept the School open probably throughout these anxious times, with the aid of his son, Henry Doughty, who performed the duties of Usher for more than two years. Subsequent generations therefore owe him an enormous debt of gratitude for these services, which are many times cordially acknowledged by the Governors in their official records.

It has been said that no rents from tenants appear to have been received from Easter, 1643, to December, 1644, which may be taken for the period when Wakefield suffered most from the war, but this was by no means the most serious loss sustained by the School. The following document has been printed already in Lupton's "Wakefield Worthies," but can hardly be omitted in a history of the School: it shows what damage was done by the soldiers to the School records and deeds in the Governors' meeting room over the South Porch in the Parish Church.

"Wakefield, the 14th day of February, 1653. Whereas in the late unnatturall warres the Counting house over the Church Poarch in Wakefield aforesaid, where the Evidences and Rights of the Free Grammar Schoole were preserved, was broken up by the Souldiery and some malevolent hands: wee the then present Schoolmaister and onely surviving Governour (whose names are subscribed) at our first comming into the said chamber after the said breaking of it up, did find severall of the Schooles donations (by Benefactors) scattered up and downe the said chamber or counting house, defaced, with the seale plucked of (though some neverthelesse we found intire), and by the examinations of the present governours some are supposed to be taken away: Therefore doe enter this evidence in this Booke of Graunts for the said schoole at the request of all the present Governours joyned with us, and are ready to attest the same when we are thereunto called. And also do hartyly desire (it tending to a publicke good), that our auntient accounts may be examined, whereby all due rents may be clearly discovered: and after such discovery that all the rights due to the said School (so cleared) may be confirmed in some court of Recoard unto the said Schoole in as good state and tenure as if the said writings and deeds of gift had not been defaced nor taken away: which wee conceave would be a just and mercyfull act, and

much conducing to the incouragement of the present and future governours of the said free School in the discharging of their duties for so publicke a good."
   Robert Doughty, Schoolmaster.
   William Waler.

"It is also this day agreed that a speciallty in writing be forthwith entered in the book of deeds of gift of the breaking up of this Chamber over the Church Porch in the tymes of the late warres and of the then rifling and abusing of the writings that doe belong to this Schole."

"Wakefield the 2 May 1654. We whose names are here-onder written present Governours having taken good notice of the abuses and wrongs done to the said evidences and deeds belonging to this said schoole, finding many seales to have beene torne cutt or plucked off from the said writings doe veryly beleeve that the testimony given above is most just and true

    John Wilson, Spoakesman
    Ed. Watkinson
    Daniell Oley
    Chr. Wilson
    John Moxon

    John Waterhouse
    John Issott
    Geo. Radcliffe
    Thomas Pease.

It is sufficiently plain from these records that many evidences of title and leases were lost to the School during these years; no doubt the soldiers who rifled the Governors' documents would be only too glad to sell such papers for whatever price could be obtained for them; and thus unscrupulous tenants were enabled to claim many lands and buildings as their own freehold property. The books of the Governors contain ample evidence of this having been done.

Thus the accounts presented by Mr. Doughty for the School rents during the period between December, 1644, and September, 1649, show that he had received £248 19s. 8d., whereas the annual rental of the School lands at that time was about £60 a year. The figures speak well for Mr. Doughty's energy and perseverance, but also show that an average of some £10 a year was lost: and this is quite well borne out by a list drawn up by the Governors in the year 1653 of various "desperate" rents, which they never hoped to recover. We may therefore safely say that from 10 to 15 per cent. of the School property was lost during the Civil War, and that the amount might easily have been increased if Mr. Doughty had not remained at his post to look after the interests of the School.

There is also ample evidence in the Governors' books of the lawless spirit produced by the war amongst the people generally, a few instances of which are appended :—

  Jan. 2, 1649-50. W. B., tenant to the School at Gawthorpe, laid claim to his land as freehold : he was ordered to bring in his "pretended assurance."

GRAMMAR SCHOOL. 93

On the same day Widow C. denied publicly that she owed any rent to the School.

Feb. 2, 1649-50. John S., whose lease had expired, was offered a new one, but refused to accept it, or to leave his lands, and said he would keep them by force : he was discharged for "medling."

July 16, 1650. A. P., tenant to the School, appeared before the Governors "and because of his peremptory language that they should come more often for their rent due to the schole out of the house in his possession," he received warning to remove at Whitsuntide.

Feb. 25, 1650-1. R. T.'s wife confessed that her husband had been "tenant diverse years to School lands, and produced only an acquittance for one whole yeare's rent received by Mr. Doughty" in 1647 ; yet she refused to pay any money.

Sep. 30, 1652. T. C. refused his copyhold rent, and when asked to pay 3s. 4d. sealing money for his lease to the Spokesman, he declined, "catching away his lease suddenly, which thing he ought not to have done."

But not only were the tenants of the School property demoralized by the war and its attendant evils, but the same results ensued in higher places.

In the first place, one of the Spokesmen of the Governors, probably the one in office in 1643, when the disturbances in Wakefield were at their height, seems to have disappeared with the balance of the School monies which he had at the time in his possession. His name is, however, unrecorded, but the extent of his indebtedness to the School must have only been small, as the Governors had long before adopted a regulation, which has done infinite benefit to the School, whereby it was ordered :—

Oct. 8, 1627. "That hereafter no Spokesman shall have in his hands above the sum of tenn pounds of the moneyes belonging to the Scole, and that the residue shall be by him disposed of for the good of the Schole to his own consideration & in some reasonable manner."

And in the next place, no less a person than Sir John Savile, of Lupset, one of the Governors, and an officer of high position in the Parliamentarian forces, as well as Sheriff of Yorkshire at the time, took advantage of his position to do the School an injury, certainly of no great extent, and perhaps by way of political reprisal, of which we have the following records :—

June 11, 1650. "In regard that Sir John Savile hath absented himself from the trust reposed in him for the Schoole since Michaelmas last, and withholdes rents due for 6 or 7 yeares in his hands from the Schoole, it is agreed that Willm Waler Spokesman shall repayre to Sir John to demand the arreares of Rent and to acquaint him that unles he come to the next meeting, which is this day five weekes, there will be another chosen in his place."

July 16, 1650. "Notwithstandinge the agreement made uppon the 11 of June last, Sir John Savile shall continue to be governor till the first publique meeting after Michaelmas, in regard of his publique imployment as Sheriff for this county. But his rents to be got in the mean time."

Sep. 30, 1650. "This day also Sir John Savile being Governour, havinge levelled the School lands to his owne, reserved his rents due to the schoole for nine yeares past, amountinge to nine pounds and eighteen shillings, and for all times disavowed the service of the schole, besides a yeare's neglect of being present with us almost a yeare after summons to severall meetings, is ejected."

Nov. 12, 1650. This day Mr Josias Rooe is elected Governor in place of Sir John Savile.

The Governors are deserving of the utmost credit for dealing with the case in so just a manner, for it could not be without great risk that they attacked so powerful a man, and, through him, the political party then in power.

At the same time it is quite clear that, although bold in the year 1650, the Governors who were left in 1647 had seriously thought it necessary to close the School and sacrifice its property; but having consulted eminent counsel upon the subject—amongst whom were Sir Thomas Widrington, of Sergeants' Inn, and Sir William Belt, Recorder of York—they ultimately decided that they were bound to endeavour to ensure its continuance. The evidence for this is the first record found in the minutes of the Governors after the Civil War had come to an end :—

Oct. 1, 1649. "This day were present William Waler and Thomas Burrowe, being the greater part of the nowe present Governers remayning 1, and Mr Robert Doughty Schoolmaster.

Whereas in the great distraction and distresse of the tymes for seaven yeares and upwardes by-past, The Free Grammer Schoole of Queene Elizabeth at Wakefield, both in matter of revenues and repayres is fallen to extreme ruine : Whereas likewise—in the sayd tymes, the most of the School Governers which were in number fourteene, are partly deceassed, partly by the statutes of the sayd Schoole avoyded : And whereas this tyme two yeares the remayning governors had severall meetings touching the selling of the Schoole affayres, but did not conclude any thing. Wee therefore above mentioned Governers being much distressed about the

(1) The only other Governor left was Sir John Savile, of Lupset.

GRAMMAR SCHOOL.

present unsetlednes of the government, According to the advice of most able and judicious Lawyers, doe (in pursuance of the good purposes of the Founders and benefactors for the promoveing of good literature as alsoe of the true intent of our Mortmayne and Statutes for preserving of the same) with the consent of our sayd Schoolmaster, Chuse for supply of the places vacant these underwritten to be Governers, viz. :—

in place of
- Mr Thomas Somester
- Mr Willm Paulden
- Mr John Story
- Mr James Lister
- Mr John Lion
- Tho: Cooke
- Leonard Wilson
- Mr John Keysar
- Mr Gervase Nevill
- Mr Cotton Horne
- Dr Brownlowe

- Edward Watkinson
- Daniel Oley
- Chr. Wilson
- Richard Wilson
- Peter Mogson
- William Harrinson
- John Issott
- Chr Holdsworth
- Tho Norton
- John Waterhouse
- John Clayton Esq.

This day Edward Watkinson, Daniel Oley, Chr. Wilson, Richard Wilson, Peter Moxon, and William Harrison took each of them the oath of Governor of the Free Schoole of Wakefield, and so tooke theyr place.

This day Willm Waler by all the present Governors above-mentioned was chosen Spokesman for the yeare following, and tooke his oath, And hath delivered into his Custodie The Common Seall, the second booke of Statutes, the Register booke, some Indentures of Accompts, And such other thinges as the unkindness of Malignants, And rudenesse of Souldiers have left, together with the Key of the Counting house-doore. And Chr. Wilson was chosen deputy Spokesman."

* * * * *

There are also one or two other characteristic entries in the records which show in what light the Governors regarded the Vicar of Wakefield appointed in place of the Rev. James Lister, who was turned out of the living during the Commonwealth, but returned amidst great rejoicings after the Restoration [1]:—

Sep. 30, 1657. "Also this day Mr, Walker, *our Vicar for the time being*, is chosen Governour in John Issott's place.

Sep. 30, 1661. This day was present . . . . Mr. James Lister, Vicar, who took his place according to a former election . . . . &c., &c.

---

(1) See Walker, p. 192.

Mr. James Clayton thereupon resigned and avoyded his place of Governor, in whose stead Mr. Lister above resumed his place by virtue of a former Election."

The Scheme issued by the Charity Commissioners in the year 1875, greatly changed the Governing Body of the School. It provided that no more Governors should be elected by the Governors themselves until their number had been reduced to eight; but these were to be co-optative for the future and hold office for life. There were also to be two ex-officio Governors, viz. :—the Mayor of Wakefield, and the Chairman of the School-Board for Wakefield for the time being. Five gentlemen were to be elected to represent the Town Council of Wakefield for a period of five years, and three to represent the School Board for a similar time.

The Amended Scheme of 1891 ordains that the Governing Body shall be further changed by limiting the tenure of office by future co-optative Governors to the period of seven years, and by adding a nineteenth Governor to represent the Council of the Yorkshire College.

The following pages contain a list of all the Governors, from the foundation of the School to the present time, as perfect as it is possible to make it, with the dates of their appointment and vacating of office, and other particulars. The only period about which there is any uncertainty in this respect is that between the years 1677 and 1721, for which there are no minute-books of the Governors now remaining: the particulars for these years have been therefore gathered from various documents bearing the Governors' names, and these are of such a character that it is not probable that more than one or two elections have been left without a record of some sort. The remarks in the foot notes have been chiefly obtained from three sources in addition to the records of the Governors, viz:—from Banks' "Walks about Wakefield," Taylor's "Rectory Manor of Wakefield," and Walker's "Cathedral Church of Wakefield": the indebtedness is acknowledged here to avoid overloading the notes with references.

LIST OF GOVERNORS OF WAKEFIELD GRAMMAR SCHOOL.

NOTE.—The first column gives the order of seniority.
,, second ,, ,, name and title of the Governor at the time of election.
,, third ,, ,, date of his election.
,, fourth ,, ,, number of the Governor whom he succeeded.
,, fifth ,, ,, reason of the termination of his office (dec. — deceased; dep. — deposed; dis. — disqualified by non-residence within proper limits or non-attendance at meetings; res. — resigned; war — died or left the district during the Civil War.)
,, sixth ,, ,, date when his office terminated; (b. — buried.)

No.	NAME.	When elected.	Vice.	How vacated.	When vacated.
1	Sir George Savile, Kt. & Bt.	Nov. 19, 1591	—	dec.	Nov. 12, 1622
2	John Savile, Esq.	do.	—	dec.	Aug. 31, 1630
3	Thomas Savile, Esq.	do.	—	dec.	in 1599
4	Robert Bradford, Esq.	do.	—	—	by 1605
5	George Savile, gent.	do.	—	dec.	Oct. 1593
6	Henry Arthington, gent.	do.	—	res.	Feb. 20, 1609-10
7	Richard Sproxton, gent.	do.	—	—	by 1605
8	Roger Pollard, yeoman	do.	—	—	by 1605
9	Richard Clayton, yeoman	do.	—	dec.	Dec. 1610
10	William Savile, yeoman	do.	—	dec.	b. Oct. 29, 1622
11	Thomas Cave, yeoman	do.	—	dec.	in 1603
12	Henry Watkinson, yeoman	do.	—	—	by 1605
13	John Battie, yeoman	do.	—	dec.	b. May 1, 1623
14	Thomas Robinson, yeoman	do.	—	dec.	June, 1623
15	Rev. William Lister, M.A.	in 1601	—	dec.	b. June 6, 1624
16	Rev. Richard Lister, M.A.	in 1601	—	res.	May 2, 1611
17	John Fleming, gent.	in 1601	—	dec.	b. Sep. 28, 1619
18	John Jackson	in 1601	—	res.	Oct. 5, 1614
19	John Mawde	in 1601	—	—	Mar. 1634-5
20	Edward Watkinson	Nov. 5, 1605	—	dec.	Apl. 1609
21	Andrew Scatcherd	Nov. 5, 1605	—	—	b. Dec. 16, 1630
22	William Rhodes	Apl. 3, 1609	6	—	about 1620
23	Hugh Cressy, Esq.	Apl. 11, 1609	20	res.	June, 1633

1—14. For particulars about these see Chap. I., pp. 8—10.   15. Vicar of Wakefield, 1598—1620.   16. Of Milnthorpe, Sandal, buried at Wakefield Aug. 26, 1632, called "clericus valde doctus"   19. Of Northgate, Wakefield.   20. Edward Watkinson is spoken of in the list of Benefactors (see p. 40) as being a Governor in 1603: there is much confusion between him and his father, Henry Watkinson (No. 12).   21. Of Northgate, Wakefield, chapman.   22. Of Crofton, chapman.   23. A barrister of Lincoln's Inn, Steward of the Rectory Manor of Wakefield: he resigned in consequence of being "sent as a judge to Ireland."

24	Christopher Naylor, gent.	Dec. 20, 1610	9	dec.	b. Oct. 2. 1638
25	George Wharton, draper	May 2, 1611	16	dep.	Sep. 30, 1612
26	George Spivie	Sep. 30, 1612	25	dec.	Oct. 1619
27	William Pollard, chapman	Oct. 12, 1614	18	—	Feb. 1639-40
28	John Greenwood	Oct. 4, 1619	26	dec.	b. Nov. 1635
29	Thomas Somaster, gent.	Oct. 4, 1619	17	war	b. July 12, 1644.
30	Robert Waterhouse	—	22	dec.	b. Nov. 7, 1621
31	Rev. Timothy Mawde, D. D.	Dec. 20, 1621	30	dec.	July, 1625
32	Richard Tayler, gent.	Nov. 6, 1622	10	dec.	b. Feb. 7, 1628-9
33	Henry Grice, Esq.	Dec. 24, 1622	1	dec.	Feb. 26, 1629-30
34	Cotton Horne	June 17, 1623	14	dep.	Apl. 8, 1624
35	John Battie, gent.	June 17, 1623	13	—	1630—1633
36	William Paulden	Sep. 30, 1624	15	war	1640—1649
37	John Storie	Sep. 30, 1624	34	war	1640—1649
38	Sir John Savile, Kt.	July 27, 1625	31	dep.	Sep. 30, 1650
39	Rev. James Lister, M.A.	Feb. 25, 1628-9	32	war	1640—1649
40	Henry Savile, gent.	Mar. 1, 1629-30	33	—	1630—1633
41	James Stansfield	Sep. 1630	2	res.	Jan. 23, 1638-9
42	Francis Hey	Dec. 21, 1630	21	dep.	Oct. 11, 1637
43	Thomas Cooke	1630-1633	35 or 40	war	1640-1649
44	John Lyon	1630-1633	35 or 40	war	1640-1649
45	Leonard Wilson	June 17, 1633	23	war	b. Mar. 28, 1643
46	John Keyser	Mar. 23, 1634-5	19	war	1640-1649
47	William Waller	Nov. 17, 1635	28	dec.	Feb. 1662-3
48	Thomas Burrow	Nov. 1, 1637	42	dec.	Mar. 1649-50

24. Joint Lord of the Rectory Manor of Wakefield with William Vernon, of Soothill: lived at Flanshaw. 25. Buried Sep. 2, 1620. 26. Of Northgate, Wakefield, chapman. 28. A French merchant, builder of Wrenthorpe Hall, or Red Hall, in 1612 (Thoresby, Duc. Leod. 170). 29. Master of the Wakefield House of Correction, succeeded by his son John in 1641. 30. Of Northgate, Wakefield, mercer. 31. Vicar of Wakefield, 1620—1625. 32. William Paulden was elected on Nov. 2, but refused to take office. 33. Of Sandal. 34. Built the Almshouses for 10 poor men and 10 poor women, in 1646 ; was re-elected Governor in Jan. 1638-9 (No. 50). 35. Lived at Alverthorpe : probably was the son of the former John Battie, yeoman (No. 13). 36. Had refused previously to hold office (see under No. 32). 37. Doubtless the father of the great benefactor of the School, who lived at Hasleborrow, in Derbyshire, was born Nov. 15, 1621, and died in 1674 (p. 50). 38. Of Lupset : the Statutes were altered to admit of his election : he was famous during the Civil War, being a local commander of the Parliamentarian forces, and holding Howley Hall against the Royalists: died May 5, 1660, and was buried at Horbury (see pp. 87, 93). 39. Educated at the School: Cave Scholar at Clare Hall, Cambridge : Usher of the School, 1621—1623 : Vicar of Wakefield from 1625 until the Civil War, when he was deprived : returned in 1660, and re-admitted as Governor (No. 72) : buried Jan. 17, 1677-8. 40. Of Lupset: son of Sir George Savile, of Thornhill and Lupset, Kt. and Bt. (No. 1). 45. Robert Kaye was elected on June 14, but declined to serve. 47. To this gentleman the School is greatly indebted for its survival of the Civil War with so little loss : he and Thomas Burrow (No. 48) appear to have been the only Governors who were left, with the exception of Sir John Savile, in 1649. Mr. Waller with the Schoolmaster of that time (Rev. Robert Doughty) took the necessary steps for the future welfare of the School, as has been pointed out earlier in this Chapter (p. 94).

GRAMMAR SCHOOL.

49	Gervase Nevile, gent.	Oct. 5, 1638	24	war	1640-1649
50	Cotton Horne, gent.	Jan. 31, 1638-9	41	war	1640-1649
51	Robert Brownlow, M.D.	Feb. 15, 1639-40	27	war	1640-1649
52	Edward Watkinson	Oct. 1, 1649	29	res.	May, 1664
53	Daniel Oley, gent.	do.	36	dec.	b. Jan. 21, 1672-3
54	Christopher Wilson	do.	37	res.	June, 1674
55	Richard Wilson	do.	39	—	Oct. 1653
56	Peter Mogson	do.	44	res.	June 22, 1658
57	William Harrison	do.	43	dec.	b. Feb. 20, 1652-3
58	John Issott	do.	45	—	Sep. 1657
59	Christopher Holdsworth	do.	46	res.	Sep. 1664
60	Thomas Norton	do.	49	res.	Apl. 5, 1653
61	John Waterhouse	do.	50	—	after Oct. 1688
62	Nathan Dodgson	June 11, 1650	51	dec.	b. July 30, 1663
63	William Mason, Lieut.	June 11, 1650	48	res.	Oct. 1664
64	Josias Rooe	Nov. 12, 1650	38	res.	May 2, 1654
65	John Wilson	Apl. 5, 1653	57	dec.	b. Aug. 7, 1671
66	George Radcliffe	Apl. 5, 1653	60	dec.	b. June 25, 1674
67	Thomas Pease	Oct. 18, 1653	55	—	before Mar. 1682
68	John Robinson	June 12, 1655	64	—	after 1676
69	Rev. Thomas Walker, D.D.	Sep. 30, 1657	58	dec.	June 25, 1660
70	James Clayton	Aug. 10, 1658	56	res.	Sep. 30, 1661
71	John Mawde, gent.	Aug. 28, 1660	69		b. Mar. 18, 1666-7
72	Rev. James Lister, M.A.	Sep. 30, 1661	70	—	before Sep. 1677
73	Richard Birkhead	Feb. 24, 1662-3	47	—	before Dec. 1683
74	Charles Naylor	Aug. 3, 1663	62	—	not before 1694
75	William Briggs	May 25, 1664	52	—	about 1678
76	Thomas Binns	Sep. 30, 1664	59	dec.	b. Jan. 16, 1668-9
77	William Denison, gent.	Oct. 24, 1664	63	—	before Dec. 1679
78	Matthew Meager	Mar. 25, 1667	71	res.	Jan. 26, 1674-5

49. Great-grandson of Sir John Nevile of Chevet, died Feb. 1676, aged 80 : no doubt he left the country during the Civil War, and returned when it was over. 50. See No. 34. 51. A well known medical man in Wakefield at the time ; died in 1663. 55. See p. 50. 57. Of Stanley. 62. John Clayton, Esq. was elected vice Dr. Brownlow on Oct. 1, 1649, but declined to serve : Joseph Holdsworth was next elected on Mar. 20, 1649-50, and likewise declined. 63. Daniel Mawde, of Alverthorpe, gent. was elected on Mar. 20 to fill this vacancy, but declared himself not to be 30 years of age until the following Sep. 14 : he was again elected on Feb. 23. 1652-3, but declined to serve : but being elected a third time on Jan. 25, 1672-3 he accepted office. 64. See above, p. 89. 65 A mercer in Wakefield. 66. Governor of the Wakefield House of Correction from 1647 to 1661, an attorney, and probably father of the famous Dr. John Radcliffe : see Chap. IX. 67. A clothier in Wakefield. 68. His initials appear on the Font in the Cathedral as a Churchwarden in 1661. Richard Norfolk was elected on May 2, 1654, but was vetoed by the Master : John Potter was next elected on Oct. 17, and likewise vetoed : see above p. 89. 69. " Our Vicar for the time being " (see p. 95) put in possession by Cromwell. 71. Son of John Mawde, of Alverthorpe, gent. 72. See under No. 39. 73. Of Newland, removed to Crofton in 1677, and perhaps became thereby disqualified for holding office. 76. A grocer in Wakefield. 77. Son and heir of Timothy Denison of Flanshaw, Steward of the Rectory Manor of Wakefield ; see p. 51 : died in 1684. 78. A Wakefield merchant, built a staircase in the Parish Church.

79	John Clough, mercer	Jan. 20, 1668-9	76	dec.	b. Mar. 16, 1674-5
80	Robert Benson, Esq.	Aug. 6, 1671	65	dec.	July, 1676
81	Daniel Mawde, gent.	Jan. 25, 1672-3	53	—	before Dec. 1710
82	Thomas Cheriholme	June 4, 1674	66	—	after Oct. 1688
83	Toby Sill, gent.	June 4, 1674	54	—	after 1679
84	Thomas Bargh	Feb. 3. 1674-5	78	—	after Sep. 1684
85	Francis Somester	Mar. 22, 1674-5	79	dec.	b. Apl. 12, 1675
86	Rev. Obadiah Lee, M.A.	Apl. 19, 1675	85	—	after Oct. 1688
87	Thomas Horsfield	July 20, 1676	80	—	before July, 1681
88	Richard Ellis	before 1680	—	—	after 1693
89	Richard Witton, Esq., sen.	before 1680	—	—	before May, 1718
90	Thomas Wheatley	before Oct. 1684	—	—	before Feb. 1715-6
91	Francis White, Esq.	before Oct. 1684	—	—	before Dec. 1692
92	John Scott, gent.	before Oct. 1684	—	—	about May, 1703
93	George Redshaw	before Oct. 1684	—	—	before Feb. 1715-6
94	Joseph Watkinson	before Oct. 1684	—	—	before Apl. 1723
95	William Turner	before Nov. 1689	—	—	before July, 1690
96	Richard Thornton	before Nov. 1689	—	—	before Feb. 1715-6
97	Francis Nevile, Esq.	before Nov. 1689	—	—	before July, 1707
98	William Haward, sen.	before Nov. 1689	—	—	before Apl. 1694
99	Thomas Brooke	before 1695	—	—	before Aug. 1703
100	Nicholas Fenay	before 1695	—	—	before Apl. 1710
101	Thomas Wilson, gent.	before 1695	—	—	before Mar. 1722
102	John Smyth, Esq.	before 1695	—	—	before Nov. 1723
103	Benjamin Watkinson, M.D.	Mar. 31, 1695	—	dec.	July 7, 1726
104	Sir Lyon Pilkington, Bt.	before 1696	—	—	before 1715
105	James Sill, gent.	before 1700	—	res.	before Nov. 1723
106	Theophilus Shelton, gent.	before 1700	—	—	before Nov. 1723
107	Rev. Thomas Scott, M.A.	Mar. 24, 1700-1	—	dec.	Apl. 14, 1729
108	William Coppendale	before 1701	—	—	before Mar. 1712-3

80. Of Red Hall, or Wrenthorpe Hall, clerk of assize for the Northern Circuit: M.P. for Aldborough: father of Lord Bingley: see Hailstone's 'Yorkshire Portraits, No. cxxxi.' 81. Son of John Mawde, of Alverthorpe, gent., born Sep. 14, 1620: Steward of the Rectory Manor of Wakefield in 1684: see under No. 63. 83. A Wakefield Mercer, buried June 21, 1695, at Wakefield, father of James Sill (No. 105). 84. Richard Norfolk was elected Jan. 26, but declined to serve; see under No. 68. 86. Vicar of Warmfield, previously Curate of Wakefield in 1671, and subsequently Vicar of Wakefield from 1677 to 1700. 89. Of Lupset Hall, a famous Barrister, Commissioner to Lord Fairfax, Lord of the Rectory Manor of Wakefield, died April 15, 1718. 91. J.P. for the West Riding, and Chief Steward of the Manor of Wakefield, died in Nov. 1692. 92. Deputy Steward of the Manor of Wakefield. 94. Of Flanshaw Hall, buried March 30, 1723. 95. Died June 21, 1690. 96. Perhaps Recorder of Leeds, who died October 7, 1710. 97. Of Chevet, son of Sandford Nevile, Esq.; died June 2, 1707. 99. Lived in Westgate; Steward of the Rectory Manor of Wakefield, buried July 25, 1703. 100 Of Fenay, died March 21, 1710. 102. Of Heath: Lord of the Rectory Manor of Wakefield: died Dec. 25, 1729. 104. Of Stanley: died in 1714, aged 54; buried in the Pilkington Chapel at Wakefield Cathedral. 105. Mercer, of Wakefield, son of Toby Sill (No. 83), see p. 51. 106. First Registrar of Deeds for the West Riding, Justice of the Peace, and Commissioner for Land Tax. 107. Educated at the School, Cave Scholar at Clare Hall, Cambridge: Vicar of Wakefield from 1701 to 1729. 108. Owner of Nether Hall, Horbury, and a Tobacconist in trade at Wakefield.

GRAMMAR SCHOOL.

109	Francis Wheatley	before 1705	—	dec. Aug. 21, 1714
110	William Haward, jun.	before 1708	—	— before July, 1713
111	Abraham Bever, gent.	before 1709	—	— before Nov. 1721
112	Richard Witton, Esq. jun.	Mar. 31, 1711	—	dec. Aug. 1, 1743
113	Jeremiah Spink	before 1713	—	— before Nov. 1713
114	Rev. Daniel Sill, M.A.	Aug 22, 1713	100	dec. Dec. 1731
115	William Spink	Oct. 28, 1713	—	dec. Jan. 5, 1738-9
116	Francis Pitt, gent.	before 1716	—	— Jan. 27, 1721-2
117	John Bromley, gent.	before 1716	—	dec. Nov. 11, 1723
118	Thomas Birkhead	Nov. 11, 1717	—	dec. b. Oct. 18, 1733
119	William Oates, gent.	Apl. 28, 1718	89	dec. Nov. 16, 1737
120	Thomas Moore, M.D.	Oct. 18, 1720	—	dec. b. Mar. 31, 1733
121	Samuel Richardson	Apl. 18, 1721	—	dec. b. Aug. 23, 1762
122	Robert Watson	Feb. 3, 1721-2	116	dec. b. Mar. 30, 1728
123	John Tilson	Feb. 16, 1721-2	—	res. Feb. 1738-9
124	Toby Sill	Apl. 1, 1723	—	res. Oct. 3, 1726
125	Ebenezer Buxton	May 10, 1723	—	dec. b. Sep. 4, 1729
126	Richard Smyth, Esq.	Nov. 20, 1723	117	dec. Apl. 15, 1730
127	John Mawde	July 15, 1726	103	dec. b. Feb. 27, 1743-4
128	Tempest Thornton	Oct. 7, 1726	124	dec. Apl. 1734
129	Francis Mawde	Apl. 5, 1728	122	dec. May 20, 1734
130	Stephen Holmes	Apl. 25, 1729	107	dec. b. Apl. 5, 1750
131	Rev. George Arnet, M.A.	Sep. 10, 1729	125	dec. b. Oct. 15, 1750
132	John Smyth, Esq.	Apl. 22, 1730	126	dec. May 31, 1731
133	William Walker	June 11, 1731	132	dec. Oct. 1732
134	Thomas Horn	Jan. 3, 1731-2	114	dec. Mar. 1740-1
135	Joseph Armitage	Nov. 1, 1732	133	dec. b. Nov. 19, 1750
136	Toby Sill	Apl. 4, 1733	120	dec. b. Dec. 2, 1736
137	Sir Lionel Pilkington, Bt.	Oct. 22, 1733	118	dis. Jan. 13, 1772
138	Matthew Wentworth	May 13, 1734	128	dec. July 26, 1749
139	Rev. Cavendish Nevile, M.A.	May 27, 1734	129	dec. Feb. 18, 1749-50

109. A draper at Wakefield, son of Colonel Thomas Wheatley (No. 90). 112. Eldest son of Richard Witton, senior (No. 89), and like him a Barrister: High Steward of the Manor of Wakefield: lived at Lupset Hall. 113. Maltster, at Wakefield. 114. Lecturer at Wakefield Parish Church from 1702, doubtless brother of James Sill (No. 105) and son of Toby Sill (No. 83). 115. Merchant, buried in Wakefield Cathedral. 116. Merchant and Cloth-Dresser; once owner of the "Six Chimneys" in Kirkgate, buried in Wakefield Cathedral. 117. Maltster, and great benefactor of the School and poor of Wakefield, buried in the Cathedral. 118. Of Newland and Crofton. 120. The chief medical man of the town at this time: lived in Kirkgate. 122. The donor of "Watson's Gift" of bread for poor people, and of the old dial at Wakefield Cathedral. 126. Mercer, of Westgate, Wakefield, son of John Smyth, Esq. (No. 102), buried in Wakefield Cathedral. 128. Son of Richard Thornton (No. 96), lived in Northgate, and died at Bristol. 129. A merchant in Wakefield. 131. Vicar of Wakefield from 1729 to 1750. 132. Of Heath, son of John Smyth, Esq. (No. 102) and elder brother of Richard Smyth, Esq. (No. 126). 133. Lived in Westgate. 134. Lived in Westgate. 135. Lived in Northgate: perhaps the builder of Outwood Hall. 137. Of Stanley originally, but purchased Chevet in 1771, and thus became disqualified by "not residing within two miles of the Parish of Wakefield": he died unmarried Aug. 11. 1778. 138. Of Wakefield, buried at Woolley. 139. Vicar of Norton, Derbyshire, the last male member of the family of Nevile of Chevet.

HISTORY OF WAKEFIELD

140	Joseph Sill	Dec. 6, 1736	136	res.	Oct. 3, 1744
141	William Charnock	Nov. 24, 1737	119	dec.	b. Apl. 21, 1746
142	Harpham Green	Jan. 12, 1738-9	115	dec.	Jan. 1772
143	John Cookson, M.D.	Feb. 26, 1738-9	123	res.	Jan. 5, 1771
144	John Smyth, Esq.	Mar. 30, 1741	134	dec.	Apl. 10, 1771
145	Christopher Hodgson, M.D.	July 27, 1743	112	dec.	Jan. 14, 1768
146	John Smith, Esq.	Mar. 3, 1743-4	127	dec.	May 26, 1746
147	Thomas Holmes	Oct. 3, 1744	140	res.	June 5, 1758
148	John Ridsdale	Apl. 29, 1746	141	dec.	May 24, 1765
149	Richard Buxton	June 4, 1746	146	dec.	b. May 27, 1775
150	James Mawde	Aug. 2, 1749	138	dec.	Jan. 1757
151	William Serjeantson	Mar. 8, 1749-50	139	dec.	b. Sep. 26, 1759
152	Thomas Norton	Apl. 11, 1750	130	res.	Jan. 15, 1765
153	Henry Thorpe	Oct. 19, 1750	131	res.	Jan. 15, 1765
154	Allan Johnson	Nov. 22, 1750	135	res.	Mar. 20, 1780
155	Francis Mawde	Feb. 2, 1757	150	res.	Jan. 26, 1768
156	Rev. Henry Zouch, M.A.	June 8, 1758	147	res.	Dec. 31, 1764
157	Richard Green	Oct. 1, 1759	151	res.	Jan. 5, 1771
158	Daniel Mawde	Sep. 27, 1762	121	dec.	Oct. 7, 1787
159	Rev. Michael Bacon, D.D.	Dec. 31, 1764	156	dec.	Aug. 19, 1805
160	William Serjeantson	Jan. 15, 1765	153	res.	Oct. 4, 1765
161	William Nevinson	Jan. 31, 1765	152	dec.	b. Apl. 21, 1785
162	Thomas Oates	May 31, 1765	148	dec.	Dec. 24, 1783
163	Alexander Hatfield	Oct. 4, 1765	160	dec.	Apl. 28, 1777
164	Samuel Zouch	Jan. 26, 1768	155	res.	Feb. 4, 1785
165	Robert Amory, M.D.	Apl. 18, 1768	145	res.	Feb. 4, 1793
166	William Serjeantson	Jan. 5, 1771	157	dec.	b. Apl. 19, 1782
167	George Charnock	Jan. 9, 1771	143	dec.	b. Feb. 14, 1783
168	Loftus Anthony Tottenham	Apl. 17, 1771	144	dis.	Mar. 25, 1780
169	Richard Burton	Jan. 9, 1772	142	dec.	b. Jan. 3, 1793

148. Lived at Cliffe House, Westgate: practised 52 years in Wakefield: buried in Wakefield Cathedral.   144. Son of Richard Smyth, Esq. (No. 126); a Justice of the Peace, buried at Kirkthorpe.   145. Buried in Wakefield Cathedral.   146. Of Newland, son of John Smith of Ecclesfield.   148. Son of Edward Ridsdale, of Ripon, buried in Wakefield Cathedral.   155. Brother of James Mawde (No. 150) whom he succeeded.   156. Of Sandal, elder brother of Dr. Thomas Zouch (see Chap. IX). The Rev. Benjamin Wilson, Vicar of Wakefield, and late Head Master of the School, was elected on June 5, but declined to serve.   158. A merchant of Wakefield: Constable in 1772.   Mr. Peregrine Wentworth was elected on Aug. 28, but declined to serve. 159 Vicar of Wakefield from 1764 to 1805.   161. Constable of Wakefield in 1750. Mr. John Rickaby was elected on Jan. 15, but declined to serve.   163. Lived in Northgate.   164. Of Sandal; Constable of Wakefield in 1760.   165. Father of the learned and eccentric Thomas Amory (Lupton's W.W., p. 165, &c): died on Feb. 14, 1805, age 74, having practised 27 years in Wakefield.   Mr. Charles Steer was elected on Jan. 22, but declined to serve.   166. Lived in Kirkgate, in the house which subsequently became the Bull and Mouth Inn.   167. A merchant; Constable in 1755.   168. Is called a Colonel in 1771, afterwards Lieutenant-Colonel: became disqualified by being sent with his regiment to America to take part in the wars: returned as General, and was re-elected in 1785 (No. 179): subsequently called Lieutenant-General.   169. Generally called Colonel Burton.

GRAMMAR SCHOOL.

170	Edward Ridsdale	Jan. 13, 1772	137	res.	June 14, 1792
171	Robert Cheetham	May 31, 1775	149	dec.	Apl. 1781
172	Samuel Armitage	May 5, 1777	163	dec.	b. Oct. 31, 1785
173	Chas.Spencer van Straubenzee	Mar. 20, 1780	154	res.	June 13, 1794
174	Thomas Hardy, sen.	Mar. 25, 1780	168	dec.	h. June 25, 1792
175	John Ellison, M D.	May 2, 1781	171	res.	Nov. 15, 1785
176	John Rickaby	Apl. 24, 1782	166	res.	May 8, 1795
177	John Smyth	Feb. 24, 1783	167	dec.	b. Feb. 23, 1811
178	Thomas Hardy, jun.	Dec. 31, 1782	162	dec.	June, 1812
179	Loftus Anthony Tottenham	Feb. 4, 1785	164	res.	Aug. 10, 1808
180	John Charnock	Apl. 29, 1785	161	res.	Apl. 27, 1807
181	Thomas Hewetson	Nov. 11, 1785	172	dec.	Nov. 16, 1794
182	John Henry Maw	Nov. 15, 1785	175	dis.	June 13, 1792
183	Matthew Robert Arnott	Oct. 15, 1787	158	dec.	May, 1800
184	William Steer	June 13, 1792	182	res.	Mar. 3, 1819
185	George Oxley	July 1, 1792	174	dec.	Jan. 1824
186	Henry Peterson	Jan. 9, 1793	169	res.	Aug. 10, 1808
187	Henry Andrews	Feb. 4, 1793	165	dec.	b. Apl. 23, 1811
188	Benjamin Kennett	June 13, 1794	173	dec.	July, 1815
189	Rev. William Wood	Nov. 28, 1794	181	dec.	June, 1825
190	Jeremiah Glover	May 8, 1795	176	dec.	Oct. 1809
191	Rev. Thomas Zouch, D.D.	June 14, 1799	170	res.	May 13, 1805
192	Rev.John Mackereth Freeman	May 16, 1800	183	dec.	Sep. 1805
193	Daniel Mawde	May 13, 1805	191	res.	Aug. 10, 1812
194	Rev.Richard Munkhouse, D.D.	Sep. 13, 1805	159	dec.	Jan. 19, 1810
195	Daniel Smallpage	Sep. 13, 1805	192	dec.	Jan. 13, 1808
196	William Charnock	Apl. 27, 1807	180	res.	Dec. 27, 1811
197	George Ridsdale	Jan. 29, 1808	195	res.	July 27, 1812
198	John Tottenham	Aug. 10, 1808	179	dec.	May, 1813
199	Andrew Peterson	Aug. 10, 1808	186	res.	Sep. 16, 1822
200	Rev. William Brown	Oct. 12, 1809	190	res.	May 14, 1818

170. Son of John Ridsdale (No. 148); Constable in 1771, died April 14, 1815. 172. Son of Joseph Armitage (No. 135). 173. Keeper of the Wakefield Prison from 1802 to 1816 (see Lupton's W. W., p. 214). 177. Of Heath; born Feb. 12, 1747-8; afterwards Lord of the Admiralty and Treasury, Master of the Mint, Member of the Privy Council, and for 25 years Member of Parliament for Pontefract; built Heath New Hall. 179. See under No. 168. 181. Major in His Majesty's Regiment of Foot. 182. Mr. Maw became disqualified by having "gone to reside in Lincolnshire." 184. Constable of Wakefield in 1792. 186. Son of Andrew Peterson, and owner of the "Six Chimneys," Kirkgate. 188. Afterwards Kennett-Dawson, Constable in 1794; Captain of Royal Wakefield Volunteers, 1798. 189. Curate of Wakefield 1791-2: lived at Woodthorpe, Sandal, in 1794. 190. Of Field Head, Stanley. 191. See Chap. IX.: son of Rev. Charles Zouch, Vicar of Sandal; educated at the School, and a most distinguished scholar and writer. 192. Curate of Warmfield in 1776, Curate of Wakefield from 1787 to 1789. 194. Vicar of Wakefield from 1805 to 1810, previously Incumbent of St. John's, Wakefield. 195. A chandler and soap-boiler, residing at Heath. 197. Of Old Hall, near Wakefield. 198. Son of General Loftus Anthony Tottenham (No. 168 and 179), and himself a Colonel. 199. Owner of the "Six Chimneys," Kirkgate. 200. Vicar of Sandal.

HISTORY OF WAKEFIELD

201	Rev. Samuel Sharp, M.A.	Feb. 16, 1810	194	dec.	Mar. 9, 1855
202	John Henry Smyth	Mar. 8, 1811	177	dec.	Oct. 20, 1822
203	William Naylor	Apl. 19, 1811	187	res.	Mar. 26, 1834
204	William Brooke	Dec. 27, 1811	196	res.	Dec. 27, 1820
205	Rev. James Drake	June 29, 1812	178	—	Jan. 1817
206	Thomas Rishworth	July 27, 1812	197	res.	Oct. 15, 1817
207	William Dawson	Aug. 10, 1812	193	res.	May 16, 1816
208	Jeremiah Todd Naylor	July 2, 1813	198	dis.	Oct. 29, 1828
209	James Teale	July 24, 1815	188	dec.	Apl. 1831
210	Joseph Hargrave	May 20, 1816	207	dec.	Jan. 1824
211	Robert Smithson	Feb. 6, 1817	205	dec.	May, 1819
212	Rev. Henry Gylby Lonsdale	Oct. 20, 1817	206	dis.	Oct. 5, 1825
213	Rev. William Snowden, M.A.	May 18, 1818	200	dis.	July 24, 1830
214	Buller Rolle Langford	Mar. 8, 1819	184	res.	Mar. 6, 1820
215	Robert Rayner	May 17, 1819	211	res.	Dec. 22, 1828
216	Thomas Barff	Mar. 13, 1820	214	dec.	Mar. 1847
217	Rev. George Beckett	Jan. 8, 1821	204	dis.	May 11, 1823
218	Rev. William Robinson Gilby	Sep. 20, 1822	199	dis.	June 23, 1824
219	Arthur Heywood	Nov. 11, 1822	202	dis.	Apl. 26, 1827
220	Jeremiah Glover	May 14, 1823	217	dec.	Mar. 1, 1869.
221	Rev. William Fox	Jan. 23, 1824	185	dis.	Sep. 11, 1826
222	John Hardy	Jan. 23, 1824	210	res.	Mar. 26, 1834
223	William Thomas, M.D.	Oct. 25, 1824	218	res.	Oct. 25, 1856
224	Rev. Thomas Kilby	July 4, 1825	189	dis.	Sep. 26, 1837
225	William Thompson Lee	Oct. 24, 1825	212	dis.	Dec. 26, 1829
226	Giles Diston Barker	Sep. 30. 1826	221	res.	Oct. 30, 1830
227	John Maude	May 12, 1828	219	dec.	Mar. 19, 1852
228	Henry Walker	Nov. 3, 1828	208	res.	Oct. 31, 1844
229	John Naylor	Dec 26, 1828	215	res.	Feb. 4, 1841
230	Joshua Smithson	Jan. 1, 1829	225	res.	Dec. 19, 1850

201. Curate of Wakefield from 1804 to 1810: Vicar of Wakefield from 1810 to 1855. 202. Son of the Rt. Hon. John Smyth, of Heath (No. 177): M.P. for Cambridge University, buried at Kirkthorpe. 203. Cloth Merchant. 205. Afterwards Vicar of Warmfield. 206. Banker, of Wakefield, of the firm Townend & Rishworth, built the old Corn Exchange; Constable in 1805. 208. A cloth merchant, of Wakefield. Constable in 1818; Captain of Royal Wakefield Volunteers, 1798. Mr. Robert Allott was elected on May 24, but declined to serve. 209. Of S. John's, Wakefield. 210. Of Sandal Hall. 212. Rector of Bolton Bolland in Craven 1826—1830: Vicar of St. Mary's, Lichfield: brother of Dr. John Lonsdale, Bishop of Lichfield. 213. Curate of Wakefield, July 1817 to Jan. 1818: Incumbent of Horbury 1817—1834: B.D. and Rector of Swillington 1834—1847. 214. Always called "Captain." 216. Woolstapler, of Wakefield; built and resided at Cliff-Field House. 217. Incumbent of Chapelthorpe in 1818: afterwards Rector of Epworth, Lincolnshire. 218. Vicar of S. Mary's, Beverley, from 1823. 219. Banker, originally from Liverpool, lived at Stanley Hall. 220. Of Field Head, Stanley. 222. Of Heath: Father of the present Viscount Cranbrook. 223. Surgeon in the 67th and 37th Regiments, 1806-1821: practised 37 years in Wakefield. 224. Curate of Wakefield, Sep. 1824 to July 1825: afterwards Vicar of St. John's, Wakefield. 225. Of Heath. 226. Generally called Captain Barker: deputy Coroner. 227. Of Moor House, Stanley: Justice of the Peace, and an enthusiastic traveller. 228. Of South Parade: afterwards Clerk to the Governors. 229. Cloth Merchant, died Feb. 4, 1856, buried in Wakefield Cathedral. 230. Colliery Proprietor, lived in Northgate, Wakefield.

GRAMMAR SCHOOL.

231	John Francis Carr	July 28, 1830	213	dec. Jan. 1863.
232	Edward Tew	Nov. 3, 1830	226	res. June 22, 1870
233	John Hardcastle	Apl. 30, 1831	209	dec. July 14, 1852
234	Thomas Tootal	Mar. 31, 1834	222	res. Oct. 15, 1840
235	Thomas Hague	Mar. 31, 1834	203	res. Mar. 24, 1851
236	Joze Luis Fernandes	Sep. 30, 1837	224	dis. Feb. 16, 1843
237	John George Smyth	Oct. 19, 1840	234	res. May 13, 1850
238	Richard Dunn	Feb. 8, 1841	229	res. Jan. 16, 1843
239	Rev. John Pullein, M.A.	Feb. 6, 1843	238	res. July 29, 1874
240	Rev. John Pemberton Simpson	Feb. 20, 1843	236	dec. Aug. 1858
241	Edward Tomlinson	Nov. 5, 1844	228	dec. May, 1870
242	John Barff	Apl. 3, 1847	216	dec. July 14, 1864
243	George Sandars, M.P.	May 17, 1850	227	res. Aug. 30, 1850
244	Thos. Giordani Wright, M.D.	Sep. 3, 1850	243	
245	Wm. Henry Leatham, M.P.	Dec. 23, 1850	230	res. Mar. 5, 1852
246	Henry Wormald	Mar. 28, 1851	235	dec. Aug. 19, 1887
247	Thomas Holy Holdsworth	Apl. 6, 1852	245	
248	Hon. and Rev. Philip Yorke Savile, M.A.	Apl. 6, 1852	227	
249	John Charlesworth Dodgson Charlesworth	Aug. 3, 1852	233	dec. Mar. 21, 1880.
250	George Hudswell Westerman	Apl. 19, 1855	201	dec. Mar. 23, 1880
251	Rev. Charles Joseph Camidge M.A.	Oct. 29, 1856	223	res. June 7, 1876
252	Daniel Burton Kendell, M.B.	Sep. 2, 1858	240	res. Mar. 16, 1868
253	Robert Bownas Mackie	Jan. 10, 1863	231	dec. June 18, 1885
254	Joze Luis Fernandes, jun.	July 27, 1864	242	res. June 3, 1891
255	Joseph Barker	Mar. 20, 1868	252	
256	John Barff Charlesworth	Mar. 15, 1869	220	

231. Of Carr Lodge, Horbury, Justice of the Peace. 232. Of Crofton Hall, Banker. 233. Lived at Westfield House, Wakefield. 234. Corn Merchant. 235. Of Sandal and Stanley Hall. 236. Born in Oporto, July 12, 1790, Grandson of the last Marquez de Tavora, died Dec. 16, 1868. 237. Son of John Henry Smyth, Esq., of Heath (No. 202): born Feb. 5, 1815, died June 10, 1869: M.P. for the city of York from 1847 to 1865: D.L. and J.P.: buried at Kirkthorpe. 238. Corn Merchant, of Wakefield, Constable in 1834. 239. Vicar of Warmfield, 1837-1871: afterwards Vicar of Weeton, Leeds. 240. Curate of Wakefield, Jan. 1826 to Dec. 1843: afterwards Rector of Crofton, 1843—1858. 241. Of St. John's, Wakefield. 242. Woolstapler, of Wakefield: Justice of the Peace: lived in St. John's: Constable in 1835. 243. Corn merchant, of Alverthorpe Hall, Wakefield: M.P. for Wakefield, 1847 to 1857: died May 14, 1879. 244. Of South Parade, Wakefield, afterwards of Milnes House; has now practised 58 years in Wakefield. 245. Of Hemsworth Hall, Pontefract: M.P. for Wakefield, 1865 to 1868. 246. Of South Parade, Wakefield. 247. Of Belle Vue and Sandal Hall: Justice of the Peace. 248 Second son of the Earl of Mexborough: now Rector of Methley. 249. Of Stanley Hall; afterwards of Chapelthorpe Hall; M.P. for Wakefield, 1857 to 1859: gave the chimes of Wakefield Cathedral: Colonel. 250. Of Sandal. 251. Vicar of Wakefield from 1855 to 1875: previously Vicar of Nether Poppleton, near York: Hon. Canon of Ripon: died Feb. 10, 1878; buried in Wakefield Cemetery. 252. Of Heath House, Wakefield: now of Walton. 253. Corn-factor, of St. John's, Wakefield: M.P. for Wakefield, 1880 to 1885: buried in Wakefield Cemetery. 254. Of Market Street, Wakefield; subsequently of Lupset and Calder Grove, Wakefield: now of Tavora House, Grange-over-Sands. 255. Of Holme Field, Thornes: Justice of the Peace: Major. 256. Of Hatfeild Hall, Stanley: Justice of the Peace.

HISTORY OF WAKEFIELD

257	Percy Tew, M.A.	May 13, 1870	241	
258	William Henry Bedford Tomlinson	June 29, 1870	232	
259	Edward Green	Aug. 5, 1874	239	res. June, 1878
260	Ven. Norman Dumenil John Straton, M.A.	Aug. 5, 1891	254	

257. Of Heath Hall, Wakefield: Justice of the Peace. 258. Of Cliff Field House, Wakefield: Justice of the Peace. 259. Lately of Heath Old Hall, Wakefield; now of Ken Hill, Norfolk and Nunthorpe, York: M.P. for Wakefield from 1885 to the present time: now Sir Edward Green, Bt. 260. Now Vicar of Wakefield, appointed in 1875; Rural Dean and late Hon. Canon of Ripon: Hon. Canon of Wakefield and Archdeacon of Huddersfield.

EX-OFFICIO GOVERNORS.

I.—As MAYOR of Wakefield.

From June, 1875. William Henry Stewart, J.P., Solicitor, Milnthorpe, Sandal.
Nov. 9, 1875. William Henry Gill, J.P., Solicitor, St. John's, Wakefield.
Nov. 9, 1876. William Henry Gill, J.P.
Nov. 9, 1877. William Henry Stewart, J.P.
Nov. 9, 1878. Thomas Taylor, J.P., Coroner for the County and Honor of Pontefract.
Nov. 10, 1879. William Hartley Lee, J.P., Worsted Manufacturer, Wakefield.
Nov. 9, 1880. William Hartley Lee, J.P.
Nov. 9, 1881. Francis Milthorp, J.P., Ink Manufacturer, Wakefield.
Nov. 9, 1882. George Mander, J.P., Solicitor, Wakefield.
Nov. 9, 1883. William Hartley Lee, J.P.
Nov. 9, 1884. George Moorhouse, Grocer, Wakefield.
Nov. 10. 1885. Reuben Reynolds, J.P., Corn Miller, Wakefield.
Nov. 9. 1886. Henry Lee, J.P., Worsted Manufacturer, Wakefield.
Nov. 9. 1887. Henry Lee, J.P.
Nov. 9, 1888. William Hartley Lee, J.P.
Nov. 9. 1889. Benjamin Watson, J.P., Grocer, Wakefield.
Nov. 10. 1890. Joseph Haslegrave, J.P., Corn Miller, Wakefield.

II.—As CHAIRMAN OF THE SCHOOL BOARD for Wakefield.

From June, 1875. Edward Green, Ironfounder, Heath Old Hall; see No. 259 above.
June, 1878. Rev. John Sheppard Eastmead, Congregational Minister, Wakefield.
June, 1881. Rev. John Sheppard Eastmead.
June, 1884. Rev. Wyndham Monson Madden, B.A., Vicar of Holy Trinity, Wakefield.
June, 1887. Jonathan Haigh Wice, Chemist, St. John's, Wakefield.
June, 1890. Jonathan Haigh Wice.

GRAMMAR SCHOOL.

Representative Governors.

I.—Representing the Town Council of Wakefield.

From June, 1875. William Stewart, Solicitor, Wakefield.
Enoch Harrison, Schoolmaster, Wakefield; died in June, 1877, and was succeeded by
William Hartley Lee, J.P.
Richard Holdsworth, J.P., House Furnisher, Castle Lodge, Sandal.
William Craven, Engineer, Wakefield.
Thomas Wilton Haigh, J.P., Maltster, Sandal.

From June, 1880. Samuel Bruce, LL.B., Solicitor, St. John's, Wakefield.
Henry Lee, J.P., resigned Sep. 6, 1882, and was succeeded by
William Hartley Lee, J.P.
Jonathan Haigh Wice.
William Stewart.
Thomas Kemp Sanderson, Maltster and Corn Merchant, Wakefield; M.P. for Wakefield, 1874 to 1880.

From June, 1885. William Henry Stewart, J.P.
William Hartley Lee, J.P.
Thomas Kemp Sanderson.
John Samuel Booth, Manufacturer, Wakefield.
Jonathan Haigh Wice.

From June, 1890. William Henry Stewart, J.P.
William Hartley Lee, J.P.
Thomas Kemp Sanderson.
John Samuel Booth.
Benjamin Watson, J.P.

II.—Representing the School Board for Wakefield.

From June, 1875. Rev. Wyndham Monson Madden, B.A.
Samuel Whitham, Ironfounder, Wakefield; resigned in August, 1887, and succeeded by
Rev. John Sheppard Eastmead.
John Connor, Estate Agent, St. John's, Wakefield.

From June, 1880. Rev. Wyndham Monson Madden, B.A.
John Connor; died in July, 1884, and succeeded by
John Capner Marks, High Bailiff of County Court, St. John's, Wakefield.
Richard Holdsworth, J.P.

From June, 1885. Rev. Wyndham Monson Madden, B.A. ; resigned in
November, 1888, and succeeded by
Herbert Beaumont, Solicitor, Wakefield.
Richard Holdsworth, J.P.
John Capner Marks.

From June, 1890. Jonathan Haigh Wice.
John Capner Marks.
Herbert Beaumont.

III.—Representing the YORKSHIRE COLLEGE.

From July, 1891. Louis Compton Miall, F.L.S., F.G.S., Professor of Biology, Hyde Park, Leeds.

THE SPOKESMEN OR PRESIDENT GOVERNORS.

The duties and privileges of the Spokesman, or Prolocutor, will be found fully described in the first section of the Statutes (printed on pp. 55-58); it has also been stated already (p. 53) that the first Spokesman was elected on Nov. 25, 1606. Since that time the elections have been regularly held on Sep. 30 or Oct. 1 in each year, according to the directions given in the Statutes, unless extraordinary circumstances have arisen and caused the election to be postponed. During the Civil War, however, there were no Spokesmen chosen for the years Oct. 1, 1642 to Sep. 30, 1649 : and the loss of minutes for the years 1677 to 1723 has made it impossible to give the names of Spokesmen for all of this period, though many have been discovered from various other sources.

No standard of eligibility for the office of Spokesman was laid down by the Statutes, but a definite principle seems to have been observed in making the choice, whereby no Governor was to be elected twice, until all the others had served in the office once, in the order of seniority : thus it came about that a Governor very frequently became Spokesman very soon after he was elected on the Governing Body. The inconvenience of this fact became so marked some 30 or 40 years ago, that a rule was adopted that no one was to be elected Spokesman until he had been a Governor at least twelve months.

During the present century the Deputy Spokesman has generally been the Governor who was Spokesman in the preceding year.

GRAMMAR SCHOOL.

LIST OF SPOKESMEN AND DEPUTY SPOKESMEN.

Spokesmen.		Deputy Spokesmen.	Spokesmen.		Deputy Spokesmen.
1606-7.	W. Savile	—	1660-1.	J. Robinson	J. Mawde
1607-8.	Rev. W. Lister	—	1661-2.	J. Mawde	C. Wilson
1608-9.	J. Mawde	—	1662-3.	C. Wilson	D. Oley
1609-10.	J. Battie	—	1663-4.	D. Oley	T. Pease
1610-1.	T. Robinson	—	1664-5.	R. Birkhead	C. Naylor
1611-2.	A. Scatcherd	—	1665-6.	C. Naylor	W. Briggs
1612-3.	J. Fleming	—	1666-7.	W. Briggs	T. Binns
1613-4.	G. Spivie	—	1667-8.	T. Binns	M. Meager
1614-5.	H. Cressy	R. Waterhouse	1668-9.	M. Meager	J. Wilson
1615-6.	W. Pollard	—	1669-70.	J. Wilson	J. Clough
1616-7.	C. Naylor	—	1670-1.	J. Clough	C. Wilson
1617-8.	R. Waterhouse	—	1671-2.	W. Denison	J. Waterhouse
1618-9.	J. Mawde	—	1672-3.	R. Benson	W. Briggs
1619-20.	J. Battie	—	1673-4.	D. Mawde	T. Pease
1620-1.	T. Robinson	—	1674-5.	T. Cheriholme	J. Robinson
1621-2.	J. Greenwood	W. Pollard	1675-6.	T. Sill	T. Pease
1622-3.	T. Somaster	J. Mawde	1676-7.	T. Bargh	T. Cheriholme
1623-4.	H. Grice	J. Battie	1677-8.	Rev. O. Lee	T. Sill
1624-5.	J. Battie	J. Storie	1678-9.	—	—
1625-6.	R. Tayler	W. Paulden	1679-80.	—	—
1626-7.	W. Paulden	W. Pollard	1680-1.	—	—
1627-8.	J. Storie	J. Greenwood	1681-2.	—	—
1628-9.	Sir J. Savile	R. Tayler	1682-3.	—	—
1629-30.	A. Scatcherd	Sir J. Savile	1683-4.	—	—
1630-1.	H. Savile	J. Storie	1684-5.	—	—
1631-2.	J. Stansfield	T. Somaster	1685-6.	—	—
1632-3.	Francis Hey	—	1686-7.	—	—
1633-4.	T. Cooke	W. Paulden	1687-8.	—	—
1634-5.	J. Lyon	J. Storie	1688-9.	—	—
1635-6.	L. Wilson	T. Cooke	1689-90.	—	—
1636-7.	W. Waller	J. Storie	1690-1.	—	—
1637-8.	C. Naylor	J. Storie	1691-2.	—	—
1638-9.	J. Keyser	T. Cooke	1692-3.	—	—
1639-40.	T. Burrow	W. Waller	1693-4.	—	—
1640-1.	G. Nevile	J. Storie	1694-5.	—	—
1641-2.	C. Horne	T. Cooke	1695-6.	T. Wilson	—
1642-3.	—	—	1696-7.	—	—
1643-4.	—	—	1697-8.	—	—
1644-5.	—	—	1698-9.	J. Sill	—
1645-6.	—	—	1699-1700.	T. Shelton	—
1646-7.	—	—	1700-1.	W. Coppendale	—
1647-8.	—	—	1701-2.	Rev. T. Scott	—
1648-9.	—	—	1702-3.	J. Watkinson	—
1649-50.	W. Waller	C. Wilson	1703-4.	W. Haward	—
1650-1.	C. Wilson	E. Watkinson	1704-5.	F. Wheatley	—
1651-2.	E. Watkinson	D. Oley	1705-6.	F. Nevile	—
1652-3.	D. Oley	R. Wilson	1706-7.	R. Witton	—
1653-4.	J. Wilson	J. Waterhouse	1707-8.	A. Bever	—
1654-5.	N. Dodgson	G. Radcliffe	1708-9.	J. Bromley	—
1655-6.	G. Radcliffe	T. Pease	1709-10.	N. Fenay	—
1656-7.	J. Waterhouse	W. Mason	1710-1.	J. Smyth	—
1657-8.	W. Mason	J. Robinson	1711-2.	R. Witton, jun.	—
1658-9.	T. Pease	J. Clayton	1712-3.	J. Spink	—
1659-60.	C. Holdsworth	J. Wilson	1713-4.	Rev. D. Sill	—

HISTORY OF WAKEFIELD

Years	Name 1	Name 2	Years	Name 1	Name 2
1714-5.	W. Spink	—	1772-3.	Lt. Col. L. A. Tottenham	Col. R. Burton
1715-6.	F. Pitt	—	1773-4.	Col. R. Burton	E. Ridsdale
1716-7.	T. Wilson	—	1774-5.	E. Ridsdale	W. Serjeantson
1717-8.	B. Watkinson	—	1775-6.	R. Cheetham	—
1718-9.	T. Birkhead	—	1776-7.	W. Serjeantson	W. Nevinson
1719-20	W. Oates	—	1777-8.	S. Armitage	Rev. Dr. Bacon
1720-1.	Rev. T. Scott	—	1778-9.	D. Mawde	Rev. Dr. Bacon
1721-2.	Dr. T. Moore	—	1779-80.	Rev. Dr. Bacon	W. Nevinson
1722-3.	S. Richardson	—	1780-1.	C. S. van Straubenzee	T. Hardy, sen.
1723-4.	R. Watson	—	1781-2.	T. Hardy, sen.	Dr. J. Ellison
1724-5.	J. Tilson	T. Sill	1782-3.	J. Rickaby	Dr. J. Ellison
1725-6.	E. Buxton	R. Smyth	1783-4.	J. Smyth	D. Mawde
1726-7.	R. Smyth	J. Mawde	1784-5.	T. Hardy, jun.	Dr. J. Ellison
1727-8.	J. Mawde	T. Thornton	1785-6.	Gen. Loftus A. Tottenham	G. Charnock
1728-9.	F. Mawde	—	1786-7.	J. H. Maw	—
1729-30.	T. Thornton	S. Holmes	1787-8.	Maj. T. Hewetson	G. Charnock
1730-1.	S. Holmes	Rev. G. Arnet	1788-9.	M. R. Arnott	Rev. Dr. Bacon
1731-2.	Rev. G. Arnet	W. Walker	1789 90.	G. Charnock	Rev. Dr. Bacon
1732-3.	T. Horne	—	1790-91.	Rev. Dr. Bacon	T. Hardy, junr.
1733-4.	J. Armitage	J. Sill	1791-2	R. Burton	E. Ridsdale
1734-5.	T. Sill	M. Wentworth	1792-3	G. Oxley	T. Hardy
1735-6.	Sir L. Pilkington	T. Sill	1793-4	H. Andrews	G. Oxley
1736-7.	M. Wentworth	Rev. C. Nevile	1794-5	B. Kennett	H. Andrews
1737-8.	Rev. C. Nevile	J. Sill	1795-6.	H. Peterson	J. Glover
1738-9.	J. Sill	W. Charnock	1796-7.	J. Glover	H. Peterson
1739-40.	W. Charnock	H. Green	1797-8.	Rev. Dr. Bacon	J. Glover
1740-1.	H. Green	Dr. J. Cookson.	1798-9.	Rev. W. Wood	Rev. Dr Bacon
1741-2.	Dr. J. Cookson	J. Smyth	1799-1800	W. Steer	B. Kennett
1742-3.	J. Smyth	S. Richardson	1800-1.	Rev. T. Zouch	Rev. Dr. Bacon
1743-4.	Dr. C. Hodgson	S. Richardson	1801-2.	Rev. J. M. Freeman	Rev. Dr. Bacon
1744-5.	J. Smith (Newland)	—	1802-3.	W. Steer	—
1745-6.	T. Holmes	—	1803-4.	T. Hardy	H. Andrews
1746-7.	J. Ridsdale	—	1804-5.	H. Andrews	T. Hardy
1747-8.	R. Buxton	J. Ridsdale	1805-6.	D. Mawde	H. Andrews
1748-9.	S. Richardson	R. Buxton	1806-7.	Rev. Dr. Munkhouse	D. Mawde
1749-50.	J. Mawde	S. Armitage	1807-8.	W. Charnock	D. Mawde
1750-1.	W. Serjeantson	T. Norton	1808-9.	G. Ridsdale	D. Mawde
1751-2.	T. Norton	R. Buxton	1809-10.	A. Peterson	▪ —
1752-3.	H. Thorpe	A. Johnson	1810-1.	Col. J. Tottenham	A. Peterson
1753-4.	A. Johnson	—	1811-2.	Rev. W. Brown	Col. J. Tottenham
1754-5.	S. Richardson	Sir L. Pilkington	1812-3.	Rev. S. Sharp	Rev. W. Brown
1755-6.	Sir L. Pilkington	H. Green	1813-4.	Rev. S. Sharp	Rev. W. Brown
1756-7.	H. Green	Dr. J. Cookson	1814-5.	W. Brooke	Rev. S. Sharp
1757-8.	F. Mawde	Dr. J. Cookson	1815-6.	W. Dawson	W. Brooke
1758-9.	Rev. H. Zouch	S. Richardson	1816-7.	W. Brooke	A. Peterson
1759-60.	Dr. J. Cookson	J. Smyth	1817-8.	J. T. Naylor	W. Brooke
1760-1.	R. Green	—	1818-9.	W. Naylor	W. Brooke
1761-2.	J. Smyth	Dr. C. Hodgson	1819-20.	A. Peterson	W. Naylor
1762-3.	D. Maude	—	1820-1.	A. Peterson	W. Naylor
1763-4.	Dr. C. Hodgson	J. Ridsdale	1821-2.	A. Peterson	Rev. S. Sharp
1764-5.	J. Ridsdale	R. Buxton	1822-3.	Rev. S. Sharp	J. Teale
1765-6.	Rev. Dr. Bacon	W. Nevinson	1823-4.	Rev. S. Sharp	J. Teale
1766-7.	W. Nevinson	T. Oates	1824-5.	Rev. S. Sharp	J. Teale
1767-8.	A. Hatfield	T. Oates			
1768-9.	T. Oates	S. Zouch			
1769-70.	Dr. R Amory	S. Zouch			
1770-1.	S. Zouch	R. Green			
1771-2.	G. Charnock	W. Serjeantson			

GRAMMAR SCHOOL.

1825-6.	Rev. S. Sharp	J. Teale	1864-5.	J.L.Fernandes,jr.R. B. Mackie
1826-7.	J. Teale	Rev. S. Sharp	1865-6.	Dr. T. G.WrightJ.L.Fernandes,jr.
1827-8.	J. Teale	Dr. W. Thomas	1866-7.	H. Wormald Dr. T. G. Wright
1828-9.	T. Barff	J. Glover	1867-8.	T. H. Holds- H. Wormald
1829-30.	J. Glover	T. Barff		worth
1830-1.	J. Hardy	J. Glover	1868-9.	Hon. & Rev. P. T.H.Holdsworth
1831-2.	Dr. W. Thomas	Rev. S. Sharp		Y. Savile
1832-3.	Rev. T. Kilby	Dr. W. Thomas	1869-70.	Major Barker Hon. & Rev. P.
1833-4.	J. Maude	Rev. T. Kilby		Y. Savile
1834-5.	H. Walker	J. Maude	1870-1.	J. B. Charles- Major Barker
1835-6.	J. Naylor	H. Walker		worth
1836-7.	J. Smithson	J. Naylor	1871-2.	P. Tew J.B.Charlesworth
1837-8.	J. F. Carr	J. Smithson	1872-3.	W. H. B. Tom- P. Tew
1838-9.	Edward Tew	J. F. Carr		linson
1839-40.	J. Hardcastle	E. Tew	1873-4.	Col. J. C. D. W. H. B. Tomlin-
1840-1.	T. Hague	J. Hardcastle		Charlesworth son
1841-2.	J. L. Fernandes	Thomas Hague	1874-5.	G. H. Wester- Col. J. C. D.
1842-3.	J. G. Smyth	J. L. Fernandes		man* Charlesworth
1843-4.	Rev. J. Pulleine	J. G. Smyth	1875-6.	Dr.T.G.Wright T.H.Holdsworth
1844-5.	Rev.J.P.Simpson	Rev. J. Pulleine	1876-7.	T. H. Holds- Dr. T. G. Wright
1845-6.	E. Tomlinson	Rev.J.P.Simpson		worth
1846-7.	Rev. S. Sharp	E. Tomlinson	1877-8.	Rev. W. M. T.H.Holdsworth
1847-8.	J. Glover	Rev. S. Sharp		Madden
1848-9.	J. Barff	J. Glover	1878-9.	P. Tew Rev. W. M.
1849-50.	Dr. W. Thomas	J. Barff		Madden
1850-1.	J. F. Carr	Dr. W. Thomas	1879-80.	P. Tew Rev. W. M.
1851-2.	Dr.T.G.Wright	J. F. Carr		Madden
1852-3.	H. Wormald	Dr. T. G. Wright	1880-1.	W.H.B.Tomlin- P. Tew
1853-4.	T.H.Holdsworth	H. Wormald		son
1854-5.	Hon. & Rev. P.	T.H.Holdsworth	1881-2.	Rev.J. S. East- W. H. B.Tomlin-
	Y. Savile			mead son
1855-6.	J.C. D.Charles-	Hon. & Rev. P.	1882-3.	J. B. Charles- Rev. J. S. East-
	worth	Y. Savile		worth mead
1856-7.	G.H.Westerman	J. C. D. Charles-	1883-4.	Rev. W. M. J. B. Charles-
		worth		Madden worth
1857-8.	Rev. C.J. Cam-	G. H. Westerman	1884-5.	Dr. T. G. Rev. W. M.
	idge			Wright Madden
1858-9.	J. Glover	Rev.C.J.Camidge	1885-6.	W. H. Lee Dr. T. G. Wright
1859-60.	D. B. Kendell	J. Glover	1886-7.	W. H. Lee Dr. T. G. Wright
1860-1.	Rev. J. Pulleine	D. B. Kendell	1887-8.	P. Tew W. H. Lee
1861-2.	E. Tomlinson	Rev.J. Pulleine	1888-9.	J. H. Wice P. Tew
1862-3.	J. Barff	E. Tomlinson	1889-90.	J. H. Wice P. Tew
1863-4.	R. B. Mackie	J. Barff	1890-1.	J. H. Wice P. Tew

CLERKS TO THE GOVERNORS.

The Spokesman was expected, according to the Statutes, to manage all the collection of rents and payments of salaries, and present his accounts on going out of office. But in 1745 the increased duties, consequent upon new Charities coming under the management

---

* Mr. Westerman resigned when the 1875 Scheme came into operation, and Dr. Wright held the office of Spokesman for the remainder of the year, June to Sept. 1875.

HISTORY OF WAKEFIELD

of the Governors, made it necessary to employ an Agent or Clerk, and since that time the office has always been continued. The names of the Clerks to the Governors are appended, with the dates of their appointment :—

Mar. 6, 1744-5	William Brown
Nov. 10, 1790	John Smallpage, Attorney-at-Law
Dec. 19, 1800	Joseph Armitage
Nov. 4, 1803	William Dawson, Attorney-at-Law
Jan. 16, 1811	John Shaw, late Master of the Charity School.
Sep. 30, 1822	Joseph Hemingway
May 14, 1823	Michael Proud
June 3, 1833	John Henry Charnock, Estate Agent.
July 28, 1846	Henry Walker
Oct. 28, 1854	William Walker, Barrister-at-Law.

Chapter 6.

THE HEAD MASTERS, USHERS AND ASSISTANTS.

THE appointment of a Head Master has always rested with the Governors of the School, with only two limitations, both of which were removed by the Scheme of the Charity Commissioners which came into force in 1875. The first limitation was that if the Governors did not elect a Master within sixty days after the office had become vacant, then the right of nomination should lapse to the Master and Fellows of Emmanuel College, Cambridge. The second limitation was that no Master appointed by the Governors of the School should commence the duties of his office until his election had been approved by the Archbishop of York, and a licence to teach obtained from him.

The qualifications required in the Head Master were thus given by the Charter—"a meete man for knowledge religion and liffe," "well reported of," and having "taken the degree of a Master of the Artes." The Statutes state the same qualifications more fully— "such a one as havinge taken the degree of a Maistre of Arts in the Universitie of Cambridge or Oxford is withall well reported of for his knowledge, religion and life, and knowne to be an enemie to popish superstition, a lover and forward imbracer of Gods truth, a man formarlie diligent and painefull in his owne studies, of a sober and amiable cariadge towardes all men, able to maintaine the place of a Scholemaister with dignitie and gravitie, given to the diligent reading of God's worde, but not called either to a pastorall charge, or hired to serve as a preacher minister or curate in the churche": but this last-mentioned condition has been sometimes modified by special resolution. The Schemes of the Charity Commissioners have required that the Head Master should have taken a degree at some University in the British Empire, and be a member of the Church of England, but not hold any benefice involving the cure of souls, or any other appointment which would interfere with the proper execution of his duties.

LIST OF HEAD MASTERS OF WAKEFIELD GRAMMAR SCHOOL.

No.	NAME.	College.	When appointed.	Why vacated.	When vacated.
1.	Rev. Edward Mawde, M.A.	S. John's, Cambridge	Nov. 19, 1591	died	in 1598
2.	Rev. John Beaumont, M.A.	Cambridge	Oct. 17, 1600	resigned	Apl. 19, 1607
3.	Rev. Jeremy Gibson, M.A.		June 4, 1607	resigned	July 20, 1607
4.	Rev. Robert Saunders, M.A.	King's, Cambridge	July 20, 1607	resigned	Oct. 30, 1607
5.	Rev. Philip Isack, M.A.	Emmanuel, Cambridge	Jan. 8, 1607-8	resigned	May 6, 1623
6.	Rev. Robert Doughty, M.A.		May 6, 1623	died	b. Feb.24,1662-3
7.	Rev. Samuel Garvey, M.A.	Emmanuel, Cambridge	July 21, 1663	resigned	Oct. 24, 1665
8.	Rev. Jeremiah Boulton, M.A.	Magdalen, Cambridge	Dec. 14, 1665	resigned	Apl. 2, 1672
9.	Rev. John Baskerville, B.D.	Emmanuel, Cambridge	May 1, 1672	died	May 15, 1681
10.	Rev. Edmund Clarke, M.A.	University, Oxford	Aug. 17, 1681	resigned	Sep. 1693
11.	Rev. Edmund Farrer, M.A.	S. John's, Cambridge	Oct. 1693	died	Apl. 7, 1703
12.	Rev. Thomas Clark, M.A.	Jesus, Cambridge	Apl. 16, 1703	resigned	Easter 1720
13.	Rev. Benjamin Wilson, M.A.	Trinity, Cambridge	Easter 1720	resigned	Mar. 29, 1751
14.	Rev. John Clarke, M.A.	Trinity, Cambridge	Apl. 8, 1751	resigned	Feb. 22, 1758
15.	Rev. Christopher Atkinson, M.A.	Queen's, Oxford	May 22, 1758	died	Jan. 1, 1795
16.	Rev. Thomas Rogers, M.A.	Magdalen, Cambridge	Feb. 6, 1795	resigned	Apl. 18, 1814
17.	Rev. Martin Joseph Naylor, D.D.	Queen's, Cambridge	May 19, 1814	resigned	Mar. 11, 1837
18.	Rev. John Carter, D.D.	S. John's, Cambridge	Apl. 8, 1837	resigned	July 2, 1847
19.	Rev. James Taylor, D.D.	Trinity, Cambridge	July 30, 1847	resigned	June 23, 1875
20.	Robert Leighton Leighton, M.A.	Balliol, Oxford	Sep. 11, 1875	resigned	Aug. 1, 1883
21.	Matthew Henry Peacock, M.A., B. Mus.	Exeter, Oxford	Sep. 10, 1883		

GRAMMAR SCHOOL.

1. REV. EDWARD MAWDE, M.A.

It has already been stated that there is ground for believing that the first Master of the School had previously been in charge of a Parish Church School at Wakefield as Curate : it is quite certain that he was engaged in teaching "poor children" at Wakefield before the foundation of the Grammar School (see pp. 5-7). It is, however, impossible to speak with certainty about his parentage, birthplace and earlier life. The name Mawde has been a common one in the district of Wakefield : a John Mawde, of Northgate, chapman, appears in the list of benefactors, and also in the list of Governors, from the year 1601 to the year 1635 : the Rev. Timothy Mawde, D.D., was Vicar of Wakefield from 1620 to 1625, and also a Governor of the School : and an Ambrose Mawde was sent as the first Cave Scholar from Wakefield Grammar School to Clare Hall, Cambridge, in the year 1603-4. Perhaps the first master was related to one or more of these; his name does not seem to appear in the published pedigrees of the Mawdes of Alverthorpe.

From Baker's "History of St. John's College, Cambridge," (p. 288), it appears that Edward Mawde, a native of Yorkshire, was admitted a Fellow of that College on March 16, 1569-70 : and I am indebted to the Rev. H. W. Reynolds, M.A., Vicar of Christ Church, Bolton, for the information that a Rev. Edward Mawde, M.A., was a schoolmaster at Halifax in the time of Elizabeth, having amongst his pupils one who afterwards became the well-known Bishop Morton (Bishop of Chester 1616, of Lichfield 1619, and of Durham 1632 to 1659), who was sent to St. John's College from Mr. Mawde's teaching at Halifax in the year 1582. The Rev. Edward Mawde was therefore probably Master of the School which in 1584 became Heath Grammar School, Halifax, and perhaps soon after that date migrated to Wakefield to assist in the foundation of another Grammar School there.

The Headmastership of the Rev. Edward Mawde must be regarded as commencing on Nov. 19, 1591, the day of the foundation of the School : but the duties of the office were probably executed in some building connected with the Church until the School Buildings were erected. Mr. Mawde was instituted Vicar of Wakefield on April 20, 1593, and held this office in conjunction with the Mastership of the Grammar School until his death, which happened about the middle of the year 1598. The lack of endowment during most of his tenure of office may be one reason why the duties of Schoolmaster were combined with those of Vicar, as they had been in earlier times with those of Chantry Priest, and probably also with those of Curate. Mr. Maude may, however, have entrusted most of his Church duties to his Curates, as did others of his successors who also held livings with their Headmasterships.

Mr. Mawde's claims to the gratitude of posterity may be based upon several grounds. There is no doubt that he took a most prominent part in procuring the Charter of Foundation by enlisting the sympathies of the Saviles and other influential Wakefield men : and when the Charter was obtained, he doubtless secured more promises of money, which came to the School, in many cases only after his death, and in various ways : besides which he himself ranks among the benefactors of the School by his gift of an annuity of ten shillings a year out of a messuage and a garden in Wrengate near Skitterick brook (see p. 37).

---

2. REV. JOHN BEAUMONT. M.A.

After the death of the Rev. Edward Mawde there was some little delay in appointing a successor. The Governors do not appear to have moved in the matter with any success, partly perhaps owing to the absence of a Spokesman and Statutes : accordingly the Master and Fellows of Emmanuel College, Cambridge, exercised their right by nominating the Rev. John Beaumond (or Beaumont), M.A., of their own University, in the following letter :—

"After our harty commendations remembred. Whereas by the letters Patents of her excellent Majestie for the foundation and erection of a free Schoole within the Towne of Wakefeild, amongst other clauses and provisoes for the better continuance therof from tyme to tyme, it hath pleased her Highnes to appoint that so oft as it shall happen the place of the School M^r to be voide, if the same shall not be presented unto according to the forme therein more at large specified within the space of 60 dayes next after the said vacancy, yt should be lawfull for the M^r and fellowes of our Colledge for the tyme being to nominate choose and elect a fitt man a M^r of Arts to be Schoole M^r of the sayd free grammer schoole at Wakefeild, as by the same letters of her Highnes graunt dated the 19th of November in the 34th yeare of her Majestie's reigne more at large may appeare. And for that as we are credibly informed after the tyme of the sayd graunt Mr Mawde enjoyed the place of the Schoole M^r there, since whose death yt hath not been assigned to any, notwithstanding the greate desyre of the inhabitants of the said Towne, that it was furnished with one able to discharge so necessarie a dutie as the trayning up of youth in good learning is knowne to be: whereby the Schoole is much decaied, and the good intention of the Petitioners to her Majestie for her royall graunt to that foundation much frustrated. Further for the good report that we heare of the sufficiency of Mr John Beaumond M^r of Arts in this University, and chiefly as we are enformed the generall desire of yow the said Governors and other the inhabitants of Wakefield to have him placed amongst yow, which especially leadeth us hereto, being otherwise willing to make choice of some of our owne Colledge. These are therefore to signifye to your wisdomes, that we the said M^r and fellowes of Emmanuell Colledge have accordingly nominated chosen and elected, and by these presents do nominate, choose and elect, so farre as lieth in us, the sayd Mr John Beaumond to the place of the Schoole M^r in the sayd Schoole of Wakefeild. Whome we do desire yow favourably to receive so nominated and elected by us and further to performe whatsoever act or acts shalbe needefull on this behaulf, for the confirming of the said place unto him with effect. And so we commend yow hartilye to God. From our Coll. this 17th of October, 1600,

To the right W^{or}, our very loving friends Sr George Savile and Sir Thomas Savile^1 Knights and to the rest of the Governours of her Maties free Schoole of Wakefield deliver these."

Your very loving friends,
WILL BRANTHWAYTE.
LAUR CHADDERTON.

From the language of this letter, it appears that the Governors had finally found a suitable Head Master, but were unable to appoint him, as considerably more than 60 days had elapsed since the office had become vacant. The local predisposition in Mr. Beaumont's favour, which induced the College authorities to pass over one of their own society, may perhaps indicate that he belonged to the neighbourhood of Wakefield, where the name is a very common one.

(1) This is evidently a mistake of the writer for 'Sir John Savile.'

During Mr. Beaumont's tenure of office—from Oct. 17, 1600 to Apl. 19, 1607—the School, which had fallen into an unsatisfactory state during the want of a Master, was thoroughly re-invigorated, and perhaps its earliest connexion with the Universities was formed through the Cave Scholarships at Clare Hall, Cambridge: for in less than three years after his appointment the first Cave Scholars were sent up, and the succession of scholars doubtless maintained. The number of benefactions given towards the endowment during these years was also very considerable; perhaps in no slight degree owing to the proviso of John Mowbray's grant (p. 38), within two years—a year less than he had stipulated—more than twenty-five pounds a year was added to the income of the School, and many unknown gifts were doubtless made during the same period. It is therefore highly probable that, by the time specified in Mr. Mowbray's gift, the School was "fully provided with a Schoolmaster and Usher for the teaching of children freely there, according to the true intent of the Letters Patent of Queen Elizabeth made for the same."

Mr. Beaumont's Headmastership terminated as follows :—

" Mr. Beaumont the Schoolmaster surrendered and resigned up his place as well in the Church in his sermon by open speache to the congregation on Sunday the 19th April, 1607, as by letter sent and delivered to the Spokesman on the 16th, 17th, or 18th day of April."

From this mention of a sermon, it may be that Mr. Beaumont held some official position in connexion with the Church, as so many of his successors have done: nothing has, however, been discovered by the writer either on this question, or on that of his subsequent history after resigning the Headmastership.

---

3. REV. JEREMY GIBSON, M.A.

The third Head Master was thus appointed :—

" Mr. Jeremy Gibson, Master of Arts, was elected Schoolmaster quarto die Junii 1607, and was presented to the Archbishop by our letters under our seale eodem die, and he was allowed by the Lord Archbishop quinto die Junii sequenti, as by the instrument of approbation under the seal of the Vicar General it appeareth."

There are still preserved in the British Museum copies of the letter sent by the Governors to the Archbishop of York on this and similar occasions, and of the Archbishop's licence to teach.

GRAMMAR SCHOOL.

"The Governours' Letter to the Lord Archbishop to allow Mr. Gibson to teach: 1607, 4 June.

Our duties to your Grace in humble manner remembred. Whereas our late Sovereign Lady Queen Elizabeth by her letters patents under her Great Seal of England bearing date the 19th day of November in the xxxiiiith year of her Majesty's reign hath given and graunted to us, being incorporated 14 in number, by the name of the Governours of the Free Grammar Schole of Queen Elizabeth at Wakefield, and to our successors for ever, that when the place of the scholemaster of the said schole should be void by what occasion soever, that then and so often we the said Governours for the time being, or the more part of us, have authority by warrant of the said graunt to choose and nominate, and under our common seal to present unto your Grace, a meet man for knowledge, religion, and life, and being a Master of Arts, for our Scholemaster, to be allowed of to that function by your Grace, or by your Vicar General in your absence, and that to be done within lx days of the vacancy thereof. And forasmuch as the said place is lately void by the resignation of our late Scholemaster Mr. Beamont, and the limited time of election and the presenting of the person now elected is not yet expired: Therefore now, according to the tenor of the said graunt, we have elected and nominated this bearer, Mr. Jeremy Gibson, Master of Arts, for our Scholemaster, whom we present to your Grace humbly beseeching you to give unto him your license and approbation to teach in our said schole. And so we humbly take our leaves. Given under our common seal this 4th of June 1607.

Licentia et Approbatio Domini Archiepiscopi.

1607. 5 June: Tobias providentia divina Eboracensis Archiepiscopus, Angliæ Primus et Metropolitanus, dilecto nobis in Christo Jeremiæ Gibson Artium Magistro Salutem. Cum major pars Gubernatorum Liberæ Scholæ Grammaticalis Dominæ nuper Reginæ Elizabethæ apud Wakefeild in Comitatu Eboracensi nostræ diœceseos modo per resignationem sive renuntiationem Magistri Johannis Beamonde nuper Ludimagistri ejusdem vacantis, et ad eorum presentationem legitime spectantis, te præfatum Jeremiam Gybson ad officium ludimagistri dictæ Scholæ juxta formam fundationis ejusdem elegerunt, et nobis hujusmodi tuam electionem debite presentarunt in scriptis sub sigillo eorum communi in Registro meo remanentibus; Te igitur memoratum Jeremiam Gybson Artium Magistrum ad exercendum munus seu officium Ludimagistri dictæ liberæ Scholæ Grammaticalis apud Wakefeild predictam, artemque Grammatices in eadem publice profitendam, bonosque auctores quoscumque de me et statutis hujus regni Angliæ approbatos ibidem publice profitendos, ceteraque omnia et singula quæ ad munus et officium Ludimagistri dictæ Scholæ spectare dinoscuntur, admittimus et Ludimagistrum ejusdem Scholæ præficimus, tibique, de cujus sana doctrina et morum probitate plenius in Domino confidimus, electionem predictam de persona tua factam acceptantes et approbantes, Licentiam et facultatem concedimus per præsentes Sigillo officii vicariatus nostri in Spiritualibus generali sigillatas. Datum Eboraci, sub sigillo predicto quo in hac parte utimur, quinto die Junii, Anno Domini millesimo sexcentesimo septimo, et nostræ translationis ad Archiepiscopatum Eboracensem anno primo."

Mr. Gibson only held office for the short period of seven weeks, some of which fell in the usual Midsummer holiday. But it has been pointed out in a previous Chapter (p. 53) that the appointment was probably made almost for the sole purpose of obtaining formal Statutes for the future management of the School, and that Mr. Gibson had perhaps had some similiar experience in this work elsewhere. The following entry in the Governors' books records his resignation, and shows that his election was only intended to be temporary.

> "Mr. Gibson the schoolmaster surrendered and resigned up his place in the school on the xxth day of July 1607, according to his promise made to the Governours at his election, for he was entreated to take the place upon him until such time as we could provide another fit person for that roome."

The antecedents and subsequent history of the Rev. Jeremy Gibson are only imperfectly known [1]. He probably was a native of the Halifax district, and perhaps belonged to the Gibsons of North and Southowram. He was Curate of Coley, near Halifax, from about 1611 to 1616, the year of his death: and married, at Halifax, some time in the year 1616, Edith, widow of Robert Hemingway, of Overbrear and Northowram, with whom he had previously resided. His burial is thus recorded in the Halifax Parish Church Register :—

> 1616. Oct. 12. "Mr. Jeremy Gibson, minister de Coley, vir bonus et concionator diligentissimus, Artium Magister."

([1]) The following details are chiefly obtained from "Chapters on the early registers of Halifax Parish Church." by Walter James Walker.

He made his will Oct. 9. 1616, apparently the very day of his death, and left £5 to his mother, £15 to his brother Richard, £15 to the children of his brother Samuel, £15 to the children of his brother-in-law Humfrey Holden, and £15 to his sister Sara Tilletson, widow; he also gave some plate to Coley Chapel, and other gifts to his friends Thomas Rawlin of Overbrear, the Rev. John Boyes, preacher at Halifax, and Samuel Lister, his wife's brother. The Rev. Oliver Heywood, a subsequent Curate of Coley, calls him "a godly man and an able minister."

4. REV. ROBERT SAUNDERS, M.A.

The only records of the Headmastership of Mr. Saunders are those which give particulars of his election and resignation, from which it will appear that he only held the office for a little more than three months:—

" Mr. Robert Saunders, Master of Arts, and Senior Fellow of the King's Colledge, in Cambridge, was elected schoolmaster the xxth day of July, 1607, and was presented to the Archbishop the said day by our writing under our common seal and signed by ix of the said Governors, and he was admitted into the school on Monday the last day of August, 1607."

"Mr. Saunders resigned up his place in the School on the xxxth day of October A.D. 1607, as by his letters it appeareth, written to Mr. Lister, William Savile, and Mr. Ratcliffe."

There is no record left to explain why Mr. Ratcliffe, whoever he may have been, was informed of this resignation: Mr. Lister was Vicar of Wakefield, and Spokesman of the Governors at the time, and William Savile had been Spokesman in the previous year : but Mr. Ratcliffe was not a Governor. Was he the Rev. Roger Ratcliffe[1] who became Incumbent of Horbury in 1623, and was also Dean of Pontefract?

5. REV. PHILIP ISACK, M.A.

More than sixty days having elapsed from the resignation of Mr. Saunders before a new Master had been found by the Governors of the School, the nomination must again have fallen to the Master and Fellows of Emmanuel College ; and this time they chose a member of their own College, which they had been unable to do in appointing

(1.) See Taylor p. 71.

the Rev. John Beaumont some years before. The following notice, however, seems to imply that the Governors elected, as a matter of form, the Master appointed by the College:—

> "Mr. Philip Isaack, Master of Arts of Emmanuel Colledge in Cambridge, was elected Schoolmaster the viiith day of January, A.D. 1607, and was presented to the Archbishop the said day by our writing under our common seal, and he was admitted into the school the fourth day after, A D. 1607."

The duration of Mr. Isack's mastership was from Jan. 8, 1607-8 until May 6, 1623, when he resigned: little is however known of his work in the School during these 15 years, beyond the fact that he educated three distinguished men, about whom some particulars will be found in a later Chapter, viz:—Hugh Paulin Cressy, Barnabas Oley, and Jeremiah Whitaker.

The Parish Church Registers contain some notices of his private life:—

> "1613. September. Nuptiæ inter Philippum Isaac ludimagistrum libere grammaticalis Scholæ et Annam Roades xxiii die.
>
> 1614. July. Ellenora filia Philippi Isaac ludimagistri libere grammaticalis schole baptizata xxx° die.
>
> 1615. November. Anna filia Philippi Isaac clerici baptizata xxx° die......sepulta vii₀ die Decembris.
>
> 1616. October. Infans Philippi Isaac non baptizat. sepult. ii° die.
>
> 1616. October. Anna uxor Philippi Isaack clerici sepulta xxiii₀ die.
>
> 1618. December. Elizabetha filia Philippi Isaack clerici baptizata xxix₀ die.

From a comparison of these entries with certain passages in Taylor's "Rectory Manor of Wakefield" (pp. 65.66. xxii. xl. &c.) it appears that Mr. Isack married the widow of William Rhodes, who was doubtless the chapman, of Crofton, who appears in the list of benefactors. Through this marriage certain property at Woodhall, near Newton and Wrenthorp, came into his hands, and this was surrendered by him and his wife for seven years from Oct. 23, 1617, to one Thomas Sonior (or Senior?); after the lapse of this period of time it was seized into the Lord's hands, and Matthew Hutton of York, draper, was admitted to it on Jan. 20. 1624-5.

Mr. Isack's term of office as Head Master closed in May 1623.

> Nov. 2, 1622. "This daye did Mr. Isaack give warning to the Governors to provide them of a Scholemaster.
>
> May 6, 1623. "Whereas Mr. Isanc the second day of November did give warning to the Governors then present to provide them of a Scholemaster, for that he would give over that place about Mayday nowe [coming], this day the said Mr. Isaac absolutelie left the said place according to his offer and warning, onelie desiring that [he might keep his] place in the Schole as Master untill Mayday of this instant May, which is graunted by the said Governors."

GRAMMAR SCHOOL.

6. REV. ROBERT DOUGHTY, M.A.

This Master was perhaps the son of a Robert Doughty, of Southowram, near Halifax, whose wife was buried at Halifax Parish Church on Apl. 29, 1603 [1]: or of the William Doughty, of Wakefield, who had a son William baptized at Wakefield Parish Church on Aug 21, 1617. The fact that his election was made on the same day as the resignation of his predecessor was given in, lends support to the idea that he was already well known in Wakefield.

> May 6, 1623. "This day Mr. Robt. Doughtie was chosen Scholemaster of this Schole by all the said Governors present, and a letter thereupon written to the Archebishoppe the same day for his approbation of him."
>
> June 17, 1623. "This day Mr. Robert Doughtie, Mr of Artes, being formerlie presented to the Lord Archebisshoppe, and by him allowed to be Scholemaster in this Schole, did take his oath according to the Statutes ministred to him by the Spokesman."

Mr. Doughty held the office for nearly 40 years, and rendered most signal service to the School during a very trying period, and in many various ways.

Within one year of his appointment he took steps to right the abuse which the endowment of Thomas Cave, at Clare Hall, Cambridge, had suffered by the wrongful nomination of two Scholars not duly qualified; some particulars about this affair are given in Chapter VIII.

Soon after this he took vigorous steps to increase the endowment of the School by securing benefactions from parents who were thought capable of paying for the education of their sons, and afterwards by the introduction of a system of school-fees in place of donations : see pp. 49, 50.

Mr. Doughty's energy and abilities were soon recognized by the Governors, who in 1626 voted him £4 a year "for his house rent, till such tyme as wee did provide him of a fitt house" (p. 27), stating that they did so "for the better encouragement of Mr. Doughtie his industrious and diligent instructing of his scollers." Again in 1627 a considerable sum was granted to Mr. Doughty "forth of the moneys in the Spokesman's hands for the speciall diligence we find in him."

Fourteen years after this, on Sep. 30, 1641, Mr. Doughty alleging "urgent occasions for money in respect of the education of his sonne [2] at Cambridge, and other charges," the Spokesman was directed to pay

---

[1] Walker's "Chapters on the Early Registers of Halifax ParishChurch,"p. 29.
[2] Probably the Henry Doughty who acted as Usher of the School from 1646 to 1649, see p. 91.

him £10 at once, £10 by St. Bartholomew's day, and £10 yearly for three years on St. Bartholomew's Day. These payments are interesting as being the forerunners of the University Exhibitions provided 33 years later by the munificence of John Storie.

But the greatest claims which the Rev. Robert Doughty has upon the gratitude of posterity have been mentioned in the previous chapter, where his devotion to duty during the Civil War has been pointed out at some length.

The Governors displayed their gratitude in many ways, but the following may be taken as typical records :—

> Oct. 12, 1652. "This day was taken into consideration the great care and paynes of Mr. Doughty present Schoolemaster, whereupon it is thought fit and ordered that in consideration thereof the Spokesman shall pay unto him the summe of seaven pounds as a gratuity from the Governors and that upon demaund."
>
> Sep. 30, 1662. "It was then ordered in consideration of Mr. Doughty the present Schoolemaster hath long lyen lame, and beene at great expenses occasioned thereby, the summe of five pounds out of the school stock shall be given him by the Spokesman for reliefe of his necessities."

Within five months after the latter record Mr. Doughty was dead, and buried in the North Quire of Wakefield Parish Church :—

> Feb. 24, 1662-3. "Robertus Doughty, generosus, Ludimagister liberæ grammaticalis Scholæ Wakfieldiensis sepultus fuit die Martis vicesimo quarto die Februarii" (Church Registers).

Mr. Doughty was the father of a numerous family, some of whose names are thus recorded in the Wakefield Parish Church Registers :— John, baptized Aug. 20, 1623, buried Sept. 1, 1623 : Timothy, baptized Dec. 27, 1624, buried Nov. 6, 1628 : Susanna, baptized Oct. 2, 1627 : Elizabeth, baptized Feb. 13, 1629 : Alice, baptized Mar. 8, 1631 : Robert, baptized July 5, 1634 : Thomas, baptized Oct. 17, 1637, perhaps M.A. of Magdalen College, Cambridge, in 1660, D.D. in 1671. He also had a son Henry, who was Usher of the School from 1646 to 1649, and therefore was probably born before his father came to Wakefield : this Henry Doughty is perhaps the one whose daughter Cicely was buried in the Quire at Wakefield Parish Church on June 20, 1641, being himself buried there on April 30, 1698. A Mr. John Doughty, perhaps another son, was offered the Headmastership of the School in 1665, as will be found recorded a few pages later ; a gentleman of the same name, and perhaps the same individual, was Head Master of Heath Grammar School, Halifax, from 1666 to 1688 :

and another John Doughty was Master of Repton School in 1681 [1].
Another Mr: Doughty was Master of Doncaster Grammar School in
1662. [2]   The name also frequently occurs in the lists of Graduates of
Oxford and Cambridge, but often in reference to families in the South of
England.

One of Mr. Doughty's pupils—the Rev. Charles Hoole, Master
of Rotherham School, and a well known author of scholastic
works—pays a high tribute to his master's ability in the preface to
"An easie entrance to the Latine Tongue" (1649), where he says
I especially respect the order I have used (these 16 years together)
in my own course of teaching, and according to which I was trained
up (by that able Schoolmaster whom I heartily reverence as my
Master, Mr. Robert Doughty, in Wakefield School.")

7. REV. SAMUEL GARVEY, M.A.

Within four weeks of the death of Mr. Doughty, the Governors
decided to ask the Master and Fellows of Emmanuel College,
Cambridge, to nominate a successor, and resolved on Mar. 24, 1662-3
that a letter should be sent in the names of the Rev. James Lister,
Vicar of Wakefield, and Mr. Thomas Pease. The original letter is
still extant, and was very kindly lent to me four years ago by Dr.
Phear, the present Master of the College : it runs as follows :—

After our most hearty commendations premised &c.,
May it please you hereby to be certifyed that the Masters
place in our free Grammar Schoole of Wakefeld is now voyde
by the death of Mr. Robert Doughty, late Master there : and
that in case election of another into the place be not made by
the Governours it devolves by the statutes of our schoole for
that turne unto Emanuel Colledge in Cambridge : and for
that the said Governours upon their best enquirie cannot
meete with a man soe quallifyed as the statutes doe require,
viz. :—A Master of Arts sufficiently furnished with such
learning as that place doth require, and of religious and Godly
conversation : Wee the Governours of the said schoole, whose
'names are here subscribed, become humble suitors to you,
that according to the trust reposed in you, you will be pleased

---

(1)   See Cox's History of Heath Grammar School p. 66 : a John Doughty
took his B.A. degree from Caius Coll. Cambridge, in 1663, and his M.A. in 1667 :
another John Doughty took his M.A. degree from Balliol Coll. Oxford, in 1662.

(2)   Admissions to St. John's College, Cambridge, by Mayor, p. 150, No. 46.

to recommend unto us (with such speede as the necessity of the place doth require) a man soe fitted and who will be content to accept of the small salary of thirty-six pounds and ten shillings per annum paid quarterly at four equall payments, besides the benefete of strangers liveing without the parish, and in so doeing we shall ever be

Wakefield
Mar. 24th, 1662.

Your affectionate friends
to serve you
Chr. Wilson   Spokesman
Ja : Lister
Danyell Oley
John Wilson
Geo : Radcliffe
Thomas Pease
John Maude
John Robinson

To the right worshipfull the Master and fellowes of Emanuel Colledge in Cambridge these humbly present.

In response to this request the Master and Fellows nominated the Rev. Samuel Garvey (or Gervey), of their own College, who took his M.A. degree in 1660. Some delay, however, took place before Mr Garvey arrived in Wakefield to take up his duties :—

June 30, 1663. "Mr. Samuel Gervye being elected by the Master and Fellows of Emmanuell Colledge in Cambridge to be schoolemaster of this schoole, and not yet entered to his place, It is thought fitt that the Spokesman desire Mr. Stapleton [1] to continue his place and imployment as formerly."

July 21, 1663. "Mr. Samuel Gerve being formerly elected Schoolmaster of this School, and showing his presentation from the Archbishop of Yorke thereunto, tooke his oath and entred to his place."

"This day Mr. Gerve the present Schoolmaster having removed his family out of Hertfordshire, and consideration being had of his great charge therein, It is agreed that the present Spokesman shall pay him five poundes towardes it."

Mr. Garvey held his post for rather more than two years only, when he resigned perhaps to take some other duties :—

Oct. 24, 1665. "Upon the receite of a letter from Mr. Samuell Garvie, bearing daite the 19th of 8br 1665, to the above saide John Wilson, part of which containes these wordes following—I desire you from me to informe the Spoaksman that I surrender my right into his handes—Wee the above said Governors takeing the premises into our consideration, do declare the said place to be voyde."

(1) I have no idea who this gentleman was, unless he was the William Stapleton, Doctor in Divinity, buried at Wakefield on July 19, 1693.

Nothing is known of Mr. Garvey's work beyond the names of some of his pupils, the most distinguished of whom was the famous Dr. John Radcliffe, who matriculated at University College, Oxford, at the age of 15 on Mar. 23, 1665-6.

8. REV. JEREMY BOULTON, M.A.

In consequence of the resignation of Mr. Garvey, a resolution was passed by the Governors on Nov. 6, 1665, that a letter should be written by the Spokesman and Mr. John Wilson, and sent to Mr. John Doughty, who was probably a son of Mr. Garvey's predecessor, to know whether he would accept the Headmastership, if he should be elected. On Nov. 20 he actually was elected, but declined the post a few days afterwards :—

> Dec. 14, 1665. "Whereas Mr John Doughty, formerly elected Skoolemaster of this Skoole, by his letter bearing daite 23 of November last did refuse the same, Wee therefore the above saide Governors have this day elected Mr Jeremie Boulton in his place."

Mr. Boulton obtained the usual licence from the Archbishop of York, and took his oath on the following Jan. 31st, having on the same day the sum of five pounds allowed to him, as it had been to his predecessor, "out of the Schoole Stock in Consideration of the charges in removing his Family hither."

It is impossible to say from what town Mr. Boulton came, but it is most probable that his family belonged to Wakefield. The Parish Church Registers contain the name of Jeremie Bolton, son of Francis Bolton, baptized June 8. 1600 (Walker, p. 278); and also that of Jeremiah, son of Michael Bolton, baptized Aug. 23, 1657. These may have been the father and nephew respectively of the Rev. Jeremy Boulton, for the conjunction of names is a remarkable one, and must have some such significance as is here suggested. Mr. Boulton himself had four children at least baptized at Wakefield Parish Church, viz. :—Margaret, on Feb. 5, 1666-7 ; Sara, on Aug. 11, 1668 ; Jeremiah, on Sept. 14, 1670 ; and Elizabeth, on Mar. 1, 1671-2 : a Susanna Bolton, married to James Bowling on Oct. 14, 1670, may have been a relative.

Mr. Boulton took the degree of B.A. in 1661, and M.A. in 1665, from Magdalen College, Cambridge. He held the Mastership of the School until April 2, 1672, when he resigned by letter to Mr. William Denison, Spokesman, in consequence of having been appointed

"Parson of Acquoth." He was not, however, instituted to the Rectory of Ackworth until May 30, 1673, and is said to have been presented by Charles II., as Duke of Lancaster. He resigned the living in the year 1694.

9. REV. JOHN BASKERVILE, B.D.

John, the son of Thomas Baskervile, was baptized at Wakefield Parish Church on Apl. 4, 1641. Perhaps he was also educated at Wakefield Grammar School under the Rev. Robert Doughty. He was a member of Emmanuel College, Cambridge, and took his B.A. degree in 1661, his M.A. in 1665, and his B.D. in 1677. His appointment is thus recorded :—

> May 1, 1672. . . . . . . " and did then take their Corporall Oath as the statutes for election of a Schoolmaister hath provided. And upon debate and serious consideration did then elect Mr John Baskervile of Drighlington Schoolmaister in the roome of Mr Jeremiah Boulton ; the Spookesman is hereby ordered to signify so much unto him."

Mr. Baskervile took his oath on Saturday, May 11, and was presented to the Archbishop of York on the same day. At the time of his election he seems to have been Incumbent of Rastrick, in the West Riding, having been appointed in the year 1666. He held the Mastership of Wakefield Grammar School until his death, which occurred on May 15, 1681, according to a tombstone in the Pilkington Chapel in Wakefield Cathedral, where he was buried on the following day. At this time the Chapel belonged to the Church-wardens :—

Hic jacet Corpus
JOHANNIS BASKERVILE, S.T.B.
Quondam Scholæ Wakefeldiensis
Ludimagistri, Qui obiit May 15, 1681.

To him belongs the credit of having educated the celebrated Dr. Bentley, the most famous classical scholar ever produced in England. His pupil, however, does not seem to have shown much respect towards his master in after years, nor to have much appreciated what was done for him in Wakefield Grammar School, if due importance is to be attached to his words, as reported by his grandson, Richard Cumberland, and printed in Dr. Jebb's "Life of Bentley," unfortunately without qualification or comment. There is, however, abundance of proof that the School at this time was in a most efficient

DR. BENTLEY.

MASTER OF TRINITY COLLEGE, CAMBRIDGE.

condition, and the reader will therefore doubtless pardon a digression, the object of which is to show what was the reputation which it enjoyed.

The ability of Mr. Doughty's administration from 1623 to 1663 is amply acknowledged by the Governors themselves, and by the testimony of his celebrated pupil, the Rev. Charles Hoole, which has been already quoted. During the last year of Mr. Doughty's rule, and the Headmastership of Mr. Garvey from 1663 to 1665, Dr. John Radcliffe was educated, and in his memoirs the school is expressly stated to have been "as famous as any whatsoever in these kingdoms, except those of Westminster, Winchester, and Eton."[1]. Shortly after this time two other famous men were produced from the School, viz. :—Joseph Bingham, who left it in 1684, and Archbishop Potter, who left it in 1688; for further particulars about whom, and for the names of other distinguished pupils, the reader is referred to Chapter IX. In the year 1715 the Governors recorded their testimony that the School had then "so great a name and credit abroad as the like hath not been remembered," and in 1717, spoke of the large number of "gentlemen and other learned persons here educated." Add to this the independent testimony of a well-known Master of University College, Oxford—Dr. Arthur Charlett—who had enjoyed excellent opportunities of judging the School by the pupils sent from it to his College, including Dr. Radcliffe, Dr. Potter, and Joseph Bingham, and by its official connection with the College through the Freeston endowment. In the year 1718 he presented books inscribed "Bibliothecæ Publicæ Scholæ celeberrimæ de Wakefield," and others in 1719 with the inscription "Scholæ eximiæ de Wakefeld." Dr. Thomas Zouch, in his life of the Rev. John Clarke[2], who was Master of Wakefield Grammar School from 1751 to 1758, and educated at it under the Rev. Thomas Clark, who was Master from 1703 to 1720, states that at both these periods "the sons of the principal gentry in the county of York, as well as those of other counties and countries" had been sent to the School to be educated. Besides this, the Master who held office during the intervening period, 1720 to 1751, who was the Rev. Benjamin Wilson, afterwards Vicar of Wakefield, is described as "one of the first Greek Scholars of the age" by the same Dr. Zouch[3]. Enough has therefore been said in this place to remove the false impression which might be created by the words of Dr. Bentley in the minds of those who do not understand what his character was.

(1) Memoirs of Dr. John Radcliffe, p. 4.   (2) Works of Dr. Thomas Zouch, vol. ii. p. 25.   (3) ibid. p. 7.

10. REV. EDWARD CLARKE, M.A.

As far as I have been able to ascertain, the name of the Rev. Edward Clarke nowhere occurs in the books of the Governors as having at any time been Head Master of this School: but this must not be considered surprising when it is remembered that the Minute-books for the years 1677 to 1723 are missing. His name is however given in the accounts of the lives of two of his pupils, Joseph Bingham and John Potter, and his appointment is recorded as follows in the Archbishop of York's register of licences :—

Aug. 17, 1681. "Licentia ad docendum et erudiendum pueros et adolescentulos in libera grammaticali Schola Reginæ Elizabethæ intra Parochiam et Vicariatum de Wakefield in Comitatu et Dioecese Eboracensi concessa Edvardo Clarke, A.M. 17mo die Augusti 1681."

There is thus a period of three months between the death of Mr. Baskervile and the licensing of Mr. Edward Clarke: it is therefore possible, but very unlikely, that another master held office during the interval.

Concerning the latter there are only fragmentary records. The following inscription in a book in the School Library seems to refer to him :—

"in usum Scholæ Wakefieldiensis E. C. d. d. Anno Domini 1686."

There is also in the Archbishop's register of licences at York the record of his appointment as Lecturer at Wakefield Parish Church, which would necessitate his resignation as Head Master :—

Sep. 17, 1693. "Edwardus Clarke A.M. Admissus fuit ad officium Prælectoris sive Concionatoris Stipendiarii in Ecclesia Parochiali de Wakefield in Comitatu et Dioecese Eboracensi."

Mr. Edward Clarke was elected a Trustee for the poor of the town and Almshouses of Wakefield on June 22nd, 1695, and was succeeded in this office by Abraham Bever on Nov. 3, 1698. He must also have ceased to be Lecturer at the Parish Church about this time or soon after, as the Rev. Thomas Clark, M.A., held that post during part of the years 1698 and 1699. He therefore probably left Wakefield in 1698, as there is no record of his death, in the Parish Registers.

I have to thank the Rev. Chas. W. Boase, M.A., Fellow and Tutor of Exeter College, Oxford, for the information that an Edward Clarke, son of Joshua Clarke, of Baconsthorp, Norfolk, matriculated as a poor boy at University College, Oxford, on July 17, 1674, aged 16: he took his B.A. degree in 1678, and his M.A. in 1681, became vicar of S. Mary's, Nottingham in 1698, was Canon of Southwell from 1701 to 1729, Rector of Haselbeach from 1711 to 1729, and of Bugbrook, Northants, 1728-9. This is very probably the Edward Clarke who was Head Master of Wakefield School from 1681 to 1693, as all the dates given encourage the identification.

11. REV. EDMUND FARRER, M.A.

The same uncertainty, which attaches to the date of the resignation of Edward Clarke, also affects the question of the time when Edmund Farrer was appointed: if the former resigned in September 1693 to accept the Lectureship at Wakefield Parish Church, we may suppose that the latter was appointed soon afterwards. There is curiously no record of his licence in the Archbishop's Registers, but he is referred to in a document printed in our last Chapter, and dated June, 1695, as apparently having been only recently appointed.

Edmund Farrer, son of Joseph Farrer, of Killington, Westmorland, was educated at Sedbergh School, and matriculated on June 1, 1668, at the age of 18, at S. John's College, Cambridge, took the B.A. degree in 1672 and the M.A. in 1687. He was married at Rotherham Parish Church, on August 29, 1683, to Martha Fowke, whose epitaph is recorded below: in the Marriage Register he is described as being a Schoolmaster, but I have not discovered to what School he then belonged.

In the absence of minute-books belonging to the Governors, the particulars of his administration are quite unknown, only the names of a few of his pupils having been preserved, and the interesting document above referred to.

Mr. Farrer held office until his death, which happened on April 7, 1703. Two days later he was buried in Wakefield Parish Church, where his wife had been buried two years before, and a monument to them was erected in the North Chancel, with the following inscription:—

Martha filia Gualteri
Fowke, gen. de Comit. Stafford: germana soror Phineæ Fowke, M.D. Coll. Med. Lond. socii
Uxor fidelissima et pientissima Edm.
Farrer A.M. Scholarchæ, matura cælo discessit
Idibus Apri. die Dominica dict. Palmarum Anno
Aeræ Christianæ 1701. Aetat suæ 50.
Quæ cui debetur vincenti palma dabatur.
Laboribus potius quam Annis confectus discessit etiam ipse
Edm. Farrer 7 Id. Apr. A. de C. 1703. Aetat suæ......
Uxoris pientissimæ desiderabili nunc consortio in
æternum fruiturus.

I am indebted to Dr. John Sykes, F.S.A., of Doncaster, for the information that Martha Fowke, whom the Rev. Edmund Farrer married, was a niece of the wife of the Rev. Luke Clayton, Vicar of Rotherham, and is mentioned as such in Mrs Clayton's will, A.D. 1682 : he also informs me that on June 15, 1703, administration of the goods of the late Edmund Farrer of Wakefield was granted to Anthony Farrer of Worsbrough, clerk, schoolmaster, and cousin-german; the latter was buried at Worsbrough, on Nov., 7, 1704: Mr. Miles Farrer, another Schoolmaster, was buried at Pocklington on April 17, 1704. Thus three schoolmasters of the same family name, and possibly all related to each other, died within 19 months.

12. REV. THOMAS CLARK, M.A.

The election of the Rev. Thomas Clark was made on April 16, 1703, only seven days after the death of the previous Master. This short interval is easily explained by the fact that the new Master was already in the service of the School as Usher, having held that post since January 1698-9. He had also previously been Lecturer at the Parish Church. His presentation to the Archbishop was made in the following form :—

"To the most reverend Father in God John Lord Archbishop of York his Grace, Primate and Metropolitan of England.

"Wee do humbly certifie your Grace that a meeting this day of the Governors of the free Grammer School of Queen Elizabeth at Wakefeld, where were present Mr. Joseph Watkinson, Spokesman, Francis Nevile, Richard Witton, Esqs., Mr. John Scott, Mr. Thomas Scott, Mr. Nicholas Fenay, Mr. Theophilus Shelton, Mr. John Smyth, Mr. Benjamin Watkinson, Mr. Thomas Brooke, and Mr. William Copindall, Governors of the said Schoole, Wee do unanimously elect the bearer hereof, Mr. Thomas Clark, Master of Arts, Schoolmaster of the said Free Grammar Schoole in the place of Mr. Edmund Farrer deceased, pursuant to the power given unto us by the Letters Patent of Queen Elizabeth of famous memory, under the great seale of England, and of the Statutes of the said Schoole in that behalfe, which said Mr. Thomas Clarke we present unto your Grace, humbly desiring you to Give unto him your Grace's Licence and Approbation to teach in our said Schoole, In Witness whereof we have hereunto caused our common Seale to be set the 16 day of Aprill Anno Domini 1703."

GRAMMAR SCHOOL.

The following entry is found in the Archbishop's Register regarding the granting of the licence :—

19 April, 1703. "Thomas Clark, Clericus, Artium Magister, admissus fuit ad officium magistri Liberæ Scholæ grammaticalis Reginæ Elizabethæ in Wakefield in Diœcese Eboracensi."

The lists of Cambridge Graduates contain the name of Thomas Clark twice during the last ten years of the 17th century: one took his B.A. degree from Jesus College in 1694, and his M.A. in 1698, and the other took his B.A. degree from the same College in 1696, and his M.A. in 1700. The latter was probably the one who came to Wakefield: and he is recorded in the Parish Registers as having married Sarah Spinke on Dec. 28, 1699, who was buried on Mar. 30, 1704, nine days after her daughter, Sarah: another daughter, Jane, was baptized on Mar. 28, 1702, and buried on July 10, 1706. Mr. Clark married a second time, and had issue:—Lucy, baptized Nov. 30, 1709, buried Jan. 12, 1714-5; Henry, baptized Feb. 15, 1710-1, buried Oct. 31, 1711; Frances, baptised May 28, 1713; Ann, baptized Oct. 18, 1714; Edward, baptized Feb. 7, 1715-6; and Beilby, baptized Feb. 7, 1718-9, buried Mar. 19, following. The last named seems to have received his Christian name from the Beilby Thompson, Esq., who presented Mr. Clark to the Vicarage of Escrick, as is recorded in the next page.

The Rev. Thomas Clark was one of the most successful of all the Masters of the School. Dr. Thomas Zouch (Works, vol. ii, p. 4.) says of him :—" The celebrity of the Rev. Thomas Clark is too well known to be here recorded. To his care the sons of the principal gentry in the county of York were entrusted. From the instructions of this eminent preceptor, young Clarke [1] acquired the most solid advantages: an improved taste, a chastised judgment, and a regulated method of study."

To him the School is indebted for the building of a separate room to be used as a Library, as will be more fully pointed out in the next Chapter, and for the acquisition of many valuable books, some of which still remain.

The flourishing state of the School under his management is clearly shown by the statute printed in full on p. 82, which states that the number of boys in the year 1717 was over 160, and provides for the employment of an extra master in consequence, in addition to the Head Master and Usher, who must indeed have had their hands full.

(1) The reference is to John Clarke, afterwards Head Master: see below.

Mr. Clark also succeeded, in conjunction with the Governors, in making an arrangement with the Master and Fellows of Clare Hall, Cambridge, with respect to the Scholarships left by Thomas Cave for the benefit of Wakefield boys: it appears that for some 20 years these had not been filled up, owing to a disagreement which existed between the College and the School authorities: see Chapter VIII.

The high opinion which the Governors held of his services is shown by the following document, a copy of which is to be found in the British Museum among the Kennett MSS., vol. xxxix., p. 50-52.

"Oct. 29, 1715. At a meeting of the Spokesman and Governors of the Free Grammar School at Wakefield present Francis Pitt gent Spokesman, Richard Witton Esq., Richard Witton, junr. Esq., the Rev. Mr. Thomas Scott, Vicar, the Rev. Mr. Dan. Sill, Lecturer, Mr. Joseph Watkinson, Mr. Benjamin Watkinson, Mr. James Sill, Mr. John Bromley, Mr. Abraham Bever, Mr. William Spink, and Mr. Tho. Wilson: Mr. Tho. Clarke the present Schoolmaster of the said Schoole attending the said Spokesman and Governors at this meeting, and acquainting them that Bielby Thompson, Esq. had lately made him an offer of the presentation to the Rectory or Parsonage of Escrick in this county, subject to a bond for resigning the same when Mr. William Thompson his brother, now scholar at this school, shall be capable to accept and enjoy the said living (which may be within seaven years or thereabouts): And the said Mr. Clarke having made it his humble request to the said Spokesman and Governors that they would give their leave and consent for his accepting the said parsonage, and dispense in this case with the statute of the school prohibiting any schoolmaster of the same from accepting any such cure: He the said Mr. Clarke promising to serve the said parsonage by a curate constantly residing there, and that he himselfe will notwithstanding live and reside at Wakefield as now and heretofore, and will duly observe and obey the statutes of the school concerning the due residence and attendance of the masters.

We the said Spokesman and Governors, taking this matter into our serious consideration, and having now read the same statute, which we much approve and think very fit to be observed generally, yet nevertheless having a just value for the great abilities of the said Mr. Clarke, by which and his great care diligence and industry he has advanced the school to such a flourishing state and condition, and to so great a name and credit abroad, as the like hath not been remembered. For these causes, and as a special mark and public testimony of our singular favour and esteeme for him in respect of such his extraordinary service to the said school, we the said Spokesman and Governors do hereby unanimously give and grant unto the said Mr. Clarke our full and free licence and consent for his accepting the same presentation, and taking institution and induction thereupon, hereby ordering and declaring that the said Mr. Clarke shall, after such acceptance institution and induction, remain and continue the schoolmaster of the said School, and enjoy all the rights and profits, to his said office belonging, in as full and ample form and manner as he now holds or enjoys the same. The statute before mentioned, or any other statute to the contrary in any wise notwithstanding: Provided always, and upon this Condition nevertheless, that the said Mr. Clarke do duly observe and obey the said statutes of the Schoole concerning the residence and attendance thereby required from the Schoolmasters thereof. Given under our common seal the day and year above written."

Mr. Clark appears to have held the Rectory of Escrick from 1715 to 1728, when he resigned.

He vacated the Headmastership of Wakefield Grammar School about Easter 1720, on being appointed to a similar post at Kirkleatham in Cleveland; the School founded there about 1710 by Sir William Turner, Lord Mayor of London, has now been transferred to East Coatham.

---

13. REV. BENJAMIN WILSON, M.A.

The Rev. Benjamin Wilson became Head Master about Easter, 1720, probably succeeding the Rev. Thomas Clark without delay, as he had been Usher of the School since the year 1717 at the latest, as appears from a list of Donors to the Library, printed in the next chapter. The exact date of his appointment is not to be found, either in the Archbishop's Register at York, or in the books of the Governors.

Mr. Wilson is called by Dr. Zouch [1] "one of the first Greek Scholars of the age;" and this is only to be expected of one who obtained a Fellowship at Trinity College, Cambridge, at a time when Dr. Bentley was Master. He took his B.A. degree from the same College in 1715, and his M.A. in 1719. During his tenure of office as Head Master—a period of thirty-one years,—the Wakefield Grammar School seems to have fully maintained the reputation which it had gained under his predecessor, and which was still further increased under his successor.

The Governors showed their "particular Esteem and Value for the said Mr. Wilson" by passing a resolution on July 5, 1727, almost exactly similar to that passed in favour of the previous Master, whereby the Statute prohibiting the Head Master from accepting a benefice was suspended, in order that Mr. Wilson might accept the offer of the presentation to the Vicarage of Normanton, which he promised to serve by a resident Curate. He appears to have held this living until his death in 1764, and in conjunction not only with his Head Mastership, but also with the Vicarage of Wakefield, which he held from 1751 to his death. Mr. Wilson was also a Prebendary of York from 1736 to 1764.

Special grants of money were frequently made to him and his Ushers by the Governors "in consideration of their Industries and

(1) Works Vol. ii. p. 7.

painfull instructing of the Scholars of the School:" this was the only means available in those days of increasing the Salaries of the Masters.

Mr. Wilson resigned the Mastership of the School on Mar. 29, 1751, on being presented to the Vicarage of Wakefield : he was instituted Vicar on July 10 of the same year, and remained in Wakefield till his death, being buried on September 6, 1764.

Those who hold that Oliver Goldsmith's "Vicar of Wakefield" is a title which means what it naturally should mean, also have reasonable grounds for believing that the portrait of Dr. Primrose is drawn from the Rev. Benjamin Wilson : but this subject has been so admirably handled by Mr. Lupton in his "Wakefield Worthies," pp. 182-8, that further reference to it here is quite unnecessary.

I find from the Wakefield Parish Registers that Mr. Wilson had a daughter, Elizabeth, baptized on Nov. 14, 1721 : another daughter, Ann, on May 8, 1723: a son, Thomas [1], on June 24, 1726, having been born on June 18 ; a daughter, Winifred, baptized on Mar. 28, 1728, and buried on the following Apl. 23 : and a son, John, baptized on June 26, 1733, and buried on the following Sep. 10.

14. REV. JOHN CLARKE, M.A.

The life of John Clarke may be found, written at great length, in the works of Dr. Thomas Zouch, one of his pupils at this School, under the title—" The Good Schoolmaster, exemplified in the character of the Reverend John Clarke, M.A., formerly Fellow of Trinity College, Cambridge, and successively Master of the Schools of Shipton, Beverley and Wakefield, in the County of York." It also appears in Mr. Lupton's "Wakefield Worthies." Under these circumstances it will be necessary only to give the most important facts concerning his work at Wakefield, supplementing them with a few particulars which have not yet been published.

He was born a mechanic's son, at Kirby Misperton, or Kirby-over-car, 3 miles south of Pickering, in the North Riding, on May 3, 1706 ; educated first at Thornton School,[2] 2 miles east of Pickering, whence he afterwards obtained a small Exhibition to the University ; removed thence to Wakefield Grammar School in order to enjoy

(1) See Chapter VIII. and also page 138.

(2) Founded in 1657 by Elizabeth, Viscountess Lumley : she left, amongst other legacies, 10 Exhibitions of £4 a year each for poor scholars of the school at Cambridge or Oxford, till they become graduates.

the tuition of the Rev. Thomas Clark, who was then Head Master, and transferred with him to Kirkleatham School in 1720. He was admitted Sizar of Trinity College, Cambridge, in 1723; took his B.A. degree in 1726; was elected Fellow of his College on October 1, 1729, after obtaining the highest praise from Dr. Bentley, who was then Master : he proceeded to the M.A. degree in 1730. His accurate knowledge of the Greek language and literature obtained for him at Cambridge the name of "the little Aristophanes." He does not seem to have undertaken any tuition at the University, but Dr. Zouch is mistaken in supposing that his first appointment was at Shipton School, as the following record of the Governors will show :—

> 1727. Sep. 30. "This day John Clark, Batcheler of Arts, of Trinity Colledge, Cambridge, was unanimously chosen Usher of the free School in the place of Mr. Thomas Murgatroyd, who has resigned the same, and was likewise chosen with the consent and approbation of Mr. Benjamin Willson, Head Master."

Mr. Clarke's appointment and acceptance of office may have been due to the recommendation of Dr. Bentley himself. He remained Usher for two years, resigning on Sep. 30, 1729, the very day before he was elected to his Fellowship. Soon after this he was appointed Head Master of Shipton School, in the Parish of Overton, near York, at a salary of £40 a year, where he remained until 1735, having, while there, married Mrs. Meek, a widow lady with three sons and a daughter, and been appointed perpetual curate of Nun-Monkton, near York, with £16 a year. In 1735 he was presented by the Mayor and Corporation of Beverley to the Headmastership of their Grammar School, and took with him thither many of his pupils from Shipton : he remained at Beverley 16 years.

On the resignation of the Rev. Benjamin Wilson, Mr. John Clarke was appointed Head Master of the very School where he had previously been both pupil and Usher.

> 1751. Apl. 8. "The Reverend Mr John Clarke of Beverley was duly elected by eight of the governors above-named, And thereupon his appointment and presentation to the Archbishop of York were ordered to be made out under the Common Seal of the Governours of the said Schole."

Nine Governors were present at the meeting when this election took place. The Archbishop's Licence was granted on June 17 following.

It appears that the Headmastership of the School had been promised to Mr. Clarke even before the resignation of his predecessor: this was doubtless owing to the fact that the presentation to the Vicarage of Wakefield, vacant by the death of the Rev. George Arnet in October, 1750, had been promised to Mr. Wilson, but not yet made. The Governors accordingly offered Mr. Clarke the Headmastership on Feb. 14. 1751, if it should become vacant within two months by the resignation of Mr. Wilson: the latter resigning on Mar. 29, Mr. Clarke was then elected according to the previous arrangement.

John Clarke did not take his oath as Head Master until June 29, and in the interval the duties of the School were performed by Mr. Thomas Wilson, son of the previous Master, who had been educated at Wakefield and sent to the University with an Exhibition from Storie's University Gift, afterwards becoming a Fellow of Trinity College, like his Father. Another Fellow of Trinity College came to the School as Usher under the Rev. John Clarke, who was also, or certainly had been, a Fellow of the same Society. There were thus in 1751 no less than four men in Wakefield who were, or had been, Fellows of the leading College in Cambridge, of which also a Wakefield Grammar School "Old Boy" had only nine years before been Master.

During the seven years in which Mr. Clarke held the Headmastership, he sent out into the world a large number of men who were well known in their time, including many of "the sons of the principal gentry in the county of York, as well as those of other counties and countries." In Wrangham's edition of Dr. Zouch's works (Vol ii. pp. 25-30) appears a list of gentlemen educated under him at Shipton, Beverley or Wakefield, and in a later chapter of the present book will be found the names of many, who, judging from dates and other circumstances, were probably educated at Wakefield Grammar School.

The number of boys in the School at the time of Mr. Clarke's Mastership, may be estimated by the fact that, when he was appointed, the Governors agreed to pay him the Usher's salary in addition to his own, on condition that he should be responsible for the remuneration of the Usher and any other Assistant Masters who might be required: he would also receive the entrance money of all boys coming to the School, and regular School fees from those who were not natives of Wakefield: and these would form the large majority. A few years after Mr. Clarke's resignation it is recorded that he had " paid for the services of two, and sometimes three Ushers or Assistant Masters," and in 1717 it had not been thought necessary to have three Masters altogether, until the number of boys had reached 160 (see pp. 82, 133.)

The School is very largely indebted to Mr. Clarke for the care with which he gathered together much of the valuable Library of books which it now possesses: amongst other means of increasing their number, he carried out most extensively the principle, adopted from very early times, and especially encouraged by the Rev. Thomas Clark, when he was Head Master, of persuading his pupils, on proceeding from the School to the Universities, or into business or professions, to present a volume to the place of their education as a memorial of them: this excellent rule has often led to the identification of gentlemen whose names would otherwise probably have been lost to the School.

Further testimony to his merits is borne by a writer in the 'Gentleman's Magazine' (Vol. lxxii. p. 122), where the scheme of religious instruction adopted by him at Wakefield School is particularly held up as a pattern for imitation in other institutions.

The Governors have also recorded their opinion of him :—

> 1758. Mar. 29. "It is ordered that the Spokesman or Deputy Spokesman do wait on Mr. Clarke, before he leaves the Town, and present him with fifty guineas out of the money belonging to the School's trust, and desire his Acceptance of it as a Gratuity for his extraordinary Diligence in the Discharge of his Duty as Master of the School, and to acquaint him that the Governors are very sorry that his bad Health will not permit him to continue the School."

Mr. Clarke had resigned his post on Feb. 22, but did not cease his work until Whitsuntide, which fell that year in the middle of May. His health had recently broken down, partly from anxiety as to the provision which he had made for his old age, and partly from the effects of preaching in Rothwell Church in a damp surplice when overheated after a sharp walk from Wakefield on a frosty morning early in 1758. This caused a stroke of apoplexy, which was repeated in the next year, and he was then quite incapacitated both in body and mind. He lived two years at Tadcaster after leaving Wakefield, and then removed to the house of his brother Francis in Scarborough, where he died without issue, on Feb. 8, 1761: he was buried in the Church of his native village three days later. He had been presented to a small vicarage in Essex by the husband of his step-daughter, Mr. Jolliffe, just before leaving Wakefield, but the state of his health made it impossible for him to accept the offer. Other patronage had been sought for him from the Duke of Newcastle, as prime minister, but his answer was that "to comply with their request would be to deprive the public of a good schoolmaster."

At a meeting of Mr. Clarke's old pupils, held at Wakefield on Aug. 29, 1793, it was decided to erect a monument to him at Kirby Misperton Church, and memorial tablets in each of the schools over which he had presided: the inscription on the latter was the composition of Dr. Zouch. The Governors of Wakefield School unanimously gave permission, on Mar. 17, 1794, for one tablet to be erected there, after an application from Dr. Zouch himself. It was removed into the new School Buildings four years since at the suggestion of the writer, and the inscription, as written by Dr. Zouch, ran as follows :—

M. S.

JOHANNIS CLARKE, A.M.

QUI

HUIC SCHOLÆ PRÆPOSITUS

SUMMA CUM OMNIUM LAUDE AC PREDICATIONE

JUVENTUTIS INSTITUENDÆ PROVINCIAM ADORNAVIT :

INTIMA LATINARUM ET GRÆCARUM LITERARUM

COGNITIONE INSTRUCTUS,

IN OPTIMIS UTRIUSQUE LINGUÆ SCRIPTORIBUS EXPLICANDIS

ET ILLUSTRANDIS DILUCIDUS, SOLLERS, PERSPICAX,

MULTIPLICI SCIENTIA

JUDICII SUBTILITATE

ET INGENII ELEGANTIA PERPOLITA

UBERRIME LOCUPLETATUS.

MORES HUMANITATE ADEO TEMPERAVIT,

UT DICIPULOS SUOS, IN GLORIÆ SPEM EDUCATOS,

INCREDIBILI QUADAM FACILITATE AD DOCTRINAM ALLICERET,

INDUSTRIAM EXCITARET ATQUE ACUERET.

HINC FREQUENTISSIMAM ADOLESCENTIUM CORONAM

SIBI CONCILIAVIT ET DEVINXIT,

QUI EUM QUASI PATREM BENIGNUM ATQUE DILECTISSIMUM

ENIXE AMARUNT ET COLUERUNT.

EX VULTU MODESTO, OBTUTUQUE SUAVI ET PLACIDO

ANIMI CANDOREM LUBENTISSIME CONJICERES :

ERAT ENIM , SI QUIS ALIUS,

INCULPABILI VITÆ INTEGRITATE ORNATISSIMUS :

IMMO PERPULCRUM PRIMÆVÆ INNOCENTIÆ EXEMPLUM.

PIGET, EHEU ! REFERRE QUAM VIRUM HUNC

OPTIME DE REPUBLICA MERITUM

INGRATA ÆTAS NEGLEXERIT,

ÆRUMNIS CONFECTUM, SINE HONORE, SINE PRÆMIO,

PAUPERTATE ET INOPIA TANTUM NON OPPRESSUM VIDERIT.

NATUS IN VILLA DE KIRBY MISPERTON

IN COMITATU EBORACENSI

iii. MAII, A.D. 1706

IN EADEM VILLA HUMATUS EST

xi FEBRUARII, A.D. 1761.

GRAMMAR SCHOOL.

The actual inscription on the stone differs slightly from the above, which is the version to be found in Dr. Zouch's biography of Mr. Clarke, and concludes with these words :—

> ALUMNI EJUS
> NE TESTIMONIUM SUÆ PIETATIS DEESSET
> HOC MARMOR POSUERE.

Nothing can be added about the personality of the man beyond what is stated by his loyal pupil, Dr. Thomas Zouch, who describes him, in different portions of his biography, as having been 'unusually proficient in classic erudition,' 'a man of exemplary application,' of 'nice and critical discernment,' 'an enlightened master of criticism,' 'breathing the very spirit of sublimity,' 'master of a polished style,' 'exquisitely nice in the choice of his language,' 'the sweet exemplar of humility and condescension,' but yet 'of awful dignity when determined to restrain petulance and to punish delinquency,' 'a man of timidity and native distrust,' 'a lovely pattern of Christian faith and Christian practice,' and of 'charming simplicity of manners.'

15. REV. CHRISTOPHER ATKINSON, M.A.

In the Cambridge Lists of Graduates there is no record of any one of this name which will suit the circumstances of the present case, but I have no doubt that the following entry from Foster's "Alumni Oxonienses" applies to the Master who succeeded the Rev. John Clarke at Wakefield :—

> Atkinson, Christopher, son of William Atkinson of Morland, Westmorland: matriculated at Queen's College, Oxford, Mar. 17, 1747-8, aged 18: B.A. 1752, M.A. 1756.

Another Christopher Atkinson, of Windermere, was also a member of the same College about this time, and became Vicar of Walton, Thorparch, in 1751: it is possible that they were relatives.

The Rev. Christopher Atkinson, of Wakefield, came to the School from Morpeth, being elected on May 22, 1758, sworn and presented to the Archbishop of York on June 1, and licensed by the latter on

> June 30, 1758. "Christopher Atkinson, Clerk, M.A., was licensed to perform the office of Master of the Free Grammar School of Queen Elizabeth at Wakefield in the County and Diocese of York, he being duly nominated thereto by the Governors of the said School." (Archbishop's Registers.)

Mr. Atkinson seems to have been appointed under the same arrangement as his predecessor, as regards the salary of himself and his Ushers, but the original custom was reverted to in a short time, as appears from the advertisement for his successor, which will be found below.

The Writing School was built very soon after he entered upon his duties, but on the whole his Headmastership does not seem to have been characterized by any unusual occurrences.

In conjunction with his duties as Head Master of the Grammar School, Mr. Atkinson obtained the permission of the Governors to hold the Assistant Curacy of Wakefield Parish Church from 1761 to 1772, and to accept the presentation, by the Mercers' Company, to the Cambden Lectureship in the last-mentioned year, on the resignation of the well-known Rev. Benjamin Forster [1] : he held this post until his death, which happened on Jan. 1, 1795.

Mr. Atkinson was thus Head Master for nearly 37 years, Curate of Wakefield for 11 years, and Lecturer for 22 years, as is pointed out by his tombstone in Wakefield Cathedral, where he was buried four days after his death.

H. S. I.
Rev[s.] Christ[s.] Atkinson, A.M.
per XXXVII Annos
Scholæ Vacfeldiensis Magister,
et per XXI Ecclesiæ ejusdem
Concionator pomeridianus;
et
Elizabetha, Uxor.
Quam boni; dicant Vicini laudantes,
Quam chari; Cognati desiderantes,
Quam pii : Liberi lugentes.
Hoc pietatis et mæroris pignus
P
Richardus Atkinson.

Ille obiit { Kal. Jan[ii.] A. D. 1795.
{ A° Ætatis, 63.

Hæc obiit { 9no Die Maii A. D. 1771.
{ A° Ætatis 40.

To make this record of Mr. Atkinson's age at his death agree with that given in the extract referring to his matriculation, we must suppose that he was only in his 18th year at matriculation, but fully 63 years old when he died.

(1) See Walker, p. 257.

GRAMMAR SCHOOL. 143

I find from the Wakefield Parish Registers that he had a son Christopher, who was baptized on Jan. 2, 1761, and buried on the following March 9 : and a son Richard, baptised on Feb. 24, 1763, educated at the School, and sent to the University with an Exhibition under Stories' Gift: he put up the tombstone above referred to. Another son, William Camplain, was baptised on Oct. 2, 1767 ; and a daughter Elizabeth, was buried on May 2, 1771, only ten days before her mother.

The following was the Advertisement inserted in "The Leeds Intelligencer" on Jan. 17, 1795, and in other papers, for a successor to Mr. Atkinson :—

> Wanted, a Master for the Free Grammar School at Wakefield.
>
> The Free Grammar School of Queen Elizabeth at Wakefield in the County of York being now vacant by the Decease of the Rev. Christopher Atkinson, M.A., the late Master ; the Governors of the said School do hereby give Notice that they will meet at the Cross Chamber in Wakefield on Saturday the 7th day of February next, by 8 o'clock in the morning, to elect a new Master. And the Candidates are desired to send sufficient Testimonials of their Abilities, Diligence and Sobriety to Mr. Smalpage, Attorney at Law, in Wakefield, as Agent to the said Governors, on or before the 28th of January inst., it being the unanimous Resolution of the Governors to make choice of such a person as shall appear to them to be in all respects the best qualified for so important a trust.
>
> The Master must be thus qualified. He must have taken the Degree of Master of Arts either in the University of Cambridge or Oxford : be well reported of for knowledge, religion and life, but not called to a pastoral charge, or hired to serve as a preacher, Minister or Curate in the Church.
>
> The Salary is £80 per annum, besides the benefit of a Dwelling house in a good State of Repair, and large enough for the Accommodation of Boarders, with suitable out-offices, Stable, Garden, Orchard, and other conveniences adjoining. The Master is entitled to the pay for teaching all Boys not belonging to the Town and Parish of Wakefield, and is provided with an Usher, whose Salary is wholly paid by the Governors.

16. THE REV. THOMAS ROGERS, M.A.

The life of this Master has been written by his son, the Rev. Charles Rogers, M.A. (Vicar of Sowerby Bridge 1829 to 1863) ; and from it we learn that he was born at Swillington, near Leeds, on Feb. 19, 1760, the youngest son of the Rev. John Rogers, Vicar of Sherburn and Fenton, and was descended from the Rev. John Rogers, once Dean of St. Paul's. In the year 1777 he was sent to Leeds Grammar School, of which the Rev. Samuel Brooke, M.A. was then Head Master, and from thence he proceeded, in 1779, to Cambridge, matriculating at Magdalene College, and taking his B.A. degree in 1783 as 8th Senior Optime, and his M.A. in 1791.

He was ordained Deacon on Trinity Sunday, 1783, and licensed Curate of Norton cum Galby in Leicestershire. His first sermon was preached for the Rev. Thomas Robinson, once a Wakefield Grammar School boy, and then Vicar of St. Mary's, Leicester, well known as the author of "Scripture Characters." He then worked for a short time at Kirkthorpe, near Wakefield, and subsequently became Curate at St. Mary's, Leicester, under the Rev. Thomas Robinson.

He was appointed to the Head Mastership of Wakefield Grammar School in 1795 :—

> 1795. Feb. 6. "The 4th Chapter of the Statutes relating to the Election of the Master, being in the first place read unto the said Governors, and They, having severally taken the oath in the said 4th Chapter expressed, according to the Direction of the said Statute, did duly and unanimously elect The Rev. Thomas Rogers, of Leicester, Clerk, M.A., Master of the School, and thereupon his appointment was made out under the Common Seal of the Corporation of the Governors."

There is no doubt that Mr. Rogers' previous residence and work at Kirkthorpe, and the recommendation of the Rev. Thos. Robinson, had told in his favour with the Governors, when the time of election came. For not only was his election unanimous, but a resolution was passed in December of the same year, allowing him to accept the post of "Lecturer in S. John's Church, Wakefield, on Sundays in the afternoon for one year certain, and afterwards until that privilege be revoked by the Governors, unless in the meantime he be nominated to the Lectureship of the Parish Church of Wakefield." This resolution was made "in consequence of the Rev. Thomas Rogers, the Schoolmaster's good character, apparent conduct, and abilities as a Preacher."

The biographer describes Wakefield as having been, at this time, full of infidels; and the work which Mr. Rogers undertook, both at S. John's Church and at the Parish Church, is described by him, and by Mr. Walker (Cath. Ch. p. 187). The Evening Lectureship at the latter Church owes its origin to the classes which Mr. Rogers held there, and he was appointed the first Lecturer when the endowment was obtained, in the year 1801. Notwithstanding the resolution referred to in the previous paragraph, he seems to have held the Lectureship at S. John's Church with that at the Parish Church until 1807, when he resigned the former : he continued to hold the latter until his death on Feb. 13, 1832.

Mr. Rogers is entitled to the credit of having formulated a plan of general education, much in advance of the times, in the year 1799. It has been previously remarked that in many Schools Greek and Latin were the only subjects of instruction until the recent legislation of the Endowed Schools Acts, and though in other Schools an attempt was made to go beyond the letter of the Charter or Statutes by which they were governed, the decision of Lord Eldon in the case of Leeds Grammar School paralysed many an effort to enlarge the scope of the education of the day. But in Wakefield School it seems that an attempt was made as early as 1750 to introduce a more liberal programme of studies: for instance, the Rev. John Clarke engaged a French Master in 1752, and from that time forward non-classical studies obtained more or less recognition in the School, there being always a Mathematical Master in addition to the Head Master and Usher, though he was only dignified by the name of the Writing Master.

The Rev. Thomas Rogers resigned the Headmastership on Apl. 21, 1814, on account of the precarious state of his health; his biographer asserts that the large and cold school-room was the cause, for no means were taken in those days to warm it by stoves or fireplaces. He became "the ill-remunerated Chaplain" of the Wakefield House of Correction in 1817, and died on Feb. 13, 1832, aged 71. There is a monument to him in the South Nave Aisle in the Cathedral:—

In memory
of
THE REVEREND THOMAS ROGERS, A.M.
Formerly of Magdalene College, Cambridge,
and
Thirty one years
Sunday Evening Lecturer in this Church,
Who died the 13th day of February
1832
Aged 71 years.

This Monument
was erected by public subscription,
As a tribute of respect
For his character,
and
a record
of his long and pious labours.

A large number of private pupils was trained by Mr. Rogers, over 50 of whom he prepared for the Church, and his work in this respect is spoken of in terms of high praise. He is also said to have been a popular preacher of the greatest ability, and a man of the most religious character. His manner in School has been described by an old pupil as dignified and commanding, and his rule as combining strictness with kindness.

Mr. Rogers married Elizabeth, daughter of Robert Long, Esq., of Norton, Leicestershire in 1785; she died on Dec. 7, 1803, leaving him with six children.

In the year 1802, Mr. Rogers published "A Course of Lectures" upon the Service for Morning Prayer, as contained in the Liturgy of the Church of England: a second course was published upon the Litany, three years later: he also drew up a collection of Family Prayers.

17. REV. MARTIN JOSEPH NAYLOR, D.D.

Was born at Batley Carr, near Dewsbury in 1763 or 1764, and educated at Queens' College, Cambridge, where he was 3rd Wrangler in 1787, and shortly afterwards elected Fellow of his College, subsequently engaging in tuition there, and filling various offices, including that of Proctor to the University: he proceeded to the M.A. degree in 1790, became B.D. in 1799, and D.D. in 1828.

He came to Wakefield in 1795, on being appointed to the Afternoon or Cambden Lectureship at the Parish Church, and held this post for no lesss than 45 years. He was elected Head Master of the Grammar School on May 19, 1814, took his oath on the following Sep. 30, and retained the position until Mar. 11, 1837, when he announced his intention of resigning at the coming Midsummer holidays. He had, in the preceding month, been presented by Lord Holland to the Rectory of Crofton, which he held until his death, which took place on Nov. 21, 1843. Dr. Naylor had also held the living of Penistone from about 1810 to his death. He was moreover Chaplain to the West Riding Lunatic Asylum, Provincial Grand Chaplain, and for more than 30 years editor of the "Wakefield Journal."

During this busy and long life Dr. Naylor earned no little reputation as a man of great ability and sound scholarship, and was especially conspicious in conversational powers and in the execution of social duties in general. A curious appreciation of his talent was

GRAMMAR SCHOOL.

shown in the year 1831, when the Trustees of Batley Grammar School invited him, assisted by Mr. R. Hall, M.A., of Leeds, Barrister, to examine candidates for the Headmastership then vacant [1] : when they reported that two gentlemen, Mr. Senior and Mr. Richardson, were practically equal, the question was decided by the Trustees drawing lots; four were drawn for the former, two for the latter, and Mr. Senior was consequently appointed.

Dr. Naylor's period of office at the Grammar School appears to have passed without any unusual events. He seems to have been the first Master who considered it necessary to record the names of his pupils at the School, and there still exist two copies of the Register drawn up by him, under rules prescribed by the Governors, of all the boys admitted from July 1814, when he commenced his duties, until his resignation in 1837: the names of a few are prefixed who were in the School when he came, and the Register has been continued to the present time : see Chapter IX.

Dr. Naylor's memory is perpetuated by a brass in the Cathedral, on the north side of the chancel, which contains the following words :—

In Memory of
Martin Joseph Naylor, D: D:
Rector of Crofton—and
forty five years Afternoon
Lecturer of this Church,
formerly Fellow of Queen's
College Cambridge, and
Head Master of Wakefield
Grammar School. He
died November 21: 1843
aged 80 years.

Also of Rebecca his
wife who died June 11
1822 aged 55 years.

One of the painted windows in the south aisle was inserted in memory of the Rev. Samuel Sharp, for 44 years Vicar of Wakefield, and the Rev. Martin Joseph Naylor, D.D. by Mr. William Stewart, a parishioner and pupil, in the year 1873 during the restoration of the Church.

The Council of the Wakefield Mechanics' Institution have very kindly given me permission to reproduce by photography the portrait of Dr. Naylor from an oil painting which they have in their possession.

(1) Yorkshire Notes and Queries I. 37.

Dr. Naylor was the author of "A Series of Discourses principally on the Evidences of Christianity," dedicated to Dr. Thomas Zouch, and published in London by Longmans in 1810. He left a son Martin Edward, who practised for a long time as a veterinary surgeon in Wakefield, and was buried at Crofton Church in Nov. 1886, having died in his 84th year. A daughter of Dr. Naylor is now resident at Carlisle.

18. REV. JOHN CARTER, D.D.

The Rev. John Carter was born in 1800, educated at Bingley Grammar School under Dr. Hartley; matriculated at St. John's College, Cambridge, in 1820, and took his first degree in 1824. He became M.A. in 1827, and D.D. "per saltum" in 1840. Immediately after leaving Cambridge he was ordained, Deacon in 1825, and Priest in 1826, by the Archbishop of York, who licensed him to the Curacy of Aberford, which he held from 1825 to 1831. In the next year he was made Vicar of Saxton, the neighbouring parish to Aberford, and held this living 46 years; he died there on Nov. 9, 1878.

He was elected Head Master of Wakefield Grammar School on Apl. 8, 1837, being at the time Vicar of Saxton: upon which he engaged a Curate to perform most of his duties at Saxton, while he himself travelled thither usually at the end of each week, when his School duties were over.

On coming to Wakefield, Mr. Carter at first lived in Westgate; but, after the lapse of a year, he occupied the usual Master's house in Almshouse Lane, where he received a number of private pupils not attending the Grammar School, in the same way as the Rev. Thomas Rogers had previously done.

The efforts which he made to secure the removal of the School from the old buildings to a more desirable site, have been described in a previous chapter; as also have the negociations for the amalgamation of the Proprietary School and the Grammar School, with which question we may suppose that Dr. Carter had something to do.

Having already a Parish under his charge before coming to Wakefield, Dr. Carter could not accept any of the appointments in connection with the Church at Wakefield, which have been held

Dʀ Naylor.
1814-1857.

Dʀ Carter.
1857-1847.

Dʀ Taylor.
1847-1875.

Mʀ Leighton.
1875-1885.

Mʀ Peacock.
1885—

HEAD MASTERS FROM 1814 TO 1891.

by his predecessors and his successor: but he often officiated in the services there, and bade farewell to his friends from the Parish Church pulpit on Tuesday evening, July 6, 1847, shortly after resigning his Headmastership.

On Feb. 10, 1847, Dr. Carter announced his intention of resigning his duties at the Grammar School at the end of the Midsummer Term, and after leaving Wakefield, spent the remaining 31 years of his life at Saxton.

Dr. Carter's portrait is provided for me by the kindness of his son, the Rev. James Henry Carter, M.A., of Weaste Parsonage, near Manchester: another son, the Rev. John Carter, M.A., resides at Raughton Head, near Carlisle.

19. THE REV. JAMES TAYLOR, D.D.

On July 30, 1847, after the usual formalities of reading the Statute, and administering the oath, the Governors of the School elected the Rev. James Taylor, M.A. of Trinity College, Cambridge, to the vacant Headmastership.

He was born at Dublin in 1810, was appointed Assistant Master at the King's School, Sherborne, Dorset, in 1834, and remained there three years under Dr. Lyon, formerly Fellow of Trinity College, Cambridge, who was then Head Master. In 1837 he opened a private School in Bristol. In Oct. 1839 he matriculated at Trinity College, Cambridge, and was a Junior Optime in the Mathematical Tripos in 1843. He took his M.A. degree in 1846 : he afterwards became B.D. in 1866, and D.D. in 1871.

Mr. Taylor was appointed Master of Kimbolton Grammar School, and ordained Deacon by the Bishop of Peterborough as Curate of Higham Ferrars in 1843, and Priest in the following year. At the time of his election as Head Master of this School, he was holding a temporary appointment at Queen's College, Birmingham.

While at Wakefield, he held the post of Sunday Evening or Jane Lecturer, first at the Parish Church, and then at S. Andrew's. He was also, for a long time, Clerical Secretary of the Church Institution.

To him the School is very greatly indebted for the acquisition of the present buildings under such favourable terms as were secured at the time of its purchase. It has been already pointed out that, with the assistance of Mr. Wm. Stewart, he secured a large number of shares in the West Riding Proprietary School as presents, and many more by purchase, as he himself explained in the columns of the Wakefield Journal in December, 1857; the consequence was that the real cost of the premises was considerably less than the nominal price bid for them by auction.

The names of his pupils, printed in Chapter IX, and the particulars of their successes, as given in the same Chapter and in the preceding one, will be sufficient evidence of the character of his work. He resigned his duties in June, 1875.

Dr. Taylor is still living, and has had a family of three sons, viz.:—James Heber, Henry Martin, William Wilberforce, all of whom have obtained very high distinction at the Universities; and a daughter who married the Rev. Thomas James Sanderson, M.A., now Rector of Brington, Huntingdonshire.

He has published several pamphlets, including "An Appeal to the Archbishop of York on the Heresies of Archdeacon Wilberforce," 1854; "A Remonstrance to the Archbishops and Bishops of the United Church of England and Ireland," 1855; "The True Doctrine of the Holy Eucharist, in reply to Archdeacon Wilberforce and Romish Views in general," 1855; and "A Summary of Evidence on the Existence of a Deity," 1855. (Crockford's Cler. Dir.)

I am able to insert his portrait by his own kindness: it is taken from a photograph by Messrs. G. and J. Hall, of this City.

20. ROBERT LEIGHTON LEIGHTON, M.A.

Was born in December, 1847, at Broughton, near Manchester, the eldest son of the Rev. J. L. Leighton (Figgins) late Rector of Blackley, near Manchester. He was educated at Manchester Grammar School from 1859 to 1866, and afterwards became an Exhibitioner of Balliol College, Oxford, where he matriculated on Oct. 21, 1867. He obtained a First Class in Classical Moderations in Trinity Term, 1869, and a First Class in Literis Humanioribus in Michaelmas Term, 1871. He took the B.A. degree in 1872, and the M.A. in 1875. He was an Assistant Master at Cheltenham College from May 1873, to September 1875, during the greater part of which time he was the First Classical Master.

On Sept. 11, 1875, Mr. Leighton was elected Head Master of Wakefield Grammar School under the new Scheme of the Charity Commissioners, and remained until July 1883, when he was appointed Head Master of Bristol Grammar School, which post he still holds.

The work of carrying out the provisions of the 1875 Scheme, which almost involved the creation of a new School, fell to Mr. Leighton's lot, and under his administration the number of boys in attendance rose from 26 in Michaelmas Term 1875, when he commenced his duties, to 125 in Lent Term 1880. Mr. Leighton was on the Governing body of the Yorkshire College as the representative of his School for several years. In 1876 he married one of the daughters of Dr. T. G. Wright, one of the Governors of the School.

His portrait is taken from a photograph by Mr. W. Gothard of Wakefield, which he has lent me for the purpose of reproducing it here.

21. MATTHEW HENRY PEACOCK, M.A., B. Mus.

The present Head Master was born at Leeds in May 1856, and is the eldest son of Matthew Peacock, of Leeds, merchant. He attended the Leeds Grammar School under the Rev. Dr. Henderson, the present Dean of Carlisle, from 1866 to 1876; and after winning the annual School Exhibition to the University, matriculated at Exeter College, Oxford, on Oct. 14, 1876. He had obtained an Open Classical Exhibition at Wadham College in the previous December, which he resigned, and an Open Classical Scholarship at Exeter College in January, 1876, which he held from that year until 1881. He was placed in the First Class in Classical Moderations in Trinity Term 1878, and in the Second Class in Literis Humanioribus in the corresponding term two years later. After remaining a year at Oxford as a private Tutor, he was appointed Senior Classical Master at Bradford Grammar School, where he was engaged from September 1881 to August 1883. He took the B.A. degree in 1880, the M.A. in 1883, and the B. Mus. in 1889.

His election to the Head Mastership of Wakefield Grammar School took place on Sep. 10, 1883, and the highest number of boys in attendance since that time was reached in Midsummer Term 1887, when there were 150 names upon the books. Like his predecessor, Mr. Peacock has been for several years a Representative Governor of the Yorkshire College: and since Feb. 1887 he has also undertaken the duties of Honorary Choirmaster at Wakefield Cathedral.

His portrait is from a photograph by Messrs G. and J. Hall, of Wakefield, who have also undertaken the responsibility of reproducing all the other illustrations of this work.

THE USHERS AND ASSISTANT MASTERS.

The qualifications of the Usher or underteacher are given in the sixth Statute (p. 67): he was to be "a man truelie fearinge God, learned in good sorte, formerly knowne to have bene painefull in teachinge of youth, att the least painfull and industrious in his owne studies, moderate in his cariadge, no minister with pastorall charge nor stipendarie preacher, nor reader in the church, save in the church at Wakefield and that not without expresse licence." His duties are also laid down in the same Statute.

The conditions under which his work in the School were done rendered it inevitable, in Wakefield as in other places, that a collision between the Head Master and Usher should sometimes take place. For, as the Endowed Schools Commissioners pointed out in their 1868 report[1], these Masters really conducted two separate Schools under the same roof, being responsible only to the Governing Body, and almost independent of each other. The first evidence of this state of affairs being felt, or foreseen, at Wakefield, was on the appointment of the Rev. John Clarke to the Headmastership in 1751, when the Usher and other Assistant Masters were made subordinate to him by special resolution of the Governors, the Statutes or anything else to the contrary notwithstanding. The same arrangement seems to have been more or less followed as long as the office of Usher lasted. the latter being appointed by the Governors on the recommendation, or with the approval, of the Head Master, and paid by them, but entirely subject to the control of the Head Master in all his School duties.

The first election of an Usher of Wakefield Grammar School, which is recorded in the Governors' Books, was made on Oct. 17, 1621: but there is no ground to suppose that Mr. James Lister, who was then elected, was the first Usher. For it has already been said that there is reason to believe that one was engaged under the Rev. John Beaumont in 1602 or 1603: and the minute, in which Mr. Lister's election is mentioned, contains no expression which leads to the supposition that he was the first Usher. Moreover, considering

---

[1] S. I. C. Report 1868, Vol. i, p. 237-8. "If a grammar school," says Mr. Fitch, "becomes large enough or rich enougi. to have a second master, it is cut boldly into two .... Many a school has two masters, but they generally sit in separate rooms and work quite independently."........"If the master has not the appointment and control of his assistants, it is impossible to hold him responsible for the good conduct and teaching of the school."

that the minute in question is the first on the first page of the earliest Minute Book in existence, the loss of the names of previous Ushers need not be considered remarkable.

The following pages represent the result of an attempt to discover the names of all Ushers of the School, and to record some details about their previous and subsequent histories. In the latter part of this task I have been very kindly aided by the Rev. C. B. Norcliffe, of Langton Hall, Malton, and the Rev. R. V. Taylor, Rector of Melbecks, Richmond.

USHERS OF WAKEFIELD GRAMMAR SCHOOL.

1. Rev. JAMES LISTER, B.A., Clare Hall, Cambridge: elected and sworn Oct. 17, 1621: resigned Aug. 2, 1623. Probably son of Mr. Joseph Lister, Doctor of Physic at Wakefield about 1600: educated at the School; Cave Scholar. Married Susanna Mawde at Wakefield, June 28, 1638. Vicar of Wakefield from 1625 to 1647, when he was ejected: Vicar of Leathley from 1647 to 1660: again Vicar of Wakefield and Prebendary of York from 1660 to his death in January 1677-8.

2. JOHN WILCOCK, B.A., elected and sworn Sep. 1, 1623: resigned July, 1634.

3. JOHN WILBIE, M.A., elected July 19, 1634, sworn Nov. 12: resigned Aug. 1635.

4. RICHARD LEAKE, M.A., elected and sworn Oct. 12, 1635: resigned Sep. 1637.

5. BRIAN CARTMELL, B.A., Balliol College, Oxford: elected Nov. 1, 1637, sworn Dec. 22. Buried at Wakefield on Feb. 16, 1639-40.

6. Rev. TIMOTHY WOOD, B.A., elected Mar. 9, 1639-40, sworn Apl. 8: perhaps resigned about 1643. Vicar of Sandal Magna from 1650 to 1660, when he was ejected and imprisoned in York Castle: perhaps Vicar of Kirk Sandall, Doncaster, from 1664 to 1680. After leaving Sandal, lived in Leicestershire for some time, and died at Belgrave, near Leicester, in 1680, aged 63. Had a great reputation for universal ability.

7. HENRY DOUGHTY, son of the Head Master, was Usher for 2½ years in the Civil War, from 1646 to 1649: perhaps buried at Wakefield on Apl. 30, 1698.

8. Rev. JOHN COLLVER, B.A., sworn Mar. 20, 1649-50: M.A. in 1654. Married Mary Ellis at Wakefield on July 19, 1653: had a son John born Apl. 7, 1654, and a son Joseph baptized Sep. 9, 1655. Incumbent of Haworth from 1653 to 1654, and from 1663 to 1675, when he died, being buried on Oct. 10. (Turner's "Haworth," p. 38).

9. ROBERT MURGATROYD, elected and sworn, Nov. 11, 1656. Buried at Wakefield on May 16, 1667.

10. WILLIAM SHELMERDINE, M.A., of Buxton, elected June 8, 1667, sworn July 3. Married Ellen Kirk at Wakefield on Nov. 29, 1674, who was buried there on May 18, 1684. Buried at Wakefield, Oct. 19, 1680.

11. .... LAWSON, ceased his duties at Midsummer, 1699 [1].

12. Rev. THOMAS CLARK, M.A., Jesus College, Cambridge; elected about January 1699; resigned on being appointed Head Master, Apl. 16, 1703. (See pp. 132-5 and 164-5 for further particulars.)

13. Rev. JOHN PALEY, B.A., Christ's College, Cambridge; elected in April or May, 1703; resigned about Christmas 1705: B.A. in 1701, M.A. in 1709. Curate of Wakefield from 1705 to 1717: Incumbent of Hunslet, near Leeds, from 1717 to 1731. Married Ann Spink at Wakefield on Aug. 22, 1717.

14. Rev. WILLIAM BURROW, M.A., St. John's College, Cambridge; elected about January 1705-6; resigned about Easter 1711. Son of Richard Burrow, of Wakefield: educated at the School: Storie Exhibitioner: B.A. in 1705, M.A. in 1709. Incumbent of Hunslet, near Leeds, from 1731 to 1741.

15. Rev. SAMUEL DRANSFIELD, B.A., St. John's College, Cambridge; elected about Easter 1711; resigned about September 1717. Son of Francis Dransfield, of Wakefield: baptized Oct. 10, 1687: educated at the School: Storie Exhibitioner: B.A. in 1710. Elected Vicar of Hooton Pagnell, Nov. 29, 1723, licensed Jan. 1, 1723-4, died in possession in 1754.

16. Rev. BENJAMIN WILSON, B.A., Fellow of Trinity College, Cambridge; elected about October 1717; resigned on being appointed Head Master about Easter 1720. (See pp. 135-6 for further particulars.)

17. Rev. RICHARD STRINGER, B.A., Trinity College, Cambridge; elected about Easter 1720; resigned about September 1723. Son of Richard Stringer, of Wakefield; baptized May 16, 1698: educated

---

(1) Probably there were other Ushers between Mr. Shelmerdine and Mr. Lawson, but in the absence of Minute Books their names have been lost.

GRAMMAR SCHOOL.   155

at the School : Storie Exhibitioner : B.A. in 1719. Head Master of Hemsworth Grammar School from 1749 to 1786, when he died.

18. Rev. THOMAS MURGATROYD, B.A., Fellow of Trinity College, Cambridge, elected about October 1723; resigned Sep. 15, 1727. Probably educated at the School: B.A. in 1722, M.A. in 1726. Curate of Kirkleatham from 1727 to 1732 : Rector of Lofthouse in Cleveland from 1732 to 1780 : and perhaps also of Kirkby in Cleveland from 1749 to 1780, when he died.

19. Rev. JOHN CLARKE, B.A., Fellow of Trinity College, Cambridge; elected Sep. 30, 1727, sworn Oct. 16; resigned Sep. 30, 1729. Educated at the School, and elected Head Master in 1751. (See pp. 136 to 141 for further particulars.)

20. Rev. JOHN HOLMES, B.A., Balliol College, Oxford ; elected Oct. 16, 1729, sworn Dec. 1 ; resigned Oct. 9, 1735. Son of Robert Holmes, of Kildwick ; matriculated Apl. 3, 1723, aged 18; B.A. in 1726. Vicar of Kirk Sandall, Doncaster, from 1748 to 1762, when he died. (Foster's Alumni Oxonienses.)

21. RICHARD HARRISON, B.A., Clare Hall, Cambridge; elected Oct. 20, 1735, sworn Apl. 12, 1736 ; resigned Dec. 22, 1737. Son of William Harrison, of Wakefield, baptized Feb. 12, 1712-3 : educated at the School : Cave Scholar : Storie Exhibitioner : B.A. in 1735.

22. Rev. RICHARD HARTLEY, B.A., Trinity College, Cambridge; elected Feb. 6, 1737-8, sworn Feb. 16 ; resigned in December 1739: B.A. in 1737. Son of William Hartley, Eldwick Hall, Bingley, born Sep. 5, 1714. Vicar of Bingley from Jan. 2, 1740-1 to Apl. 20, 1789, when he died, aged 75. Married (1) Ann, daughter of John Perkins, M.D., of Netherton, near Wakefield ; (2) Martha, daughter of the Rev. Thomas Hudson, B.A., Head Master of Bingley Grammar School. His son Richard was 6th Wrangler, Vicar of Bingley, and Head Master of Bingley Grammar School. (Whitaker's Craven p. 194, &c.)

23. JOHN GARLICK, M.A., Fellow of Clare Hall, Cambridge; elected Feb. 7, 1740-1 ; resigned Apl. 22, 1751. Son of James Garlick, of Wakefield : baptized Oct. 14, 1719 : educated at the School : Cave Scholar : Storie Exhibitioner : B.A. in 1740, M.A. in 1744. Perhaps the clergyman of that name who was about 1770 living at Stanley, and made a topographical collection of local interest and importance.

24. Rev. HENRY WILSON, M.A., Fellow of Trinity College, Cambridge; elected May 11, 1751, sworn June 19 : resigned about

Christmas 1756. Son of Henry Wilson of Kilham, Yorks. B.A. in 1742, M.A. in 1746. Usher of Beverley School before 1751. Vicar of Otley from 1761 to 1781, when he died.

25. JAMES HORRAX, B.A., Fellow of Trinity College, Cambridge, elected Feb. 2, 1756-7. Probably a Wakefield man and educated at the School : 6th Wrangler in 1755 : M.A. in 1758.

26. DIXON REDDALL, B.A., St. John's College, Cambridge: was Usher in 1758. Was 12th Junior Optime in 1756, M.A. in 1759.

27. .... BROCKLEBANK was Usher in 1763.

28. Rev. WILLIAM BROWN, M.A., Clare Hall, Cambridge : elected Jan. 5, 1771[1]; resigned in August, 1795 : B.A. in 1760, M.A. in 1763. Vicar of Hooton Pagnell from 1816 (elected Sep. 30) to Jan. 18, 1823, when he died. Perhaps Vicar of Sandal Magna from Oct. 1793 to 1818.

29. RICHARD SNAPE, B.A., Magdalene College, Cambridge: elected in August, 1795, resigned about Christmas 1796[2]. Was 8th Junior Optime in 1793.

30. WILLIAM SHACKLETON, elected Jan. 26, 1805 ; resigned Aug. 21, 1807. Was previously an Assistant Master at Heath Grammar School, Halifax, under Mr. Wilkinson, who was Head Master there from 1789 to 1839.

31. Rev. FRANCIS RAWLING, of Easingwold, was offered the Ushership on Nov. 2, 1807.

32. .... MEADE, elected July 27, 1814, a temporary appointment.

33. Rev. JOSEPH LAWSON SISSON, M.A., Clare Hall, Cambridge ; elected Sep. 30, 1814, sworn Aug. 14, 1815 ; resigned July 3, 1834. Educated at Leeds Grammar School: B.A. in 1810, M.A. in 1814, D.D. in 1827. Sunday Evening Reader at Wakefield Parish Church. Author of the " Historic Sketch " of the same Church and other works. Curate of Duntsbourn Abbotts, Cirencester, from 1834 to 1843 : Perpetual Curate of Coleford near Newland, in the diocese of Gloucester and Bristol, from 1843 to his death in May 1886, aged 80. (Lupton's W.W. p. 233.)

34. RICHARD SNOWDEN, B.A., of Queen's College, Oxford ; elected Aug. 11, 1834 ; resigned Oct. 3, 1835. Son of the Rev. W. Snowden, of Doncaster. Matriculated at Oxford July 6, 1829, aged 18. Hastings Exhibitioner. Educated at the School. B.A. in 1834.

(1) Mr. Brown's name appears as Usher in the year from Sep. 1769 to Sep. 1770, but he was not formally elected until this day.

(2) There appears to have been no Usher from this time to the election of Mr. Shackleton.

35. O. C. SIM, elected Sep. 21, 1835; resigned Feb. 24, 1840.

36. WILLIAM ALLISON, elected Apl. 6, 1840; resigned Mar. 1, 1855. Died at Wakefield in December 1861.

37. Rev. THOMAS WADE, M.A., Exeter College, Oxford; elected Aug. 7, 1855; resigned Jan. 6, 1857. Eldest son of Richard Wade, of Marylebone, London; matriculated June 4, 1846, aged 18: B.A. in 1850, 2nd Class in Literis Humanioribus, and 3rd Class in Mathematics: ordained Deacon and Priest in 1853 by the Bishop of Manchester: Assistant Master of Marlborough College: M.A. in 1853: Senior Curate at St. Andrew's, Wells St., London from 1863 to 1869: now of Albany House, Caterham, Surrey. (Crockford's Cler. Dir. Foster's Al. Ox.)

38. JOHN SAMUEL LILLISTONE, B.A., Jesus College, Cambridge; elected Feb. 23, 1857: resigned Feb. 5, 1858: Scholar of his College, 1st Class Classical Tripos 1855, M.A. in 1858: Fellow of his College from 1861 to 1869. Ordained Deacon and Priest in 1861 by the Bishop of Ely: buried in Willesden Parish Church in 1889. (Crockford's Cler. Dir.)

39. JOSEPH HIRST LUPTON, B.A., Fellow of St. John's College, Cambridge: elected Apl. 27, 1858; resigned Apl. 5, 1859. Son of Joseph Lupton (Master of the Greencoat School, Wakefield, from Feb. 19, 1827 to Apl. 5, 1859, when he resigned). Educated at the School, and at Giggleswick School: Storie Exhibitioner: Scholar of St. John's College, Cambridge: 5th Classic and Members' Prizeman, 1858: Fellow of his College from 1860 to 1863: M.A. in 1861. Ordained Deacon in 1859 and Priest in 1860 by the Bishop of London. Second Classical Master of the City of London School, and Curate of S. Paul's, Hampstead, from 1859 to 1864: Sur-Master of S. Paul's School, London, from 1864 to the present time: Curate of S. Matthew's, Friday St., London, from 1868 to 1879: Hulsean Lecturer at Cambridge in 1887: Preacher at Gray's Inn, 1890. Author of "Wakefield Worthies," 1864; "Life of Dean Colet," 1887: contributor to the "Speaker's Commentary." (Crockford's Cler. Dir.)

40. JOHN LANGHORNE, B.A., Christ's College, Cambridge: elected Apl. 12, 1859; resigned Mar. 27, 1860. Scholar of his College, 1st Class Classical Tripos, 1859; M.A. in 1862. Ordained Deacon in 1862 and Priest in 1864 by the Archbishop of Canterbury. Assistant Classical Master at Tonbridge School from 1861 to 1877: Curate of Tudeley, Kent, from 1871 to 1877. Head Master of King's School, Rochester, from 1877 to the present time. (Crockford's Cler. Dir.)

41. JOHN COOPER WOOD, B.A., St. John's College, Cambridge : elected May 18, 1860 ; resigned Sept. 30, 1862. Scholar of his College, 2nd Class Classical Tripos, 1860 ; M.A. in 1863. Ordained Deacon in 1861, and Priest in 1862 by the Bishop of Ripon : Curate of S. John's, Wakefield, 1861—1862 ; Head Master of Prescot Grammar School in 1863, and of Halesowen Grammar School from 1863 to 1866. Rector of S. Kenelm in Romsley, Worcestershire, from 1867 to 1872 ; Vicar of Grinshill, Salop, 1872—1873 : Vicar of the Clive, Shrewsbury, from 1873 to the present time. (Crockford's Cler. Dir.)

42. RICHARD FRANCIS WOODWARD, B.A., Trinity College, Cambridge : elected May 26, 1863 ; resigned Feb. 11, 1864. 2nd Class Classical Tripos in 1862.

43. Rev. JOHN ADDISON RUSSELL WASHBOURN, B.A., Pembroke College, Oxford : elected Apl. 7, 1864 : resigned Dec. 7, 1865. Fourth son of William Washbourn, of Gloucester ; matriculated June 23, 1859, aged 17 : Scholar of his College ; 2nd Class Classical Moderations 1861, 2nd Class in Literis Humanioribus, and Hon. 4th Class in Mathematics in 1863, M.A. in 1866. Ordained Deacon in 1864 and Priest in 1865 by the Bishop of Ripon. Curate of St. Mary's, Wakefield, 1864—1865 ; Assistant Master at St. John's College, Hurstpierpoint, from 1866 to 1873 ; Senior Assistant Master at Bromsgrove School, 1873—1874 : Assistant Master at Rossall School, 1874—1875 ; Head Master, Collegiate School, Gloucester from 1875 to 1886. Rector of Rudford, Gloucester, from 1885 to the present time. (Crockford's Cler. Dir. and Foster's Al. Ox.)

The office of Usher was abolished, by order of the Charity Commissioners, dated Dec. 22, 1865.

ASSISTANT MASTERS AT WAKEFIELD GRAMMAR SCHOOL.

The following list contains the names of all the Assistant Masters which have come under my notice, but it is not to be expected that there are no omissions. It is not, however, likely that any appointments in recent years have been lost sight of.

1. CHARLES ZOUCH, B.A., Trinity College, Cambridge, Assistant in 1717 ; B.A. in 1714, M.A. in 1718 : Vicar of Sandal Magna from 1718 to 1754 : died July 27, 1754, and buried at Sandal.

GRAMMAR SCHOOL.

2. JOHN SKELTON, B.A., Clare Hall, Cambridge; Assistant in 1751. Educated at the School: Cave Scholar: Storie Exhibitioner: Junior Optime in 1750.

3. DAVID QUENEDY, M.A., French Master in 1752.

4. MR. GARGRAVE, Writing Master [1] in 1758.

5. MR. WOOD, Writing Master, resigned in 1795.

6. WILLIAM PHILLIPS, Writing Master, appointed May 19, 1814: resigned at Christmas, 1819.

7. JOHN WATERALL, Writing Master, appointed Jan. 12, 1820.

8. JOSEPH RICHARD ATHA, Writing Master, appointed Nov. 20, 1826.

9. E. PILLING, Writing Master, appointed Jan. 6, 1834: resigned Feb. 2, 1835 [2].

10. MR. TOOTAL, Drawing Master in 1855.

11. JULIEN GOLDSTEIN, French Master in 1855.

12. KARL DAMMANN, German Master in 1855.

13. W. B. JONES, Drawing Master in 1857.

14. M. FIERVILLE, French Master in 1857.

15. E. E. DENYER, Drawing Master in 1859.

16. WILLIAM BICKERSTAFF, B.A., Trinity College, Dublin: Third Master from 1861 to 1871: B.A. in 1866, M.A. in 1872. Ordained Deacon in 1868, and Priest in 1870 by the Bishop of Ripon. Curate of St. Andrew's, Wakefield, 1868-71: Curate of Chapelthorpe, 1871-5: Curate of Pateley Bridge, 1875-81: Vicar of Marr, Doncaster, 1881 to the present time. (Crockford's Cler. Dir.)

17. Rev. BRIAN CHRISTOPHERSON, B.A., St. John's College, Cambridge: Mathematical Master 1863—4: B.A. 1862, M.A. 1865: ordained Deacon in 1863, and Priest in 1864, by the Bishop of Ripon. Curate of Thornes, 1863—4: Head Master of Batley Grammar School, 1864—9: of Moulton Grammar School, Lincs., 1869—73; and of the Royal Grammar School, Newcastle-on-Tyne, 1873—83. Rector of Falmouth, 1882 to the present time. (Crockford's Cler. Dir.)

18. WILLIAM LEVESON GOWER MORGAN, Dublin University: Assistant Master from August to December 1863.

19. ARTHUR JONATHAN EDMONDS, B.A., Clare College, Cambridge: Second Master from January to June 1866. Scholar of his College, 3rd Class Classical Tripos, 1866, M.A. in 1869. Ordained Deacon in 1871 and Priest in 1872 by the Bishop of Gloucester and Bristol. Curate of Stroud, Gloucester, 1871—7: Curate of Weston-

---

(1) The Writing Master also taught Mathematics. (2) At that time the Writing Mastership was abolished, and the duties given to the Usher and Assistant Masters.

Super-Mare, 1879—84 : Vicar of Great Gransden, St. Neots, 1884 to the present time. (Crockford's Cler. Dir.)

20. Rev. THOMAS JAMES SANDERSON, B.A., Fellow of Clare College, Cambridge: Second Master from June 17, 1866 to Jan. 1, 1868. Educated at the School, Cave Scholar, Storie Exhibitioner, Foundation Scholar; Goldsmiths' Exhibitioner : 19th Wrangler in 1866, M.A. in 1869. Ordained Deacon and Priest in 1867 by the Bishop of Ely. Vicar of Litlington, Cambridgeshire, 1867—83 : Rector of Brington, Kimbolton, 1883 to the present time. (Crockford's Cler. Dir.)

21. JOHN HENRY LESTER, B.A., St. John's College, Cambridge: Second Master from Jan. 22 to Christmas, 1868. Was 38th Wrangler in 1868, M.A. in 1871. Ordained Deacon in 1868 by the Bishop of Ripon, and Priest in 1870 by the Bishop of Exeter. Second Master at Crediton Grammar School, 1869—72 ; Curate of St. James, Litchurch, Derby, 1872—5 ; Curate of Normanton, Derby, 1875—7 : Perpetual Curate of Normanton, 1877—80 : Lichfield Diocesan Missioner, 1880—5 : Chaplain to the Bishop of Lichfield, 1885 : Prebendary of Whittington in Lichfield Cathedral, 1884 : Rector of South Hackney, 1885 to the present time. (Crockford's Cler. Dir.)

22. HENRY WILKINSON BULL, B.A., Corpus Christi College, Cambridge : Second Master from Feb. 18, 1869 to June 26, 1872. Scholar of his College, 17th Senior Optime in 1869, M.A. in 1872. Ordained Deacon in 1870, and Priest in 1872 by the Bishop of Ripon. Curate of Holy Trinity, Wakefield, 1870-4 : Curate of Holy Trinity, Bournemouth, 1874-84 : Vicar of Hook with Warsash, Fareham, 1884 to the present time. (Cockford's Cler. Dir.).

23. JAMES KERSHAW, B.A., Clare College, Cambridge : Second Master from June 26, 1872 to May 6, 1874. Son of John Kershaw of Kirkthorpe : educated at the School : Cave Scholar and Storie Exhibitioner: B.A. in 1872. Died on Jan. 8, 1875, aged 27; buried at Kirkthorpe.

24. THOMAS STEVENS, B.A., S. John's College, Cambridge: Second Master from July 29, 1874 to June 1875. Scholar and Exhibitioner of his College : 23rd Wrangler in 1863, M.A. 1881. Ordained Deacon by the Bishop of Ripon in 1874, and Priest by the Bishop of Rochester in 1877. Sub-Master of St. Saviour's School, Southwark, 1864-74 : Curate of South Ossett, 1874-5 : Second Master of King Edward's School, Great Berkhamsted, 1875-7 : Curate of St. Thomas, Charterhouse, 1877-9 : Curate of Grange, 1879-82 : Second Master of Queen Elizabeth's School, Sevenoaks, from 1882 to the present time. (Crockford's Cler. Dir.)

GRAMMAR SCHOOL.

25. F. DE BAUDISS, Modern Languages Master from September 1875 to July 1876: now Assistant Master at University College School, London. Author, with Mr. H. W. Eve, of a well-known French Grammar.

26. JOHN WILLIAM YOUNG, Senior Master of the Junior Department from September 1875 to Christmas 1888. Previously Head Master of St. Mary's National Schools, Wakefield: Head Master of the Greencoat School, Wakefield, from July 13, 1860 to its abolition in June 1875. Died Sep. 8, 1889, aged 54, and buried at St. John's, Wakefield.

27. JAMES SAMUEL STOLLARD, M.A., Queens' College, Cambridge: Senior Mathematical and Science Master from Jan. 1876 to the present time. Educated at Chesterfield and Derby Schools: 18th Wrangler, and 4th in the Second Class of the Natural Sciences Tripos in 1875: M.A. in 1880.

28. Rev. THOMAS ALEXANDER LACEY, B.A., Balliol College, Oxford: Classical Master from April 1876 to July 1878. Son of George Frederick Lacey, of Nottingham: Exhibitioner of his College, 1871-5: matriculated Oct. 18, 1871, aged 17: 2nd Class Literæ Humaniores in 1875, M.A. in 1885. Ordained Deacon in 1876 by the Bishop of Ripon, and Priest in 1879 by Bishop Ryan. Curate of St. Michael's, Wakefield, 1876-9: Curate of Caunton, Notts, 1879-80: Curate of St. Benedict, Ardwick, Manchester, 1880-3: Assistant Master at Denstone College, 1885-8: Fellow of the College of St. Mary and St. John, Lichfield, 1885-8: Second Master at Taunton School, 1888-9: Lecturer of Holy Trinity, Stroud Green, London, from 1889 to the present time. (Crockford's Cler. Dir.: Foster's Al. Ox.).

29. M. CAUMONT, Modern Languages Master from September 1876 to April, 1877.

30. J. M. MADDEN, Drawing Master from January 1887 to July 1880. Son of the Rev. W. M. Madden, Vicar of Holy Trinity, Wakefield: educated at the School: now in New Zealand.

31. F. STEINGASS, Modern Languages Master from September 1877 to July 1879.

32. WILLIAM WILKINSON, Junior Assistant Master from January 1878 to July 1879.

33. T. E. JACOB, B.A., S. Catharine's College, Cambridge. Classical Master from September 1878 to July 1880. Second Class, Classical Tripos in 1878.

34. F. W. STRONG, Modern Languages Master from September 1879 to April 1880.

35. JAMES JONES MORGAN, B.A., Jesus College, Oxford: Classical Master from September, 1879 to December, 1882 : B.A. in 1879, M.A. in 1884. Ordained Deacon in 1884 and Priest in 1885 by the Bishop of Worcester. Curate of St. Jude, Birmingham, 1884-5 : Curate of Much Wenlock, 1885-8 : Curate of Holmer, Hereford, from 1888 to the present time. (Crockford's Cler. Dir.)

36. CADWYAN POWELL PRICE, B.A., Lincoln College, Oxford: Fifth Form Master from January to July 1880. 3rd Class Classical Moderations, 1877 ; B.A. 1879, M.A. 1883. Ordained Deacon in 1880 by the Bishop of Bangor, and Priest in 1881 by the Bishop of St. Asaph. Curate of Llanidloes, 1880 to the present time. (Crockford's Cler. Dir.)

37. WALTER HUNGERFORD DAUBENY, Magdalen College, Oxford: Assistant Master from May to December 1880. Demy of his College; 2nd Class Classical Moderations, 1870.

38. REGINALD PHILLIMORE PHILLIMORE, B.A., Queen's College, Oxford: Drawing and Assistant Master from September, 1880 to December, 1882. Matriculated as Unattached Student in 1876, B.A. from Queen's College in 1880. (Foster's Al. Ox.)

39. WILLIAM EDWARD POWELL, M.A., London University : Fifth Form Master from September, 1880 to December, 1888. Was educated at Owen's College, Manchester; 19th in Honours, London Matriculation. Assistant Master at Manchester Cathedral School : Head Master of Hindley Grammar School. 1876—80. Died at Southport, Mar. 15, 1889, aged 42, buried at Manchester.

40. EDWARD MELVILLE LYNCH, M.A., Lincoln College, Oxford : Modern Languages Master from January to July, 1881. Scholar of his College, 1871—5 ; matriculated Oct. 18, 1871, aged 19 : 2nd Class Classical Moderations, 1873 : B.A. and M.A. in 1879. (Foster's Al. Ox.).

41. W. H. HARWOOD, B. ès L., Paris University : Modern Languages Master from September 1881 to December 1882.

42. SAMUEL BENJAMIN SLACK, B.A., Balliol College, Oxford: Classical Master from January to December, 1883. Scholar of his College 1877—82, matriculated Oct. 30, 1878, aged 18 : 1st Class Classical Moderations, 1879, 3rd Class Literæ Humaniores, 1882 : M.A. in 1885. (Foster's Al. Ox.).

43. JAMES GOODLIFFE, B.A., London University : Assistant Master from January 1883 to the present time: now Fifth Form

GRAMMAR SCHOOL.   163

Master. Ordained Deacon in 1888 and Priest in 1890 by the Bishop of Wakefield. Curate of S. James, Thornes, 1889—90.

44. LEON KLEM, of Lemberg University : Modern Languages Master from January, 1883 to April 1884.

45. ARTHUR McCULLOCK HUGHES, B.A., Oriel College, Oxford : Modern Languages Master from April to December 1884. Exhibitioner of Queen's College ; Adam de Brome Exhibitioner of Oriel College, 1878—81 ; 2nd Class Classical Moderations, 1879 : B.A. 1881. Assistant Master at Faversham Grammar School, 1881—4.

46. JOHN GREENWOOD BOURNE, London University ; Student-Teacher from September 1884 to July 1886. Assistant Master at Neath Proprietary School, 1886—90. Lay Reader at Christ Church, Wakefield, 1891.

47. GEORGE JAMES TOSSELL, London University ; Modern Languages Master from January 1885 to December 1888. Previously Assistant Master at Margate High School. Author of various Schoolbooks.

48. JAMES CHRISTOPHER JAQUES, Durham University : Student-Teacher from September 1886 to July, 1888.

49. CHARLES HENRY HEAD, B.A., Oxford University : Assistant Master from September 1887 to the present time. Previously Assistant Master at the Oxford Central School, and Bristol Grammar School.

50. FRANK CROSLAND LEAROYD, Student Teacher from September 1888 to July 1890. Now Assistant Master at Rugby House, Bexley.

51. HENRY ANDREW BROOKE, Drawing and Assistant Master from January 1889 to the present time.

52. OSWALD METCALFE, Modern Languages Master from January to April, 1889.

53. WILLIAM ARTHUR RUSSELL, B.A., St. John's College, Cambridge : Fifth Form Master from January to December 1889. Exhibitioner of his College, Senior Optime, Second Class Classical Tripos, Third Class Theological Tripos. Assistant Master at Bath College, 1890 : Head Master of the South African College School, Capetown, 1891.

54. HERMANN DONATT, Modern Languages Master from May to December 1890. Previously Assistant Master at Ripon Grammar School.

55. ARNOLD RIDLEY DAVIES, London University: Student-Teacher from September 1890 to the present time.

56. JOHN BOWERS KERSHAW, M.A., Brasenose College, Oxford: Modern Languages Master from January 1891 to the present time. Hulme Exhibitioner of his College, 2nd Class Classical Moderations, 2nd Class Literæ Humaniores, 2nd Class Modern History.

Since the earlier part of this Chapter was printed, I have discovered that the Rev. Thomas Clark, M.A., the 12th Head Master, was Rector of Kirkheaton, Rector of Swillington, and Prebendary of York, from the time of his leaving Kirkleatham School until his death on Nov. 25, 1756. And in the chancel of Kirkheaton Church there is a monument to his memory, which, according to Whitaker's Loidis and Elmete, p. 340, runs as follows:—

>   Monendus es, Amice Lector, hic subtus jacere
>   Reliquias (quot quot Mortales)
>   Viri Reverendi Thomæ Clarke A.M.,
>   Hujusce & Ecclesiæ de Swillington dignissimi Rectoris,
>   Et Eboracensis Prebendarij :
>   Qui ab ineunte ætate usque ad annum septuagessimum,
>   Ludimagister tam publice quam privatim,
>   Functus est officiis.
>   In quo Munere obeundo ita Fideliter se gessit,
>   Ut quid Doctrina, quid Virtus, quid Pietas possit,
>   Clarissimum posteris reliquerit Exemplum.
>   Per primos viginti Annos
>   Regiæ Scholæ Wakefeldiensi Præpositus
>   Disciplinæ totus incubuit :
>   Dein eandem apud Kirkletham in se Curam recepit ;
>   Et is fuit Amor Discipulorum, quos direlicturus erat,
>   Ut Præceptorem suum quasi gregatim
>   Illo Sequerentur.
>   Ad hanc Ecclesiam regendam tandem vocatus
>   Ac divisis pariter Laboribus
>   Inter Res Sacras
>   Et in Adolescentulis quibusdam lectis instituendis,
>   Ea Animi Tranquillitate et Felicitate,
>   Quam cæteris omnibus Impertivit,
>   Ipse auspicatissime fruebatur.

GRAMMAR SCHOOL.

Vixit Annos octaginta,
Tum demum, nulla Vixdum Senectutis Mala,
Præter ipsam Senectutem perpessus,
Haustis viribus ex hac vita
In alteram feliciter transiit,
Die Novembris xxv^{to} et Salutis nostræ Anno MDCCLVI^{to}
Ne tam chari Capitis Memoria funditus periret,
Vidua illius mæstissima, et Filiarum Par,
Marmor hoc non mendax
Flentes Posuere.

Chapter 7.

THE LIBRARY.

FROM the earliest years of the School's history the necessity of a good Library has always been recognized, and through the energy of many Head Masters, and the loyal affection of many pupils, there is now in the possession of the School a very valuable selection of books on all necessary subjects.

The deeds, under which the original benefactors of the School made their gifts, contained mention of the Library, as one of the objects to which the money was to be applied, and in the following words :—"Necnon pro reparatione domus Scholæ predictæ, augmentatione Librarii sive Bibliothecæ ejusdem, ac aliis necessariis ejusdem Scholæ."

There is also an interesting list of books acquired up to the year 1607, or about that time :—

1. Inprimis, Mr. Joseph Lister, Doctor of Physic, hath given one Greek Lexicon to the perpetuall use of the schole.
2. Item, Mr. Streete, preacher of the word of God in Emlay Parish, who is now deceased, hath given one book called Commentaries upon Terence.
3. Item, Mr. Harrison hath given one book called Natalis Comes.
4. Item, Mr. Ambrose Mawde gave, the same day he went to Cambridge, one book called Terentius Christianus.
5. Item, one book called Lycosthenes Apothegms.
6. Item, one book called Flores Poetarum.
7. Item, another Adage Book.
8. Item, one Commentary of Lubin upon Juvenal and Persius.
9. Item, one Greek Grammar called the Grammar of Theodorus.
10. Item, one book called Maturantius upon Tullie's Epistles ad Herennium.
11. Item, one commentary upon Tullie's Epistles.
12. Item, one common book called Textoris Officina.

OLD BUILDING AND LIBRARY ROOM IN 1820.
(Photographed from an engraving in "Buckler's Endowed Schools".)

GRAMMAR SCHOOL.

13. Item, a large English Bible, given by Mr. Batty.
14. Item, Clenard's Greek Grammar.

A little afterwards "William Savile, gentleman, one of the Governors, did give the great large dictionary made by Bishop Cowper, called in Latin Thesaurus Linguæ Romanæ et Britannicæ, of the last edition Anno Domini 1565, and it was given in December 1608."

One other gift only is recorded before the commencement of the eighteenth century, and this was probably made by the Rev. Edward Clarke, who was the Head Master in 1686.

The Rev. Thomas Clark must, however, be regarded as the real founder of the Library, as it was owing to his efforts that a separate building was provided for the preservation of the volumes that had been given already, or were in the future to be given for the use of the School. The appeal which the Governors issued has been preserved, and it is here printed, with the names of the Subscribers: the date is 1717 or 1718.

"The great usefulness and advantage of publick Libraries being universally acknowledged, all the considerable Scholes and many of the market townes in the kingdom have of late vied with one another in the encouraging so good a work: and in this neighbourhood Leeds, Hallifax, Bradford and Skipton have already gone before us.

We, whose names are hereunto subscribed, desire to imitate and recommend to others this zeal for learning, being unwilling our town should be excelled in the promotion of a design so truly commendable and so generally beneficial. And being perswaded that the gentlemen and other learned persons here educated would in a few years furnish us with books at the least equal in number and value to the best provided of our neighbours, had we but a spacious and commodious room wherein to place them.

This work is recommended to us by our Schole, which has been a great ornament and benefit to the town, and has never towards its repairs or otherwise required at our hands for a hundred years or upwards any contributions: we could not refuse this first request. In order therefore to the erecting of such a building, we promise and oblige ourselves to pay to Mr. Clark, our present Schoolmaster, the several sums over against our names:—

HISTORY OF WAKEFIELD

John Smyth, Esq., Governor	02	02	0
R. Witton Esq., Governor	02	02	0
Mr. Rich. Smyth ..	.. 01	01	0
Mr. Wm. Spinke, Governor	01	01	0
Mr. Benj. Watkinson, Spokesman	.. 01	01	0
Mr. Wm. Coppendale	.. 01	01	0
Mr. Saml. Moore ..	.. 00	10	6
Mr. Abra. Bever, Governour	01	11	6
Mr. J. Watkinson, Governour	01	01	0
Mr. Robt. Milnes ..	.. 01	11	6
Mr. Wm. Oates, Governour	01	01	0
Mr. John Milnes ..	.. 01	00	0
Mr. Ebenezer Naylor	.. 00	10	0
Mr. Fra: Maud ..	.. 01	01	0
Mr. Fra: Pitt, Governour	.. 01	01	0
Mrs. Doro: Clarke	.. 00	10	0
Mrs. Richardson ..	.. 00	10	6
Mr. Willm. Charnock	.. 01	00	0
Mr. Ebenezer Buxton	.. 01	01	0
A Gentleman Mr. Bromley, Governour	01	01	0
Mr. Saml. Richardson	.. 00	10	0
Mr. Tilson	.. 00	10	0
Mr. Fairbourne	.. 00	10	0
Mr. Linley	.. 01	01	0
Mr. Abra: Barber ..	.. 02	02	0
Mr. Jos: Watkinson, jun...	01	01	0
Sir Arthur Kay ..	.. 01	01	0
Charles Savile, Esq.	.. 01	01	0
John Lowther, Esq. of Ackworth	.. 01	01	0
Mr. Robt. Hopkinson	.. 01	01	0
Mr. George Cotton ..	.. 00	10	0
Mr. Tho: Clarke, Schoolemaster ..	.. 02	02	0
Mr. B. Wilson, Usher	. 01	01	0
Mr. Robt. Read ..	.. 01	01	0
Mrs. Lawson ..	.. 00	10	6
Mrs. Green	.. 01	01	0
Mrs. Woollen	.. 00	10	0
Mr. James Maude ..	. 00	10	6
Mr. Toby Sill ..	.. 01	01	0
Mr. Jo: Spooner ..	.. 00	10	6
Mr. Abra: Wilson	.. 00	05	0
Mrs. Smurfet ..	.. 00	10	0
Mrs. Bargh	.. 00	10	0
Mr. Samuel Knowles	.. 00	10	0
Mr. St: Shepard ..	.. 00	05	0
Mr. John Walker ..	.. 00	05	0
Mr. John Maude ..	.. 01	01	0
Mr Jer: Barstow ..	.. 00	10	6
Mr. John Scott ..	.. 00	10	6
Mr. Rey: Newstead	.. 00	10	6
Mr. Samuel Usher ..	.. 00	10	6
Mr. T. Birkhead, Governor	01	01	0
Mr. Nevinson ..	.. 01	03	0
Mr. Ja: Clayton ..	.. 00	10	0
Mr. Tho: Bragg ..	.. 00	10	6
Mr. Chr: Driffield ..	.. 00	10	6
Mrs. Mary Wheatley	.. 00	10	0
Mr. Willm. Lupton	.. 00	10	0
Mrs. Elizabeth Wheatley ..	00	10	0
Mr. Hudson ..	.. 00	10	6
Mr. Willm. Ingram	.. 00	10	6
Mr. Ubank	.. 00	10	6
Mr. Josias Oates ..	.. 00	10	6
Mr. Tho: Horne ..	.. 00	10	6
Mr. Allan Johnson ..	.. 00	10	6
Mr. John Waddington	.. 00	10	6
Mr. John Cowpe ..	.. 00	10	6
Mr. John Foster ..	.. 00	10	6
Mr. Saml. Thompson	.. 00	10	0
Mr. J. Walker ..	.. 00	05	0
Mr. R. Gargrave ..	.. 00	15	0
Mr. Tho: Warberton	.. 00	10	6
Mr. R. Bevers ..	.. 00	10	0
Mr. Abra: Wilson ..	.. 00	05	0
Mr. Jer: Dixon ..	.. 00	10	0
Mr. Addinell. the painting of the room			
Mr. Cyrill Wood ..	.. 00	10	6
Mr. W. Gill ..	.. 00	05	0
Mrs. Houlden ..	.. 00	05	0
Mr. Robt. Browne ..	.. 00	10	6
Mr. John Scrooby ..	.. 00	10	6
Mr. Shillito	.. 00	10	0
Mr. J. Smyth, jun ..	.. 01	01	0
Capt. John Burton ..	.. 01	01	0
Mr. Middleton ..	.. 00	5	0
Mr. Mar: Shepley ..	.. 00	10	6
Mr. Char: Zouch, Assistant	01	01	0
Mr. Joseph Sager ..	.. 01	01	0
Mrs. Clareborough ..	.. 00	10	0
Mr. Jo: Chibchase ..	.. 00	10	0
Mr. J. Dawson ..	.. 00	10	6
Mr. J. Smyth, of Maningam	00	10	6

GRAMMAR SCHOOL. 169

Soon after the Library room was erected by the aid of the above subscriptions, as actually happened in the years 1717 and 1718, gifts of books were doubtless made in large numbers : but the names of donors do not appear to have been generally preserved until after 1751, when the Rev. John Clarke became Head Master: and his zeal in this direction has already been pointed out. There will be found below a list of names which appear written in various volumes, some with an explanatory note, some merely with the date appended. The presumption is that the very great majority of the donors were educated at the School: many of the names appear in the list of old pupils of the Rev. John Clarke, which is given by Dr. Zouch : many also are the names of pupils who won Cave Scholarships or Storie Exhibitions from the School, some occur in other University records in such a way as to make it certain that they refer to Wakefield Grammar School boys : and the custom of pupils presenting books on leaving school has already been referred to. Some names, however, are clearly those of Governors, others are those of Ushers or Assistant Masters who were not previously pupils at the School, and others belonged to certain University Officials : these will be found at the end of our list, which is otherwise chronologically arranged.

1690. William Woodcock, of Hatfeild in the County of York.

1722. J. J. Lowther, Sidney Sussex College, Cambridge.

About 1722. Goodriche Ingram, and Edward Hoyland.

1725. Mr. Wm Sacheverel.

1727. Rev. Thomas Murgatroyd, Fellow of Trinity College, Cambridge, lately Usher in the School.

1727. Godfrey Wentworth, Esq.

1729. Sandys Hutchinson, Fellow of Trinity College, Cambridge.

1729. " Almæ suæ Nutrici Scholæ Publicæ in Wakefield in Com. Eborac. hunc librum gratitudinis ergo d. d. d. Edm. Dring, Trin. Coll. Cantab. Socius."

1729. Strelley Pegge, of Beauchieff in the County of Derby, Esq.

1729. Christopher Hodgson, Fellow of Trinity College, Cambridge.

1729. John Coppendale, Fellow of Trinity College, Cambridge.

1734. Robert North, of Scarborough, gent.

1735. Thomas Lilley.

1737. J. Hotchkis.

1739. William Haward, B.D.

1750. G. Neville, and John Skelton.

1751. Henry Robinson, Thomas Cayley, and William Gill.

1752. "JOHANNES WEBSTER, MDCCLII: inter Baccalaureos Artium comitiis prioribus Academiæ Cantabr. MDCCLVI., cum Philosophiæ tum Literarum amœniorum nomine, qui primum honorem et præmium retulit." SENIOR WRANGLER and SENIOR CLASSIC in 1756.

1752. John Ambler, Robert Wells, Francis Bland, and William Green.

About 1752. Thomas Preston, Edmund and Edward Edmunds.

1753. John Banister, Roger Pocklington, Robert Mackenzie, Thomas Ball, Samuel Carr, Richard Mattison, and Marmaduke Tomline.

1754. Ambrose Uredale, Antony Trollope, Edmund Barker, John Brewster Darley, William Horn, John Hepworth, William Fenton, Thomas Dade, William Tomlinson, Edward Seymour, and Dr. Thomas Perkins.

1755. Langhorne Burton, Joseph Pocklington, Richard Wilsford, Christopher Wandesford, James Horrocks, Samuel Riley, Robert Bolling, William Wighton and Roger Swire.

1756. George Routh.

1757. Edward Norton, Joshua Newby, John Field, Joseph Lord, Barnard Foord, and Robert Beverley.

1758. Charles Burton, Richard Thorold, John Lonsdale, Leonard Burton, Robert Burton, Anthony Hall, Edward Cottoril, and Thomas Nevile.

1759. "The gift of Mr. Wm. Ellerby to Wakefield School Library as a Memorial of his Gratitude and a proof of his Veneration for the place of his Education, in which he was qualified to enter a member of Oxford, May 31, 1759."

1759. "The gift of Thomas Smith of Virginia to Wakefield School, upon his leaving it and entering a member of Trinity College, Cambridge."

1759. Charles Favell, John Rickaby and Theodore Bland.

1760. "Richardus Roundell, Coll. Univ. apud Oxon. superioris ordinis commensalis, et ejusdem Scholæ super alumnus July 14, 1760."

1760. James Collins.

1761. John Ramsden, of University College, Oxford, and Robert Tucker, of Virginia.

1768. William Walker, October 1768.

1769. "The gift of Mr. Thomas Hardcastle to Wakefield School upon his entering commoner of Queen's College, Oxford, Dec. 6, 1769."

GRAMMAR SCHOOL.

1770. "John Sheppard upon his entering a member of Trinity College, Cambridge."

About 1770. Rev. John Simpson, Canon of Lincoln.

1773. "The gift of Mr. Jno. Knowles to Wakefield School (Library), in which he had his education."

1775. John Goodair, "on his entering a pensioner of Trinity College, Cambridge, Oct. 1775."

1779. Samuel Smalpage, "Trin. Coll. Camb. Oct. 27, 1779."

1782. Thomas Comber, November 28; Andrew Peterson, Utrecht.

1790. Henry Lumb.

1793. "Mr. Robinson presents respectful compliments to Mr. Atkinson, and begs his permission for a set of Scripture Characters, (which accompanies this note) to stand in the Library of Wakefield School, as a small testimony of the Author's gratitude for the valuable instructions which he received in that seminary of Learning. Leicester, Nov. 15, 1793."

1819. "The gift of Charles Lawson to Wakefield School Library on his entering a sizar at St. John's Coll., Cambridge, Oct., 1819."

1819. "The gift of Egremont Richardson to Wakefield School Library, A.D., 1819."

1820. "Given to the Library of the Wakefield Free Grammar School by John Day Hurst on his entering at Trinity College, Cambridge, October, 1820."

1822. James Burdakin.

1832. "John Sharp, Magd. Coll. Camb., Jan. 28, 1832."

1847. "Presented by the Rev. W. E. Coldwell, Rector of Stafford, June 24, 1847."

1887. J. H. Lupton.

1889. H. M. Chadwick.

In addition to the above gifts from those who were, or may be supposed to have been, pupils at the School, there were others from Masters:—

1686. "in usum Scholæ Wakefieldiensis E(dwardus) C(larke) d.d. Anno Domini, 1686." (see p. 130).

1751. Henry Wilson, Fellow of Trinity College, Cambridge, and Usher in the School.

1751. John Skelton, Assistant Master (p. 159).

1752. David Quenedy, Teacher of the French Language in the School.

1758. Dixon Reddall, B.A., of St. John's College, Cambridge, and Usher in the School.
1885. G. J. Tossell.
1891. J. S. Stollard.

The next three gifts are from Governors of the School :—
Bought with the money left by John Bromley, gent. late Governor of the School (p. 51).
Richard Birkhead, gent., Governor of the School.
Tempest Thornton, Esq., Governor of the School.
1728. Rev. Cavendish Nevile, of Chevet.

The following inscriptions, occurring in several volumes, savour of economy in School management :—
1753. Bought with the Coal money.
1755. Bought with the Coal and Catalogue money.

Many friends, not directly connected with the School, have presented volumes at various times. Of these no one has been more liberal or complimentary than Dr. Arthur Charlett, Master of University College from 1692 to 1722, whose name appears, generally with an elaborate dedication or quotation, in many books: he always speaks of the School as "illustrious," "most celebrated," "most famous," or with some such epithet: and once or twice calls its Library an excellent one, as it must have been. Volumes also came more than once from " Cornelius Crownfield, Printer to the most celebrated University of Cambridge," and from the Rev. Stephen Whisson, Fellow of Trinity College, Cambridge, and Public Librarian to the University.

One of the purposes of this Chapter may be mentioned in conclusion: a knowledge of what former pupils of the School did for its Library in days gone by may rouse some of their successors to an imitation of an example which has been too seldom followed during the present century. The bare list of names, which has been given above, may be elucidated by turning to the index; this will be found to contain references to other pages in this book, where further details as to the careers of the various donors may be found.

It only remains to be stated that the School came into possession of a large number of books when the premises of the late West Riding Proprietary School were acquired, and that many more have since been added by purchase from time to time.

Chapter 8.

SCHOLARSHIPS AND OTHER ENDOWMENTS.

FEW Schools have been more fortunate in respect of their endowment of Scholarships than Wakefield Grammar School. From the very earliest period of its history it has been able to offer to the most deserving of its pupils the means of continuing their studies at the Universities of Oxford or Cambridge, which were, until recent times, almost the only places in England where advanced teaching was provided for those who had finished their School course. And although some of these endowments have been unfortunately lost —let us hope not beyond recovery—the School possesses at the present time a large number of Scholarships and Exhibitions tenable either at Oxford or Cambridge, or some other of the centres of higher education in the country.

It is now purposed to give some account of these in the order of their foundation, and to add a list of their holders, as complete as it has been found at present possible to make it.

I. THE FREESTON SCHOLARSHIPS OR EXHIBITIONS AT UNIVERSITY COLLEGE, OXFORD.

As has been briefly stated on p. 34, John Freeston, of Altofts, Esquire, gave by deed, dated September 12, 1592, his estate called the Trinities at Pontefract to the Master and Fellows of University College, Oxford, under trust to make several payments. Amongst these was included a payment of £20 a year to "a Fellow and two Scholars at University College": out of this sum £10 a year was probably assigned to the Fellow, and five [1] pounds a year to each Scholar, as was the case with a similar endowment at Cambridge. Mr. Freeston directed that his Scholars should be chosen out of the Normanton Grammar School, or else out of the Free School at Wakefield, or else out of the Free Schools at Pontefract and Swillington, or else out of the free schools in the County of York. An ordinance of the University Commissioners (17 and 18 Vict. c. 81) somewhat modified these provisions by deciding that no Candidates were to be

---

[1] On p. 34, line 6, for ten pounds read five pounds: and similarly on p. 48, line 22. The document there quoted omits all mention of the Fellowship.

entitled to any preference, unless they had been educated at one of the four Schools mentioned by name in the instrument of foundation, and no candidates from any of the four privileged Schools were to be entitled to any preference, unless they had been educated at such a School for two years at least next preceding the day of election. The Statutes made for University College, under the Universities of Oxford and Cambridge Act, 1877, state that the election shall be confined in the first instance to Candidates from the four Schools named in the deed, and that such Candidates shall compete on an equal footing : no Candidate is to claim any preference by reason of his place of birth, or being of the name or kindred of John Freeston : and no one is to claim preference unless he has been educated, for the two years immediately preceding the day of election, at one or more of the privileged Schools; moreover, all candidates are to be under 19 years of age on the day of election. In the event of no candidate from one of the four Schools being considered eligible after examination, candidates under 21 years of age from any School may compete, if they have not completed six terms from matriculation.

Since the year 1847, the Freeston Exhibitions, as they were then called instead of Scholarships, have been augmented out of the general revenues of the College, so as to make up the number of three Exhibitions of £50 a year each, tenable for two years, when they are renewable for a further term of two years; and after this period has elapsed, they may be held for a fifth year, under special circumstances.

I have unfortunately been able to discover no names of Freeston Scholars or Exhibitioners sent from Wakefield to University College until quite recent times : but these are as follows :—

1860. T. C. P. PAYNE.

1865. GEORGE BREWERTON, eldest son of William B., Alverthorpe, matriculated Oct. 15, 1864, aged 18. Storie Exhibitioner : 2nd Class Classical Moderations, 1866; 2nd Class Mathematical Moderations, 1866 : 3rd Class Literæ Humaniores, 1868. Now Assistant Master at King Edward's School, Birmingham. (Foster's Al. Ox.)

1878. RICHARD GEORGE PARKER BULLOCK, son of the Rev. Richard B., Chaplain of H.M. Prison, Wakefield: born at Banbury: matriculated Jan. 25, 1879 : 3rd Class Classical Moderations 1880, 3rd Class Theology, 1882. Ordained Deacon in 1883, and Priest in 1884 by the Bishop of Carlisle. Curate of S. Cuthbert's, Carlisle, 1883-5 : of S. Martin's, Leeds, 1885—1891 : Vicar of S. Luke's, Leeds, 1891. (Crockford's Cler. Dir. : Foster's Al. Ox.)

GRAMMAR SCHOOL. 175

1879. WILLIAM BASIL WORSFOLD, son of the Rev. John Napper W., Haddlesey Rectory, Selby: 1st Class Classical Moderations 1881; 2nd Class Literæ Humaniores, 1883.

1880. JOHN PATRICK O'DONOHOE, eldest son of Martin O'D., Supervisor of Excise, Wakefield: born at Shutford, Oxon: matriculated Oct. 16, 1880, aged 19: B.A. 1884. Storie Exhibitioner. Now Assistant Master at Stonyhurst College (Foster's Al. Ox.)

1883. FRANCIS ARTHUR MORTON, son of Charles M., Southport: B.A. 1887.

1884. ROBERT THORLEY JOHNSON, son of James Henry J., Southport: 2nd Class Classical Moderations, 1886: 3rd Class Literæ Humaniores, 1888. Storie Exhibitioner. Now Assistant Master at Bristol Grammar School.

1887. GEORGE WILLIAM SYKES, son of Richard S., Castleford: 3rd Class Classical Moderations, 1889: 4th Class Modern History, 1891. Storie Exhibitioner. Now Assistant Master at Leeds Middle Class School.

1888. JOHN THORNTON, son of Joseph T., Dewsbury. Storie Exhibitioner.

1889. CHARLES HENRY HIRST WALKER, son of Charles James W., Wakefield. Storie Exhibitioner.

In addition, however, to the above, it is possible that Freeston Scholarships were held by some of the following Wakefield boys, who are known to have matriculated at University College: more details about them will be found in this and the next chapter:—

About 1663. Richard Thompson: Dean of Bristol.
— 1663. William Pindar, Fellow.
— 1665. John Radcliffe, Scholar: the famous physician.
— 1684. John Bingham: the great Ecclesiastical Historian.
— 1688. John Potter, Servitor: Archbishop of Canterbury.
— 1719. James Scott, see Storie Exhibitioner for 1719.
— 1751. John Ramsden.
— 1755. Samuel Swire, Fellow: Rector of Melsonby.
— 1760. Edmund Cartwright,: Inventor of the power loom.
- 1760. Richard Roundell, Fellow-Commoner.
— 1761. William Ellerby: see Storie Exhibitioner for 1761.

II. THE FREESTON FELLOWSHIP AND SCHOLARSHIPS AT EMMANUEL AND SIDNEY SUSSEX COLLEGES, CAMBRIDGE.

Having established a Fellowship and two Scholarships at Oxford during his lifetime, John Freeston, of Altofts, Esq., by will dated

Nov. 26, 1594, founded similar endowments at Emmanuel College, Cambridge. He directed that the sum of £500 should be laid out in the purchase of an estate which would bring in an income of £25 a year: out of this sum £10 a year was to be devoted to a Fellowship, £10 a year to two Scholarships, and £5 a year to the general funds of the College. Boys from Normanton, Wakefield, Pontefract, and Rotherham Schools were to have the preference in the order named, both for the Scholarships and for the Fellowship. Sir Edward Heron, Knight, Baron of the Exchequer, and John Brown, B.D., Fellow of University College, Oxford, were named Executors. On June 22, 1607, Emmanuel College relinquished all claim to Mr. Freeston's legacy, and gave permission to the executors to transfer it to Sidney Sussex College. And on the next day, by the consent of Richard Freeston, Esq , of Mendham, and William Freeston, of the Middle Temple, gent., kinsmen and heirs of the late John Freeston, Esq., Sir Edward Heron conveyed to Sidney Sussex College lands and tenements in Stamford, of the yearly value of £25, to be employed according to Mr. Freeston's will. Scholars of the donor's name and kin were to have the first claim, and then Scholars from Normanton, Wakefield, Pontefract, and Rotherham Schools, then those born in the West Riding, or in Yorkshire, and no others to have them.

From Potts' "Liber Cantabrigiensis" I find that in the year 1855 the value of the Fellowship was £52 a year, and that of the Scholarships £26 a year: in 1857 they were said to be worth £76 and £38 respectively.

But the University Commissioners who were appointed by an Act 17 and 18 Vict. ordered that " From the date of the confirmation of this Statute[1] there shall be no further elections to the Fellowship at Sidney Sussex College, founded by John Freeston, nor to either of the two Scholarships founded by him at the same College. All the emoluments derived from the foundation of the said John Freeston shall be consolidated and carried to the general funds of the College, to be applied in the manner directed by the Statutes of the College."

No list of Freeston Scholars or Fellows at Sidney Sussex College seems to have been kept, and I can therefore only append the names of a few pupils of the School who matriculated at the College, and may perhaps have benefited by this endowment: (see the next chapter for more particulars).

(1) It was approved by the Queen in Council, in 1858.

About 1615. Jeremiah Whitaker: Puritan Divine.
— 1615. Joseph Naylor: Fellow.
— 1725. J. J. Lowther.
— 1837. George Andrews Hewett.

III. THE CAVE SCHOLARSHIPS OR EXHIBITIONS AT CLARE HALL, CAMBRIDGE.

According to a copy to be found in the British Museum, the terms of the will, by which these Scholarships were founded, were as follows :—

"In the name of God. Amen. The 6th day of February, in the year of our Lord God 1602, annoque regni Dominæ Elizabethæ dei gratia Reginæ Angliæ, &c., quadragesimo quinto. I, THOMAS CAVE, of Wakefield, in the county of York, chapman . . . . . give and bequeathe, to the Master Fellowes and Schollers of Clarehall, in Cambridge, and to their successors for ever, all that my half Rectorie or Parsonage of Warmefeild in the countie aforesaid, together with all the tithes, oblacions, obventions and emoluments whatsoever to the same belonginge, (my glebe lands belonginge to the said parsonage onelie excepted), to the intent and purpose that two of the poorest schollers of the fre gramer Schole of Wakefeild, the one of them beinge of kin unto me, and havinge bene brought up in the said fre schoole by the space of three yeres, (if any such be), and in defalt thereof one which is or shalbe born in the towne and parishe of Wakefield aforesaid, and the other of them also borne, or to be borne, within the said towne or parishe of Wakefeild, being both of them fit for the Universitie may be contynuallye for ever maynteyned and kept att learninge within Clarehall aforesaid, with the rents, yssues, profitts, and commodities, arisinge, cominge and growinge of the same Rectorie or Parsonage. And my will and mynde is that the said two schollers shall from tyme to tyme forever hereafter be chosen and taken out of the free schole in Wakefeild aforesaid, upon election and choice of the Vicar of Wakefeild, and the Scholemaster of the said fre schole, and their successors, and four of the most honest and substantiall men of Wakefield aforesaid; in which said election I will that my Cossen Mr. Lyster, Preacher, nowe Vicar of Wakefield, shall have during his life a negative voice, and after him all his successors for ever a casting voice."

The form of the nomination of the first Cave Scholars has been preserved both in the Governors' Books and in the British Museum: it is dated Feb. 4, 1603-4.

"To the right Worshipfull Mr. Doctor Smythe, the Master, and to all the fellowes of Clare-hall in Cambridge.

Our heartie commendacions premised. Whereas your friend and ours, Thomas Cave, late of Wakefield, deceased, one of the Governours of our Fre Schole of Queene Elizabeth at Wakefeild, by his last will and testament, bearinge date the sixthe day of February 1602, did give and bequeath to the Master, Fellowes and Scholars of Clare-hall in Cambridge, and their successors for ever, All that parte of the half rectorie or parsonage of Warmefeild in the countie of Yorke, together with all the tithes, oblacions, obventions and emoluments whatsoever to the same belonginge, (his glebe land belonginge to the said parsonage onelie excepted) of the yearlie valew of xii*li*. to the intent and purpose that two of the poorest scholars of the Fre Grammar Schole of Queene Elizabeth att Wakefeild, the one of them beinge of kin unto him, and havinge bene brought up in the said Fre Schole by the space of three yeares (if any such be), and in defalt thereof one which is, or shalbe, borne in the towne and parishe of Wakefeild aforesaid, and the other of them also borne, or to be borne, within the said towne or parishe of Wakefeild, beinge both of them fit for the Universitie, may be contynuallie for ever maynteyned and kept att learninge within Clare-hall aforesaid, with the rents, issues, profitts and commodities, arisinge, cominge and growinge of the same rectorie and parsonage, And his will and mynde was further that the said two Scholers should from tyme to tyme for ever heareafter be chosen and taken out of the said fre Schole in Wakefeild aforesaid, by the elleccion and choice of the Vicar of Wakefeild for the tyme beinge and the Scholemaster of the said fre Schole, and their successors for ever, and fower of the most honest and substantiall men of Wakefeild aforesaid: in which said eleccion his will and mynd was that William Lister, now Vicar of Wakefield, should have duringe his life a negative voice, and all his successors after him but castinge voices: We therefore the Vicar and Scholemaster, with the consent of the Governors of the said Schole, have chosen those which were by himself in his lifetime named to be scholars, to witt, Ambrose Mawde and John Ryley, to be the first scholars elected by vertue of this grant, desiringe your favourable acceptance and kind usage of them, according to the trew meaninge of his said gifte and trust reposed in you. And so shall we be bound unto you, and others shalbe moved hereby to shewe more liberalitie and kindnes to your Colledge, which we desire God hartelie to blesse, with you all and these yonge ones whome we send unto you. In testimonye whereof we have setto our common seall. Dated att Wakefeild the 4th day of February, Anno Domini 1603.

Your wel-willinge freinds in the Lord.

A certificate to
Mr. Doctor Smyth
and the Fellows of
Clarehall."

Owing to a change of Head Masters in 1623, it appears that an informal nomination of the two Cave Scholars was made about that time: for in the next year Mr. Doughty, the new Master, reported to the Governors that "the sonne of Mr. Ouldfield of Newlande and the sonne of Mr. Milton of Pudsey, whereof the former was never at the said Schole, and the other but one quarter of a yeare onely," had been accepted at Clare Hall as duly elected, though they had by no means fulfilled the requirements of Thomas Cave's will. An inquiry was held by the Governors into the matter, and it was decided that Mr. Cotton Horne, at that time one of the governing body, having made the nomination in the name of the Vicar and Master of the School, had acted contrary to his office and duty, and his place as Governor was consequently declared vacant. He was however subsequently re-elected upon the governing body, and became a benefactor of the town by establishing Almshouses for poor men and women.

Some time before the middle of the seventeenth century[1] the Master and Fellows of Clare Hall claimed the right of electing the Cave Scholars themselves, and this was not conceded by the Governors without some tedious disputes[2]: but an agreement was arrived at in the year 1716, by which the power of nomination was still preserved to the persons mentioned in Thomas Cave's will, but

(1) The date is thus surmised from the fact that Hugh Cressy, Barrister-at-Law, and one of the Governors, was applied to for his opinion on the question, and the document in which he gave it still exists: but he left Wakefield in 1633, being appointed to a Judgeship in Ireland : see p. 97.

(2) An account of these, though not altogether correct, was supplied by Dr. Taylor to the "Wakefield Journal," in 1857.

the Master and Fellows were to judge whether the candidates were fitly qualified to be admitted. The Scholarships were to be tenable for seven years, unless before the lapse of that time the holders became Fellows of the College, or Masters of Arts. This dispute may account for the fact that no elections have been discovered between the years 1623 and 1678.

In the year 1700 the value of the Scholarships had increased to £10 8s. od. each per annum : in 1818 it had become £1 11s. 6d. each per week during residence, equivalent to about £40 a year : but since 1861, when a new Statute came into force, having become law three years before, the two Scholars have each received £50 a year. They were, however, then called Exhibitioners, and the tenure was limited to four years.

For many of the names upon the following list of Cave Scholars or Exhibitioners I am indebted to the kindness of the Rev. Dr. Atkinson, Master of Clare College, as it is now called, and the Rev. H. W. Fulford, Fellow and Tutor. In cases where a Cave Scholar has been subsequently appointed Usher or Assistant Master at the School, the details of his career are not repeated, but a reference made to the place in which these may be found.

1. AMBROSE MAWDE, elected Feb. 4, 1603-4.
2. JOHN RYLEY, elected Feb. 4, 1603-4.
3. JAMES LISTER, elected about 1615 : afterwards Usher of the School, and Vicar of Wakefield, (see p. 153).
4. ...... OULDFIELD, of Newland, elected about 1623 ; not duly qualified.
5. ...... MILTON, of Pudsey, elected about 1623 ; not duly qualified.
6. GEORGE BENLOWES, elected Jan. 17, 1677-8 : B.A. 1681.
7. RICHARD KIRSHAW, elected Jan. 12, 1681-2 : B.A., 1681, M.A. 1685, D.D. 1702. Rector of Ripley, 1694-1736, when he died, aged 72. Father of Dr. Samuel Kirshaw, Vicar of Leeds from 1747 to 1786.
8. RICHARD ELLERSHAW, elected Jan. 18, 1682-3 : B A. 1682, M.A., 1688. Vicar of Giggleswick from Apl. 20, 1686. to his death in 1719.
9. OBADIAH LEE, elected Jan. 17, 1688-9 : B.A. 1691, M.A 1695. Son of the Vicar of Wakefield of the same name. Born June 2, 1671 ; Lecturer of Wakefield Parish Church from 1698 to 1703 : buried at Wakefield, Jan. 29, 1702-3.

GRAMMAR SCHOOL.

10. THOMAS SCOTT, elected Jan. 21, 1691-2: B.A. 1691, M.A. 1695. Vicar of Wakefield from 1700 to 1729: married Katherine Smith there on May 25, 1709: she was buried on Sep. 3, 1710: and he on Apl. 17, 1729

11. JOHN MARROW, elected Jan. 17, 1694-5.[1]

12. JOHN WILSON, elected about 1713: B.A. 1716: Storie Exhibitioner. Son of Thomas Wilson, of Wakefield. Vicar of Hooton Pagnall from May to November, 1723; buried at Wakefield on Nov. 21, 1723.

13. JOHN WRAY, elected Jan. 18, 1715-6: B.A. 1718.[2]

14. WILLIAM RUECASTLE, elected Jan. 23, 1728-9: B.A. 1731, M.A. 1750: Storie Exhibitioner. Son of John Ruecastle, who was Master of the Storie Petty Scholars [3], Wakefield, and died in March, 1728. Baptized Oct. 24, 1710.

15. SAMUEL PAUL, elected Jan. 23, 1728-9: Storie Exhibitioner. Son of Luke Paul, barber, of Wakefield. Master of the Storie Petty Scholars from 1757 to his death in November, 1762.

16. RICHARD HARRISON, elected Jan. 18, 1732: B.A. 1735: Storie Exhibitioner. Afterwards Usher (see p   ).

17. THOMAS DENTON, elected Jan. 17, 1733-4: Storie Exhibitioner. Son of Richard Denton. Afterwards Curate of some Church near Wakefield.

18. JOHN BUXTON, elected Jan. 22, 1735-6: B.A. 1738, M.A. 1742: Fellow of his College. Storie Exhibitioner.

19. JOHN GARLICK, elected Jan. 19, 1737-8: B.A. 1740: M.A. 1744: Fellow of his College. Storie Exhibitioner. Afterwards Usher, (see p. 155).

20. JOHN COPPENDALE, elected Jan. 22, 1740-1: B.A. 1743, M.A, 1748: Storie Exhibitioner. Son of Daniel Coppendale, baptized Nov. 7, 1726. Curate of Wakefield from 1751 to 1754. Vicar of Hooton Pagnell from 1754 to 1768, when he died there.

21. WILLIAM HARGREAVES, elected Jan. 19, 1743-4; B.A. 1746: Storie Exhibitioner. Son of Joseph Hargreaves, Innkeeper, of Wakefield: baptized September 29, 1724.

22. BENJAMIN WRIGHT, elected Jan. 17, 1744-5: 4th Wrangler, 1748; M.A. 1751: Fellow of his College. Storie Exhibitioner. Son of William Wright, of Northgate; baptized Dec. 15, 1726.

---

(1) Probably Charles Naylor and James Hargreaves (see Storie Exhibitioners) were the Cave scholars between John Marrow and John Wilson.

(2) Probably Benjamin Dawson (see Storie Exhibitioners) followed John Wray.

(3) An explanation of the term will be found below, p. 186.

23. JOHN SKELTON, elected Jan. 21, 1747-8: Junior Optime, 1751; Storie Exhibitioner. Afterwards Assistant Master (see p. 159).

24. SAMUEL CARR, elected Jan. 24, 1754, 6th Wrangler, 1758: Fellow of his College: M.A. 1761: D.D. 1782. Storie Exhibitioner. Son of Robert Carr, of Horbury.

25. BENJAMIN TIDSWELL, elected Jan. 22, 1756: B.A. 1759. Storie Exhibitioner. Son of Robert Tidswell, of Westgate: baptized, Apl. 4, 1734. .Vicar of Chapel Allerton, Leeds, where he died in Feb. 1777.

26. CHARLES FAVELL, elected Jan. 17, 1760: 10th Wrangler, 1763: M.A. 1766: Fellow of his College. Storie Exhibitioner. Son of Henry Favell; baptized, Feb 28, 1739-40.

27. WILLIAM WALKER, elected Jan. 19, 1769: Junior Optime, 1772; M.A., 1798. Storie Exhibitioner. Son of Thomas Walker: baptized Aug. 20, 1751.

28. SAMUEL POLLARD, elected Jan. 17, 1771: B.A. 1774. Storie Exhibitioner. Son of Samuel Pollard, of Horbury.

29. CHRISTOPHER BELL, elected Jan. 19, 1793. Storie Exhibitioner. Son of Robert Bell, Supervisor of Excise: died Sept. 13, 1794.

30. GEORGE AMBLER, elected Jan. 19, 1799: B.A. 1802. Storie Exhibitioner. Son of Richard Ambler; baptized Oct. 28, 1776. Died Jan. 8, 1855 (Banks, p. 162).

31. BENJAMIN PULLAN, elected Jan. 19, 1805: Senior Optime, 1808, M.A. 1811: Fellow of his College. Master of Holt Grammar School, Norfolk, in 1837.

32. JAMES BURDAKIN, elected Jan. 18, 1817; 11th Wrangler, 1820; M.A., 1823. Fellow of his College; Proctor in 1838, and Classical Examiner in 1840. Storie Exhibitioner. Son of Benjamin Burdakin, of Wakefield.

33. SAMUEL SUNDERLAND, elected Jan. 21, 1826; Junior Optime, 1829. Storie Exhibitioner. Curate of Penistone up to 1843.

34. THOMAS FOLJAMBE, elected Jan. 22, 1831: B.A. 1834. Son of Thomas Foljambe, of Holme Field, Wakefield, Solicitor, M.A., D.L., J.P. Of Acomb, near York, where he died in 1890.

35. JAMES BUTLER KELLY, elected Jan. 25, 1851: son of the Rev. John Kelly, Minister of Zion Chapel, Wakefield, and afterwards Curate of the Parish Church. Foundation Scholar, Storie Exhibitioner; B.A., 1854; M.A., 1858; D.D., 1867. Ordained Deacon in 1855, and Priest in 1856 by the Bishop of Peterborough. Curate of Abington, Northants, 1855-6: Domestic Chaplain to the

GRAMMAR SCHOOL.

Bishop of Sodor and Man, 1856-64: Vicar of Kirk Michael, Isle of Man, 1860-4: Archdeacon of Newfoundland, 1865-7: Coadjutor Bishop of Newfoundland, 1867-76: Bishop of Newfoundland, 1876-7: Vicar of Kirkby, Lancs., 1877-80: Bishop Commissary for the Bishop of Chester, 1879-84: Archdeacon of Macclesfield, 1880-4: Bishop Commissary for the Bishop of Salisbury, 1884-5: Coadjutor Bishop of Moray, Ross and Caithness, and Provost of S. Andrew's Cathedral, Inverness, 1885-6: Bishop of Moray, Ross and Caithness, 1886 to the present time. (Crockford's Cler. Dir.)

36. ROUTH TOMLINSON, elected Jan. 31, 1860. Storie Exhibitioner; 3rd class Classics 1863; M.A., 1866. Ordained Deacon in 1863, and Priest in 1864 by the Bishop of Peterborough: Curate of St. Mary's Peterborough, 1863-6: Curate of Wrotham, Kent, 1866: Curate of Lutterworth, 1866-71: Curate of S. Barnabas, Rotherhithe, 1871-2: Vicar of Warmfield, 1872-82: Curate of Husbands Bosworth, Leicestershire, 1883-7: Vicar of Finchampstead, 1887 to the present time. (Crockford's Cler. Dir.)

37. THOMAS JAMES SANDERSON, elected May 30, 1861: 19th Wrangler, 1866; M.A., 1869. Foundation Scholar, Goldsmith's Exhibitioner, Storie Exhibitioner, Fellow of his College. Afterwards Assistant Master. (See p. 160.)

38. THOMAS HENRY SHAW, elected June 5, 1863: 8th Wrangler, 1867; M.A., 1870. Foundation Scholar, Storie Exhibitioner, Fellow of his College. Carus Greek Testament Prizeman, 1865. Ordained Deacon in 1871, and Priest in 1874 by the Bishop of Ely. Lecturer at S. Bees College, and Curate of S. Bees, 1871-5: Vicar of Everton, Beds., from 1876 to the present time. (Crockford's Cler. Dir.)

39. WILLIAM LAMPREY BOWDITCH, elected June 9, 1865: son of the Rev. William Renwick B., Vicar of S. Andrew's, Wakefield. Foundation Scholar, Storie Exhibitioner; 28th Wrangler, 1871. Ordained Deacon in 1871, and Priest in 1872 by the Bishop of Winchester; Curate of Rotherhithe, 1871-5: Curate of S. Mary Magdalen, Paddington, 1875-7; Warden of Native College, and Canon of S. Saviour's Cathedral, Maritzburg, 1877-86: Lecturer in Mathematics and Natural Philosophy in Trinity Coll., Melbourne, and Mathematical Master in the Church of England Grammar School, Melbourne, from 1887 to the present time. (Crockford's Cler. Dir.)

40. JAMES KERSHAW, elected June 7, 1867: Foundation Scholar, Storie Exhibitioner, B.A. 1872. Afterwards Second Master. (See p. 160).

41. JAMES BEVERLEY, elected Mar. 19, 1869: Foundation Scholar, Storie Exhibitioner, Junior Optime, 1873. Now of S. John's, Wakefield, Barrister-at-Law.

42. FREDERICK WILLIAM AINLEY, elected Mar. 26, 1871 : Storie Exhibitioner: Senior optime in 1875; Ordained Deacon in 1876 and Priest in 1877 by the Bishop of Ripon. Curate of Huddersfield, 1876-7: Missionary in Travancore, 1877-9: Curate of St. John the Baptist, Newtown, Leeds, 1879-80: Curate of St. Luke, Cork, 1881-3: Incumbent of the Free Church, Cork, 1883 to the present time. (Crockford's Cler. Dir.)

43. CHARLES MILNER ATKINSON, elected Mar. 28, 1873: Storie Exhibitioner: Foundation Scholar: 16th Wrangler in 1877. Now a Barrister in London.

44. WILLIAM HEY ALDERSON, elected Mar. 23, 1877 : son of the Rev. William Thompson A., Chaplain of H.M. Prison, Wakefield: Storie Exhibitioner: Foundation Scholar: 3rd Senior Optime in 1881, M.A. 1884. Ordained Deacon in 1884, and Priest in 1887 by the Bishop of Carlisle. Second Master of St. Bees Grammar School, 1881 to the present time. (Crockford's Cler. Dir.)

45. BOWMAN HENRY MADDEN, elected Apl. 4, 1879: son of the Rev. Wyndham Monson M., Vicar of Holy Trinity, Wakefield: Storie Exhibitioner: Foundation Scholar: 26th Wrangler in 1882. Now Assistant Examiner in the Patent Office, London.

46. GEORGE JOHN BURGE CHRISTIE, elected Mar. 16, 1883: son of the Rev. James John C., Vicar of Pontefract: Foundation Scholar: 2nd Class Classics, 1886. Ordained Deacon in 1888, and Priest in 1890 by the Archbishop of York: Curate of Thirsk, 1888-9: Curate of Kirby on the Moor, Boroughbridge, 1889 to the present time. (Crockford's Cler. Dir.)

47. HERBERT MILNES WALKER, elected Mar. 21, 1885: B.A. 1889: son of Thomas W., Surgeon, of Wakefield. Ordained Deacon in 1890 and Priest in 1891 by the Bishop of Durham. Curate of Bishop Wearmouth, 1890 to the present time. (Crockford's Cler. Dir.)

48. JAMES EDWARD BRIGGS, elected Oct. 16, 1886: son of Francis B., of Ossett: Storie Exhibitioner: 2nd Class, Natural Science, Part I, 1888; 3rd Class, Part II, 1890.

49. HECTOR MUNRO CHADWICK, elected Mar. 16, 1889: son of the Rev. Edward C., Vicar of Thornhill Lees: Storie Exhibitioner: Foundation Scholar.

50. WILLIAM HOLMES WALKER, elected Mar. 14, 1891: son of John Younger W., Schoolmaster, Wakefield. Resigned.

51. FREDERICK MASLIN BEILBY CARTER, elected Aug. 10, 1891. Son of Henry Mark C., of Outwood Hall.

IV. THE STORIE EXHIBITIONS.

This valuable endowment, which has perhaps benefited the the School more than any other, was left by John Storie in the year 1674, according to the following terms:—

"I, John Storie, of Hasleborrow, in the parish of Norton in the County of Derby, merchant, do make and ordain this my last will and testament . . . . . . I give and bequeath the profits of all my lands, both copyhold and freehold, lying within the county of York, to my loving sister Margaret Wingfield, for and during her natural life; and after the death of my said sister I give and bequeath the said lands, both copyhold and freehold, within the said county of York, for the maintaining and bringing up of three boys (the children of such parents as are not able to bring them up) at one of the Universities of this nation, viz: Cambridge or Oxford, for three years. And my mind and will is that the said three boys be chosen out of those poor children that I have lately settled lands upon for their teaching at a petty school, until they be fit to go to the Free School in Wakefield, and to be sent from thence and maintained in one of the Universities aforesaid for three years. And after that time three other boys of the same to be sent up and maintained there three years successively for ever. And I desire my loving friends, Mr. John Morewood, of Alfreton, and Mr. Andrew Morewood, of the Hallows, to see that the same be settled accordingly . . . . . . I give and bequeath to my niece Margaret Wingfield one thousand pounds, upon condition that she marry with the consent and approbation of her mother, my loving sister Margaret Wingfield aforesaid, and my aforesaid loving friends Mr. John and Andrew Morewood. Otherwise my mind and will is that the said one thousand pounds shall be bestowed upon lands, and settled by the discretion of my aforesaid loving friends, Mr. John and Andrew Morewood, for the maintenance of three other poor boys, [1] besides the former already mentioned, and also of those poor children I maintain at a petty school in Wakefield aforesaid, at one of the Universities of Cambridge or Oxford for three years, and after that time other three boys for three years successively for ever . . . . Dat. 29 April 1674. Probat. 26 June 1674."

Immediately after the proving of the above will, the Governors of the School took steps to carry out John Storie's intentions; and on Sept. 30, 1674, resolved "that John Pickergill, Schoolmaster, be admitted to teach and instruct the twelve boys included in John Story, gent, his gift." It was also resolved on the same day "that

---

[1] Nothing was ever received under this head.

Francis Greene, son of Widdow Greene; Thomas Stead, son-in-law₁ to William Robinson; Timothy Brooke, son of John Brooke; William Martin, son of Joseph Martin; Edward Clayton, son of Edward Clayton; John Arnall, son of Israell Arnall; John Smith, son-in-law to William Hague; Elias Wood, son of George Wood; Isack Ridleden, son of Joseph Ridleden; Jaine Broadley's son in Kirkgate, and Robert Broadley, son of the same, and Edward Anley son; in number twelve, be admitted as free petty schollars to be taught by the foresaid Pickergill, till they be fitt for the free Grammar Schoole. And also the said Pickergill is ordered to gather the rents given by the said Mr. Story out of the lands mentioned in the said deed and gift and one surrender, bearing date with the date of the said deed or deeds, and is to buy books for the said twelve children untill they and every of them be fitt for the free Grammer Schoole aforesaid." On Oct. 4, 1675, William Adcock, John Craven, and Michael Dabens were ordered to "be taught by Pickergill in place of Timothy Brooke, Thomas Wade, and John Smith," and on June 11, 1677, Peter Browne and John Stead were sent to take the places of John Dabring and John Arnall.

Up to this time the number of twelve boys seems to have been kept up, but there is an absence of records after 1677 for some years, and in 1698 Mr. Pickersgill was only teaching three boys: in 1704 Mr. William Lambert is teaching one petty scholar, and Mr. Pickersgill one or two others: in 1707 the teachers are Mr. Lambert and Mr. Varley, in 1708 Mr. Ruecastle₂ and Mr. Bever: in 1709 Mr. England was employed to teach four Northgate boys only, and he remained in this occupation some 30 years, until the Charity or Greencoat School was thought to be the best place for the boys to be prepared for the Grammar School.

The reason why the original number of twelve petty scholars was reduced to four in a very short time, and the Petty School merged in the Greencoat School, is clearly stated by the Commissioners for Charities in their 1827 Report, vol. xvii., p. 695.

"Storie's Petty Gift. By Indentures of the 25 and 26 May, 1674, and surrender, John Storie conveyed a house and nine acres of freehold land at Ardsley, and surrendered one acre two roods of copyhold land in Sandal to the Governors of the Free Grammar School in trust, for teaching twelve children at a petty school until they should be fit to go to the Free Grammar School: the children to be chosen out of Northgate, next out of Kirkgate, and then out of Westgate. The house and land at Ardsley, mentioned in the will, never came into the possession of the Governors, and the identical

(₁) We should now say "step-son."   (²) See page 181.

property and the present possessor of it are unknown. . . . . . There never was a school for twelve children established, in consequence, probably, of the property at Ardsley not coming into the possession of the Governors, and the property at Sandal being of small value. . . . . . The income of the estate has long been carried to the general account of the Charity School and Trust."

From the same report it appears that the total income available for teaching the petty scholars was not quite £2 a year, so that the Governors must have educated the first twelve boys, and probably many others after them out of the proceeds of Storie's University Gift, or from the general income of the Grammar School.

There is no evidence that any of the petty scholars above-mentioned ever proceeded to the University as Storie Exhibitioners: the Governors' books are, unfortunately, defective just at the time when the first elections must have been made, and a search in the list of Oxford and Cambridge Graduates has also proved fruitless. The fact seems to be that the boys did not always show themselves fit for the University, or care to proceed thither. Accordingly the Commissioners for Charities reported in 1827 that it had been "the custom to give Storie Exhibitions to boys brought up at the Grammar School, though not educated under the charity called Storie's Petty Gift," in default of candidates from those so educated, special permission having been given by the Court of Chancery for this purpose. At the same time names will be found in the following list of Storie Exhibitioners, which will suggest that when candidates were forthcoming, who fulfilled the description given by John Storie, at least in the spirit, if not in the letter, they were chosen in preference to others in more prosperous circumstances: for in many cases it is quite clear that the Storie Exhibitioner was not the cleverest pupil of his year, and some of the most famous men educated at the School never won the Exhibition at all. The scheme, issued by the Charity Commissioners in 1891, confirms this practice by ordering that in future elections of Storie Exhibitioners, if two or more candidates are equal, preference shall be given to boys who have previously been educated for three years at one of the Public Elementary Schools of Wakefield. During the earlier part of this century the Governors seem to have given the preference (1) to boys born in the township of Wakefield, (2) to boys born in the ancient parish of Wakefield, (3) to any boys in in the School who were considered eligible.[1]

(1) S. I. C. Report, 1868. Vol. xviii., p. 290.

The value of the Storie Exhibitions was originally £20 a year,[1] and the tenure was for three years; in 1769 the value was increased to £40 under special circumstances,[2] and maintained at the same sum until 1780, when it was £50 a year; in 1798 it became £63; in 1816 it was £52 10s.[3]; in 1840 the tenure was extended to 4 years, and the value increased to £80 annually; in 1849 the term was again reduced to three years, and in 1853 the election was made for ten University terms of residence at £24 a term.[4] The number of Exhibitioners has varied according to the number of applicants and the state of the fund, but the scheme of 1875 fixed the annual amount to be awarded, and since then there have been four Exhibitions of £60 a year each, tenable for three years.

The following may be considered a complete list of Storie Exhibitioners from 1697, as since that time the names have always been carefully recorded. No election can have been made until 1677 at the earliest, so that only the names for the first 20 years are lost. It will be noticed that some Exhibitioners were not elected until they had taken their B.A. degree, and others, on the contrary, a considerable time before proceeding to the University. This shows the great importance which was attached to the Exhibition, both by the Governors and by the candidates.

1697. THOMAS DOUGHTY, son of William D., baptized [5] Nov. 5, 1677: B.A. Jesus Coll. Cambridge, 1699.

1698. DAVID WATERHOUSE, son of John W., B.A. Christ's Coll., Cambridge, 1701, M.A. 1705.

1702. BENJAMIN BAYNES, son of William B., baptized Dec. 19, 1683.

1703. WILLIAM BURROW. Usher, No. 14.

1705. JOHN BRADSBURY, son of Nicholas B., tailor, baptized Sep. 30, 1684: entered S. John's Coll. Cambridge, July 6, 1703: B.A. 1706.

1708. SAMUEL DRANSFIELD, son of Francis D., blacksmith: entered S. John's Coll. Cambridge, June 6, 1707, aged 19: Usher, No. 15.

1709. CHARLES NAYLOR, son of William N., mercer, baptized May 14, 1691: B.A. Clare Hall, Cambridge, 1711: M.A. 1715. Probably Cave Scholar. Dean of Winchester and Chancellor of

---

(1) Lupton, W. W., p. 198.   (2) Ibid; and above, p. 52.   (3) Carlisle's Endowed Grammar Schools, ii., 911.   (4) S. I. C. Report, 1868, Vol. xviii., p. 290.   (5) The dates of baptism are taken from the Parish Church Registers.

GRAMMAR SCHOOL. 189

Salisbury: died in 1739: buried in Winchester Cathedral. (Lupton's W. W., p. 209.)

1710. JAMES HARGREAVES, son of Nathaniel H., B.A. Clare Hall, Cambridge, 1711 : M.A. 1715 : D.D. 1728. Probably Cave Scholar.

1714. JOHN WILSON, son of Thomas W., Cave Scholar, No. 12.

1717. JAMES WOOLLEN, son of James W., deceased: baptized July 26, 1697. Afterwards Rector of Emley, and Benefactor. (p. 52.)

1717. RICHARD STRINGER, son of Richard S.: Usher, No. 17.

1719. JAMES SCOTT, son of John S.: entered University Coll. Oxford, Dec. 11, 1717, aged 17: B.A. 1721 ; M.A. 1724. Vicar of Bardsey, and first Minister of Trinity Church, Leeds, 1727–1782, when he died, Feb. 11, Father of Dr. Scott, Rector of Simonburn, 1771. (Whitaker's Loidis and Elmete, pp. 67–8. Foster's Al. Ox.)

1720. WILLIAM HALL, son of Swaile H., entered Christ Church, Oxford, April 9, 1720, aged 17.

1722. STEPHEN COOPER, B.A. Emmanuel Coll. Cambridge, 1724.

1723. BENJAMIN DAWSON, son of John D., B.A., Clare Hall, Cambridge, 1723: M.A. 1727. Fellow of his College. Probably Cave Scholar.

1725. WILLIAM WADE, B.A., Clare Hall, Cambridge, 1724: M.A. 1731. Probably Cave Scholar.

1729. WILLIAM RUECASTLE, Cave Scholar, No. 14.

1729, SAMUEL PAUL, Cave Scholar, No. 15.

1731. .... ROBINSON,

1731. JOHN SHEPARD, son of Stephen S., tobacconist.

1733. RICHARD HARRISON, Cave Scholar, No. 16: Usher, No. 21.

1734. THOMAS DENTON, Cave Scholar, No. 17.

1735. JOHN BUXTON, Cave Scholar, No. 18.

1738. JOHN GARLICK, Cave Scholar, No. 19: Usher No. 23.

1739. ROBERT HARRISON, son of Thomas H., baptized June 20, 1719: B.A. Trinity Coll. Cambridge, 1741. Incumbent of Hartshead 1744—1762, when he died.

1740. THOMAS WHITE, son of Richard W., B.A., Trinity Coll. Cambridge, 1741 : M.A. 1745.

1741. JOHN COPPENDALE, Cave Scholar, No. 20.

1742. JOHN ROBINSON, son of Joseph R., B.A. Trinity Coll. Cambridge, 1743.

1742. GEORGE SHAW, son of William S., B.A. Trinity Coll. Cambridge, 1744.

1743. JOHN COOKE, son of Robert C.
1744. BENJAMIN WRIGHT, Cave Scholar, No 22.
1746. WILLIAM HARGREAVES, Cave Scholar, No. 21.
1749. THOMAS WILSON, son of the Rev. Benjamin W., Head Master: born June 18, 1726: entered Trinity Coll. Cambridge, Oct. 17, 1743: B.A. 1747; M.A. 1751; B.D. 1768. Fellow of his College; Sublector, 1754; Lector Linguæ Latinæ, 1757; Lector Primarius, 1760.

1750. JOHN BRIGGS, son of John B., B.A. Trinity Coll. Cambridge, 1749: M.A. 1753. Fellow of his College.
1753. JOHN SKELTON, Cave Scholar, No 23.
1754. SAMUEL CARR, Cave Scholar, No. 24.
1756. BENJAMIN TIDSWELL, Cave Scholar, No. 25.
1760. JOSHUA GIBSON, son of William G., B.A. Trinity Coll. Cambridge, 1762.

1761. WILLIAM ELLERBY, son of Thomas E., baptised Feb 25, 1739-40: entered University Coll, Oxford, May 31, 1759: B.A. 1763.
1761. CHARLES FAVELL, Cave Scholar, No. 26. Afterwards Rector of Brington, Hunts.
1769. WILLIAM WALKER, Cave Scholar, No. 27.
1769. THOMAS ROBINSON, fourth son of James R., hosier: entered Trinity Coll. Cambridge as sizar, 1768: Scholar of his College, Apl. 1771: Hooper Medal for English declamation, Dec. 1771: 7th Wrangler, 1772: Fellow of his College, Oct. 1772: Latin Essay Prize, 1773: M.A. 1775. Curate of Witcham and Wichford, Ely: Afternoon Lecturer at All Saints, Leicester, and Chaplain to Leicester Infirmary, 1773-8: Lecturer of S. Mary's, Leicester, 1778: Incumbent of S. Mary's, Leicester, 1778 to 1813. Died Mar. 24, 1813. Author of "Scripture Characters." (p. 171 and Lupton's W.W. pp. 197—206.)

1772. JOHN SHEPARD, Son of Joseph S., baptized Sep. 7, 1751: B.A. Trinity Coll. Cambridge, 1774: M.A. 1778.
1770. SAMUEL POLLARD, Cave Scholar, No. 28.
1780. SAMUEL SMALPAGE, son of Samuel S., 5th Senior Optime, Trinity Coll. Cambridge, 1783: M.A. 1786.
1781. RICHARD PEARSON, son of Robert P., 4th Wrangler, Trinity Coll. Cambridge, 1784: M.A. 1787.
1781. JOHN POPPLEWELL, son of Edward P., baptized Oct. 20, 1761: B.A. S. John's Coll. Cambridge, 1784.
1783. RICHARD ATKINSON, son of the Rev. Christopher A., Head Master: 7th Senior Optime, Trinity Coll. Cambridge, 1786: M.A. 1791.

GRAMMAR SCHOOL. 191

1788. JOHN DIXON, son of John D., Junior Optime, Trinity Coll. Cambridge, 1790.

1788. JOSEPH ARMITAGE, son of Joseph A., Woolstapler, baptized June 18, 1772 : B.A. Trinity Coll. Cambridge.

1792. CHRISTOPHER BELL, Cave Scholar, No. 29.

1793. JOHN BELL, son of Robert B., supervisor of excise; entered Queen's Coll. Oxford, Oct. 14, 1794, aged 18: B.A. 1798: M.A. 1801. Hastings Exhibitioner.

1798. HENRY ARMITAGE, son of Joseph A., of Alverthorpe: ceased residence at Cambridge in 1799.

1799. GEORGE AMBLER, Cave Scholar, No. 30.

1799. WILLIAM TATE, son of James T.

1801. JOHN MATTHEWS, matriculated at Cambridge.

1804. THOMAS ROGERS, son of the Rev. Thomas R., Head Master: B.A. Clare Hall, Cambridge, 1808.

1814. WILLIAM EDWARD COLDWELL, B.A. Catharine Hall, Cambridge, 1818: M.A. 1821: M.A. of Oxford by incorporation, 1854. Prebendary of Lichfield and Rector of Stafford in 1847. (See p. 171.)

1816. JAMES BURDAKIN, Cave Scholar, No. 32.

1817. JOHN DAY HURST, Trinity Coll. Cambridge. (See p. 171.) B.A. from Caius Coll. 1825: M.A. 1829.

1817. Mar. 8. CHARLES LAWSON, Scholar of S. John's Coll. Cambridge, 1823; 11th Senior Optime, 1824; M.A. 1827: M.A. of Oxford by incorporation, July 2, 1829. Preacher at the Foundling Hospital, London. Perhaps Archdeacon of Barbados.

1819. May 17. EGREMONT RICHARDSON, B.A. S. Catharine's Coll. Cambridge, 1823.

1824. Feb. 16. WILLIAM ROBERT ELLISS, Senior Optime, Jesus Coll. Cambridge, 1829 : M.A. 1832.

1825. Nov. 14. SAMUEL SUNDERLAND, Cave Scholar, No. 33,

1825. Nov., 14. JOSEPH HASLEGRAVE, B.A. S. Catharine's Coll. Cambridge, 1828 : M.A. 1838 : Vicar of St. Peter's, Islington, in 1835, where he died.

1827. Feb. 19. FREDERICK LUMB, B.A. Caius Coll. Cambridge, 1831 : Solicitor, of Gray's Inn, London : Solicitor of the Wakefield Rolls Office, and Deputy Steward of the Manor. Died April 19, 1872, aged 65.

1829. Sept. 30. JOHN SHARP, son of the Rev. Samuel Sharp, Vicar of Wakefield. Scholar of Magdalene Coll. Cambridge, 4th Junior Optime, 1833: M.A. 1836. Ordained Deacon in 1833, and

Priest in 1834. Perpetual Curate of Horbury from 1834 to the present time. Hon. Canon of Wakefield, late Hon. Canon of Ripon.

1829. Sep. 30. WILLIAM HURST, Junior Optime, Clare Hall, Cambridge, 1834: M.A. 1847. Ordained Deacon in 1836 and Priest in 1838 by the Bishop of Lincoln. Vicar of St. Martin, Chirk, 1842 to 1884 (Crockford's Cler. Dir.)

1830. Sep. 30. WILLIAM SHARP, son of the Rev. Samuel Sharp, Vicar of Wakefield: Scholar of Magdalene Coll. Cambridge, B.A. 1836. Ordained Deacon in 1836 by the Archbishop of York, and Priest in 1837 by the Bishop of Ripon. Vicar of Addingham, 1839-1855; Rector of Hutton. 1846-1855: Rector of Mareham-le Fen, Lincs, 1855 to the present time. (Crockford's Cler. Dir.)

1833. Sep. 30. JOSEPH LAWSON SISSON, son of the Rev. Joseph Lawson Sisson, Usher.[1] Born Jan. 10, 1816, at Leeds: B.A. Jesus Coll. Cambridge, 1840: Ordained Deacon in 1840, and Priest in 1841 by the Bishop of Hereford. Curate of Monmouth, 1840-1: Curate of Hunstanton, 1841; Vicar of Swafield, Norfolk, 1841-8: Rector of Edinthorpe, North Walsham, 1849-1890, when he died. English Chaplain at Lausanne, 1857. (See "The British Bee Journal," April 10, 1890).

1833. Sep. 30. DAVID GOODMAN DIXON, S. Catharine's Coll. Cambridge.

1836. Sep. 30. WILLIAM SPICER WOOD, Scholar of St. John's Coll. Cambridge: Chancellor's Medal for English Poem, 1838: Browne Medal for Epigram, 1839: 7th Wrangler, 3rd Classic, and 2nd Chancellor's Medallist, 1840: M.A. 1843: D.D. 1862. Fellow of his College, 1841-75. Ordained Deacon in 1844 by the Bishop of Ely, and Priest in 1845 by the Bishop of Hereford. Head Master of Oakham School, 1846-75. Curate of Brooke, Rutland, 1853-65. Vicar of Higham, Rochester, 1875 to the present time. Rural Dean of Gravesend, 1877. (Crockford's Cler. Dir.)

1837. Sep. 30. HENRY HARDCASTLE, Scholar of St. John's Coll. Cambridge. Senior Optime, 1841. Son of John H., Westfield House, Wakefield. Died June 20, 1843, aged 24: buried at Thornes.

1837. Sep. 30. GEORGE ANDREWS HEWETT, Sidney Sussex Coll. Cambridge, B.A. 1842.

1840. Sep. 30. FRANCIS HENRY DUNWELL, son of John D., of Stanley: entered Queen's Coll. Oxford, June 6, 1839, aged 20: 4th

(1) A Chancery suit was commenced to overthrow this election, but dismissed with costs: the contention was that the Exhibition was for natives of Wakefield only, and Mr. Sisson had been "accidentally" born at Leeds, as he himself says in the paper quoted above.

Class Literæ Humaniores, 1843. Hastings Exhibitioner. Vicar of Hensall, York, 1870-80, when he died, May 29. (Foster's Al. Ox.)

1841. Sep. 30. EDWIN BITTLESTON, 4th son of Thomas B., of Hunslet: entered S. Edmund's Hall, Oxford, Oct. 29, 1841, aged 19: B.A. 1845, M.A. 1848. Ordained Deacon in 1846, and Priest in 1847 by the Bishop of Durham. Curate of Long Benton, 1846-7: Perpetual Curate of Halton Gill, Skipton, 1847-66: Vicar of South Stainley, Yorks, 1873 to the present time. (Crockford's Cler. Dir.: Foster's Al. Ox.)

1841. Sep. 30. THOMAS WOODCOCK, Junior Optime, Catharine Hall, Cambridge, 1845: M.A. 1848. Curate of S. Peter's, Normanton, Derby. Now resident at Harrogate.

1844. Sep. 30. EDWARD SNOWDEN, Clare Coll. Cambridge: died Sep. 1846.

1845. Sep. 30. GEORGE ALEXANDER HOLDSWORTH, B.A. S. John's Coll. Cambridge, 1850: M.A. 1854. Ordained Deacon in 1852, and Priest in 1854 by the Bishop of Ely. Curate of S. James, Upper Edmonton: Curate of Bicester: Perpetual Curate of Sevenhampton, 1862-73: Curate of St. Mary-de-Lode, 1869-74: Curate of Stonehouse, Gloucester, 1874 to the present time. (Crockford's Cler. Dir.)

1845. Sep. 30. JAMES HENRY CARTER, eldest son of the Rev. John C., Head Master: born at Aberford: entered Trinity Coll. Oxford, May 19, 1845, aged 18: B.A. 1849, M.A. 1865. Ordained Deacon in 1849, and Priest in 1850 by the Archbishop of York. Curate of Helmsley, 1849-52: Curate of Waghen, 1852-9: Curate of Eccles, Lancs. 1859-65; Perpetual Curate of Weaste, Manchester, 1865 to the present time. (Crockford's Cler. Dir. Foster's Al. Ox.)

1847, Oct. 5. JOHN WILLIAM TAYLOR, 12th Classic and Junior Optime, St. Peter's Coll. Cambridge, 1851: M.A. 1854. Fellow and Tutor of his College. Ordained Deacon in 1852 by the Bishop of Worcester, and Priest in 1853 by the Archbishop of Canterbury. Vicar of All Saints', Cambridge, 1862-5: Rector of Exford, Somerset, 1865-6: Rector of Stathern, Leicester, 1866 to the present time. (Crockford's Cler. Dir.)

1849. Oct. 1. JOHN WALTER RHODES, Junior Optime, Trinity Coll. Cambridge, 1853. Now resides at Hill Brow, East Liss, Hunts.

1850. May 17. JAMES BUTLER KELLY, Cave Scholar, No. 35.

1851. May 6. RALPH HALL KILBY, son of the Rev. Thomas K., Vicar of S. John's, Wakefield: entered at S. Catharine's Coll. Cambridge.

1852. Sep. 7. THOMAS DUNN, son of Henry D., of Wakefield: enterered Worcester Coll. Oxford, May 12, 1852, aged 19: B.A. 1856, M.A. 1858. Ordained Deacon in 1857, and Priest in 1858 by the Bishop of Ripon. Curate of Thorner, Leeds, 1857–9: Curate of S. John the Baptist, Hulme, 1859–65: Curate of S. Philip's, Hulme, 1865–70: Curate of Mirfield, 1870–3: Vicar of Burton, Cheshire, 1876 to the present time. (Crockford's Cler. Dir.: Foster's Al. Ox.)

1853. May 3. JOSEPH HIRST LUPTON, Usher No. 39.

1853. May 3. FRANCIS THOMAS HURST, Scholar of S. Catharine's College, Cambridge: 19th Wrangler 1857, M.A. 1860. Fellow of his College. Ordained Deacon in 1859, and Priest in 1860 by the Bishop of Ripon: Curate of Holy Trinity, Richmond, Yorks, and 2nd Master at Richmond Grammar School, 1859–60. Vicar of Ridgewell, 1862 to the present time. (Crockford's Cler. Dir.)

1855. May 3. JOSEPH RAYNER, Clare Coll. Cambridge, afterwards of Magdalene Coll.: B.A. 1858, M.A. 1862. Now resides at Sharlston, near Wakefield.

1856 June 20. JOHN HODGSON, S. John's Coll. Cambridge: died in 1859.

1857. June 30. ARTHUR BUCKLEY, S. John's Coll. Cambridge: 6th Senior Optime, 1861. Once Chaplain on H.M.S. Britannia.

1858. June 18. ROUTH TOMLINSON, Cave Scholar, No. 36.

1859. June 28. JOSEPH WESTMORLAND, eldest son of Joseph W., of Wakefield [1] entered Lincoln Coll. Oxford, Oct. 20, 1859, aged 18.

1860. May 18. JAMES HEBER TAYLOR, son of the Rev. James T., Head Master: born at Bristol. Hastings Exhibitioner, Queen's Coll. Oxford; 1st Class Classical Moderations, and 1st Class Mathematical Moderations, 1861; 2nd Class Literæ Humaniores, 1863. Scholar of Trinity Coll. Cambridge: Browne Medal for Greek Ode, 1866; 1st Class Classical Tripos and Senior Optime, 1868; 1st Chancellor's Medal, 1868.

1861. June 18. HENRY MARTYN TAYLOR, son of the Rev. James T., Head Master. Scholar of Trinity Coll. Cambridge: 3rd Wrangler, and 2nd Smith's Prize, 1865; Fellow of his College, Tutor, and Examiner in the Mathematical Tripos.

---

(1) This election was appealed against by a Chancery Suit, which the Governors defended successfully: an appeal was then made to the House of Lords by the parties non-suited, and this was allowed: the whole of the costs of both trials came out of the Storie University Fund.

GRAMMAR SCHOOL.

1862. June 17. THOMAS JAMES SANDERSON, Cave Scholar, No. 37.

1863. June 20. THOMAS HENRY SHAW, Cave Scholar, No. 38.

1864. June 23. GEORGE BREWERTON, Freeston Exhibitioner.

1865. June 29. WILLIAM WILBERFORCE TAYLOR, son of the Rev. James T., Head Master. Hastings Exhibitioner, Queen's Coll. Oxford: 1st Class Mathematical Moderations, 1867; 1st Class Mathematics, 1869. Scholar of Trinity Coll. Cambridge; 7th Wrangler, 1872. Lately Assistant Master at Ripon Grammar School.

1866. July 4. WILLIAM LAMPREY BOWDITCH, Cave Scholar, No. 39.

1867. June 5. JAMES KERSHAW, Cave Scholar, No. 40.

1868. July 1. WYNDHAM MONSON MADDEN, son of the Rev. Wyndham Monson M., Vicar of Holy Trinity, Wakefield. Scholar of Queens' Coll. Cambridge; 17th Wrangler, 1872.

1869. June 21. JAMES BEVERLEY, Cave Scholar, No. 41.

1870. June 22. FREDERICK WILLIAM AINLEY, Cave Scholar, No. 42.

1871. June 21. HENRY EVERINGHAM ALDERSON, son of the Rev. William Thompson A., Chaplain of H.M. Prison, Wakefield. Junior Optime, S. Catharine's Coll. Cambridge, 1875: M.A. 1878. Ordained Deacon in 1875 aud Priest in 1878 by the Bishop of Oxford. Chaplain of S. Paul's Coll. Stony Stratford 1876-82: Curate of Beachampton, Bucks, 1878-82: Curate of Mirfield, 1882-87: Vicar of Peel, Bolton-le-Moors, 1887 to the present time. (Crockford's Cler. Dir.)

1872. July 31. WILLIAM MOXON WADSWORTH, B.A., Queens' Coll. Cambridge, 1875: M.A. 1880. Ordained Deacon in 1880, and Priest in 1881 by the Bishop of Durham. Assistant Master at Durham School, 1877-82: Curate of Chester-le-Street, 1882-6: Curate of Christ Church, Sunderland, 1886 to the present time. (Crockford's Cler. Dir.)

1873. July 9. CHARLES MILNER ATKINSON, Cave Exhibitioner, No. 43.

1874. July 1. HERBERT WICE, son of Jonathan Haigh W., of Wakefield. Junior Optime, Trinity Coll. Cambridge, 1878: M.A. 1881. Ordained Deacon in 1879, and Priest in 1880 by the Bishop of Lichfield: Curate of Christ Church, Derby, 1879-85: Curate of S. Mary's, Lichfield, 1885-6: Curate of S. Mary Magdalene, Taunton, 1887 to the present time. (Crockford's Cler. Dir.)

1875. July 27. WILLIAM JOSEPH GOMERSALL, S. Edmund Hall, Oxford: 3rd Class Classical Moderations, 1877.

1877. Sep. 5. WILLIAM HAY ALDERSON, Cave Exhibitioner, No. 44.

1877. Sep. 5. GEORGE HOLKEY HUNTER, Owens College, Manchester.

1878. Nov. 6. RICHARD GEORGE PARKER BULLOCK, Freeston Exhibitioner.

1879. Oct. 6. BOWMAN HENRY MADDEN, Cave Exhibitioner, No. 45.

1880. Sep. 22. JAMES PATRICK O'DONOHOE, Freeston Exhibitioner.

1880. Sep. 22. GEORGE HENRY SCOTT, son of Henry Castile S., of Ossett. Of Owens College, Manchester. Now Surgeon in Sheffield.

1881. Oct. 5. RALPH HORATIO BOWDIN, 2nd son of William B., Supervisor of Inland Revenue, Wakefield: Scholar of Balliol Coll. Oxford, matriculated Oct. 18, 1881, aged 19: 1st Class Mathematical Moderations, 1882: Junior Mathematical Scholarship, 1883: 1st Class Mathematics, 1884: 1st Class Natural Science, 1886. Died at Harrogate in April, 1889.

1882. Sep. 6. RICHARD ELLIS HOLMES, son of Richard Hind H., of Pontefract. Unattached Student at Oxford, matriculated Oct. 14, 1882, aged 19: Exhibitioner of Trinity Coll. Oxford: 3rd Class Modern History, 1885. Ordained Deacon in 1887, and Priest in 1888 by the Bishop of Adelaide: Curate of Holy Trinity, South Shields, 1887 to the present time. (Crockford's Cler. Dir.)

1883. Aug. 1. CHARLES MILLER GRACE, 2nd son of William G., of Wakefield. Hastings Exhibitioner, Queen's Coll. Oxford: matriculated Oct. 22, 1883, aged 18: B.A. 1887.

1883. Aug. 1. JAMES EDWARD WILKINSON, Scholar of Downing Coll. Cambridge: 1st Class Natural Science Tripos, 1886.

1884. July 29. ROBERT THORLEY JOHNSON, Freeston Exhibitioner.

1885. Aug. 5. JOHN WILLIAM ASHTON, son of William A., of Wakefield. Scholar of University Coll. Oxford: 2nd Class Mathematical Moderations, 1886; 1st Class Mathematics, 1889; now resides at Fakenham, Norfolk.

1885. Aug. 5. LEONARD TECK REID, son of Thomas R., Normanton. Exhibitioner of King's Coll. Cambridge: 19th Wrangler, 1888.

1886. Nov. 3. JAMES EDWARD BRIGGS, Cave Exhibitioner, No. 48.

1887. Aug. 3. GEORGE WILLIAM SYKES, Freeston Exhibitioner.

GRAMMAR SCHOOL.

1888. Aug. 1. JOHN THORNTON, Freeston Exhibitioner.

1889. Sep. 4. HECTOR MUNRO CHADWICK, Cave Exhibitioner, No. 49.

1889. Sep. 4. CHARLES HENRY HIRST WALKER, Freeston Exhibitioner.

1890. July 31. GEORGE THOMAS MANLEY, son of the late George M., of Wakefield. Scholar of Christ's Coll. Cambridge. Akroyd Scholar.[1]

1891. July 30. FREDERICK WILLIAM PEARSON, son of William P., Broom Hall, Wakefield. Scholar of Exeter Coll. Oxford.

V. THE HASTINGS EXHIBITIONS AT QUEEN'S COLLEGE, OXFORD.

Lady Elizabeth Hastings, daughter of Theophilus, 7th Earl of Huntingdon, gave by a codicil to her will, dated Apl. 24, 1739, all her "Mannors Lands and Hereditaments in Wheldale, otherwise called Queldale, in the West Riding of the County of York . . . . to the Provost and Scholars of Queen's Colledge in the University of Oxford for ever . . . . One Hundred and Forty Pounds out of the clear Rents and Profits of the same shall from time to time be applied for Exhibitions towards the maintenance of Five poor Scholars of the said Colledge to be nominated and elected in manner herein after directed . . . . Eight of the principal Schools in the County of York, namely those of Leeds Wakefield Bradford Beverly Skipton Sedborough Rippon and Sherborne, and Two more in the County of Westmoreland, namely Appleby and Haversham and Two more in Cumberland, namely St. Bees and Penrith, shall each of them have the Priviledge or liberty of sending one poor Scholar every five Years to the place of Nomination . . . . . And I make it my earnest request that the Rectors of Berwick Spofforth and Bolton Percy, and the Vicars of Leeds, Ledsham, Thorp-Arch and Collingham in the County of York will . . . . meet together at the best Inn in Abberford or Abberforth in the same County, namely on Thursday in Whitson-Week before Eight of the Clock in the morning, Also all the Boys to meet at the said best Inn at Abberforth the Night preceding the Day of Nomination in order to be ready to begin their Exercises the next Morning. And I intreat the Rectors and Vicars aforenamed will be there half an hour after Seven that They may choose the Boys Morning Exercise and put them upon beginning the same by Eight of

[1] This Scholarship is open to candidates from any endowed School in Yorkshire, and is of the value of £50 a year.

the Clock. And my Will is that their Exercise be a part of an Oration in Tully not exceeding Eight or Ten Lines to be translated into English and part of an Oration in Demosthenes about the said number of Lines to be translated into Latin, And two or Three Verses of the Latin Testament to be translated into Greek, And whilst the Boys are making their Morning Exercise the said Rectors and Vicars or the greater number of them shall proceed to chuse the Afternoon's Exercise (which shall be upon Two Subjects) One of Practical Divinity out of the Church Catechism upon which each Boy shall give his Thoughts in Latin in not fewer than Eight Lines nor more than Twelve, The other Subject some distinguished sentence of a Classick Author upon which each Boy shall write Two Distichs of Verses. All which translations and Compositions are to be written out fair upon One Sheet of Paper and signed by the name of each Boy they belong to and then shewed to every nominating Rector and Vicar, who are desired impartially to weigh and consider and return Ten of the best of the said exercises (each of which ten to be signed by the greater Number of the Rectors and Vicars present) to the Provost and Fellows of Queen's Colledge in the University of Oxford, And when the said Provost and Fellows have received the same they are hereby required to meet together as soon after as conveniently may be to examine into them carefully and impartially and choose out of them Eight of the best Performances which appear the best, which done the Names subscribed to those Eight shall be fairly written each in a distinct Paper and the Papers rolled up and put into an Urn or Vase by the Provost or in his absence by the Vice-Provost or Senior Fellow, and after having been shaken well together in the Urn shall be drawn out of the same by some Person whom he or they shall appoint, And those Five whose Names are first drawn shall to all Intents and Purposes be held duly Elected and intitled to the whole Profits each of his Exhibition for the space of Five Years as before provided from Pentecost then next preceding the Election. And though this Method of choosing by Lot may be called by some Superstition or Enthusiasm, yet as the Advice was given me by an Orthodox and Pious Prelate of the Church of England as leaving something to Providence and as it will be a means to save the Scholars the trouble and expence of a journey to Oxford under too great an uncertainty of being elected, I will this method of Balloting be for ever observed." The rest of the codicil contains much that is interesting and well worth perusal.

  Various changes have been made in the Schools entitled to send in candidates, owing to some having decayed: thus the place of

GRAMMAR SCHOOL. 199

Beverley was taken by Richmond in 1789, York substituted for Richmond in 1804, Pontefract for Skipton in the same year, Hipperholme for Ripon in 1784, Giggleswick for Sherborne in 1849, and Ripon, Carlisle and Doncaster in recent years for Hipperholme, Penrith and Pontefract.[1] It will thus appear that Wakefield has never lost its right to send in candidates; though, as a matter of fact, it has sent in only few, doubtless because it has always had other Exhibitions or Scholarships to depend upon at Oxford and Cambridge.

From 1764 to 1859 the election was held only once in five years, but since that time it has been held every year, and the system of drawing by lot abolished: since the same time prizes of £5 have been awarded to unsuccessful candidates who have been judged "meritorious."

The following list of successful and meritorious Candidates from Wakefield has been very kindly sent to me by the Rev. Dr. Magrath, the present Provost of the College :—

1769. June 5. THOMAS HERON, son of Thomas H. of Pontefract: matriculated June 30, 1769, aged 19 : B.A. 1773.

1789. JOHN BUTTERFIELD SCHOREY, son of Thomas S. of Sandal Magna : matriculated July 11, 1789, aged 19 : B.A. 1793, M.A. 1796.

1794. JOHN BELL, Storie Exhibitioner for 1794.

1799. JOSEPH STEPHENSON, son of Christopher S. of Rowley Regis, Stafford: matriculated July 10. 1799, aged 16: B.A. 1803, M.A. 1806.

1824. WILLIAM MONKHOUSE, 3rd son of the Rev. William M., of Stockdale Wath, Cumberland: matriculated June 22, aged 19. Scholar of the College 1826–39: 3rd class Literæ Humaniores, 1828: Fellow of the College 1839–62 : M.A. 1832, B.D. 1853 ; Bursar 1842, Proctor 1842: Rector of Goldington, Beds. 1836–62. (Foster's Al. Ox.)

1829. RICHARD SNOWDEN, Usher, No. 34.

1843. FRANCIS HENRY DUNWELL, Storie Exhibitioner.

1859. JAMES HEBER TAYLOR, Storie Exhibitioner.

1865. WILLIAM WILBERFORCE TAYLOR, Storie Exhibitioner.

1868. CHARLES JAMES BALL, eldest son of Charles B. of Guildford, Surrey: matriculated Oct. 23, 1868, aged 17 : 2nd class Classical Moderations, 1870 ; 1st class Literæ Humaniores 1872 : M A. 1876. Ordained Deacon in 1874, and Priest in 1875 by the Bishop of London. Curate of St. Gabriel, Pimlico, 1874–5 : Head Master's Assistant at Merchant Taylors' School 1873–5 : Curate of S. Clement, Eastcheap, 1875–6 : 2nd Classical Master at Merchant Taylors'

[1] See Mr. W. Claridge's articles in the "Yorkshire Weekly Post." 1885.

School 1875–8: Townsend Lecturer, St. Magnus the Martyr, London Bridge, 1877–8: Censor and Chaplain of King's Coll. London, 1878–9: Chaplain of Lincoln's Inn, 1880 to the present time. Author of various Hebrew Grammars, Contributor to the "Commentary for English Readers," and "Dictionary of Christian Biography" (Crockford's Cler. Dir.: Foster's Al. Ox.)

1883. CHARLES MILLER GRACE, Storie Exhibitioner.

In addition to the above-mentioned successful candidates, the following Wakefield boys have been judged "meritorious," viz:—Henry Martyn Taylor in 1860, Thomas James Sanderson in 1861, William Lamprey Bowditch in 1865, and again in 1866, James Kershaw in 1867, Robert Thorley Johnson in 1884, and Hector Munro Chadwick in 1888.

Moreover, John Day Hurst's lot was not drawn in 1819, though he was selected at Aberford, and Joseph Lawson Sisson was disqualified in 1834 as not having attended the School for the previous four years. All these eight names appear in the list of Storie Exhibitioners.

Chapter 9.

REGISTER OF PUPILS.

AN attempt will be made in this Chapter to record the names of all those who are known, or supposed, to have been educated at the School. Up to the year 1814 there appears to have been no Register kept, and the details here given have therefore been obtained from a variety of sources, such as the biographies of the most famous of its pupils, the Oxford and Cambridge Calendars, Foster's "Alumni Oxonienses," "Graduati Cantabrigienses," the Matriculation Registers of various Colleges, the lists of Cave, Freeston and Hastings Scholars and Exhibitioners, the account-books of the Governors, the life of the Rev. John Clarke, and the inscriptions in various books in the School Library.

On Mar. 2, 1829, the Governors of the School ordered that the Master and Usher should " immediately make out a List, to the best of their power, of all such Scholars as have been instructed by them during the time they have held their respective situations . . . . . . The Master and Usher are held responsible that from henceforth the Register and Duplicate are kept in the most correct manner." From this it will appear that the entries from 1814, the year of Dr. Naylor's appointment as Head Master, to 1829, the year when the Register was first written, were made from memory: but that after the latter year the names have been regularly inserted, as occasion demanded.

Various abbreviations have been used in the following pages :— C, F, H, S, after the names, denote that the Scholar in question obtained a Cave, Freeston, Hastings or Storie Exhibition, and particulars will therefore be found about them in the preceding chapter. The letters L and Z denote that the name is inserted here on the ground that it occurs in the list of Donors to the Library, or in Dr. Zouch's list of pupils of the Rev. John Clarke, a consideration of dates and other facts rendering it probable that the insertion is justifiable. The dates given, up to the year 1814, are the approximate ones of leaving School.

REGISTER OF PUPILS OF WAKEFIELD GRAMMAR SCHOOL.

1604. AMBROSE MAWDE C., JOHN RILEY C.

1612. JOSEPH NAYLOR, born at Wakefield in 1594: Fellow of Sid. Sus. Coll. Cambridge: Archdeacon of Northumberland in 1632. Prebendary of Durham in 1636: Rector of Sedgefield in 1634: ejected by the Puritans, and restored in 1662: Chaplain to Bishop Morton (p. 115): died and buried in Sedgefield Church in 1667. (Lupton's W.W.) Was perhaps Freeston Scholar and Fellow.

1615. JEREMIAH WHITAKER, born at Wakefield in 1599: Sizar of Sid. Sus. Coll. Camb., in 1615; B.A. in 1619: Master of Oakham School, 1619-30: Vicar of Stretton in Rutland, 1630-43: Rector of S. Mary Magdalene, Bermondsey, 1644-54: Member of the Assembly of Divines, 1643, and Moderator in 1647: died on June 1, 1654, buried in S. Mary Magdalene's, Bermondsey. A great Oriental Scholar and Puritan Divine. (Lupton's W.W.) Perhaps a Freeston Scholar.

1616. JAMES LISTER C.

1619. HUGH PAULIN CRESSY, son of Hugh C., Governor and Benefactor (p. 45), born at Wakefield in 1605: entered Magd. Hall, Oxford, Jan. 21, 1619-20: B. A. in 1623, M.A. in 1629: Fellow of Merton College in 1626: Domestic Chaplain to the Earl of Strafford in 1629, and to Viscount Falkland in 1638: Canon of Windsor in 1642, Dean of Laghlin in Ireland in 1643: a zealous Royalist: became a Roman Catholic in 1646, and a Benedictine Monk at Douay: afterwards Chaplain to Queen Katharine; died Aug. 10, 1674, buried in East Grinstead Church, Sussex. (Lupton's W.W.)

1620. BARNABAS OLEY or HEYOLT, born at Kirkthorpe in 1601: probably Cave Scholar of Clare Hall, Camb., where he was afterwards Fellow, Tutor and President: Taxor in 1634 and Proctor in 1635: Vicar of Great Gransden, Hunts.: a zealous Royalist: ejected from his living and Fellowship by the Puritans, but restored in 1659: Prebendary of Worcester in 1660: Archdeacon of Ely in 1679: died Feb. 20, 1685-6. A great benefactor of his College and native parish. (Lupton's W.W.)

1623. ....MILTON C.

1627. .....HORNE, ... COPLEY, ... SUNDERLAND, ... DENISON, (p. 50.) The last named may be the WILLIAM DENISON, who was Governor and Benefactor. (p. 51.)

GRAMMAR SCHOOL.

1627. GODFREY WINTER, son of the Rev. Richard W., Rector of Spotborough; at Wakefield School 2 years: entered Chr. Coll. Camb. in 1627, aged 17, and Caius Coll. Apl. 7, 1629: B.A. in 1632.

1627. MATTHEW WHITLEY, son of John W., born at Halifax: B.A. of Emm. Coll. Camb. in 1631: entered as Pensioner of S. Jo. Coll. Dec. 1, 1632, aged 21.

1628. CHARLES HOOLE, born at Wakefield in 1610, entered Linc. Coll. Oxford, in 1628: Rector of Ponton Magna in Leicestershire in 1642; ejected by the Puritans: Head Master of Rotherham Free School: Master of private Schools in Aldersgate St. and Lothbury: Rector of Stock near Chelmsford in 1660: Prebendary of Lincoln in 1661; died and buried at Stock, Mar. 7, 1666-7. A famous Scholar and author of School-books. (Lupton's W.W.)

1631. INGRAM HOPTON, son of Ralph H., of Armley; at Wakefield School 4 years: Fellow-Commoner of S. Jo. Coll. Camb., May 12, aged 16: afterwards a Colonel in the Royalist Forces: Knighted by Charles I., and killed at Winceby in Lincolnshire, Oct 24, 1643.

1632. WILLIAM ALLOTT, son of Edward A., farmer, Sandal: at Wakefield School 2 years: Sizar of S. Jo. Coll. Camb., May 12, aged 19: Fellow in 1637.

1632. GEORGE MARSDEN, son of Thomas M., Thornhill; born at Newhall Manor, Thornhill: at Wakefield School 5 years: Sizar of S. Jo. Coll. Camb., May 23, aged 16.

1632-3. ANDREW HARE, son of Robert H., born at Calverley; at Wakefield School 2 years: Sizar of Caius Coll. Camb., Feb. 12, aged 16.

1633. RICHARD ALLOTT, son of Bartin A., born at Clayton in July, 1617: at Wakefield School 3 years: Pensioner of S. Jo. Coll. Camb., May 2.

1633-4. THOMAS CALLIS, son of Robert C., farmer, Wakefield: born at York: at Wakefield School 7 years: Sizar of S. Jo. Coll. Camb., Feb. 22, aged 15.

1636. WILLIAM WENTWORTH, son of Thomas W., Esq., of Kirkby: at Wakefield School 2 years: Pensioner of S. Jo. Coll. Camb., Sept. 1, aged 16. A Captain in the Royalist Forces, died in 1660.

1638-9. ROBERT WILBORE, son of Lawrence W., gent. of Balne, Yorks: born at Norton: at Wakefield School 4 years: Pensioner of Caius Coll. Camb., Jan. 28, aged 24.

1640. JOHN STORIE, son of John S., Governor of the School: baptized at Wakefield Parish Church, Nov. 15, 1621: probably educated at the School, and one of its greatest benefactors (p. 50.) Was "sequestred and imprisoned for his constant Loyalty to the King, and often plundered and had many writeings and goods both of his owne and of the Mounsons and Saviles taken away from him," for whom "he had done much business in the late rebellious times." He died at Hasleborrow, Derbyshire, in 1674, and left £6000 value in lands.

1641. HENRY DOUGHTY, Usher No. 7.

1641. ROBERT CASSON, son of Robert C., yeoman, of Thorpe on the Hill, Rothwell: at Wakefield School 2 years: Sizar of S. Jo. Coll. Camb. June 19, aged 17. A zealous supporter of the King against Parliament: see Batty's Rothwell p. 60.

1641. SAMUEL BATTISON, son of Giles B., weaver, of Hemsworth: born at Hiendley: at Wakefield School 1 year: Pensioner of S. Jo. Coll. Camb. June 19, aged 18.

1642. RICHARD CLARKE, son of William C., farmer, of Sandal: at Wakefield School 6 years: Sizar of S. Jo. Coll. Camb. Apl. 12, aged 18.

1642. RICHARD COATES, son of Thomas C., draper, of Wakefield: at Wakefield School "a primordiis literarum": Sizar of S. Jo. Coll. Camb. June 20, aged 18. Ejected in 1645, perhaps for his political views.

1643. RICHARD WORSOPPE, son of Edward W., mercer, of Batley, entered University College, Oxford in 1643: Sizar of S. Jo. Coll. Camb. Jan. 5, 1645-6, aged 17.

1644. JOSEPH MOXON, born at Wakefield Aug. 8, 1627, and probably educated at the School; perhaps the son of Peter M., a Governor. An excellent mathematician, and hydrographer to Charles II.: often quoted in Johnson's Dictionary: planned a canal from the Thames to the Severn in 1667. Fellow of the Royal Society in 1678; died in 1700 (Lupton's W.W.)

1645. ROBERT HOBSON, son of Edmund H., of Smallfield near Penistone: Sizar of S. Jo. Coll. Camb. Sept. 8, aged 20.

1648. CHARLES WILSON, son of Christopher W., of Broadfield: Sizar of S. Jo. Coll. Camb. Sept. 8, aged 17.

1650. WILLIAM BOOTH, son of Matthew B., clerk, of Knaresborough: Sizar of S. Jo. Coll. Camb. July 1, aged 17.

1651. DANIEL PELL, son of William P., of Sandal: born at Walton: Sizar of S. Jo. Coll. Camb. May 31, aged 19.

1652. THEODORE BROWNELOW, son of Robert B., M.D. of Wakefield and Governor of the School: born at Leeds: Pensioner of S. Jo. Coll. Camb. Feb. 6, aged 17.

1653. JOHN FRANKE, son of Charles F., of Pontefract, gent: born in Hertfordshire: Pensioner of S. Jo. Coll. Camb. May 12 aged 17.

(Photographed from an engraving of a painting by Kneller.)

GRAMMAR SCHOOL. 205

1653. THOMAS DOUGHTY, son of Robert D., Head Master of the School: born in 1637: perhaps M.A. of Magd. Coll. Camb. in 1660, and D.D. in 1671.

1653–4. NICHOLAS WINTERBOURNE, son of Leonard W., blacksmith, of Wakefield: at Wakefield School 6 years: Sizar of S. Jo. Coll. Camb. Feb. 14, aged 17.

1654. THOMAS HARDCASTLE, son of William H., of Kirkby Malzeard: at Wakefield School 2 years: Sizar of S. Jo. Coll. Camb., July 3, aged 15.

1655. JOSIAH HOLDSWORTH, son of John H., clothier, of Wakefield: Sizar of S. Jo. Coll. Camb., Apl. 9, aged 17. Ejected from Sutton in Yorkshire in 1662, died in 1685.

1658. JOHN BASKERVILE, son of Thomas B., of Wakefield: born in 1641, and probably educated at the School. Afterwards Head Master. (p. 128.)

1660. ELISHA ROBINSON, son of Thomas R., clerk, of Tong: at Wakefield School 5 years: Sizar of S. Jo. Coll. Camb., June 11, aged 15: B.A. in 1663, and M.A. in 1667.

1661. RICHARD MILNER, son of Richard M., farmer, of S. Hiendley: at Wakefield School 2 years: Sizar of S. Jo. Coll. Camb., Apl. 29, aged 18.

1663. RICHARD THOMPSON, born at Wakefield about 1645; Scholar of Univ. Coll. Oxford: B.A. in 1667; M.A. of Magd. Coll. Cambridge in 1670, and D.D. in 1684: Curate of Brington, Northants: Vicar of S. Mary's, Marlborough; of Bedminster near Bristol: and of S. Mary Redcliffe, Bristol: Prebendary of Sarum in 1676: Prebendary of Bristol in 1683, Dean in 1684: died Nov. 29, 1685, and buried in Bristol Cathedral. A "zealous upholder of the Church of England," suspected of joining in Popish Plots, and "brought on his knees in the House of Commons and blasted for a papist." (Lupton's W.W.)

1663. JOSEPH ROBINSON, son of Thomas R., of Kirkthorpe, Clerk: at Wakefield School 6 years: Sizar of S. Jo. Coll. Camb., Mar. 31, aged 14: B.A. in 1666, M.A. of King's College in 1670.

1664. WILLIAM PINDAR, son of Nicholas P., of Wakefield: born about 1646: entered Univ. Coll. Oxford in 1664: B.A. in 1667: Fellow of his College. Rector of S. Ebbe's, Oxford: Chaplain to Lord Grey: died Sep. 23, 1678, buried at Gosfield in Essex. (Lupton's W.W.)

1665. JOHN RADCLIFFE, son of George R., of Wakefield, Governor of the House of Correction from 1647 to 1661, an attorney, and Governor of the School from 1653 to his death in 1674. Born in the house now occupied by Mr. W. H. Milnes, and baptized at the Parish Church on May 1, 1650. Entered Univ. Coll. Oxford, on Mar. 23, 1665-6 : B.A. and Senior Scholar in 1669, M.A. in 1672, M.B. in 1675, M.D. in 1682. Fellow of Lincoln College from 1670 to 1677. Practised in Oxford until 1682, when he settled in Bow St., Covent Garden, and became immediately famous. Had the offer of the post of Royal Physician to William III. and a baronetcy, but declined both : yet was often called in to attend the King. Was Physician to Princess Anne of Denmark from 1686. Elected M.P. for Buckingham in 1713, and died on Nov. 1, 1714, at Carlshalton, where he had gone to reside: buried at S. Mary's, Oxford, on Dec. 3, following. Left very large bequests for charitable purposes, such as £40,000 for founding the Radcliffe Library at Oxford (built in 1737-47), £150 a year to the librarian, £5000 to complete the front of his College buildings, £600 a year to found the Radcliffe Travelling Fellowships, £600 a year to S. Bartholomew's Hospital, and other smaller sums. Dr. Radcliffe made "many repeated promises in his Life Time" to leave money to his School, but nothing was ever received from him. In 1801, however, the Radcliffe Trustees gave £1000 towards S. John's Church in this city. Dr. Radcliffe is said, in Ingledew's "History of North-allerton," to have been partly educated at Northallerton School : he however himself says, in a letter to Mr. Obadiah Walker, Master of University College, Oxford, dated May 25, 1688, that he was " bred up a Protestant at Wakefield, and sent from thence in that Perswasion to Oxford." He was therefore probably at Northallerton first, if at all : for there is perhaps some confusion of names, seeing that Mr. George Radcliffe, his father, was resident in Wakefield from 1647, three years before Dr. Radcliffe's birth, until his death in 1674, and it would be unlikely that a boy was sent away from Wakefield at a time when its Grammar School was "as famous as any whatsoever in these Kingdoms, except those of Westminster, Winchester, and Eton." (p. 129.) (Lupton's W.W.)

1669. FRANCIS RAYNEY, son of Henry R., of Darfield : at Wakefield School 2 years : entered S. Jo. Coll. Camb. on May 7, aged 17 : B.A. in 1672, M.A. in 1676.

1670. MICHAEL WENTWORTH, son of John W., Esq., born at York : Fellow-Commoner of S. Jo. Coll. Camb. Apl. 25, aged 15. Of Woolley, knighted at Windsor, for his military services, in 1681 : died Sep. 1696, and buried at Woolley.

1671. MATTHEW DODSWORTH, son of Edward D., of Badsworth, clerk : entered S. Jo. Coll. Camb. Mar. 30, aged 14.

GRAMMAR SCHOOL.   207

1671. RICHARD BEAUMONT, son of Adam B., of Heaton, Esq.: Fellow-Commoner of S. Jo. Coll. Camb. May 13, aged 17.

1671. GEORGE WALKER, son of George W., of Wakefield: entered S. Jo. Coll. Camb. May 13, aged 16.

1672. THOMAS SENIOR, son of Thomas S., of Dodworth, clerk: entered S. Jo. Coll. Camb. Apl. 1, aged 17: M.B. in 1677.

1674. CHRISTOPHER ARMITAGE, son of Sir John A., Kt. and Bt.: born at York: entered S. Jo. Coll. Camb. July 10, aged 16: Fellow-Commoner and B.A. in 1680. Fellow of Peterhouse and M.A. in 1682.

1674–5. JOSHUA HOBSON, son of John H., currier, of Dodworth: entered S. Jo. Coll. Camb. Mar. 11: B.A. in 1678, M.A. in 1682: Fellow of his College.

1675. JOHN SENIOR, son of George S., of Selbrooke: entered S. Jo. Coll. Camb. Apl. 19, aged 18: LL.B. in 1680.

1675. THOMAS SLINGER, son of Thomas S., of Sharlston: entered S. Jo. Coll. Camb. June 18, aged 17.

1676. RICHARD BENTLEY, son of the late Thomas B., of Oulton, near Wakefield: born Jan. 27, 1661–2: sub-sizar of S. Jo. Coll. Camb. on May 24, 1676, educated at a day-school in Methley, and subsequently at Wakefield Grammar School: in 1680 he was 3rd Wrangler, and took his B.A. degree: M.A. in 1683: and M.A. of Wadham College, Oxford, in 1689: D.D. (by the Archbishop of Canterbury) in 1696. Head Master of Spalding School in 1682: ordained Deacon in 1690, and appointed Chaplain to the Bishop of Worcester. First Boyle Lecturer and Prebendary of Worcester in 1692: Keeper of the Royal Library at S. James's in 1693. Master of Trin. Coll. Camb. and Vice-Chancellor in 1700: Archdeacon of Ely in 1701: Regius Professor of Divinity in 1717: died on July 14, 1742. "The greatest of English critics in this, or possibly any other, age." (Hallam's Lit. of Europe, iii. 251). See Monk's and Jebb's "Life of Bentley," and Lupton's "Wakefield Worthies," where lists of Dr. Bentley's works and details of his eventful life may be found. (p. 128).

1676. JOHN BEEVER, son of William B., dyer, Penistone: entered S. Jo. Coll. Camb. June 12, aged 17: B.A. in 1679, M.A. in 1683.

1676. NATHAN DRAKE, son of Joseph D., of Pennigent: entered S. Jo. Coll. Camb. Nov. 27, aged 16: B.A. in 1680, M.A. in 1684.

1677. GEORGE BENLOWES C.

1677. JOHN WASTELL, son of the late Leonard W., Esq., of Bolton, Yorks: Fellow-Commoner of S. Jo. Coll. Camb. June 1, aged 16: B.A. in 1680.

1678. WILLIAM ALLOTT, son of George A., of Crigglestone, gent., entered S. Jo. Coll. Camb. April 11, aged 19.

1678-9. HENRY AWDSLEY, son of Thomas A., schoolmaster, of Worsbrough: entered S. Jo. Coll. Camb. Feb. 1, aged 15: B.A. in 1682.

1681. JAMES HARGREAVES, son of James H., of Colne, clerk: entered S. Jo. Coll. Camb. Apl. 16, aged 16: B.A. in 1684, M.A. in 1700.

1681. RICHARD KIRSHAW C.

1682. RICHARD ELLERSHAW C.

1684. JOSEPH BINGHAM, son of Francis B., of Wakefield: born in Sept., 1668: entered Univ. Coll. Oxford, May 26, 1684: B.A. in 1688: Fellow of his College in 1689: M.A. in 1691, and Tutor, having the future Archbishop Potter under his charge. Resigned his Fellowship in 1695, and presented by Dr. Radcliffe to the Rectory of Headbourne Worthy, near Winchester: Rector of Havant, near Portsmouth, in 1712: died Aug. 17, 1723, and buried at Headbourne Worthy. Author of the learned and voluminous "Origines Ecclesiasticæ." (Lupton's W.W.)

1686-7. THOMAS EDMUNDS, son of Thomas E., of Worsbrough, gent.: entered S. Jo. Coll. Camb. Feb. 12, aged 16.

1686-7. WILLIAM TAYLOR, son of Thomas T., of Worsbrough, farmer: entered S. Jo. Coll. Camb. Feb. 12: B.A. in 1690, M.A. in 1694.

1688. JOHN POTTER, son of Thomas P., draper, of Wakefield: born in the house now called "The Black Rock," in the Market Place, about 1674: servitor at Univ. Coll. Oxford, Lent Term, 1688: B.A. in 1692: Fellow of Linc. Coll. in 1694: ordained Deacon in 1698: Chaplain to Archbishop Tenison in 1704: D.D. in 1706, and Chaplain in Ordinary to Queen Anne: Regius Professor of Divinity, and Canon of Christ Church, Oxford, in 1708: Bishop of Oxford in 1715: Archbishop of Canterbury in 1737: died Oct. 10, 1747. When Dr. Bentley became Regius Professor of Divinity at Cambridge, the Wakefield Grammar School enjoyed "the singular distinction of having produced two scholars who held the office of Regius Professor of Divinity in their respective Universities at the same time" (Monk's "Life of Bentley"). Dr. Potter published several classical books, the most important being his "Archæologia Græca," a Dictionary of Greek Antiquities, which was in great request until quite recent times. (Lupton's W.W.)

DR. POTTER.
ARCHBISHOP OF CANTERBURY.

(From a Photograph in Hailstone's "Portraits of Yorkshire Worthies.")

GRAMMAR SCHOOL.

1688. OBADIAH LEE C, and WILLIAM WOODCOCK L.

1691. DANIEL SILL, son of Toby S., of Wakefield: B.A. Magd. Coll. Camb. 1694, M.A. 1698. Afterwards Governor (p. 101).

1691-2. THOMAS SCOTT C.

1693. GEORGE WALKER, son of Thomas W., shoemaker, Wakefield: entered S. Jo. Coll. Camb. June 15, aged 18: B.A. in 1696, M.A. in 1706.

1694. JOHN MARROW C.

1698. THOMAS DOUGHTY S, and DAVID WATERHOUSE S.

1702. BENJAMIN BAYNES S.

1703. WILLIAM BURROW S, Usher of the School (p. 154.)

1703. JOHN BRADSBURY S.

1707. SAMUEL DRANSFIELD S.

1709. CHARLES NAYLOR S.

1709. WHETLEY HEALD, son of Thomas H., of Wakefield, clerk: entered S. Jo. Coll. Camb. Oct. 28, aged 15: B.A. in 1713, M.A. in 1717, B.D. in 1724. Fellow of his College.

1710. JAMES HARGREAVES S.

1710. WILLIAM SHAW, son of Samuel S., draper, Shelley: entered S. Jo. Coll. Camb. May 24, aged 22: B.A. in 1713.

1711. ABRAHAM SHAW, son of Abraham S., of Edlington, clerk: entered S. Jo. Coll. Camb. May 23, aged 18: B A. in 1714.

1714. JOHN WILSON CS.

1714. RICHARD CAYLEY, son of Matthew C., of Knottingley, gent.: entered S. Jo. Coll. Camb. May 6, aged 19: B.A. in 1717, M.A. in 1721, B.D. in 1729. Fellow of his College.

1715. JOHN WRAY C.

1715-6. WILLIAM MOMPESSON, son of George M., of York, clerk: at Wakefield School two years: entered S. Jo. Coll. Camb. Mar. 20, aged 18. B.A. of Peterhouse in 1719, M.A. in 1723.

1715-6. JOHN WOOLLEN, son of James W. of Wakefield, baptized June 6, 1699: entered Mert. Coll. Oxford, Jan. 19, aged 16: B.A. in 1720: M.A. of Oriel Coll. in 1722: B.D. in 1735. Proctor in 1729.

1716. JOHN COPPENDALE L, B.A. of Trin. Coll. Camb. in 1720, M.A. in 1724: Fellow of his College in 1729. Perhaps son of William C., Governor of the School.

1717. RICHARD STRINGER S.

1717. JAMES WOOLLEN S.

1718. THOMAS MURGATROYD, Usher of the School (p. 155).

1718. WILLIAM THOMPSON (p. 134).

1718. JOHN DEWHIRST, son of John D., chapman, of Colne: entered S. Jo. Coll. Camb. June 26, aged 18.

1719. JAMES SCOTT S.

1720. WILLIAM HAWARD, son of William H., of Wakefield gent., entered Mert. Coll. Oxford, Apl. 7, aged 17 : B.A. 1723, M.A. 1727, B.D. Magd. Coll. 1735, D.D. 1742.

1720. WILLIAM HALL S, and GOODRICHE INGRAM L.

1720. JOHN CLARKE, afterwards Head Master (p. 136, &c.)

1720. EDWARD HOYLAND, son of John H., of Brearley: entered S. Jo. Coll. Camb. Apl. 22, aged 19 : B.A. in 1723, M.A. in 1727.

1720. WILLIAM LAMPLUGH, son of William L., of Spotborough, clerk: at Wakefield School two years: entered St. Jo. Coll. Camb. July 9 : B.A. in 1724, M.A. in 1728.

1720–1. RALPH CREYKE, son of Ralph C., of Marton, near Bridlington, gent. : at Wakefield School three years: entered S. Jo. Coll. Camb. Feb. 25, aged 18.

1721. JOHN LISTER, son of James L., of Halifax, gent.: entered S. Jo. Coll. Camb. Mar. 25, aged 18: B.A. in 1724, M.A. in 1728.

1721. JOHN LOWTHER L, M.B., Sid. Sus. Coll. Camb., 1725.

1721. RICHARD BENTLEY, son of Joseph B , of Oulton, and nephew of Dr. Bentley: entered Trin. Coll. Camb. Sep. 23, aged 17. Afterwards Fellow of his College. (Lupton's W. W.)

1722. STEPHEN COOPER S.

1722. GODFREY WENTWORTH, son of Godfrey W., of Brodsworth, gent.: born Oct. 17, 1705 : entered S. Jo. Coll. Camb. July 21. Of Woolley and Hickleton: died Jan. 18, 1789 (Thoresby's Duc. Leod. p. 197.)

1722–3. JOHN FLEMING, son of William F., of Kippax, barrister: entered S. Jo. Coll. Camb. Mar. 14, aged 17 : B.A. in 1726.

1723. SANDYS HUTCHINSON L, B.A. of Trin. Coll. Camb. in 1727, M.A. in 1731 : Fellow and Librarian of his College.

1723. EDMUND DRING, B.A. of Trin. Coll. Camb. in 1723, M.A. in 1727 : Fellow of his College in 1729.

1723. BENJAMIN DAWSON S.

1725. WILLIAM WADE S.

1725. WILLIAM SACHEVEREL, drowned and buried at Wakefield, July 3, 1725.

1725. CHRISTOPHER HODGSON L, B.A. of Trin. Coll. Camb. in 1729, M.A. in 1733.

1725, STRELLEY PEGGE L, of Beauchieff, Derbyshire : High Sheriff of Derbyshire in 1739. (Nichols' Lit. Anec. vi. 224.)

1728. WILLIAM RUECASTLE C S, and SAMUEL PAUL, C S.

GRAMMAR SCHOOL.

1728. WILLIAM THOMPSON, son of Samuel T., of Middleton, farmer: entered S. Jo. Coll. Camb. June 27, aged 22: B.A. in 1731, M.A. in 1735.

1731. .... ROBINSON S, and JOHN SHEPARD S.

1730. JOHN COWPE, Master of the Wakefield Charity School in 1766.

1732. RICHARD HARRISON CS, and THOMAS DENTON CS.

1733. WILLIAM JESSOP, son of George J., Esq.; born at Thurnscoe, Yorks., entered S. Jo. Coll. Camb. June 29, aged 18.

1734. ROBERT NORTH L, and THOMAS LILLEY L.

1735. WILLIAM HAWARD L, and JOHN BUXTON CS.

1737. JOHN GARLICK CS, ROBERT HARRISON S, and J. HOTCHKIS L.

1740. JOHN COPPENDALE CS, and THOMAS WHITE S.

1740. EDWARD SILL, son of the Rev. Daniel S., Governor.

1741. JOHN ROBINSON S, GEORGE SHAW S.

1741. MATTHEW ROBERT ARNOTT, doubtless son of the Rev. George Arnet (often spelt Arnott), and educated at the School: B.A. of Clare Hall, Camb in 1744, M.A. in 1748. Fellow of his College, afterwards Governor of the School.

1742. HENRY ZOUCH, son of the Rev. Charles Z., Vicar of Sandal (p. 158), probably educated at the School: B.A. Trin. Coll. Camb. in 1746, M.A. in 1750: afterwards Governor of the School.

1743, JOHN COOKE S, WILLIAM HARGREAVES CS, THOMAS WILSON S.

1744. JOHN BRIGGS S, BENJAMIN WRIGHT CS.

1746. JOHN SKELTON CS, and THOMAS PERKINS L.

1751. THOMAS CAYLEY L, of Brompton, Scarborough, 5th Baronet: born Aug., 1731: died Mar. 15, 1792: married in 1763 Isabella, daughter of Sir John Seton, of Parbroath. (Foster's Pedigrees.)

1751. JAMES HORRAX (or HORROCKS), Usher, No. 25.

1751. HENRY ROBINSON, LZ, B.A. Emm. Coll. Camb. 1756.

1751. WILLIAM GILL LZ, B.A. S. Jo. Coll. Camb. 1755, M.A. 1758: afterwards Vicar of Sherburn, Yorks.

1752. JOHN AMBLER L, FRANCIS BLAND L.

1752. ROBERT WELLS LZ, son of the Rev. Thomas W., of Willingham, Lincs.: entered Linc. Coll. Oxford, Nov. 9. aged 18: B.A. 1756: M.A. 1774: B.D. and D.D. 1774. Vicar of East Rasen and Rector of Springthorpe, Lincs., 1775: Rector of Willingham, 1781: died Mar. 26, 1807. (Foster's Al. Ox.)

1752. WILLIAM GREEN LZ, Senior Optime, S. Jo. Coll. Camb. 1757, M.A. 1760. Or perhaps son of Samuel G., of Cawthorne, entered Mert. Coll. Oxford, July 6, 1752, aged 18.

1752. [Thomas] HUDSON Z, Junior Optime, Chr. Coll. Camb. 1756, M.A. 1759. Fellow of his College. Afterwards a clergyman at Scarborough.

1752. JOHN WEBSTER, son of Thomas W., of Wakefield: baptized at Wakefield Parish Church, Mar. 8, 1735: entered Corp. Chr. Coll. Camb. in 1752. SENIOR WRANGLER and FIRST CHANCELLOR'S MEDALLIST, which in those days was equivalent to SENIOR CLASSIC, in 1756: M.A. in 1759. Fellow of his College, and for some time Chaplain to Dr. John Green, Bishop of Lincoln. Died in 1766, having "by a habit of study brought a weak constitution to a premature end." (Lamb's History of Corpus Christi College, Cambridge) See also p. 170.

1752. GEORGE MADDISON Z, afterwards Colonel of the 4th Foot, and served with distinction in the American War.

1753. JOHN BANISTER L, SAMUEL CARR C S, ROBERT MACKENZIE LZ, RICHARD MATTISON L, THOMAS PRESTON L.

1753. THOMAS BALL L, Junior Optime, Magd. Coll. Camb. 1757: M.A. 1760; D.D. 1777.

1753. ROGER POCKLINGTON LZ, born Oct. 25, 1734: LL.B. Jes. Coll. Camb. 1759. Afterwards of Winthorpe, Newark.

1753. MARMADUKE TOMLINE LZ, afterwards of Riby Grove, Caistor.

1754. EDMUND BARKER L, EDMUND EDMUNDS L, EDWARD EDMUNDS L, WILLIAM FENTON LZ, WILLIAM HORN L, EDWARD SEYMOUR LZ.

1754. AMBROSE UVEDALE LZ, B.A., Trin. Coll. Camb. 1758: afterwards a clergyman in Suffolk.

1754. ANTONY TROLLOPE LZ, Junior Optime, Pemb. Coll. Camb. 1758, M.A. 1761. Afterwards Vicar of Cottered, Herts. Grandfather of the well-known novelist, Thomas Anthony Trollope.

1754. THOMAS DADE, son of the Rev. Thomas D., of Scampston: entered S. Jo. Coll. Camb. Jan. 16: Junior Optime 1759, M.A. 1785. Afterwards Rector of Barmston, Yorks. and F.S.A.

1754. WILLIAM TOMLINSON LZ, B.A. Jes. Coll. Camb. 1758, M.A. 1761. Afterwards Vicar (?) of Waltham, Grimsby.

1754. JOHN HEPWORTH, LZ, B.A. Corp. Chr. Coll. Camb. 1758, M.A. 1761. Afterwards Vicar (?) of Graffham, Hunts.

GRAMMAR SCHOOL.   213

1754. GEORGE COOKE Z, son of George C., of Arksey, Esq.: entered Bras. Coll. Oxford, Feb. 21, aged 18. Afterwards of Streethorpe, Yorks.: of Lincoln's Inn, 1759. Assumed the name Yarborough in 1802, died Jan. 19, 1818 (Foster's Al. Ox).

1754. THOMAS LUMLEY Z, Senior Optime, Jes. Coll. Camb. 1757, M.A. 1760. Fellow of his College. Afterwards Vicar (?) of Dalby, Yorks.

1755. ROBERT BOLLING L, JOHN BREWSTER DARLEY L (afterwards of Aldby Park), SAMUEL RILEY, L, BENJAMIN TIDSWELL CS, CHRISTOPHER WANDESFORD L.

1755. WILLIAM WIGHTON LZ, LL.B. Magd. Coll. Camb. 1764: afterwards of Selby.

1755. JOSEPH POCKLINGTON LZ: afterwards of Muskham, Newark.

1755. LANGHORNE BURTON L, eldest son and heir of William B., of Somersby, Lincs., Esq.

1755. RICHARD WILSFORD LZ : afterwards of Pontefract.

1755. ROGER SWIRE, son of Samuel S. of Cononley, gent., entered Univ. Coll. Oxford, June 6, aged 19. Afterwards of Cononley: died Jan. 22, 1778, aged 42.

1755. MILES STAVELEY Z, son of Miles S., of Staineley, Yorks., gent: entered Univ. Coll. Oxford, June 6, aged 17. Afterwards of Staineley Hall: General, and Colonel of the 4th (Royal Irish) Dragoon Guards, and Royal Horse Guards: died May 26, 1814. (Foster's Al. Ox.)

1755. FRANCIS MOLYNEUX Z, afterwards Baronet, of Wellow Park, Nottingham. For 46 years Gentlemen Usher of the Black Rod in the House of Lords; died in 1812, aged 74.

1755. GEORGE NEVILE LZ, afterwards of Thorney; J.P. and D.L.; Lieutenant-Colonel of Notts. Militia, High Sheriff of Notts. in 1772, died June 29, 1806, aged 66.

1756. GEORGE ROUTH L, perhaps 6th Wrangler, Caius Coll. Camb. 1762; M.A. 1765.

1756. BRIAN ALLOTT, son of the Rev. Brian A., of York: entered S. Jo. Coll. Camb. Mar. 31, aged 19: LL.B. in 1770.

1757. ROBERT BEVERLEY L, JOHN FIELD L, JOSEPH LORD L.

1757. JOHN DOBBS, born at Bucknall, Lincs: entered S. Jo. Camb. June 3, aged 19.

1757. JOSHUA NEWBY L, son of Henry N., of Kildwick, gent: entered Bras. Coll. Oxford, Mar. 28, aged 18: B.A. 1760, M.A. 1763: Fellow of his College. Rector of Great Rolwright, Oxon.: died Aug. 12, 1811.

1757. BARNARD FOORD LZ, B.A. Trin. Coll. Camb. 1761, M.A. 1764, D.D. 1790. Afterwards of Beverley.

1757. EDWARD NORTON L, son of Edward N., of Knaresborough, gent.: entered Univ. Coll. Oxford, June 6, aged 19.

1757. THOMAS ZOUCH, son of the Rev. Charles Z., Vicar of Sandal, and previously Assistant Master in the School. Born Sep. 12, 1737: entered as Pensioner of Trin. Coll. Camb. in 1757: elected Scholar in 1758: Craven Scholar in 1760: 3rd Wrangler in 1761: Fellow in 1762: Member's Prizeman in 1762 and 1763: Seatonian Prize in 1765: Assistant Tutor of Trin. Coll. in 1763. M.A. in 1764, D.D. in 1805. Rector of Wycliff, Yorks. in 1770–93: Rector of Scrayingham, Yorks. in 1793. Retired to live at Sandal in 1795. Prebendary of Durham in 1805. Was offered the Bishopric of Carlisle in 1808. Died Dec. 17, 1815. Governor of the School, and founder of Sandal Endowed School. (Lupton's W.W.)

1757. SAMUEL SWIRE, son of Samuel S., of Cononley, gent.: entered Univ. Coll. Oxford, Mar. 28, aged 17: B.A. 1760, M.A. 1763, B.D. 1771, D.D. 1805. Fellow of his College. Vicar of Coleshill, Berks: Rector of Melsonby and Barningham, Yorks., in 1787: died Feb. 19, 1816. (Lupton's W.W., p. 196. Foster's Al. Ox.)

1757. BENNET LANGTON Z, son of Bennet L., of Langton, Lincs., Esq.: entered Trin. Coll. Oxford, July 7, aged 20: created M.A. in 1765, D.C.L. in 1790. Afterwards of Langton, Lincs; Captain of Lincolnshire Militia, and the well-known friend of Dr. Johnson. (Foster's Al. Ox.)

1758. CHARLES BURTON L, EDWARD COTTORIL L, ANTHONY HALL L, RICHARD THOROLD L. THOMAS NEVILE L.

1758. LEONARD BURTON LZ: afterwards of Ringstead, Thrapston.

1758. ROBERT BURTON LZ, LL.B. Trin. Coll. Camb. 1762: brother and heir of Langhorne Burton, of Somersby, Lincs., Esq.

1758. JOHN LONSDALE LZ, Senior Optime Trin. Coll. Camb. 1761: afterwards of Newmillerdam, Wakefield, and Clapham, Surrey. Father of Dr. John Lonsdale, Bishop of Lichfield from 1843 to 1867.

1759. HENRY SHEPHERD Z, Junior Optime, S. Jo. Coll. Camb. 1763; M.A. 1766; B.D. 1774. Fellow of his College. Archdeacon.

1759. CHARLES CARTWRIGHT Z, son of William C., of Marnham, Notts. Lieutenant in the Royal Navy, captured the Dutch Fort of Commenda, W. Africa: died at Storrington, Sussex, in 1807, aged 63.

1759. THEODORE BLAND L, WILLIAM ELLERBY S (p. 170), CHARLES FAVELL CS.

DR. EDMUND CARTWRIGHT.
INVENTOR OF THE POWER LOOM.
(Photographed from an engraving in Knight's "Gallery of Portraits".)

GRAMMAR SCHOOL. 215

1759. THOMAS SMITH "of Virginia" (p. 170): B.A. Trin. Coll. Camb. 1763.

1759. JOHN RICKABY LZ : afterwards of Bridlington Quay, and Governor of the School.

1760. WILLIAM BECHER Z, Senior Optime, S. Jo.. Coll. Camb. 1764, M.A. 1769. Fellow of his College. Afterwards a clergyman at Southwell.

1760. RICHARD GEE Z, LL.B. S. Jo. Coll. Camb. 1766: Rector of Thornton in Ribblesdale from 1813 to 1832, when he died.

1760. JOSHUA GIBSON S.

1760. RICHARD ROUNDELL, baptized at Marton, Mar. 5, 1740. Fellow-Commoner of Univ. Coll. Oxford, 1760. Afterwards of Marton, Esq.: died unmarried Feb. 11, 1772.

1760. JOHN SIMPSON L, Senior Optime Corp. Chr. Coll. Camb. 1763. Fellow of his College. Afterwards Canon of Lincoln.

1760. JAMES COLLINS LZ, afterwards of Knaresborough.

1760. ALEXANDER THOMSON, born about 1744. Master in Chancery, 1782: Accountant-General of the Court of Chancery, 1786: Baron of Exchequer, 1786, and Knighted: Lord Chief Baron of Exchequer, 1814. Died at Bath, April 15, 1817.

1760. EDMUND CARTWRIGHT, son of William C., of Marnham, Notts., born in Apl. 1743: entered Univ. Coll. Oxford, July 19, 1760, aged 17: B.A. and Fellow of Magd. Coll. 1764: M.A. 1766: B.D. and D.D. 1806: F.R.S. and F.R.L.S Rector of Goadby Marwood, Leicester, 1779: Prebendary of Lincoln, 1786. Died at Hastings, Oct. 30, 1823. The reputed inventor of the Power Loom. (Foster's Al. Ox.) Government granted him £10,000 for his inventions.

1761. JOHN RAMSDEN, L, son of John R., of Southowram: entered Univ. Coll. Oxford, Mar, 14, aged 18.

1761. ROBERT TUCKER L, "of Virginia" (p. 170), THOMAS PRESTON L.

1763. FRANK STANDISH Z, son of Thomas S., of Preston, Lancs.: entered Bras. Coll. Oxford, Jan. 31, aged 17. Third Baronet: died May 18, 1812.

1764. JOHN DISNEY, born Sep. 17, 1746; LL.B. Pet. Camb. 1770. Afterwards Vicar of Swinderby, and Chaplain to the Bishop of Carlisle. Adopted Unitarian views in 1782: died at Ingatestone, Essex, Dec. 26, 1816.

1765. SAMUEL BUCK Z, LL.B. Trin. H. 1770. Afterwards of Leeds.

1768. THOMAS ROBINSON S, WILLIAM WALKER CS.
1769. THOMAS HERON H.
1769. THOMAS HARDCASTLE, son of William H., of Masham, gent.: entered Queen's Coll. Oxford, July 14, aged 18: B.A. 1773, M.A. and Fellow of Mert. Coll. 1776: Proctor in 1782: Professor of Anglo-Saxon 1800–3. (Foster's Al. Ox.) See p. 170.
1770. JOHN SHEPARD S.
1771. SAMUEL POLLARD CS.
1773. JOHN KNOWLES (p. 171).
1775. JOHN GOODAIR, B.A. Trin. Coll. Camb. 1780. Afterwards Vicar of Penistone.
1775. WILLIAM WOOD, son of Michael W., Coal Merchant, Ardsley: entered S. Jo. Coll. Feb. 20, aged 18.
1779. SAMUEL SMALPAGE, Trin. Coll. Camb. B.A. 1783, M.A. 1786.
1781. RICHARD PEARSON S, JOHN POPPLEWELL S.
1782. THOMAS COMBER, B.A. Jes. Coll. Camb. 1787.
1782. ANDREW PETERSON L, of Utrecht: afterwards of "Six Chimneys," Wakefield.
1783. RICHARD ATKINSON S.
1788. JOSEPH ARMITAGE S, JOHN DIXON S.
1790. HENRY LUMB L, JOHN BUTTERFIELD SCHOREY H.
1793. CHRISTOPHER BELL CS.
1794. JOHN BELL H S.
1794. DANIEL CRESWELL, son of Daniel C., of Crowden-le-Booth, Derby: born in 1775. Exhibitioner of Trin. Coll. Camb: 7th Wrangler in 1797, Member's Prize in 1798, Proctor in 1813, Taxor in 1814. M.A. 1800, D.D. 1823. Fellow of his College. Vicar of Enfield in 1822, Justice of the Peace, and Fellow of the Royal Society in 1823. Died Mar. 21, 1844. Author of various mathematical works. (Lupton's W.W.)
1798. HENRY ARMITAGE S, WILLIAM TATE S.
1799. GEORGE AMBLER CS, JOSEPH STEPHENSON H.
1801. JOHN MATTHEWS S.
1804. THOMAS ROGERS S.
1805. BENJAMIN PULLAN C.
1810. HENRY GILBY LONSDALE, son of the Rev. John L., of Newmillerdam, Wakefield: B.A. Jes. Coll. Camb. 1814, M.A. 1817. Afterwards a Governor (p. 104).

GRAMMAR SCHOOL. 217

The remainder of this Chapter will contain a copy of the School Register, which, as has been pointed out before, begins in the year 1814 : the same abbreviations will be used as hitherto, and a few notes appended, as occasion seems to demand, with reference to boys' subsequent careers. The dates given are those of entry into the School.

Before JULY, 1814. Chas. Malcolm Kennedy (C.B., Foreign Office, London), Jas. Kennedy (2 Cl. Law Trip. Trin. H. Camb. 1817 : Judge at Havannah), Mich. Kennedy, Rich. Kennedy, Wm. Dawson, Rob. Dawson, Wm. Edw. Coldwell S, Jos. Robinson, Jas. Burdakin CS, Phil. Dawson. Fredk. Holdsworth, Chas. Lawson S, Corn. Binns, Frank Billam, Egremont Richardson S, Fredk. Dawson, Jas Scott, Jno. Day Hurst S, Thos. Sanders, Jno. Sanders, Thos. Dawson, Rich. Beatson Mann, Thos. Jno. Milnes Johnstone, Thos. Ross, — Pearson, Robt. Hurst.

1814. JULY. Martin Edwd. Naylor (Vet. Surgeon, Wakefield), Wm. Statter (Snapethorpe Hall, J.P.). SEPT. Jas. Kennet Dawson (B.A. Cath. H. Camb. 1825).

1815. JAN. Thos. Marsden, — Moxon. MAR. Edwd. Foljambe. JULY. — Driffield, — Driffield.

1816. JAN. Jno. Hy. Foljambe, Saml. Sunderland CS. JULY. Jno. Marsden, Geo. Swinden, Thos. Billington, Jno. Billington, Thos. Foljambe C, Geo. Craven.

1817. JAN. Jno. Acton, Wm. Day, Robt. Austwick, Edwd. Sykes. JULY. — Birkinshaw, Wm. Rawsthorne, Edwin Harrison, Robt. Lumb, Fredk. Lumb S, Rowland Hurst.

1817-1821. — Fowler, Saml. Oxley, Wm. Oxley, Wm. Hurst, Edw. Marsden, Geo. Walker, Wm. Fawcett, Wm. Stafford, Jas. Oates, Wm. Oates, — Blakeborough, Jno. Batty, Hy. Walton, Wm. Scholefield, Aug. Mellor, Jno. Mellor, Jos. Jackson, Jos. Senior (LL.D., Cambden Lecturer, Wakefield Cath.), Horatio Trafalgar Taylor, Hy. Taylor, Beatson Nichols, Hy. Wormald (Governor), Hy. Harrison, Jno. Wood Berry (Solicitor, Wakefield), Jos. Burrell (Barrister, Lincoln's Inn), Wm. Ottley, Jno. Palmer, Wm. Robinson, Wm. Lawton, Edwin Lawton, Hy. Lawton, Saml. Shuttleworth, Wm. Elliss S, — Mellor, Jas. Stafford, Thos. Shaw, — Wilby, Edwin Green, Fra. Champion, Jos. Atkinson, Geo. Arnold, Wm. Chapple, Chas. Denison, Nowell Luis Fernandes (Crofton Hall), Joze Luis Fernandes (Governor), Adolphus Langford, Jno. Dibb, Thos. Hargreaves, Jno. Aydon, Jno. Taylor, Benj. Simpson, Jno. Sharp S, Wm. Sharp S, Geo. Haigh, Wm. Monkhouse H, — Haigh, Rich. Wormald, Edwd. Wormald, Wm. Hepworth, Jos. Dobson, Thos. Cromek, — Clay, Jno. Smith, Chas. Clapham, Alf. O'Dwyer (Master in Wakefield Prop. School), — Logan, Jno. Shackleton, Jno. Allison (Schoolmaster in Northgate), Tim. Clegg, — Armitage, Wm. Calladine, Jno. Watson, Geo. B. Rheinhardt (Chemist, Leeds), And. Thos. Turton Peterson (Judge in India), Wm. Todd Naylor.

1821. AUG. Giles Diston Barker (Dep. Coroner, Wakefield), Jno. Moxon, Jos. Booth, Jno. Smith, Geo. Roach, Rob. Haynes.

1823-1825. Jos. Lawson Sisson S, Rich. Cope, Edwd. Cope, Aug. Cope, Fredk. Wood, Jas. Potter, Jno. Potter, Wm. Rhodes, Wm. Heald, Saml. Stead, Chas. Nichols, — Waterworth, Fredk. Dalton, Jno. Hardcastle (Governor), Jos. Haslegrave S, Saml. Jackson, Jos. Walker, Hy. Walker (Governor), Jno. Cuttle,

Robt. Craven (J. P., F. R C. S., Kendal), Wm. Walker, Jno. Bramhald, Jno. Barras, Thos. Barras, Alf. Clarkson, Wm. Blaky, Wm. Pannell, Wm. R. H. Johnstone, Edwd. Shepherd (Governor H.M. Prison, Wakefield).

1825-1831. Rich. Saml. Sisson (Physician, Edinbro'), Jno. Sowden, Jno. Pullon, Hy. Hardcastle S, Hy. Lumb, Wm. Lumb, Jos. A. Beaver, Rich. Snowden H, Clifton Wilkinson (of Newall Hall), — Barker, — Linley, — Linley, Thos. Brown, Benj. Brown (Draper, Manchester), Jas. Oakes, Johann Rheinhardt (Chemist, Leeds), Saml. Oates, Chas. Holdsworth, Jno. Kendall, Chas. Nevile, Geo. Nevile, Jno. Jackson, Thos. Ambler Bolton (Vicar of New Basford, Notts), Wm Spicer Wood S, — Nevile, Jas. Kendall, Jos. Wainwright (Solicitor, Wakefield), Jno. Bevers, Saml. Milnes Marshall, — Rowley, Edm. Kaye, Chas. Phillips, Saml. Glover, Wm. Wiseman, Jer. Wiseman, — Lister, Jno. Nevins, Penrose Nevins, Jos. Watson Shaw, Jno. Walton, Saml. Hill, Wm. Bakewell (of Seaton), Jno. Starkey, Jas. Armitage, Wm. Fennell (Wine Merchant, Wakefield), Rich. Eccles, Jos. Billinton, Jas. Billinton, Edwd. Taylor, — Woodcock, — Abson, Geo. Barker, — Barras, Wm. Hurst S, Paul Geo. Atkinson, — Clayton, Jno. Mosley, Jas. Mosley, Jos. Atkinson, Thos. Gill, Rich. Gill, Saml. Stafford, Geo. Andrews Hewett S, Thos. Dobson, Wm. Weeds, Edwd. Taylor, Peter Marsden, — Billinton, — Billinton.

1831. JAN. — Wright, — Oakes. MAR. — Watson. APL. — Alderson, — Horn. MAY. — Neil (Manager of Wakefield and Barnsley Bank), — Armitage. AUG. — Brown, — Shaw, — Hartley, — Bolland, — Jackson, — Johnson, — Shaw, — Shaw, — Mosley.

1832. JAN. — Coe, — Hartley, — Hartley, Wm. Hartley (Solicitor, Settle), Fra. Hy. Dunwell H S. FEB. — Hardcastle. MAR. - Holdsworth, — Holdsworth, — Gill. JULY. — Bennett, — Watson, — Watson, — Rhodes, — Nelson, — Atkinson, — Cawthorne, — Gill, Benj. Kemp (Surgeon, Wakefield), — Kemp, — Stafford, — Fennell.

1833. JAN. — Dawson, — Wood. FEB. — Binney, — Hewitt, Dav. Goodman Dixon S, — Holdsworth. APL. Rhodes, — Marshall. JULY. — Taylor, — Wittington. AUG. — Tennant, — Flockton, — Weeds.

1834. JAN. — Oldfield, — Bingley, — Ground. AUG. — Illingworth, — Sisson, Jos. F. Howgate (S. John's, Wakefield). SEPT. — Burnell, — Burnell.

1835. JAN. Chas. Priest, — Atkinson, Alf. Moxon. JUNE. — Illingworth.

1836. JAN. Robt. Hurst, Wm. Hurst (Crofton Old Hall), Jno. T. Huxley, R. F. Haigh, Hy. Walker, Jno. Walker, Thos. Holdsworth, Chas. Darley, Thos. Harrison Jno. Robinson, Fra. Bell, Jno. Cuthbert, Hy. Becket, Geo. Haldane (Clark Hall, Stanley), G. S. Pollock, Geo. Wm. Alder (South Parade, Wakefield), Sidney Alder, N. Thos. Fennell, Chas. Hurst. FEB. Thos. H. Angell, Jno. H. Wood, Jno. Wilson, Jas. Gregory, Geo. Nichols, Thos. Linley. MAR. G. A. Lawton, H. A Lawton. APL. Hy. Wilson, Wm. Poppleton (Horbury), Fred. Gill, Wm. Briggs, S. H. Haxby (Solicitor, Leicester), Jas. A. Green, A. H. Rheinhardt. MAY. Jno. Robinson. JULY. Hy. Lister (Vicar of Stanley), — Halliday, J. S. Holdsworth, W. B. Holdsworth, — Neill, Thos. Howden (Ironfounder, Wakefield), — Cowell, J. Brierley, A. Brierley, F. Gill (Doctors' Commons, E.C.). AUG. — Firth, Thos. Pollock. SEPT. T. G. Hamer (Solicitor, Barnsley). OCT. Jno. Pollock, A. Neill, H. Marsden, Jno. Wyrill, — Towning.

GRAMMAR SCHOOL. 219

1837. JAN. J. H. Cookson (C.C., Stanley), Jer. Waterhouse, Ch. Clay (Walton). FEB. J. H. Wice (Governor), — Blackburn, Jno. Hy. Wilson, Jos. Watson (B.A. Caius Coll. Camb. 1844). MAR. J. Briggs. APL. H. Brown, Potter, — Moss, Jno. Pullon (Grand Stand, Wakefield), H. Tootal MAY. P. Kendall, Wm. Crawford. AUG. Geo. Alex. Holdsworth S, Edwd. Holdsworth, Jas. Hy. Carter S, Jno. Carter (Vicar of Raughton Head, Carlisle), Thos. Woodcock S, Wallace Hampson, Wm. Cooper, Thos. G. Robinson, Joe Gill.

1838. AUG. Gilbert Hill Broughton. OCT. Geo. Beckett.

1839. JAN. Edwin Bittleston S, Geo. Tennant, Walt. Thos. Shaw, Wm. Winter, Jno. Hallilay. FEB. Jno. Broughton. AUG. Jos. B. Atkinson (d. June, 1842).

1840. AUG. Wm. Saville, Jos. Jaggar, Wm. Barnes, F. G. Taylor, Jno. Bell, Thos. Secker (Vicar of St. Peter's, Bishop Wearmouth), Thos. Binney, Rich. E. Goldthorpe, Jos. Firth, Jas. H. Haldane (Clark Hall, Stanley). OCT. Jno. Hy. Lake, Jackson Muspratt Williams. NOV. Wm. Smith, Jas. Smith.

1841. JAN. Wm. Fox, Thos. Bramah, Hy. Andrew, Jno. Wm. Taylor S, Thos. Ramsden Walker, F. E. Rishworth, Edwd. Snowden S, Jabez Watson. FEB. Thos. Link. APL. Wm. Perkin, Dan. Wilson, Hy. Sykes. AUG. Fred. Wm. Gill, Thos. Senior (Solicitor, Wakefield), Thos. Wm. Atkinson, Wm. Haldane, Fred. Hy. Storry, Rob. Walker, G. S. Marriott, Jno. Billington (Toole's Theatre, London). OCT. Rich. Binney, Rich. Halliday.

1842. JAN. J. W. Rhodes S, Geo. Clayton, Chas. Enoch Moss, Wm. Cuthbert, Geo. Cuthbert, Jno. Pitchforth, Fra. Walker, Jno. Cogill, Jos. Shaw, Edm. Asquith, Geo. Graytrix Sykes. AUG. Thos. Dunn S, Saml. Hurst, Edwd. Walker, Jno. Crossland, Ch. Saml. Crossland. SEP. Ralph Hall Kilby S. OCT. Wm. Hy. Oxley, Jno. Lockwood. Hy. Drummond Wolff (G.C.B., G.C.M.G., British Ambassador at Madrid).

1843. JAN. Arth. Jas. Holdsworth, Jno. Rich. Clayton, Jno Hy. Clay, Wm. Cawood, Jos. S. Freeman, Rob. Clarence Buckley (Chemist, Todmorden), Arth. Buckley S, Joe Harrap, Thos. Sellars Higgins (Chemist, Huddersfield), Thos. Sellars, Benj. Fawcett Glover (Alverthorpe), Wm. Glover, Iliff Hopton, Hy. R. Whitworth, Edwd. Pet. Burrell, Wm. Connor, Jas. B. H. Kelly CS, Geo. Holt, Ch. Holt, Jos. Dobson, Godfrey B. Berry. AUG. Jackson Mason (Vicar of Settle), Wm. Mason, Benj. Fawcett Clegg, Wm. Atkinson, Geo. Perkin, Jas. Barlow Goldthorp, Wm. R. Dodgson, Jno. H. Ridsdale, Jno. Jos. Winter, Tom Firth, Jos. Cookson, Chas. Norcliffe.

1844. JAN. Jos. Leach, Chas. Sorby Dawson, Wm. Dawson, Wm. Graham, W. O. Armitage, Jos. Balmforth, Wm. Taylor, Jno. Wilcock APL. Rob. Beaumont, Chas. Heptonstall. AUG. Isaac Preston, Geo. Chas. Hick, Wm. Stawman, Jno. Walker, Jos. Hirst Lupton S.

1845. JAN. Hy. Graham, Thos. Stones, Thos. Firth, Hy. Thos. Whiting, FEB. Rob. Dodgson. AUG. Dav. Stephenson (Eastmoor), Wm. Blanshaw.

1846. MAR. Jno. Nettleton Terry (Surgeon, Bradford). AUG. Wm. Hy. Middleton, Chas. Jas. Walker, Septimus Walker, Rowland R. Walker, Fred. Decimus Walker, Wm. Andrew, Arth. Goldthorp (Westgate), Wm. Owston, Edwd. Napier Dibb. SEP. Chas. Flatman (Saltley House, Wakefield), Saml. Bramah, Chr. J. Dibb (Official Receiver, Manchester).

1847. JAN. Geo. Victor Ellerton (S. John's, Wakefield,) Saml. Dawson, Hy. M. Thompson. MAR. Jos. Rayner S. APL. Geo. Dyson, Alf. Wilson,

AUG. Thos. Wilton Lee, Arth. Lee, Thos. Milsom, Fred. Wm. Towler, Wm. Matthewman, Joseph Matthewman (S. John's, Wakefield), Jas. Heber Taylor HS, Hy. Martyn Taylor S. SEP. Wm. Watson.

1848. JAN. Tom Jones Holdsworth, Owen Jones Holdsworth, Fredk. Jones Holdsworth, Hy. Avison, Rich. Webster, Jos. Twibill, Saml. Northin, Joseph Turner Ward. FEB. Hy. Ogden, Chas. Edwd. Emmett, Hy. Nevison Harrison. MAR. Benj. Buckley. APL. Jas. C. Thompson. AUG. Fra. Thos. Hurst S, Geo. Jas. Atkinson (Town Clerk, Liverpool), Wm. Wilkinson, Jno. Lockwood, Edwin S. Norcliffe, Alf. Berry, Thos. Billinton, Jas. Broadbent, Edwin Lister, Dan. Ledgard, Wm. Wood, B. B. F. Clarkson. OCT. Routh Tomlinson CS, Phil. R. Tomlinson, J. G. Horsfall (Indian Civil Service), S. T. Horsfall.

1849. JAN. Joseph Leighton, Walt. Angel, Jno. Kershaw, Vinson Hartley, T. R. W. Gawthorpe, Jno. Ellerton, T. A. Bramley, Wm. Havers Pope (Everton, Bucks), Chas. Wm. Baker. FEB. Jno- Woodley, W. S. Bramley (Vicar of Crumpsall, Manchester). APL. C. B. L. Fernandes (Solicitor, Wakefield), Jos. Perkin. AUG. Frank S. Cooper.

1850. JAN. Jno. Hodgson S, A. T. Cartwright, Chas. Angel. FEB. A. R. Burkill. APL. Edgar Cannon, Mont. Cannon. AUG. Jno. Haslegrave, G. H. Armytage. SEP. Edwd. Vaux.

1851. JAN. Alb. J. Bower, J. A. Burkill, Thos. W. Orwin, Jos. Haslegrave, (J.P., Stanley Hall), Geo. Brook. APL. Godfrey Carlin, C. Wm. Graham. AUG. Jos. Westmorland S, Robt. Westmorland, W. J. Heptonstall, Saml. Kershaw. SEP. Edwin Winter.

1852. APL. Jos. Norcliffe. AUG. Fredk. Buckley, Fredk. Craven, Wm. Rhodes (Duncan House, Thornes), Alb. Micklethwaite ("The Yorkshire Post") Geo. B. Doughty (Vicar of Wanstead), Chas. Edwd. Burkill.

1853. JAN. F. R. Halliday, Rich. Edwd. Garvey, Jno. H. Burrell, Benj. Thompson, J. B. Barraclough (Chaplain, London Jews' Soc.), Wm. Ash (Heathfield, Wakefield), R. R. Bramley. AUG. W. Jno. Stead, W. W. Stead, Jas. Harrison, R. P. Linfield (Vicar of Elton, Lancs.), Jno. Scott (Solicitor, Sandal). SEPT. Thos. Hy. Shaw CS. OCT. Edwin Ledgar.

1854. JAN. G. H. Secker, Wm. Collins, A. W. Dawson, T. C. P. Payne F. FEB. Jno. Taylor.

1855. JAN. A. W. Lupton, W. W. Taylor HS, Wm. Smith, Robt. Smith. FEB. C. E. P. Simpson, Jonathan Haigh (St. John's, Wakefield), Wm. Dyson Wood (Med. Officer of Health, Oxford). AUG. W. H. Beaumont, A. F. Clarkson, J. A. Holdsworth, Arth. Micklethwaite (Chaplain, House of Mercy, Horbury), Burnley Rayner, Jno. L. Wood, W. H. Taylor, Rich. Wilks, Thos. Hy. Wright. OCT. F. Micklethwaite (Somerset House, Strand).

1856. JAN. Hy. Booth, J. C. Cuttle, W. Ellinor, J. W. Hardcastle, Evan Hunter, Robt. Jackson, Robt. V. Reynolds, F. Robinson, C. G. Smith, J. Smithson, Wm. Hy. Stewart (Solicitor, Milnthorpe, and Governor), Thos. Taylor (Surgeon, Methley), J. T. Thresh, Chas. Thompson. FEB. Squire Jackson. MAR. J. W. Beckett (Solicitor, Liverpool), Fitzherbert Astley Cave Browne Cave (Vicar of Longridge, Preston), T. Hart, S. S. J. Marsden, T. H. Matthews, C. H. Simpson (Solicitor, Manchester). MAY. Isaac Burnley, Eugene Storer. AUG. Jas. M. Draper, Hy. Atkinson, Wm. Lamprey Bowditch CS, Wm. Chadwick, Chas. Edwd. Hodson (Trin. H. Camb., Chaplain on Arctic Expedition), Geo. Fredk. Rayner, Harry Scott, Geo. H. Ward (Solicitor, Glasgow), Robt. Wilson, W. T. Howden, Chas. Edwd. Nettleton (Solicitor, Wakefield). NOV. Hy. B. Payne.

GRAMMAR SCHOOL.

1857. JAN. Walt. Bold, Arth. Bold, Geo. Hy. Heald, Jno. Fenton Heald, Wm. Thos. Heald (Badsworth) APL. E. S. Hall. MAY. Walt. Richard, Jno. Wm. Park, Geo. Hy. Park. AUG. Thos. Dear, Jas. Leonard Park.

1858. JAN. Arth. Wm. Ellis, Geo. Dreaper, J J. L. Fernandes, Hervey Ellis, E B. Randell (Higham Ferrers), Walt. Rowley (C.E. Leeds). Thos. Jas. Sanderson CS, Walt. H. Wright (Banker, Hull), Alb. Thompson. APL. J. H. Hall. AUG. Yel Hallilay, M. M. Hick, F. Ibbotson, .T. S. Whitehead, A. Whitehead, Wm. E. Thresh, Dav. Duncan. OCT. Jas. Kershaw CS, Rich. Kershaw.

1859. JAN. Geo. Emmerson. FEB. Cecil Hardcastle (Solicitor, London), Tom Williams, Geo. Vialls (Architect, Ealing, W.). MAR. J. S. Saville (Artist, Southport). APL. Geo. Hayley, Jno. Lee. AUG. Benj Burton, G. W. Hart, Arth. Jones, W. M. Madden S, Walt. Spong (Higham Ferrers), Edwd Collett Bridgeman. SEP. J. Wm. Jackson.

1860. JAN. Wm. Aked Statter (Surgeon, Wakefield), Alf. Wm. Statter (Physician, Rotherham), J. G. Womack, Geo. Brewerton S. MAR. Baron Walker, Fredk. Wright. APL. Geo. Dale. MAY. Arth. Methley, Jos. Lee. AUG. Geo. Wm. Harrison, Geo. Milsom, Jos. Milsom. SEP. Wm. Hy. Madden (32nd Wrangler, 1874, now Master at Marlborough Coll.), Fredk. Child.

1861. JAN. T. Oliver Bennett, Herb. Beaumont (Solicitor, Wakefield, and Governor), W. Ford, Wm. Gilderdale (Alverthorpe), Neville Green (Freemasons' Hall, W.C.), Herbert G. E. Green (St. John's, Wakefield), Jno. Wm. Lake (killed in threshing machine), Fred. S. Parker, T. Sigston Smith, L. Smith, C. Oxley Smithson (Curate, Dishforth, Thirsk), Hy. Wales, Hy. P. Holt, Benj. Kemp (Solicitor, Wakefield), Jos. Kemp, Thos. Edwd. Taylor, J. Winde Taylor. APL. Jno. Hunter. MAY. T. Shackleton, Marm. Gibson, F. W. Dyson. AUG. Haydn Brear (Organist, Wakefield), W. Barff, Jno. Chipstead, J. W. Hart, Jno. Marks, Wm. W. Marks (Clerk to County Council, Beds.), G. Marsland, G. Nowers, E. Row, Chas. Taylor, Ernest Taylor, Thos. Haigh Connor (Chemist, Doncaster), Jno. Connor, Walt. E. Denham (Solicitor, Leeds), E. O. Denton (drowned in Thames), Arth. Rob. Lake (Solicitor, Wakefield), T. S. Saville. SEP. A. Row, V. W. Woodcock (Banker, Ossett), Hy. B. Payne. OCT. W. South. -

1862. JAN. Chas. Chapman (Auctioneer, Wakefield), C. Clapham, Murray Clayton, R. B. Horner, Howard Horner (Solicitor, Wakefield), J. H. Pottage, W. H. Purchas, C. S. Purchas, Oct. Row. T. Wilkinson, R. Wilkinson, G. Wilkinson, W. Wilson (Corn Mercht., Wisbech), J. G. Hesling. AUG. T. Garside, H. Kelly, T. E. Rennie, T. C. Richardson, J. Harrison, C. Harrison, Francis H. Wood (Surgeon, Wakefield). SEP. H. Lockwood, A. Lockwood, G. Pearson (The Glen, Harrogate). OCT. G. Swallow. DEC. — Swallow.

1863. JAN. Edwd. Burrows, Jno. Grimes, Fredk. Geo. Milnes (Curate of Dewsbury), Halford Parker, W. Rhodes, Arth. Malim (Curate of Stowe, Weedon), W. B. Chamberlain (Chaplain, Monte Video), W. Chipstead. APL. W. E. Poppleton, Frank Taylor, W. Secker. MAY. E. M. Wadsworth, W. H. Wadsworth. AUG. C. E. Battye. Edwd. T. Clark (Solicitor, Snaith), Hy. W. L. Fernandes (Crofton Grange), Hugo Green, G. Herb. Harrison, Wm. B. Moorhouse, W. Sutcliffe Ramsden. OCT. Chas. Jas. Ball H.

1864. JAN. Wm. Briggs (Red Hall, Wakefield), Jas. E. Burniston, J. E. Hollidge, Saml. Rayner, Saml. Secker, Frank O. Scott, L. W. Woodcock. APL. Thos. Dunwell, Wm. Athron, J. Oakes, Wm. Saville (Chapeltown, Leeds), Walker Hy. Shaw, J. Sykes. AUG. W. H. Blakey, Aug. Cardwell, And. Wm.

Leighton, Walt. Moorhouse, G. A. Moorhouse, W. H. Nowers, Thos. Normington, Francis Smith (Chief Justice, Gold Coast Colony), T. Smith, R. Walton, J. Wilce, H. Whitehead, Fredk. Wm. Ainley CS. AUG. W. Amys, Jas. Blackburn. OCT. Bayldon Taylor, F. Saml. Stahlschmidt.
1865..JAN. Robt. T. Barratt, Edwd Lake, Walt. Lake, Illingworth Redfern, Wm. Shaw, Wm. E. Wright. FEB. A. Hick, H. Hick (Physician, New Romney), Wm. King, Watson King (Curate, Tunbridge Wells). APL. J. B. Walker. AUG. Jas. Beverley CS, Walt Clark, C. A. Lambert (Vicar of Weeton, Leeds), A. Park, W. H. Radcliffe, Lionel Walker, Frank West. SEPT. Jos. White. T. P. Moorhouse (Vicar of Mosser, Cockermouth).
1866. JAN. W. Hollidge, H. Dunn, J. H. Holden, J. Westerman. MAR. A. W. Taylor. AUG. Dav. Avison, T. Avison, G. Barff, H. Clapham. J. Ellis, H. Ellis, G. H. Gill, C. W. Hall (Curate of S. Lowestoft), W. Hudson, J. W. Whitehead. SEP. W. Riddell. OCT. Saml. Heald.
1867. JAN. Walt. Beverley, Hy. A. Beverley (Walton House), J. E. Driver, J. J. Penny. APL. J. W. Firth, T. W. Firth. AUG. Hy. E. Alderson S, Alb. Beverley, Geo. W. Haldane, J. M. Madden, Oliver Moxon, Fredk. Wm. Smith, Jno. Haigh Smith, Harry Smith, H. Stahlschmidt, T. Mich. Wood. NOV. Wm. M. Wadsworth S.
1868. JAN. H. E. Ainley, C. H. Marshall, Richmond Smith. MAY. W. Place (Auctioneer, Nottingham), Chas. Lester (Vicar of S. John's, Bootle). AUG. Walt. Gilbert, Jas. Hawkes, H. W. Kenworthy (Ackworth), W. E. Micklethwaite, R. S. Piddock, J. Shaw, Ern. Statter. SEP. J. R. Handley, T. H. Wadsworth. OCT. – Crowther, E. Milnes (Radcliffe House, Wakefield).
1869. JAN. R. Booth, W. Corbitt, T. Depledge, G. W. Knowles, J. W. Stead (Solicitor, Leeds), E. H. Thompson, Alf. Thompson. APL. J. S. Roberts, H. Redfern, J. W. Saville, J. Walker. MAY. W A. Boyce, — Wadsworth. AUG. Jos. Hawkes, B. H. Madden CS, R. Schofield. OCT. H. B. Statter.
1870. JAN. P. J. Crossley, H. Dodds, W. S. Race, J. Shaw, E. C. Tattersall, J. W. Wilcock. MAR. F. West Firth. APL. C. M. Atkinson CS, S. Pickersgill. AUG. G. Beverley, J. W. Buckley, T. J. Chambers, H. Heptonstall J. Heptonstall, Alb. Lee, W. Neary, H. Wice S, B. H. Wright. OCT. Geo. Hy. Bays.
1871. JAN. T. Andrews, W. Dawson, R. Holdsworth, F. Lister. APL. S. Hampshire, Chas. Hampshire, Wm. Blanche Hodgson. AUG. T. H. Beverley, F. A. Bowditch, Joe Brook, H. M. Carter (Solicitor, Leeds), E. M. Ellis, W. J. Gomersall S, W Greenwood, E. O. Wright. OCT. F. H. Glew.
1872. JAN. H. S. Holt, C. E. Holt, H. G. Keighley (Solicitor, Wakefield), J. F. Ianson (Solicitor, Wakefield), R. Barker, T. Kershaw, C. Johnson, M. C. Thornes, J. P. Thornes. APL. E. Farrer, R. Robinson, A. Robinson. AUG. Philip Marsden. SEP. J. S. Smith, Jno. G. Statter, A. Warburton. OCT. Geo. Green.
1873. JAN. T. E. England, W. H. Gillott, W. H. Alderson CS, F. W. Bowdin, R. H. Bowdin S, B. Ramsden, J. E. Wilkinson S, Geo. H. Hunter S. APL. C. H. Hatfield, F. W. Hatfield, J. Furniss. AUG. J. W. Whitaker.
1874. JAN. W. Townend (Solicitor, Wakefield). APL. R. H. C. Dawson. AUG. B. Brook, W. Cawthorn, W. E. Hartley, Thos. Mark Carter. OCT. P. Rhodes, J. H. Stead, A. Simpson, F. Smith.
1875. JAN. Geo. Marsden, H. Clarke, G. Clarke. APL. J. H. Dibb (B.Sc. Lond., and of Pet., Camb.), J. B. Jagger. SEPT. J. P. O'Donohoe FS,

GRAMMAR SCHOOL. 223

Jos. Hy. Howden, R. G. P. Bullock FS. OCT. Arth. Jno. Chas. Stanfield, Jno. Ramsden, Wm Hy. Hallilay, Thos. L. Leighton, Sydney Alb. Gammell, Hy. Slade Childe (C.E., Wakefield). NOV. Chas. Miller Grace HS, Walt. Wm. Goodwill. DEC. Herb. Hy. Theaker, Harry Firth.
1876. JAN Geo. L. Earle, Thos. P. Ingham, Isaac Robson, Wm. Jas. Baker, Marm. Marsden, Wm. Evelyn Parker Bullock, Arth. Chas. Parker Bullock, Edwd. Teall Tomlinson, Hy. Secker Walker (Physician, Leeds), Wm. Thos. Depledge, Hy. Hutchinson, Phil. Arnold Taylor, Jos. Hy. Stringer, Graham B. Moore, Lionel G. Moore, Jas. Hy. Wade, Jas. V. B. Twamley, Geo. Aug. Beverley, Colin C. Roberts, Percy M. Roberts, Hy. N. Secker. MAR. Jno. Hy. Cuthbert. APL. Chas. D. Machell, Herb. G. Allen, Fra. Hy. Moore, Jos. Hy. Howden, Matt. Liddon, A. G. C. Hunter, Joe Balmforth, Geo. H. Scott S. MAY. Thos. Z. Walker. SEPT. Alf. E. Roberts, Chas. Wm. Fennell, Fra. H. Gale, Jas. P. Maddison, Robt. Thompson, R. J. Roberts, J. H. Cairns, W. H. Varley, A. H. Pettinger, Jno. Charlesworth, Jno. Wm. Hollings, R. S. Hollings, Wm. Woodhead, Robt. T. Johnson FS, Alf. E. Johnson, Walt. Milsom, Jos. S. Sheard. NOV. Edwin Davison, Jas. W. Davison, Wm. D. Davison DEC. M. L. Morton.
1877. JAN. Wm. A. Boyce, Jno. Hy. Richardson, Jno. Whitton, Jas. Whittton, E. L. Gale, Jno. Widdop, A. M. Lawrence, Wilf. Smith, J. R. Woodhead, J. H. Craven, Fred. Roberts, J. H. Twamley, T. C. Sheard. FEB. A. Ferguson, J. A. Tonge. APL. Jno. Fowler, Wm. Berry, C. W. Duffin, S. C. Ashton, C. J. Holt, A. E. Elvey, S. J. Gammell, A. H. Roberts, W. Kay, Herb. M. Walker C, A. H. Brook, A. J. Grace. MAY. L. Wilson, H. H. Baker, E. A. Broadhead, H. T. Hirst, W. B. Worsfold F, A. E. Cass, A. Cass, C. A. Rhodes. JUNE. T. W. Phillips, M. P. Stonehouse. SEPT. G. E. Webster, H. W. Day, H. H. Gledhill, Percy Greaves, B. Marshall, F. T. Hayley, W. G. Nuttall, T. F. Tiplady, Wm. Senior (Solicitor, Wakefield). OCT. W. H. Gilby, Jacob Ross, E. W. W. Bell, R. C. Roberts. NOV. G. E. Charlesworth.
1878. JAN. H. J. E. Marsden (B.A. Clare Coll. Cambridge), H. E. Brown, W. H. Saville, A. Saville, J. H. Giggal, H. Briggs, H. Robb, W. H. Clafton, J. A. Masterman, H. Whiteley, A. H. Carpenter, B. Glover, W. E. Coates, E. Coates, H. P. Coates, Hy.A. Halliwell (Dentist, Wakefield), H. R. Howroyd, J.W. Swindells, A. R. Ingham, L. Cripps, R. W. L. Fernandes. FEB. Wm. Marsden, H. Norris, E. Whitton. APL. H. S. Elliott, A. S. Elliott, A. F. A. Hollings, R. H. Blakeley, Alf. F. Tattersall, H. B. Edwards, Jos. L. Day, Ch. Hy. H. Walker FS, Fred Tomlinson, D. Wadsworth, Jno. W. Stringer. AUG. Geo. I. Playfair. SEPT. Fra. Edw. Robinson, Hy. Dews, J. E. Baines, L. S. Baines, C. H. B. Fowler, J. M. Grace, O. Holmes, R. E. Holmes S, R. H. Hewitt. OCT. Robt. Thorley. NOV. Jos. H. Glover, Hy. P. Riley. DEC. A. E. Ash.
1879. JAN. Wm. R. Benington, P. Backshell, M. R. Carter, Wm. Dews, E. G. Manley, W. J. Rothery, R H. Rothery, S. E. Rutter, M. L. E. Silver, G. H. Thornton (Clothworkers' Scholar, City and Guilds Institute, London), N. B. Twist, Hy. Walker (Scholar and Demonstrator, City and Guilds Institute, London), A. Whitlow. FEB. J. W. Ashton S. APL. B. D. Aspdin, Joe Clayton, Hy. Moorhouse, Chas. D. Machell. MAY. Norman Berry, C. P. Spink (B.Sc., London). AUG. Alf. Webster. SEPT. J. T. Arundel, W. E. Baines. S. M. Baines, E. Baines, Hy. Baines, Chas. Carter, N. Carter, Fred Ross, Jno. G. Sanderson, Jno. Thornton FS, R. R. Warrington, Herb. C. Woolf, Reg. N. Woolf. OCT. Wm. Henderson.

1880. JAN. Geo. Wm. Ashton, Joe Dobson, Jno. R Green, S. W. Hutchinson, E. Hill, Harold T. Kaberry, Sept. Kendall, Hy. S. Morrison (B.A., Clare Coll. Cambridge), R. P. Morrison, Fred. Wm. Sanderson, J. R. Sykes, Geo. Wm. Sykes FS, Kitson Smith, Fred. Walker. MAR. Jas. E. Briggs CS. MAY. Ern. Backshell, F. R. Carter, II. S. Moxon A. E. Moorhouse, Hy. M. Walker (Solicitor, Barnsley). SEPT. Rich. J. Barker, G. J. B. Christie C, Jno. W. Cussons, Ern. Howden, A. J. Hughes, G. T. Manley S, A. Rushworth, S. C. Scott, P. Woolf.

1881. JAN. A. W. Broadhead, Geo. M. Benington, Phil. Benington, Reg. L. Brotherton, Benj. Crowther, W. N. Clayton, Hy. Davison, Fred. Fawcett, A. S. Hutchinson. L. C. Haigh, Joe Hirst, F. W. Hanstock, P. C. Jessop, C. W. Midgley, L. T. Reid S, D. D. Ramsden, H. L. Tolson, G. P. Wood. FEB. Alex. Mackenzie (B.A. Caius Coll. Cambridge, 1890), W. S. Mackenzie. APL. Wm. Jno. Ainsworth, Chr. Atkinson, J. B. Oxley, Fred. Geo. Pilley (Scholar of Downing Coll. Cambridge), J. M. Sheard, Alf. Smith, T. R. Sykes. SEPT. Rufus Burnley, Jos. Fowler (Durham University), H. W. Hall, Jno. Hall, Hy. Hind, L. A. Johnson. OCT. T. C. Howard.

1882. JAN. C. E. Birkby, Geo. Cradock, F. Cumberbirch, J. E. Knight, Hy. Loxley, E. W. Lockwood, F. A. Morton F, J. H. Midgley, J. H. Norbury, J. Stephenson, J. A. Whiteoak, W. H. Wraith. FEB Edm. Murray, Thos. Murray, Rich. Murray. APL. Jno. Dobson, Hy. Jos. Morton, A. H. Webster, Wm. P. Walker. JUNE. P. C. Langton. SEPT. Ern. Parkin (Brown Scholar, Yorks. Coll.), Wm. H. Rhodes, T. W. Swales, R. P. Sykes, H. E. Appleton.

1883. JAN. Herbert Arundel (Medical Scholar, Yorks. Coll.), E. C. Carr, Chas. Johnson, J. E. McInnes, Fred. Oldroyd. MAR. P. S. Cradock, H. S. Desprez, A. R. Holliday, Geo. H. Littlewood, Jos. Lodge, G. H. Proctor, A. Thornton. JUNE. A. J. Powell, Jos. Winterbottom. SEPT. H. T. E. Bell, T. F. Coupland (B.A. Clare Coll. Camb. 1888), T. P. Duffin, G. R. Denton, O. M. Denton, H. Harrop, G. Harrop, W. H. Hattersley. E. Holmes, R. C. McInnes, F. W. Pearson S, G. E. Pearson, Joe Rhodes, C. R. Skene, E. Whiteoak, W. J. Walker.

1884. JAN. E. V. Baines, W. T. Butler, C. E. Elliott, A. E. Gardiner, L. N. Gardiner, Hy. J. Haslegrave, W. Lodge, F. Lodge, H. P. Metcalfe, W Roulson, W. Robb, H. Sanderson, H. Sidebottom, G. Saville. FEB. Geo. Leslie, Jas. Leslie. MAY. H. P. G. Brakenridge, F. J. Brakenridge, J. G. Bourne, J. G. Denton, J. S. Flower, Alf. Greenwood, H. Nell, A. Oldroyd. SEPT. H. Edmondson, R. G. Fotherby, H. E. Gill, F. W. Metcalfe.

1885. JAN. J. N. Cumberbirch, J. G. Chappell, G. Firth, G. N. Ianson, H. T. A. Lupton, R. Mitchell, R. C. Prest, H. Rhodes. MAY. C. W. Beaumont, R. P. G. Batho, G. F. W. Batho, H. M. Chadwick CS, Jas. Denton, G. le C. Grace, B. Hardy, G. Haslegrave, A. Myers, P. R. Reynolds, F. A. Rhodes, R. S. White. SEPT. G. A. W. Gould, J. L. B. Gould, W. J. Metcalfe, E. Simpkin, H. Topham, E. D. Whiteoak, F. D. Walker.

1886. JAN. H O. Bracey, J. A. Burnley, A. T. Cussons, Jno. Clayton, A. Dearnaly, A. E. Dearnaly, Geo. Gill, B. Haigh, E. Halliwell, H. Holmes, H. Johnson, J. A. Kilner, T. G. Leedal, J. G. Musham, C. J. Rhodes, T. D. Sanderson, Geo. Sanderson, A. E. Whiteley, W. H. Walker C, G. W. Wilson MAY. F. B. Burton, L. Cradock, R. W Fearnley, E. Haslegrave, Geo. Lyde, W. W. Lyde, J. A. Lyde, C. H. Latimer, W. A. Tolson, G. T. Wilson, R. Wigglesworth. SEPT. C. F. Carr, H. H. Denton, W. B. Falding, H. W.

GRAMMAR SCHOOL.

Gould, W. I. Hardwick, R. A. C. Heslop, H. G. Jeffery, J. C Jaques, C. N. Kennedy, P. K. Kennedy, C. E. Milsom, A. Mellor, S. Stephenson, W. Wrigley, J. O. Walker.

1887. JAN. H. D. Atkinson, J. Croysdale, J. P. Crouch (Brown Scholar, Yorks. Coll.), P. R. Crossland, J. H. Greaves, A. E. Greaves, W. Malkin, C. E. Sykes, C. H. Schofield. MAR. E. S Benington, F. St. J. E. W. Fitzpatric, P. W. Macvay. MAY. G. Beaumont, J. A. Croysdale, H. M. Clarke, F. M. B. Carter C, C. W. Hall. W. H. Kaye, H. Oxley, Geo. Simpson, F. Y. Stanger, W. H. Watson, A. Schofield. SEPT. C. T. T. Allen, J. F. Briggs, G. A. Fearnley, W. L Fotherby, Jno. Greig, R. H. Goodyear, C. Hey, Jas. Holdsworth, H. Haigh, C. Hudson, F. W. R. Hurt (County Council Scholar, Yorks. Coll.), H. D Job, E. W. Kemp, C. H. Lockwood, M. Lee, F. E. Manning, C. E. Manning, J. W. Percival, E. S. Perkin, G. W. Perkin, G. L. Rhodes, J. N. Shaw, F. W. Smith, R. W. H. Walker.

1888. JAN. M. F. Burgin, Jno. Clark-Barnacle, J. H. Corden, W. Dickinson, S. D. Hey, J. H. Haigh, S. Hampshire, S. W. S. Hall, N. Hardcastle, P. E. Johnson, W. Iredale, C. Mitchell (Akroyd Scholar, Yorks. Coll.), H. G. Myers, A. Murray, J. C. Patterson, R. W. Pearson, P. Pollard, A. W. Smith, G W. Wilson, E. C. White, E. A. Wraith, H. Wood, G. F. Walmsley, J. G. Walker. MAR. H. Slater, A. G. Valentine. MAY. C. Croysdale, T. H. G. Fulton, C. T. C. V Fulton, J. B. P. Harrison, Tom Haigh, Jim Ross, A. Snowden, C. Stewart, Wm. Sheard, A. D. Tansley, H. J. B. Wadsworth, L C. E. Wadsworth, C. B. White. SEPT. F. H. Bond, J. Hillas, E. S. Hey, L. Lett. F. C. Learoyd, C. A. Mackenzie, A. S. Manfield, H. Sugden, W. Simpson, M. Scott.

1889. JAN. V. L. Addison, J. R. L. Allott, V. Bateson, A. E. Bennett, A. H. Green, P. Halliwell, G. W. C. Lane, A. W. T. Prest, T. H. Simpson. J. Walmsley, G. W. White, D. L. Williams. MAY. W. Akeroyd, W. Duffin, C. B. Lennox, H. S. Moss, W. Powell, P. R. Smith. SEPT. H. A. Close, E. Froggatt, E. N. R. Hurt, V. G. F. Head, F. W. Hardman, W. H. Kingswell, G. E. Tansley, J. W. Talbot, A. L. Wylde, H. Wilkinson, H. B. Whittington.

1890. JAN. H. Akeroyd, C. Collins, A. Collins, H. Crawshaw, G. A. Charles, P. L Day, W. O. Pearson, J. W. Sterland, J. W. Wordsworth, C. E. E. Wilkinson. MAY. A. Brook, B. Brook, L. W. Bradshaw, C. H. Close, C. Forsyth. A. H. Lee. SEPT. W. Burton, H. W. Crouch, A. R. Davies, J. D. Goldthorp, G. E. Guest, A. Harrap, F. Harrap, J. H. Horner, W. Horner, D. Leslie, B. J. Littlewood, J. Murray. H. Mason, G. R. Spurr, F. Waide.

1891. JAN. W. K. L. Clarke, H. L. Clarke, T. O. Dickenson, F. W. B. Frankland, P T. Hopkins, H. T. Lee, D. H. C Macarthur, D. Mitchell, C Mitchell, A. P. Robinson, W. B. Robinson, F. Simpkin, R. D. Sheard, H. Stanger, B. Taylor. P. J. Whitehead, E. R. Wales, P. M Walker. APL. H. Cockell, H. S. Haworth, W. Helliwell, P. Lunn, B. Stephenson, F. H. E. Torbett, A. L. White. SEPT. C. A. Blackburn, H. Brown, R. J. H. Bunt, N Clapham, G. D Dobinson. R. Goodliffe, S. H. Gascoigne, J. Gill, H. W. Howe, H. C. Harrap, A. E. Hodgson, M. H. Hein, L. Holdsworth, J. H. Holdsworth, E. B. Horsfield, S. W. Hardwick, H. Kenyon, H. B. Kemp, F. Milnes, V. Mellor, A. J. Shuttleworth, A. Smith, E. M. Sterland, E. I. Williams, R. Wilson.

Chapter 10.

MISCELLANEOUS.

IT may well be imagined that in the records of 300 years many interesting particulars in connection with the history of this School have been found, which do not readily fall under the heads selected for the previous chapters of this book, but which may be fittingly put together in a concluding chapter.

SCHOOL FEES.

At various times various means have been taken at Wakefield, as at other places, to ensure a just incidence of this payment. It has already been pointed out [1] that this School was intended to provide free education only for boys born and residing in the Parish of Wakefield, whilst "foreigners" were expected to pay for the privilege of enjoying the teaching which it offered. But exceptions were made to this rule in two directions; for, in the first place, residents in the Parish who were in prosperous circumstances were expected either to become benefactors of the School, or to pay for their sons at least one third more than the usual charge for boys from the neighbourhood [2]; and, on the other hand, residents outside the Parish, if benefactors to the School, were allowed the privilege of having their sons educated without further payment. Thus, in 1609, Mr. Hugh Cressy [3] gave "durante vita sua xxs., sub conditione to have the placing of 2 scholars though hereafter he remove his Dwelling out of the towne and parishe." Similarly, the Governors made a grant to "Martin Lister and his heires for the education of a child [4] in consideration of 10$li.$ given by him." A similar grant made in favour of the Rev. Richard Lister is here printed in full :—

"A graunt to Mr. Richard Lister [4] to have a scholler frely taught in the Schole for ever."

To all Christian people to whome theis presents shall com, Wee the Governours of the free Grammer Schole of Quene Elizabeth att Wakefeild send greetinge in our Lord God everlastinge. Whereas Richard Lister of

---

(1) pp. 49, 50.   (2) Ibid.   (3) p. 45.

(4) In p. 153 I have said that James Lister, Usher, and afterwards Vicar of Wakefield, was probably the son of Doctor Joseph Lister : he may also have been connected with this Martin Lyster and Rev. Richard Lister.

PRESENT MASTER'S HOUSE.
(From a Photograph by Messrs. G. & J. Hall.)

GRAMMAR SCHOOL. 227

Milnethorpe in the Countie of Yorke, Clerke, for the good will he bearith to the mayntenaunce of learninge and for the augmentacion of the Revenewe of the sayd Schole, by his deed ₁ sealled with his seall bearinge date the 20 day of Dec. last past, hath given, granted, and confirmed to us and our successors for ever, One annuitie or yearlie rent of twentie shillinges by yeare, yssuinge out and to be taken of, in, and upon one Messuage or tenement sett, lying, and beinge in Woodthorpe in the sayd Countie of Yorke, And of and in all the landes, medowes, and pastures lyinge neare to Woodthorpe, or in the feild of Sandall called Carre and Carrflattes, late the landes of Richard Wilcocke, conteyninge by estimacion thirtie sixe acres, to the sayd messuage or tenement belonginge or apperteyninge, with their appertenances in Woodthorpe and Sandall in the sayd countye of Yorke, and nowe in the tenure and occupacion of the sayd Richard Lister, or his assignes, att the feasts of Pentecost and Sainte Martyn the Bushoppe in winter by even porcions, as by the same deed more fullie it appearith : Nowe knowe you that we the said Governors of the said free Grammer Schole of Quene Elizabeth att Wakefeild, in consideracion thereof have granted, and by theis presents doe graunt for us and our successors to the said Richard Lister, his heires and asssignes of his now dwellinge house commonly called Mylnthorpe Hall in Milnthorpe aforesaide for the tyme being, that he and they shall or may have theire sonne or sonnes being Grammer schollers from tyme to tyme from henceforth for ever hereafter freely taught by the Mayster and Usher of the sayd Schole for the tyme being as other schollers of Wakefeild, or in the parish of Wakefeild, there learninge grammer, are or shall be taughte : So that we the sayd Governors or our successors shall or may for ever quietlye and peaceablie enjoye and receive the sayd annuitie according to the true intent and effect of the graunte thereof to us made, without any lawfull lett, interrupcion, recovery, or avoyding of the same annuitie, or any parte thereof by the sayd Richard Lister, his heires or assignes, or by any other person or persons lawfully clayminge by, from, or under the title of hym the sayd Richard Lister, his heires or assignes. In wittnes whereof hereunto wee have setto our common seall the . . . . day of . . . . in the yeare of the reigne of our sovereigne Lord James by the grace of God Kinge of England, Fraunce and Ireland, defender of the faith &c, the third, And of Scotland the xxxixth. (A.D. 1605.)

The intentions of the founders of Grammar Schools in various parts of the country, when they left money for the gratuitous education of all their scholars, or of a privileged number only, were defeated by various causes. In some cases the money left was found to be utterly inadequate to provide for the needs of the School, either owing to changes in the value of money and property, or to the increased numbers of boys under teaching. In other cases the more enlightened wisdom of a subsequent age discovered that Latin and Greek were not the only subjects of education required to fit boys for the different spheres of life. Therefore school-fees were charged

(1) quoted on p. 43.

either to supplement the income of the endowment, or to entitle boys to receive teaching in non-classical subjects, or to accomplish both objects.

At Wakefield the establishment of a Writing School in 1758 for the teaching of Writing, Accounts, and Mathematics, seems to have been the "fons et origo mali" in this respect : for the Writing Master paid the Governors a rent for the building, and apparently made his own terms with the parents of the Grammar School boys, who were all (whether town boys or "foreigners") expected to "attend the Writing School one Hour in the forenoon and another hour in the afternoon of each Day at such times of the Day as the Head Master shall direct." The Writing Master was also "permitted to open the Writing School for the benefit of Town Scholars, as well as those belonging to the Free Grammar School, but not to admit any girls as Scholars into his School." The principle adopted was therefore the same as that confirmed 50 years later by the famous decision of Lord Eldon, already quoted,[1] that "if scholars required anything more than the founder directed, they might be required to pay for it." Latin and Greek were thus to be taught gratuitously to town-boys, but other subjects must be paid for, even by them.

When the office of Writing Master was abolished, the Usher was entrusted with the duty of teaching boys Mathematics and Writing, and allowed to make an annual charge of two guineas for every boy who came under his instruction; but this charge was altered in 1840, when a fee of two guineas a year for "free boys," and four guineas a year for "foreigners" was substituted, and the extra subjects to be taught were defined as Writing, Arithmetic, English, Reading, and Geography. The next change came in 1855, when a new Statute was made by which the whole Scheme of Education was remodelled, and a definite scale of fees drawn up: an account of this, and of subsequent changes in this direction, may be found at the conclusion of the chapter dealing with the Statutes (pp. 83-5).

But in addition to these charges for subjects not mentioned in the Statutes, many other payments have been made at different Schools under different heads in order to augment the income of the Masters. These may be found given with some detail in Carlisle's "Endowed Grammar Schools," and in the Schools Inquiry Commissioners' Report of 1868 (I. 123-5). Sometimes a fee for admission was charged; so at Wakefield the Statutes [2] say :—

"Everie scholler entered into the Schole to be taught grammer beinge of the Towne or parish or freed by graunt of the governors under theire

(1) p. 25.   (2) p. 69.

GRAMMAR SCHOOL.

common seale for some liberall contribution given to the Schole shall the daie of his admittance paye to the hands of the maister or usher under whose teachinge he is to be entered Twelve pence as his admission money. Unles he be the sonne of a day taile man or one of like povertie: and then his admission shalbe free. And everie forrenour admitted whatsoever be the state or condicion of his father shall paye two shillings."

The sums thus received were "accounted for" by the Master and Usher to the Spokesman from time to time, but returned to them in addition to their usual salaries and other payments.[1]

At other Schools a variety of quarterly payments were enforced, so at Coventry in 1628—

"The scholars are to pay quarterages to the sweeper of the school for ringing of the bell, for making of fiers there, and for roddes, as hath been accustomed." (S.I.C. Report I. 124.)

Or at Guildford in 1608—

"Every scholar shall pay 8d. yearly, viz:—1d. quarterly towards the providing of brooms and rods, and also 4d. at the Feast of St. Michael yearly, wherewith shall be bought clean waxen candles to keep light in the school in the winter " (ibid).

Likewise at Camberwell in 1615 —

"The Schoolmaster's duties to be paid at the entrance of every Scholar —5s., and 3d. a quarter towards brooms and rods—and the week after Michaelmas, a pound of good candles." (Carlisle ii. 561.)

At Wakefield no payments of this nature have been discovered, but there are traces of others in the present century :—

"The Head Master (and probably the Second) is usually complimented with a small donation at Christmas." (Carlisle ii. 911.)

"The Master is authorized at his discretion to levy a Fine of One Penny each time that any Scholar is not present at the regular hour of Attendance at the Grammar School : and should the said fines be unpaid to the amount of half-a-crown, the Boy shall be expelled."

Instead of fines for late and irregular attendance, in some schools a second payment of admission money was enforced, in others the offending boys, if free scholars, were made to pay fees, or if "foreigners," were compelled to pay on a higher scale. In a few Schools, as in the Mercers' School, and at Southampton, "breaking up money" was paid to the Masters at the end of each term.

Finally, there were payments of a more discreditable nature, such as cockpence, victor pence, and potation pence, which will be explained in a future page.

(1) See bottom of page 66.

SCHOOL HOURS.

A memorandum in the Governors' Minute-Books, dated Jan. 21, 1820, gives a clear account of the original rules, and subsequent alterations, with respect to hours of school, holidays, and so on :—

"It having been ordained by the Original Statutes made for the good Government of the Free Grammar School, founded in the year of our Lord 1591, that from the tenth Day of March till the tenth day of October the Master and Usher shall begin to teach at or upon Six o'clock in the morning, and shall continue so till at, or upon, Six in the Evening (saving betwixt Eleven and One o'clock)—and from the tenth of October till the tenth of March again they shall begin from, or soon after Sun-rising till, or near, Sunsetting (save between Eleven and One o'clock,) which Statutes were kept in full force from the year 1777 till 1782—and, even, within a very few years, saving that consideration being had by the Governors to the Change in the Times and general Modes of living in these Realms, the Hour of Six in the Morning from the tenth of March till the tenth of October was altered to Seven o'clock, and one Half Hour was allowed from Eight till Half-past Eight for Breakfast.—The Dinner Respite was also altered from Eleven and One to from Twelve till Two, and from thence till Six o'clock—and from the tenth of October till the tenth of March the Hour of assembling in the Morning was fixed for Eight o'clock, allowing no time for Breakfast; and the hour of Departure continued till or near Sunsetting.

Of late years, however, from sundry causes, not material to be recited, numerous Innovations having crept into the Establishment by the Want of Masters and Scholars attending at the fixed Hours, and when so attending neither parties continuing till the times of Departure fixed by the Statutes—We the Governors of the Free Grammar School, anxious for the Prosperity of that Establishment do, with the Assent of the Master, order and appoint

That in future, from the second Monday in October to the second Monday in March, the Hours of attendance at the School for the Master, Usher, and Scholars shall be, in the Morning from Nine o'clock precisely till Twelve; and, in the Afternoon, from Two till Five, or in the shorter Days, till at, or near Sunsetting.

That, from the second Monday in March to the second Monday in October, the Hours of Attendance shall be, in the Morning from Eight o'clock precisely till Twelve, and in the Afternoon from Two till Six o'clock.

That an Avocation from the Business of the School be allowed on Wednesday and Saturday Afternoons, and on Saint Days, as usual.

That such of the Scholars, as wish to receive Improvement in Writing and Arithmetic, shall be allowed to attend the Writing School under the Order and Jurisdiction of the Governors, and no other, in the Morning from Ten till Eleven, and in the Afternoon from Three till Four."

The vacations, as fixed by the Statutes, were originally one of 10 days at Midsummer, commencing June 20, and another of 14 days at Christmas, commencing Dec. 20. But in 1694, owing to the custom of allowing 10 days at Whitsuntide, the Midsummer vacation was reduced to 7 days, and 7 days were also given at Allhallow tide, commencing Oct. 30 (see p. 80). In 1751 the Whitsuntide and Christmas holidays were each made a month in duration, and the others were apparently abolished, or made so short as not to deserve recognition in the School rules.

Additional holidays were however sometimes allowed, as for instance on the 17th November (see p. 72), the day of the accession of Queen Elizabeth, when it was ordered by the Statutes that the boys "shall play the whole daye and those which are able shall upon that daye sett upp verses[1] in honour and commendacion of Quene Elizabeth the blessed founder of this Schole." Also on two afternoons in each quarter the Master had power to give a holiday, in addition to the usual ones on Thursdays and Saints' days. And at other times the boys could obtain leave to play by consent of three of the Governors. This consent was given in writing, and when obtained was considered a justification of that summary proceeding known as "barring out the Master," which is thus referred to in Carlisle's Endowed Grammar Schools (ii. 631. 2):—

"Dr. Johnson in his 'Life of Addison' describes an innocent and harmless custom, which is not yet altogether relinquished in the North of England, with some degree of harshness. 'The practice of Barring-out was a savage licence, practised in many Schools to the end of the last Century, by which the boys, when the periodical Vacation drew near, growing petulant at the approach of liberty, some days before the time of regular recess, took possession of the School, of which they barred the doors, and bade their Master defiance from

---

[1] I am anxious to obtain a collection of as many of these boyish productions as are still in existence, and should extremely value any addition to my present stock.

the windows. It is not easy to suppose that on such occasions the Master would do more than laugh: yet, if tradition may be credited, he often struggled hard to force or surprise the garrison.'"

Perhaps we may suppose that Dr. Johnson was subjected to a very harsh form of "barring out" when he was Usher of Market Bosworth School. On one occasion, indeed, at Birmingham School, the boys went to violent extremes, by making an "assault to enter the schoole and then and theire did, not onely threaten to kill theire Master beeing gott into the Schoole, but for the space of neare two howers made such attempts by casting in stones and bricks, as well as breaking the wall and wenscote of the saide Schoole, as might indanger his life." In most Schools the practice was, however, of a less unpleasant nature, being merely an ocular demonstration to the Master that his boys had obtained the leave of the Governors of the School to have a holiday.[2] There is a Statute for this School which deals with the subject in such a way (see p. 81) as to fully justify Carlisle's opinion of its "innocent and harmless" nature: it enacts that the Governors shall not give orders for holidays contrary to the Statutes, that the boys shall not show their orders before Nov. 6 in any year, that the Master shall grant the holiday at once, but that if the boys bar him out before showing their orders, they shall be expelled.

SCHOOL GAMES.

It is a most interesting fact that one of the best descriptions of School games in vogue early in the 17th century is written by a Wakefield Grammar School boy, and may therefore be considered to be an account, more or less accurate, of the games which the author himself used to indulge in when a School boy here. The work in which this account is given is an edition of "Johannis Amos Commenii Orbis Sensualium Pictus," and the author is the Rev. Charles Hoole, M.A., some time Head Master of Rotherham School, whose career will be found summarized on p. 203. The book is a sort of illustrated pocket dictionary, divided into a large number of sections, each headed by an illustration, and having a description of the picture in Latin and English: from it a most complete idea can be obtained of the habits and life of the time. In section 130 Hoole describes stage-plays, "ludus scenicus," in section 131 tumbling or "prestigiæ," in section 132 wrestling or "palæstra," in section 133 various games of ball, "ludus pilæ," the text here running as follows:

(1) Carlisle's End. Gr. Schools, ii. 632.   (2) Chambers' Book of Days, i. 238.

"In a Tennis Court they play with a ball, which one throweth and another taketh and sendeth it back with a racket, and that is the sport of noblemen to stir their body. A winde ball being filled with air by means of a Ventil is tossed to and fro with the Fist in the open air." Section 134 deals with games of dice, "ludus aleæ." while section 135, on race-running, "cursus certamina," says—" Boyes exercise themselves in running either upon the Ice, in Scrick-shoes (*i.e.* skates) where they are carried also upon Sleds, or in the open field, making a line which he that desireth to win ought to touch, but not to run beyond it. Heretofore runners ran betwixt railes to the goal (a stone wall in the illustration) and he that toucheth it first, received the prize from him that gave the prize. At this day tilting, or the quintain, is used, where a hoop is struck at with a Trunchion, instead of Horseraces, which are grown out of use." Section 136 deals with small boys' games, "ludi pueriles." "Boyes use to play either with Bowling stones (large marbles in the illustration) or throwing a Bowl, at Nine pins, or striking a ball thorow a Ring with a Bandy, or scourging a Top with a Whip, or shooting with a Trunck (*i.e.* a tube) and a bow, or going upon Stilts, or tossing and swinging themselves upon a Merry-totter," (*i.e.* a swing).

Hoole's work was published in 1658, and in 1801 appeared an edition of Strutt's "Sports and Pastimes," which gives us further particulars about school and other games, often referring to Hoole's account. Amongst other games mentioned we find base, or bars, or prisoners' bars, which is alluded to in Cymbeline, Act I., Sc. 2, and needs no description here. A note by Fitz-stephen is quoted as follows:—"Annually on Shrove Tuesday London shoolboys go into the fields immediately after Dinner, and play at the celebrated game of ball: every party of boys carrying their own ball." It does not appear certain what particular game is here meant: some think it is golf or bandy ball, others say it is football, others take it to be hand ball or hand tennis, adding that in this game cords and tendons were wrapped round the hands to protect them. Strutt also mentions "stool-ball," a sort of cricket, the striker being out if the bowler hit the stool. Then there was "hurling or hand-football," in which the ball was carried from goal to goal by being passed from partner to partner, the opposite side trying to gain possession.[1] There was also a similar game played with bats, corresponding to our hockey. Football is described as being "once popular, but now in disrepute." Golf is next referred to; then a sort of croquet with a ring on a swivel instead

(1) See also Chambers' Book of Days, i. 238.

of a hoop; club ball and cricket; trap ball, which is called a childish pastime; Northern spell and tip-cat; bowling, nine-pins, skittles; nine-holes, in which marbles were rolled on to a board with holes and arches in it; swinging on merry-totters, or tetter-totters, the latter being the same as our see-saw; shuttlecock, which is called a boys' sport of great popularity since the reign of James I.; cards, chess, dice, merrelles, dominoes. Finally comes a long list of children's games, including pot-guns or pop-guns, hunt the fox, hide and seek or harry-racket, barley brake, thread the tailor's needle, puss in corner, leap frog, hop scotch, skipping, trundling hoops, marbles, tops, kites, bob-cherry, hoodman blind, hot cockles, and the like.

From these two works we may therefore derive a satisfactory idea of the harmless amusements of school boys during the 17th and 18th centuries. But there remain to be noticed amusements of a more disgraceful and degrading character.

Cockfighting was formerly a most popular sport, not only in public places of amusement, but especially in schools, and the most discreditable feature of the sport was the fact that the masters of schools often used it as a means of augmenting their income. This source of gain was even recognized and allowed in the Statutes of some Schools, as at Hartlebury,[1] where the rules, made by "twenty of the most discreet and honest men of the Parish, with the advice and consent of the Right Revd. Father in God Edwin Lord Bishop of Worcester," in the year 1564, contain the provision—

> "Also that the said Schoolmaster and Usher shall and may have, use and take the profits of all such cock-fights and potations, as are commonly used in Schools, and such other gifts as shall be freely given them by any of the friends of their Scholars, over and besides their wages, until their salary and stipend shall be augmented."

In one of the reports[2] of the Schools Inquiry Commissioners of 1868, it is stated that in—

> "the original statutes of Sir T. Boteler's School at Warrington, founded in A.D. 1526, it is declared lawful for the schoolmaster for the time being to take of any scholar 4 pence in the year, viz.:—in the quarter after Christmas a cock-penny at Shrove tide, and in the other three quarters one potation penny, and for the same it is added he shall make a drink for all the said scholars."

The same report adds that at Heversham the school cock-pit could still be seen, while at Lancaster it existed until very recent times.

---

(1) Carlisle's End. Gr Schools, ii. 759
(2) Mr. Bryce's General Report, p. 469.

GRAMMAR SCHOOL.

It is also remarked in more than one of these reports that cock-pence were paid even in 1868 to the Masters in many Schools, though there were no longer any cock fights. Thus at Sedbergh [1] the boys had to pay one guinea to the Master and half a guinea to the Usher every quarter as cock-pence, but they got no sport. At Preston, Blackburn, and Clitheroe [2] the cock-pence amounted to two guineas a quarter. At Wreay School, near Carlisle, a Mr. Graham gave a silver bell, weighing two ounces, upon which was engraven "Wrey Chapple, 1655," to be fought for annually on Shrove Tuesday by cocks: the bell was presented to the owner of the victorious bird.[3]

On the other hand, many School Statutes are entirely without mention of cock-pence, whilst in some the practice of exacting it is expressly forbidden, as at Manchester and Witton, near Chester.

I am pleased to be able to add that neither in the Statutes of Wakefield Grammar School, nor in any other of the numerous documents which I have seen relating to it, have I found the slightest reference to either cock-pence or cock-fighting, or the more cruel pastime of cock-throwing, which is thus condemned by Brady (Clavis Calendaria, i. 102) :—

"Cock-throwing, the other barbarous amusement of the day was even yet more barbarous than that of cock-fighting: in the latter diversion the contesting birds were prompted to destroy each other by their natural propensity for fighting and by that invincible spirit which upheld them throughout the severity of their sufferings, while they had likewise some chance of surviving the almost general slaughter: but in cock-throwing the poor sufferer could not receive any such natural and invigorating stimulus, and had no rival bird to inflame his jealousy and call forth his powers, but fastened to a stake he was compelled to endure the batterings of sticks and other missiles until by repeated bruises or broken limbs he lay prostrate before his savage tormentors, writhing in agonies from which he could only be relieved by some lucky blow that terminated at once his sufferings and his life."

"The boys at School," says Carlisle,[4] "now throw at a wooden, instead of a living Cock, and near the metropolis even the vulgar have long disused this brutal custom, substituting in its stead oranges,

(1) Mr. Fitch's General Report, p. 144.
(2) Mr. Bryce's General Report, p. 469.
(3) Chambers' Book of Days, i. 239.
(4) Historical Account of the Origin of the Commission appointed to enquire into Charities in England and Wales, p. 272.

tobacco, boxes, and other articles placed upon sticks, all of which, out of compliment to the original, are denominated Cocks, and as such are thrown at with bludgeons by those who are tempted to strive for their possession."

These amusements provided another source of income for the under-paid Schoolmasters of a former age, which is known by the name of Victor-penny. This was apparently paid to the Masters by their boys for the privilege of celebrating the result of a contest in cock-fighting or cock-throwing by some sort of a procession, in which the owner of the victorious bird, in the one case, or the most successful thrower, in the other case, was conducted from the scene of battle in triumph: the practice is called "riding about of victory" in Dean Colet's Statutes for S. Paul's School.

SCHOOL ROUTINE.

This School being, as the Statutes point out, "not ordained for petties but for grammarians," or, as we might now say, not being in any sense an elementary or preparatory school, was open to no boy "unles he be able in tolerable sorte to read Englishe and be promoted to the accidence," *i.e.* the Latin accidence. Hence we may suppose that few boys entered before the age of 7 or 8, the age for entering the "Petty" or preparatory school being 5 or thereabouts, at the end of the 16th century. When a boy had entered the School, he was put either under the Usher or the Master, according to his proficiency. If he was put in the Usher's class, he was taught Latin grammar before anything else, including, according to the directions of the Statutes, the declensions of nouns, conjugations of verbs, agreement of substantive and adjective, of antecedent and relative, of verb and subject, and so on. Being fairly proficient in this, he was practised in writing Latin exercises from the Usher's dictation; and after due training therein, he was taught to translate Cato, or some like book, into English, and to turn his English again into Latin. One hour in every afternoon was devoted to writing copies set by the Usher, or some of the scholars. These were the sole subjects of teaching, as far as can be gathered from the Wakefield Statutes, for boys under the Usher's care, being "groundes and beginnings of good learninge, as they are most unpleasant for the Schollers to learn, so are they most troublesome for the schoolmaister to teach, and require a long and unpleasant tyme of carefull instruction."

When promoted to the Master's class, the 17th century Schoolboy still continued his career in Latin grammar, using the famous text-book by Lyly, and reading Terence, Cicero, Cæsar, Livy, Ovid, Virgil, and Horace. He was not to be taught Latin Verses until he could write in Latin "an epistle and theame of good force and congruitie," and not to be taught Greek until he was "able of a theme in reasonable time to make halfe a score or a dozen of tollerable, if not of good verses." When Greek was commenced, no particular grammar was specified for adoption, but the one most commonly used in Cambridge from time to time was selected: the authors to be read included Isocrates, Demosthenes, Hesiod, and Homer. In both languages exercises were to be written by the boys, corrected by the Master, and compared with fair copies of his own, "and thus the displeasinge hardnes of learninge shalbe made easie in the welpleasinge mannor of teachinge."

When proficient in Greek, the best boys were taught Logic and Hebrew. On Saturdays, from one to two o'clock, lessons were given by the Master in the principles of Christian religion. On Sundays the boys were taken by him to Church, and the elder ones took notes of the sermon, which were produced for examination on the Monday morning, when questions were also asked upon the lessons given on the two previous days in School and in Church. The boys under the Master were also always expected to speak in Latin, both in the School and in the playground.

Lastly, the Master and Usher were to inculcate respect towards superiors in all places, courteousness of speech to all men, cleanliness of apparel, decency, modesty, and good manners as well as good learninge.

School was opened every morning with prayers,[1] including a thanksgiving for benefactors, which were followed by the reading of a Chapter from the Bible: in the afternoon, at the close of School, prayers were again said, and a Psalm sung by the boys.

Such was the School routine, as fixed by the Statutes in 1607: the following document gives us an account of the conduct of the School nearly a century later:—

June 11, 1695. "Whereas complaint hath been made that for some years last past severall laudable customes have been omitted relating to the good order and government of the free school, which

---

[1] Dr. Taylor, one of my predecessors, compiled a series of Prayers to be used in the School on different days of the week: a copy has very kindly been lent to me by the Rev. T. H. Shaw, M.A.

being represented to Mr. Farrar the present master, he thereupon made his request to the Governours to be informed of the said customes and usages of the Schole, together with what may further be requisite for the good government thereof. They have therefore thought fitt that these following directions be observed.

Of the Monitor of the Free Schole and his duty.

That there be a monitor for each end of the Schole, and their office to continue for a week, to be chosen out of one of the three first formes in each end.

Their office on Sundays.

To see how the Boys behave themselves at Church, and to note down the absent: to goe out once or oftener in Sermon time to see if there be no idle persons about the Schole, breaking the windows, &c.

On School-dayes.

To call the boys into the Schole at the usual times, morning and afternoon, and more especially if the Master be not there.

To take care the Boys keep every one their proper place, that they make no noise in the school, and this as well in the absence as presence of the Master.

To note down all offenders, *videl.*, such as swear, curse, use filthy and obscene words, give bad names, fight, game for money, break the Schole windows, teare the school books, speak English, come late or are absent.

To laye up the Schole-Books carefully, and to see that the doors be duely locked.

Not to permitt more to go out than two at a time, and they to stay no longer than their necessityes require, and none to go into the town and churchyard in schole hours.

Short Memoranda for the Master to observe.

1st. To have a generall eye over the schole but particularly see that the monitor do his duty, and to correct him severely if he be found negligent and faulty, sparing any for favour, or accusing falsely. To enquire how the boys behave themselves out of schole, not to abuse any one nor to make a noise in Companyes in the Streets, nor to carry themselves irreverently towards those who are above them either in years or Authority.

GRAMMAR SCHOOL.

To keep up the Usher's Authority in the Schole, and that the upper boyes reverence him.

2nd. To have prayers morning and evening constantly, and to bee present at them.

To have a chapter read in the morning in English, and another at one o'clock afternoone by a boy of the low end.

To be carefull in the Schole Exercises, to observe the faults in them, and to cause the boyes to correct them themselves, if they be able, or if they cannot, to do it in their presence, to make them now and then an Exercise for their Imitation, and to take care they do not get others to make them.

That such as are able to make Speeches and Declamations, repeat them memoriter, and take particular care of their Pronuntiation.

That the boyes in repeating their parts and Lessons memoriter be not permitted to prompt one another, or to hold their bookes so as they who are repeating may looke on.

That the Master admits of no Exercises but what is fair written and true Orthography, and made of such Subjects only as he shall impose.

That such as read Greeke, make use of Lexicons for the Signification of words, and not the Latine Translations, except the sense of the Author cannot well be explained without it, and then to be sent to look the difficult words in the Lexicon notwithstanding.

That the Master permitt none besides himselfe, or the Under Master, to send for ale, or Club in the Schole Chamber During schole time, it being a thing of ill Example to the Schollars, and discreditt to the Schole."

Let us hope that this document deals not with offences which had actually occurred,[1] but with such as might occur in the future: it certainly cannot be criticized for a want of straightforward language.

Little more has been recorded in the Governors' books on the subject of School discipline beyond a few references to the attendance of boys at Church, which was always strictly insisted upon. The seats occupied by them were at the East end of the South Gallery, where the four pews belonging to the School had brass plates

---

[1] Those who are curious may, however, find the faults and failings of Schoolmasters described in the Schools Inquiry Commissioners' Reports of 1868.

upon them, with the inscription "Free Grammar School." Similar brass plates were provided by the Governors for all the pews in the Parish Church belonging to the different Trusts under their control.

But the management of the School during the Headmastership of the Rev. John Clarke (1751-8) has been described at some length in his biography, by Dr. Zouch, and in the "Gentleman's Magazine." In the latter a discussion was started (in Vol. 72) concerning religious education in English Schools, and it is interesting to note that the Schools quoted as examples were Eton, Winchester, Westminster, Rugby, Manchester, and Wakefield. Mr. Clarke's system at Wakefield is especially commended. Dr. Zouch describes it as follows:—"It was one of his employments to begin the mornings of the three first days in each week with explaining to his scholars a select portion in the Version of the LXXII, and another in the Greek New Testament. Hence they became familiarized, in their more tender years, to the language of the sacred penmen. Many of them, intended for the Church, in conformity to his advice, continued to dedicate a brief portion of every day to the careful perusal of the Scriptures, and the regular use of an interleaved Bible for the insertion of incidental remarks and illustrations. If this plan of study were universally adopted in our public schools, might it not enable the candidates for orders to acquit themselves with superior credit?"

It only now remains to be added, respecting this subject, that until the present century periodical Examinations seem to have been unheard of, except as tests for Scholarships and Degrees at the University. The first record of a School Examination at Wakefield is—

> Mar. 12, 1832. "Resolved, that an eminent classical Scholar be appointed by the Spokesman for the time being to examine all the boys in the Grammar School previous to the Midsummer and Christmas Vacations in every subsequent year, and that the first examination take place at Midsummer next."

But there was an institution which to some extent served the purpose of an examination of the best boys in different schools, that of "disputing abroad," as it was called, a custom which is thus described in Strype's edition of Stow's "Survey of London" (pp. 123-4):—

"Upon Festival days, the Masters made solemn meetings in the Churches, where their Scholars disputed logically and demonstratively. The boys of divers Schools did cap or pot verses, and contended of the principles of Grammar. The same was long since discontinued. But the arguing of the School-boys about the principles of Grammar hath been continued even till our time: for I myself, in my youth, have yearly seen (on the eve of St. Bartholomew the Apostle) the Scholars of divers Grammar Schools repair unto the Church-yard of St. Bartholomew the Priory in Smithfield, where (upon a bank boarded about under a Tree) some one Scholar hath stepped up, and there hath opposed and answered, till he were by some better Scholar overcome and put down. And then the overcomer taking the place, did like as the first: and in the end, the best opposers and answerers had rewards, which I observed not. But it made both good Schoolmasters, and also good Scholars, (diligently against such times) to prepare themselves for the obtaining of this Garland."

In Dean Colet's Statutes for St. Paul's School, London, a different opinion is expressed :—"I will they use no Cockfightinge, nor rydinge about of victorye, nor disputing at Saint Bartilimewe, which is but foolish babbling, and losse of time;" but Carlisle mentions several Schools where such "disputing" was common, and it was certainly a custom in connection with Wakefield School, as the following extract shows, from Smith's "Old Yorkshire" (Vol. ii. p. 150) where an account of Lee Fair, held at Woodkirk, is given :—

"On St. Bartholomew's day, on which the fair ended, the Scholars from the Grammar Schools of Leeds, Wakefield, and other places, were brought to Lee Fair for disputation, or to ascertain their proficiency in classical learning, yearly down to the early part of last century."

There is no need to comment upon the contrast between the un-examined School of the last century and the much-examined School of the present day: much could be said on both sides of the question.

Nor is there any necessity for speculating upon the important changes which may be in store for this School and others in the coming years: whatever they be, may every reader of this work join its author in the prayer—

FLOREAT SCHOLA WAKEFIELDIENSIS.

I. INDEX OF SUBJECTS.

Accounts, School 23–5, 73
Acts of Parliament 2–4, 26, 53, 84, 174
Admission Money 68–9, 228–9
American Wars 102, 212
Arctic Expedition 220
Assembly of Divines 202
Assistant Masters 82, 138–164

Ball, Games of 233–4
Barring Out 81, 231–2
Beadle of School 24, 57
Benefactors 19, 20, 33–52
Black Rod, Gent. Usher of 213
Books of School 70, 166–172
Boyle Lectures 207
Breaking Up Money 229
Broom Money 229
Buildings of School 18–32

Canal, Thames–Severn 204
Candle Money 229
Catalogue Money 172
"Cathedral Church of Wakefield" 96, &c.
Cathedral Schools 2
Chancery, Court of 25, 192, 194, 215
Charity Commission 53, 84, 113, 186–7
Charity School 112, 211
Charter of Foundation 10–15
Cholera in Wakefield 29
Civil Wars 4, 10, 48, 90, 92–3, 96, 98–9, 108
Clerks to Governors 104, 111–2
Coal Money 172
Cock-fighting and throwing 234–6
Cock-pence 234–5
Croft of School 22, 26

Deputy Spokesmen 56, 109–111
Disputing Abroad 240–1
Dissolution of Religious Houses 2–4
Dodsworth MSS. 21

Endowed Schools Act 26, 53, 84
"Endowed Gr. Schools," Buckler's 21, 160
  Do. Carlisle's 21, 54, 228, 231, &c.
Examinations 83–4, 240
Exchequer, Court of 215
Exhibitions, Cave 10, 36, 38, 48, 98, 100, 115, 118, 123, 134, 177–184
—— Freeston 34–5, 48, 129, 173–7
—— Hastings 197–200
—— Storie 50, 84–5, 185–197

Fellowships, Freeston 35, 48, 175–7
Football 233
"Foreigners" 50, 69, 70 226
Foundation of School 1–17
"Free Grammar School," Meaning of 15–17
Free Scholars, 49, 69, 226

"Gentleman's Magazine" 139, 240
Goldsmiths' Company 2
Governors, Duties of 60–2
—— Election of 86–96
—— List of 97–108
—— Meetings of 57
—— Oath of 60, 63
—— Qualifications of 58–60, 78–9, 89
Grammar Schools, Origin of 4, 5
Guinea, Value of 23

Head Masters, Election of 79, 113
—— Faults in 61, 241
—— House of 22, 26–8, 241
—— Leave of Absence 72
—— List of 114
—— Lives of 115–151
—— Oath of 64
—— Power over Usher 77
—— Qualifications of 62, 113
—— Salary of 29, 66, 82, 228–9
—— Veto of 59, 88–9
"History of Corp. Chr. Coll." 212
" —— Northallerton" 206
" —— S. John's Coll." 115
Holidays 71–2, 80, 83, 120, 230–2

Inscription on Old School 22
Instruction, Course of 15, 25–6, 65, 68, 83–4, 145, 228, 236–9

Jewish Schools 54

Kennett MSS. 134
Keys of School Chests 56

Late Boys Fined 229
Lay for Endowment 47–8
Leases 62, 92–3
"Lectures on Hist. of Wakefield" 8
"Leeds Intelligencer" 28, 143
"Liber Cantabrigiensis" 176
Library 22, 51, 129, 130, 133, 139, 166–172
Licence to Teach 119
"Life of Bentley" 128, 207

INDEX OF SUBJECTS.

"Life of Dean Colet" 157
"Loidis and Elmete" 164
London Jews' Society 220
Lot, Scholars Elected by 198, 200

Mercers' Company 2, 142
Middle Ages, Education in 1, 2
Monastic Schools 2, 4
Monitors 24, 238

Number of Scholars 82, 151

"Old Yorkshire" 241
"Origines Ecclesiasticæ" 208

Parish Church Schools 2
Petty School, 181, 186
Plague in Wakefield 88
Popery Abjured 64
Potation Pence 234
Power Loom Invented 215
Prayer Book of Edward VI. 4
Prayers in School 71, 237
President of the North 12, 59
Proprietary School 28-31, 217

Quarry in School Croft 22, 35

Radcliffe Fellowships 206
"Rectory Manor of Wakefield" 96, 122, &c.
Register of Pupils 201-225
Rods, Money for 229

"Savilian, the" 20
Scholarships, Foundation 84-5
    (and see Exhibitions)
School Fees 49, 50, 69, 83-5, 226-9
—— Games 232-6
—— Hours 65, 71, 83, 230-2
—— Routine 236-241

Schools Inquiry Commission 4, 16, 152, 228, 239
"Scripture Characters" 144, 171, 190
Senior Classic and Senior Wrangler 170, 212
"South Yorkshire" 19
Spokesmen of Governors 9, 18, 53, 55-8, 93, 108
—— List of 109-111
—— Oath of 56
"Sports and Pastimes" 233
Statutes of School 53-85
"Survey of London" 240

Town Crier 24
Towneley Mysteries 3, 22
Trade Guilds 2, 3

Usher, Duties of 67-8, 77, 236
—— Faults in 61
—— Leave of Absence 72
—— List of 132, 135, 137, 153-8
—— Oath of 67
—— Qualifications of 67, 152
—— Salary of 69, 82, 228

Victor Pence 236

Wages, Rate of 21
"Wakefield Journal" 28-9, 146, 150, 179
"Wakefield Worthies" 3, 91, 136, 157, 207, &c.
"Walks about Wakefield" 33, 38, 96, &c.
Windows Broken 20, 24, 25, 70
"Works of Dr. Zouch" 133, 135-6, 138
Writing Master, 26. 145, 159, 228
—— School 126, 142, 228, 231

"Yorkshire Worthies" 100

II. INDEX OF PLACES.

Aberford 148, 197
Abington 182
Ackworth 128, 222
Acomb 182
Addingham 192
Aldborough 100
Aldby Park 213
Alfreton 185
Altofts 34–5
Alverthorpe 41, 44, 105, 219, 221
Appleby Sch. 197
Ardsley 216
Ardwick, S. Benedict's, 161
Arksey 213
Armley, 203

Badsworth 206, 221
Balne 203
Barbados, Archd. of, 191
Bardsey, Vicar of, 189
Barmston 212
Barningham 214
Barnsley 218
Bath 163, 215
Batley 8, 146, 204
— Sch. 147, 159
Beachampton 195
Beauchieff 210
Bedfordshire C. Council 221
Bedminster 205
Belgrave 153
Bentley Grange 39
Bermondsey, S. Mary M., 202
Berwick Rectory 197
Beverley 104, 214
— Sch. 136–7, 156, 159
Bexley 163
Bicester 193
Bingley Sch. 148, 155
— Vicar of, 155
Birmingham, Queen's Coll., 149
— S. Jude's, 162
— K. Ed. Sch., 174, 232
Birstall 36, 41
Bishop Wearmouth 184, 219
Blackburn Sch. 3, 235
Blackley, 150
Bolton 208
— Bolland 104
— Percy 197
Bootle 222
Bournemouth 160

Bradford 1, 8, 219
— Sch. 151, 197
Bradley Hall 8
Brearley 210
Bridlington 210, 215
Brington 150. 160, 190, 205
Bristol 101, 149
— Dean of, 205
— Preb. of, 205
— Sch. 150, 163, 175
— S. Mary Redc., 205
Broadfield 204
Brodsworth 210
Brompton 211
Bromsgrove Sch. 158
Brooke 192
Brotherton 45
Broughton 150
Buckingham 206
Bucknall 213
Burton 194
Buxton 154

Caistor 212
Calverley, 36, 203
Camberwell Sch. 229
Cambridge, All Saints', 193
— Caius Coll., 193, 203, 213, 219, 224
— Cath. Coll., 161, 191–5
— Chr. Coll., 154, 157, 188, 197, 203, 212
— Clare Coll., 10, 34, 48, 98, 100, 115, 134, 153, 155–6, 159, 160, 177–8, 188, 191, 192, 194, 202, 211, 223–4
— Corp. Chr. Coll., 160, 212, 215
— Down. Coll., 196, 224
— Emm. Coll., 13, 18, 35, 48, 65, 113, 116–7, 121–2, 125–6, 128, 176, 189, 203, 211
— Jes. Coll., 133, 154, 157, 188, 191–2, 212–3, 216
— King's Coll., 121, 196, 205
— Magd. Coll., 124, 127, 144–5, 156, 171, 191–2, 194, 205, 209, 212–3
— Queens' Coll., 146–7, 161, 195
— S. John's Coll., 18, 115, 131, 148, 154, 157–9, 160, 163, 171–2, 188, 190–4, 203–16

Cambridge, S. Pet. Coll., 193, 207, 209, 215, 222
— Sid. Sus. Coll., 35, 48, 169, 176, 192, 202, 210
— Trin. Coll., 135–8, 149, 154–6, 158, 169, 170–1, 189, 190–1, 194–5, 207, 209–12, 214–6
— Trin. H., 215, 217
Canterbury, 52
— Archb. of, 207–8
Capetown 163
Carlisle, Bish. of, 214–5
— Dean of, 151
— S. Cuthbert's, 174
— Sch., 2, 199
Carshalton 206
Caterham 157
Caunton 161
Cawthorne 212
Chapel Allerton 182
Chapelthorpe 52, 104–5, 159
Chapeltown 221
Charterhouse 160
Cheltenham Coll. 150
Chester, Bish. of, 115
Chesterfield Sch. 161
Chester-le-Street 195
Chevet 99–101
Chirk, S. Martin, 192
Clapham 214
Clayton 203
Clitheroe Sch. 235
Clive, The, 158
Coleford 156
Coleshill 214
Coley 120–1
Collingham 197
Colne, 208, 210
Commenda 214
Cononley 213–4
Cork, Free Ch., 184
— S. Luke's, 184
Coventry Sch 229
Crediton Sch. 160
Crigglestone 208
Crofton 44, 97, 99, 101, 218
— Grange 221
— Hall 105, 148, 217
— Lister Close 44
— Rector of, 105, 146–7
Cromer Sch. 2
Crowden-le-Booth 216
Crumpsall 220

(245)

INDEX OF PLACES.

Dalby 213
Darfield 206
Denstone Coll. 161
Derby, Chr. Ch., 195
— Sch. 161
Derbyshire, High Sheriff, 210
Dewsbury 221
Dishforth 221
Dodworth 207
Doncaster 221
— Sch. 125, 199
Douay 202
Drighlington 128
Dublin, Trin. Coll., 159
Duntsbourn Abbots 156
Durham, Bish. of, 115
— Preb. of, 202, 214
— Sch. 195
— Univ. 224

Ealing 221
Easingwold 156
East Grinstead 202
East Liss 193
East Rasen 211
Eccles 193
Ecclesfield 102
Edinboro' 218
Edinthorpe 192
Edlington 209
Edmondton, Upper, 193
Eldwick Hall 155
Elton 220
Ely, Archd. of, 202, 207
Emley 52, 166, 189
Enfield 216
Epworth 104
Escrick 133-5
Eton Coll. 8, 129, 206, 240
Everton 183, 220
Exford 193

Faireburne 45
Fakenham 196
Falmouth 159
Faversham Sch. 163
Fenay 100
Fenton 143
Finchampstead 183
Flanshaw 37, 98-100
Fryston 45

Gawkethorpe 18, 37
— Wheateroyd Close, 37
Giggleswick Sch. 157, 199
— Vicar of, 180
Glasgow 220
Gloucester Sch. 158

Goadby Marwood 215
Gold Coast 222
Goldington 199
Gosfield 205
Graffham 212
Grange-over-Sands 160
Gravesend 192
Great Berkhampstead 160
Great Gransden 160, 202
Great Rolwright 213
Grinshill 158
Guildford Sch. 229

Haddlesey 175
Halesowen Sch. 158
Halifax 1, 120, 123, 203, 210
Hallows 185
Halton Gill 193
Hampstead, S. Paul's, 157
Harrogate 221
Hartlebury Sch. 234
Hartshead 187
Hasleborrow 50, 98, 185, 204
Hastings 215
Hatfield 105, 169
Havannah 217
Havant 208
Haworth 154
Headbourn Worthy 208
Heath, Halifax, 115, 124-5, 156
— Wakefield, 100-6
Heaton 207
Heckmondwike 41
Helmsley 193
Hemsworth 204
— Hall 105
— Sch. 155
Hensall 193
Heversham Sch. 197, 234
Hickleton 210
Hiendley 204-5
Higham 192
Higham Ferrars 149, 221
Hindley Sch. 162
Hipperholme Sch. 199
Holmer 162
Holt Sch. 182
Hook with Warsash 160
Hooton Pagnell 19, 31, 36, 154, 156, 181
Horbury 42, 100, 218, 220
— Carr Lodge, 105
— Curate of, 192
— Incumbent of, 104, 121
— Milnefield, 42
— Westfield, 42
Howley Hall 8, 98
Huddersfield 219

Huddersfield, Archd. of, 106
— Curate of, 184
Hull 221
Hulme, S. John's, 194
— S. Philip's, 194
Hunslet 154, 193
Hunstanton 192
Hurstpierpoint Coll. 158
Husband's Bosworth 183
Hutton 192

Ingatestone 215
Inns of Court 49
Inverness Cath. 183
Islington, St. Peter's 191

Kendal 218
Ken Hill 106
Kildwick 155, 213
Kilham 156
Killington 131
Kimbolton Sch. 149
Kippax 210
Kirby Misperton 136, 139, 140
— on-Moor, 184
Kirkby 155, 183, 203
Kirkby Malzeard 205
Kirkleatham 135, 137, 155, 164
Kirk Michael 183
— Sandal 153, 155
Kirkthorpe 102, 104-5, 144, 160, 202, 205
Knaresbro' 204, 214-5
Knottingley 209

Laghlin, Dean of, 202
Lancaster, Duke of, 128
— Sch. 234
Langton 214
Launceston Sch. 3
Lausanne 192
Leathley 153
Ledsham 197
Leeds 1, 8, 100, 204, 215, 217-8, 221-4
— Gr. Sch. 15, 25, 143, 145, 151, 156, 197, 241
— Middle Class Sch. 175
— S. Luke's 174
— S. Martin's 174
— Trinity Ch. 189
— Vicar of, 36, 180, 197
— Yorkshire College 85, 151, 224-5
Leicester 218
— All Saints', 190
— Infimary 190
— St. Mary's, 144, 190

(246)

INDEX OF PLACES.

Lichfield 104, 160, 191
— Bish. of, 104, 115, 214
— Coll. 161
— St. Mary's, 195
Lincoln, Bishop of, 212
— Canon of, 171, 215
— Preb. of, 203, 215
Litchurch 160
Litlington 160
Liverpool Sch. 3
Llanidloes 162
Lofthouse 155
London, Aldersgate, 203
— Blackwall Hall, 9, 21, 49
— Bow Street, 206
— Brit. Mus., 118, 134, 177
— City and Guilds' Inst., 223
— City Sch., 157
— Doctors' Comm., 218
— For. Office, 217
— Foundling Hosp., 191
— Freemasons' Hall, 221
— Gray's Inn, 157, 191
— King's Coll., 200
— Lincoln's Inn, 97, 200, 213, 217
— Lord Mayor of, 135
— Lothbury, 203
— Marylebone, 157
— Merch. Taylors' Sch., 199
— Pat. Office, 184
— S. Andrew's, 157
— S. Barth. Ch., 241
— S. Barth. Hosp, 206
— S. Clement's, 199
— S. Gabriel's, 199
— S. James's Pal., 207
— S. Magnus', 200
— S. Matthew's, 157
— S. Paul's Cath., 143
— S. Paul's Sch., 2, 157, 241
— Somerset House, 220
— Stroud Green, 161
— Toole's Theatre, 219
— Univ. Coll. Sch., 161
Long Benton 193
Longridge 220
Lowestoft 222
Lupset 100-1, 105
Lutterworth 183

Macclesfield, Archd. of, 183
Madrid Ambass. at, 219
Manchester 218–220. 240, 235
— Cath. Sch. 162
— Owens Coll., 196
Mareham le fen 192
Margate 163

Maritzburg 183
Market Bosworth Sch. 232
Marlborough Coll. 157, 221
— St. Mary's, 205
Marnham 214-5
Marr 159
Marston Moor 91
Marton 210, 215
Masham 216
Melbourne 183
Melsonby 214
Methley 105, 207, 220
Middleton 211 .
Mirfield 194-5
Monmouth 192
Monte Video 221
Moray and Ross, Bish. of, 183
Morland 141
Morpeth 141
Mosser 222
Moulton Sch. 159
Much Wenlock 162
Muskham 213

Neath Sch. 163
Nether Poppleton 105
Netherton 155
Newall Hall 218
New Basford 218
Newcastle Sch. 159
Newfoundland, Bish. of, 183
Newhall Manor 203
Newland 9, 99, 101-2, 179
Newmillerdam 214, 216
New Romney 222
Newton 42
Newtown 184
Normanton 160, 193
— School 34-5, 173, 176
— Vicar of, 135
Northallerton 206
Northowram 120
Northumberland, Archd. of, 202
Norton 50, 101, 144, 185, 203
Nostell 2, 44
Nottingham 222
Notts, High Sheriff of, 213
Nunmonkton 137
Nunthorpe 106

Oakham Sch. 192, 202
Oporto 105
Ossett 160, 221
Oswestry Sch. 1
Otley Sch. 10
— Tithes 36
Ouchthorpe 45
Oulton 207, 210

Outwood Hall 101, 184
Overbrear 120-1
Overton 137
Oxford 220
— Ball. Coll., 150, 153, 155, 161-2, 196
— Bish. of, 208
— Bodl. Library, 21, 48
— Bras. Coll., 164, 213, 215
— Central Sch., 163
— Ch. Ch., 189, 208
— Exeter Coll., 151, 157, 197
— Jesus Coll., 162
— Linc. Coll., 3, 162, 194, 203, 206, 208, 211, 214
— Magd. Coll., 4, 162, 210, 215
— Magd. Hall, 202
— Mert. Coll., 8, 202, 209, 210
— Oriel Coll., 163, 209
— Pemb. Coll., 158
— Queen's Coll., 141, 156, 162-3, 170, 191-2, 196-200, 216
— Radcliffe Library, 206
— S. Ebbe's, 205
— S. Edm. H., 193, 195
— S. Mary's, 206
— Trin. Coll., 193, 196, 214
— Univ. Coll., 34, 48, 139, 170, 172-5, 189, 190, 196, 204-6, 208, 213-5
— Wadh. Coll., 151, 207
— Worc. Coll., 194

Paddington. S. Mary's, 183
Parbroath 211
Pateley Bridge 159
Peel 195
Penistone 146, 182, 204, 207, 216
Pennigent 207
Penrith Sch. 2, 197
Peterbro', S. Mary's, 183
Pocklington 132
Pontefract 204, 213
— Dean of, 33-4, 121
— Honor of, 106
— Sch. 34-5, 173, 176, 199
— Steward of, 8
— Trinities, 34, 173
— Vicar of, 184
Ponton Magna 203
Prescot Sch. 158
Preston 215, 235
Pudsey 179

Rastrick 128
Raughton Head 149, 219
Repton Sch. 125
Richmond Sch. 194, 199

(247)

INDEX OF PLACES.

Richmond, Trinity Ch. 194
Ridgewell 194
Ringstead 214
Ripley 180
Ripon 102, 105
— Canon of, 106, 192
— Sch. 163, 195, 197
Rochester Sch. 157
Romsley 158
Rossall Sch. 158
Rotherham 32, 221
— Sch. 35, 125, 176, 203
Rotherhithe 183
Rothwell 139, 204
Royston Sch. 3
Rudford 158
Rugby Sch. 240

S. Bees' Coll., 183-4, 197
S. Mary de Lode 193
Salisbury, Chanc. of, 189
Sandal, passim
— Carre 43, 227
— Castle Lodge 106
— Endowed Sch. 214
— Hall 104-5
— Milnethorpe 9, 43, 46, 97, 106, 220, 227
— Vicar of, 103, 153, 156, 158, 214
Sarum, Preb. of, 205
Saxton 148-9
Scampston 212
Scarboro' 139
Seaton 218
Sedbergh Sch. 131, 197, 235
Sedgefield 202
Selbrooke 207
Selby 213
Settle 218-9
Sevenhampton 193
Sevenoaks Sch. 1, 160
Sharlston 207
Shelley 209
Sherborne Sch. 149, 197
Sherburn 143, 211
Shipton Sch. 136-7
Skipton Sch. 197
Smallfield 204
Snaith 221
Snapethorpe 217
Somersby 213-4
Soothill 98
Southampton Sch. 229
South Hackney 160
Southowram 120, 123, 215
Southport 221
South Shields 196

South Stainley 193
Southwark Sch. 160
Southwell 215
Sowerby Bridge 143
Spalding School 207
Spofforth 197
Spotborough 203, 210
Springthorpe 211
Stafford 171, 191
Staincliffe 42
Staineley 213
Standley (Stanley) 7
Stanley, passim.
— Clarke Hall, 9, 218-9
— Field Head, 103-4
— Hall, 104-5, 220
— Moor House, 29, 52, 104
— Vicar of, 218
— Windehill, 40
Stathern 193
Stock 203
Stockport Sch. 2
Stonehouse 193
Stonyhurst Coll. 175
Stony Stratford 195
Storrington 214
Stowe 221
Streethorpe 213
Stretton 202
Stroud 159
Sunderland 195
Sutton 205
Swafield 192
Swillington 104, 143, 164
— Sch., 34, 173
Swinderby 215

Tadcaster 139
Taunton, S. Mary's, 195
— Sch., 161
Thames 221
Thirsk 184
Thorner 194
Thornes, passim.
— Curate of, 159, 163
— Farholme, 42,
— Holme, 41
— Holmefield, 105, 182
— Lawefield, 42
— Moor, 41
— Morecroft, 41
— Narholme, 42
— Netherfield, 42
— Rishie Lands, 42
Thorney 213
Thornhill 8, 36, 203
— Lees, 184
Thornton-in-Ribblesdale 215

Thorparch 20, 36
Thorparch, Vicar of, 197
Thorpe-on-the-Hill 204
Thrapston 214
Thurnscoe 211
Todmorden 219
Tonbridge Sch. 159
Tong 205
Travancore 184
Tudeley 157
Tunbridge Wells 222

Utrecht 216

Virginia 215

Wakefield, passim.
— Allyson Rawe, 40
— Almshouse Lane, 27
— Asylum, 146
— Battle of, 90
— Bitchehill, 38
— Black Rock, 208
— Black Swan, 40
— Borough Market, 26
— Breadbooths, 37, 43
— Brooksbank, 38
— Broom Hall, 197
— Bull and Mouth, 102
— Bull Ring, 43
— Butcher Rawe, 39
— Calder Grove, 105
— Cambden Lecturer, 142, 146
— Canon of, 106, 192
— Cathedral (see Par. Ch.)
— Cemetery, 105
— Christ Ch., 163
— Church Inst., 149
— Church Porch, 6, 20, 45, 55, 91
— Church Sceele, 37
— Cliffe Hill, 30
— Cliffe House, 102, 104, 106
— Cliffield, 40-1, 45, 51
— Constable of, 102-5
— Corn Exch., 29
— Corporation, 97
— Cross Chamber, 143
— Cross Keys, 40
— Curate of, 5, 50, 100, 103-5, 115, 142, 154, 181-2
— Gaol, 98-9, 103, 145, 184, 195, 205, 218
— Golden Cock, 40
— Goodybower, 19, 21, 35-6
— Greencoat Sch., 157, 161, 186
— Haselden Hall 9, 19, 21, 36
— Horshead, 40

INDEX OF PLACES.

Wakefield, Lecturer of, 83, 101, 130, 132, 142, 144-6, 149, 217
— Manor, 9. 97-100, 191
— Mayor of, 96-100, 106
— Mechanics' Inst., 147
— Milnes House, 105?
— Northgate Head, 10
— Old Hall, 103
— Outlane, 39
— Parish Ch. (or Cathedral), 3-6, 18, 33, 36, 99, 105, 128, 131, 149, 151, 203, 206, 212
— Parish Registers, 122, 124, 127, 130, 133, 136
— Parson Flatt, 42
— Pilkington Chapel, 100, 128
— Radcliffe House, 222
— Reader of, 156
— Rectory, 43
— Red Hall, 221
— Rolls Office, 191
— S. Andrew's, 149, 159
— S. John's, 158, 161, 193, 206
— S. Mary's 158, 161
— S. Michael's, 161
— School Board, 96
— Six Chimneys, 101, 103, 216
— Skitterick Brook, 37, 116

Wakefield, Softs, 37
— Swalling Stones, 45
— Swan Lane, 40
— Trinity Ch., 106, 160-1, 184
— Vicar of 4, 5, 50-1, 89, 90, 95, 98, 100-6, 114, 129, 135-8, 153, 177-8, 180-1, 191-2, 226
— Westfield House, 105
— Zion Chapel, 182
Waghen 193
Waltham 212
Walton 105, 141, 204, 219, 222
Wanstead 220
Warmfield 38-9
— Vicar of, 100, 104-5, 177-8
— Curate of, 103
Warrington Sch. 234
Weaste 149, 193
Weeton 105, 222
Wellow Park 213
Westminster 1, 3, 129, 206, 240
Weston-super-Mare 159
Wheldale 197
Willesden 157
Willingham 211
Winceby, Battle of, 203
Winchester Coll. 2, 129, 206, 240

Winchester, Dean of, 188
Windermere 141
Windsor 202, 206
Winthorpe 212
Wisbech 221
Witcham and Wichford 190
Witton Sch. 235
Woodhall 122
Woodkirk 2, 3, 241
Woodthorpe 43, 103, 227
Woolley 101, 206, 210
Worcester, Bish. of, 207, 234
— Preb. of. 202, 207
Worsbrough 132, 208
Wotton-under-Edge 17
Wreay Sch. 235
Wrenthorpe Hall 98, 100
Wrotham 183
Wycliff 214

York 105, 203, 206-7, 209, 213
—Archb. of, 3, 13, 39, 59, 87-8, 113, 118, 121, 130, 132-3, 135, 137, 141, 148
— Castle, 153
— Preb. of, 135, 153, 164
— Recorder of, 94
— S. Peter's Sch. 199
Yorkshire, Sheriff of, 93

III. INDEX OF PERSONS.

Addinell Mr. 168
Ainley F. W. 184, 195
Alder G. W. 218
Alderson P. 39; H. E. 195; W. H. 184, 196; W. T. 184, 195
Allison J. 217; W. 157
Allott B. 203, 213; E. 203; G. 208; J. 39; R. 104, 203; W. 203, 208
Ambler G. 182, 191; J. 170, 211; R. 182
Amory R. 102; T. 102
Andrews H. 103
Anne, Princess 206; Queen 208
Armitage C. 207; H. 191; J. 101, 103, 112, 191, 207; S. 103; W. 41, 46
Arnett (Arnott) G. 101, 138, 211; M. R. 103, 211
Arthington H. 7-9, 45, 87, 97
Arundel (-ll) H. 224; R. 37
Ash W. 220
Ashton J. W. 196; W. 196
Askewe R. 43
Atha J. R. 159
Atkinson C. 28, 141, 143, 190; C. M. 184, 195; E. 142, 180; G. J. 220; R. 142-3, 190; W. 141; W. C. 143
Awdesley R. 46
Awdsley H. 208; T. 208

Bacon M. 89, 102
Bakewell W. 218
Ball C. 199; C. J. 199; T. 170, 212
Banister J. 170
Banks W. S. 33, 38
Barber A. 168
Barff (Bargh) J. 83, 105; T. 80, 100, 104
Barker E. 170; G. D. 104, 217; J. 105
Barraclough J. B. 220
Barstow J. 7
Baskerville J. 114, 128-30, 205; T. 128, 205
Bate L. 38
Battison G. 204; S. 204
Batty (Battie, Battye) E. 44; J. 7, 8, 10, 34, 37, 41-4, 75-6, 78-9, 87, 97-8, 167

Baudiss F. de 161
Baynes B 188; W. 188
Beaumont (-d) A. 207; H. 108, 221; J. 114-9, 152; R. 207
Becher W. 215
Beckett G. 104; J. W. 220
Beeston R. 46
Beever (Bever) A. 82, 101, 130, 134, 168; J. 207; Mr. 186; W. 207
Bell C. 182, 191; J. 191, 199; R. 182
Belt W. 94
Benlowes G. 180
Benson J. 47; R. 100
Bennett J. 39
Bentley (Bentlay) J. 210; M. 46; R. 128-9, 135, 137, 207-8, 210; T. 207
Berry J. W. 217
Bestwicke J. 43
Beverley H. A. 222; J. 183, 195; R. 170
Bevers R. 168
Bickerstaff W. 159
Billington J. 219
Bingham F. 208; J. 129, 130, 175, 208
Bingley Lord 100
Binns T. 99
Birkdall K. 39
Birkhead (-de) M. 45; N. 45; R. 80, 99, 172; T. 101, 168
Bittleston E. 193; T. 193
Bland F. 170; T. 170
Booth J. S. 107; M. 204; W. 204
Boteler T. 234
Boulton (Bolton) E. 127; F. 127; J. 27, 114, 127-8; M. 127; S. 127; T. A. 218
Bourne J. G. 163
Bowdin R. H. 196; W. 196
Bowditch W. L. 183, 195, 200; W. R. 183
Bowling (Boll-) J. 127; R. 170
Boyes J 121
Bradford (-rde, -rth) E. 39; Mr. 46; R. 8, 9, 97
Bradley J. 39, 46
Bradsbury J. 188; N. 188
Brady R. 235
Bragg T. 168

Bramley T. 39, 40; W. S. 220
Branthwayte W. 117
Brear H. 221
Brewerton G. 172, 195; W. 172
Briggs (-es) F. 184; J. 190; J. E. 184, 196; M. 42; W. 99, 221
Brocklebank Mr. 156
Bromhead J. 47; W. 39
Bromley J. 51, 101, 134, 168, 172
Brook (-ke) G. 38; H. A. 163; S. 143; T. 81, 100, 132; W. 104
Brown (-ne) B. 218; J. 176; Mrs. 47; W. 103, 112, 156
Brownlow R. 95, 99, 204; T. 204
Buck S. 215
Buckley A. 194; R. C. 219
Buckler 21
Bull H. W. 160
Bullock R. 174; R. G. P. 174, 196; W. 23
Bunny (-ye) R. 20
Burdakin B. 182; J. 171, 182, 191
Burnley 32
Burrell J. 217
Burrow (-we) R, 42, 89, 154; T. 46-7, 89, 94, 98; W. 154
Burton Capt. 23, 168; C. 170; H. 7; L. 170, 213-4; R. 102, 170, 214; W. 213
Buxton E. 101, 168; J. 181, 189; R. 102

Callis R. 203; T. 203
Camidge C. J. 105
Carlisle N. 21, 54, 228, 231, 235
Carr J. F. 105; Mr. 23, 182; S. 170, 182, 190
Carter F. M. B. 184; H. M. 184, 222; J. 28, 148, 193, 219; J. H. 193
Cartmell B. 153
Cartwright C. 214; E. 175, 215; W. 214-5
Casson H. 47; R. 204
Caumont M. 161
Cave C. 39; F. A. C. B. 220; T. 7-9, 34, 36-8, 97, 177
Cayley M. 209; R. 209; T. 169, 211

(250)

INDEX OF PERSONS.

Chadburne R. 41
Chadderton L. 117
Chadwick E. 184; H. M. 171, 184, 197, 200
Chamberlain W. B. 221
Chapman C. 221
Charles I. 90, 203; II. 128, 204
Charlesworth J. B. 105; J. C. D. 32, 52, 105
Charlett A. 129, 172
Charnock G. 102; J. 103; J. H. 112; W. 102-3, 168
Cheetham R. 103
Cheriholme (Chieri-) T. 80, 100
Childe H. S. 223
Chipchase J. 168
Christie G. J. B. 184; J. J. 184
Christopherson B. 159
Clark (-ke) A 1, 133; B. 133; D. 168; E. 130, 131, 133, 167, 171; E. T. 221; F. 133, 139; H. 133; J. 24, 27, 129, 133, 136-41, 145, 152, 155, 169, 201, 240; L. 133; R. 204; S. 133; T. 22-3, 82, 129, 130, 132-5, 137, 139, 154, 164, 167-8; W. 38, 204
Clay C. 219
Clayton (Cle-, Clai-) J. 95-6, 99, 168; L. 132; R. 8, 9, 20, 34, 36-7, 39, 87, 97
Clough J. 100
Coates R. 204; T. 204
Cockill R. 45
Coldwell W. E. 171, 191
Colet Dean 236, 241
Collins J. 170, 215
Collyer J. 154
Comber T. 216
Commenius J. A. 232
Connor J. 107; T. II. 221
Cooke G. 213; J. 190; R. 36, 39, 47, 190; T. 95, 98
Cookson J. 102; J. II. 219; L. 35
Cooper S. 189
Copley E. 50
Coppendale D. 181; J. 169, 181, 189, 209; W. 100, 130, 168, 209
Cotton G. 168
Cottoril E. 170
Coupland F. T. 224
Cowpe J. 168, 211
Cowper H. 43
Cranbrook Visc. 104
Craven R. 218; W. 107
Cresswell D. 216

Cressy (-ye) H. 45, 76, 78, 88, 97, 179, 202, 226; H. P. 122, 202
Creyke R. 210
Crompton Mr. 36
Cromwell O. 90
Crouch J. P. 225
Crownfield C. 172
Cudworth J. 44
Cumberland R. 128

Dade T. 170, 212
Dammann K. 159
Darley J. B. 170, 213
Daubeny W. H. 162
Davies A. R. 164
Dawson B. 181, 189; J. 168, 189; J. K. 217; W. 104, 112
Denham W. E. 221
Denison T. 50, 99; W. 51, 80, 99, 127
Denton E. O. 221; R. 181; T. 181, 189
Denyer E. E. 159
Dewhirst J. 210
Dibb C. J. 219; J. H. 222
Dickson R. 36
Dighton D. 42, 46
Dinisoun T. 46
Disney J. 215
Dixon D. G. 192; J. 168, 191
Dobbs J. 213
Dodgson N. 99
Dodsworth E. 206; M. 206; R. 9, 19, 21, 47
Dolliffe R. 42
Donatt H. 163
Doughty (-tie) A. 124; E. 124; G. B. 220; H. 91, 123, 153; J. 124-5, 127; R. 27, 49, 50, 78, 88-92 98, 114, 123-5, 128-9, 179, 205; S. 124; T. 124, 188, 205; W. 123, 188
Drake J. 104, 207; N. 207
Dransfield F. 154, 188; S. 154, 188
Driffield C. 168
Dring E. 169, 210
Dunn E. 194; R. 105; T. 194
Dunwell F. H. 192, 199; J. 192
Dymond R. 46

Eastmead J. S. 106-7
Edmonds (-munds) A. J. 159; E. 170; T. 208
Edward VI. 4
Eldon Lord 15, 25, 145, 228
Elizabeth Queen 8, 10, 54, 231

Ellerby T. 190; W. 170, 175, 190
Ellershaw R. 180
Ellerton G. V. 219
Elliott W. 20, 46
Ellis (-iss) M. 154; R. 80-1, 100; W. R. 191
Ellison J. 103
Elmsall R. 47
England Mr. 186
Eve H. W. 161

Fairborne Mr. 168
Fairfax T. 90
Falkland Visc. 202
Farrer A. 132; E. 81, 131-2, 238; J 131; M. 132
Favell C. 170, 182, 190; H. 182
Fenay N. 81, 100, 132
Fennell W. 218
Fenton W. 170
Fernandes C. B. L. 220; H. W. L. 221; J. L. 105; N L. 217
Field (-e, Feild) J. 4, 23, 170; R 41-2, 46
Fierville M. 159
Fitz-Stephen 233
Fitzwilliam Earl 28
Flatman C. 219
Fleming (-ynge) J. 45, 75, 86, 97, 210; R. 3, 37; W. 210
Foljambe T. 182
Foord B. 170, 214
Forman J. 3
Forster B. 142
Foster J. 168
Fox W. 104
Fowke M. 131; P. 131
Fowler J. 224
Franke C. 204; J. 204
Freeman J. M. 103
Freeston J. 34-5, 173, 175; R. 176; W. 176
Frobisher M. 4
Fulford H. W. 180

Gargrave Mr. 26, 159, 168; R. 44
Garlick J. 155, 181, 189
Garnet B. 47
Garvey (Gervy) S. 114, 125-7, 129
Gee R. 215
Gerrarde S. 14
Gibson J. 53-4, 75, 114, 118-121, 190; R. 39, 121; S. 121
Gilby W. R 104

(251)

INDEX OF PERSONS.

Gilderdale W. 221
Gill F. 218; W. 168-9, 211;
 W. H, 106
Glendower 15
Glover B. F. 219; J. 83-4,
 103-4
Goldsmith O. 136
Goldstein J. 159
Goldthorp A. 219
Gomersall W. J. 195
Goodair J. 171, 216
Goodison B. 24
Goodliffe J. 162
Goodwyn W. 39
Gothard J. 151
Grace C. M. 196, 200 : W. 196
Grant (Graunt,-te) A. 34; F. 6,
 33, 37
Green (Grene) E. 106; H. 102;
 H. G. E. 221; J. 212;
 M. A. E. 1; N. 221; R. 102;
 T. 46 : W. 170, 212
Green (Grene-) J. 79, 98; M.
 42
Grey Lord 205
Grice (-yce) H. 19, 33, 35, 45,
 98

Haigh (Hagge, Hague) A. 89;
 J. 220; T. 105; T. W. 107
Haldane G. 218; J. H. 219
Hall A. 170; C. W. 222; G. &
 J. 150-1; R. 147; S. 189;
 W. 189
Halliwell H. A. 223
Hamer T. G. 218
Hamshier E. 40
Hardcastle C. 221; H. 192;
 J. 83, 105, 192; T. 170, 205,
 216; W. 205, 216
Hardy (-ye) F. 42; J. 104; T.
 103
Hare A. 203; R. 203
Hargraves (-ave, -eaves) J. 104,
 181, 189, 208; N. 189; W.
 181, 190
Harrison E. 107; R. 155, 181,
 189; T. 37, 44, 189; W. 95,
 99, 155
Hartley R. 148, 155; W. 155
Harwood, W. H. 162
Haslegrave J 106, 191, 220
Hastings E. 197
Hatfeild A. 102; G. 43
Haward W. 100-1, 169, 210-11
Hawkesworth T. 39, 45
Haxby S. H. 218
Head C. H. 163

Heald T. 209; W. 23, 209;
 W. T. 221
Hemingway E. 120; J. 112;
 R. 120
Henderson W. G. 151
Henry VIII. 1, 3, 4
Hepworth J. 170, 212
Heron E. 176; T. 199
Hewetson T. 103
Hewett G. A. 177, 192; J. 42
Hey F. 88-9, 98
Heyolt (see Oley)
Heywood A. 104; O. 121
Hick H. 222
Higgins T. S. 219
Hill G. 43
Hobson E. 204; J. 207; R.
 204
Hodgson C. 102, 169, 210; J.
 194
Hodson C. E. 220
Hoile N. 40
Holden H. 121
Holdsworth (Haldes-) C. 95,
 99; G. A. 193; J. 37, 99,
 205; T. H. 105
Hollings C. 41
Holmes J. 155; R. 155; R. E.
 196; R. H. 196; T. 102
Hoole C. 125, 129, 203, 232-3
Hopkinson R. 168
Hopton I. 203; R. 203
Horn (-ne) C. 50, 95, 98, 100,
 179; T. 101, 168; W. 170
Horner H. 221
Horrax (-ocks) J. 156, 170,
 211
Horsfall T. G. 220
Horsfield T. 80, 100
Hotchkis. J. 169, 211
Howden T. 218
Howgate J. F. 218
Hoyland E 169, 210; J. 210
Hudson M. 155; T. 155, 212
Hughes A. McC. 163
Hunter G H. 196
Huntingdon Earl 197
Hurst F. T. 194; J. D. 171,
 191; W. 192, 218
Hurt F. W. R. 225
Hutchinson S. 169, 210
Hutton M. 122

Ianson J. F. 222
Ingram G. 169, 210; W. 168
Isaac (Isack) A. 122; E. 122;
 P 49, 76-8, 114, 121
Isott, J. 92, 95, 99

Jackson J. 41, 75-6, 86, 97
Jacob T. E. 161
Jaques J. G. 163
Jebb R. C. 128
Jenkinson J. 46
Jessop G. 211; W. 211
Johnson A. 102, 168; J H. 175;
 R. T. 175, 196, 200; S. 15,
 214, 231
Jolliffe Mr. 139
Jones W. B. 159

Katharine Queen 202
Kay A. 168; R. 43, 46, 88, 98
Keighley H. G. 222
Kelly J. 182; J. B. 182, 193
Kemp B. 218, 221
Kendell D. B. 30 105
Kennedy C. M. 217; J. 217
Kennett B. 103
Kenworthy H. W. 222
Kershaw (Kirs-) J. 160, 183,
 195, 200; J. B. 164; R. 180;
 S. 180
Keyser (-ar) J. 88-9, 95, 98
Kilby R. H., 193; T. 104
King W. 222
Kirk E. 154
Klem L. 163
Knowles (-olles) J. 271; S. 168;
 T 4

Laburn (-orne, Lay-) O. 7, 37, 43
Lacey G. F. 161; T. A. 161
Lake A. L. 221; J. W. 221
Lambert C. A. 222; W. 186
Lamplugh W. 210
Lane R. 28, 32
Langford B. R. 104
Langhorne J. 157
Langton B. 214
Lawson C. 171, 191; Mr. 154
Learoyd F C. 163
Leatham W. H. 8, 30, 105
Lee (Leigh) H. 106-7; O. 80,
 89, 100, 180; R. 23-5; W.
 H. 106-7; W. T. 104
Leighton J. L. 150; R. L. 114,
 150-1
Lester C. 222; J. H. 160
Lilley T. 169
Lillistone J. S. 157
Linfield R. P. 220
Linley Mr. 168
Lister (Lyster) H 218; J. 95,
 99, 125-6, 152-3, 180, 210,
 226; M. 46, 226, ; R. 4, 43,
 75, 86, 97, 226; W. 39, 45,
 54, 75-6, 78, 97

(252)

INDEX OF PERSONS.

Lockwood and Mawson 32
Long E. 146 ; R. 146
Longley J. 46
Lonsdale H. G. 104, 216 ; J. 170, 214
Lord J. 170
Lowther J. 168, 210 ; J. J. 169, 177
Lumb (Lomme, Lumme) F. 191 ; H. 171 ; R. 46–7 ; T. 39
Lumley T. 213
Lumley Viscountess 136
Lupton J. 157 ; J. H. 1, 3, 91, 136, 157, 171, 194 ; W. 168
Lynch E. M. 162
Lyon (Lion) Dr. 149 ; J. 88, 95, 98

Mackenzie A. 224 ; R. 170
Mackie R. B. 105
Madden B. H. 184 ; J. M. 161; W. H. 221 ; W. M. 106–8, 161, 184, 195
Maddison G. 212
Magrath Dr. 199
Malim A. 221
Mander G. 106
Manley G. 197 ; G. T. 197
Marks J. C. 107–8 ; W. W. 221
Marrowe J. 181
Marsden G. 103 ; H. J. E. 223; J. 37 ; T. 203 ; W. 27
Mason J. 219
Mathew T. 119
Matthewman J. 220
Mattison R. 170
Maude (Mawde) A. 114, 166, 178, 180 ; D. 80, 99, 100, 102–3 ; E. 6–7, 18, 36–7, 87, 114–6 ; F. 101–2, 168 ; J. 7, 20, 29, 30, 42, 52, 75–6, 86, 88, 97, 99, 101–2, 104, 115, 126, 168 ; S. 153 ; T. 98, 115
Maw J. H. 103
Meade Mr. 156
Meager M. 99
Meek Mrs. 137
Mercer R. 6, 33
Metcalfe O. 163
Mexborough Earl 28, 105
Miall L. C. 108
Micklethwaite A. 220 ; F. 220
Milner R. 205
Milnes E. 222 ; F. G. 221 ; J. 168 ; R. 168 ; W. H. 206
Milthorp F. 106
Milton 179, 180

Mitchell C. 225
Molyneux F. 213
Mompesson G. 209 ; W. 209
Monkhouse (Munk-) Dr. 89, 90, 103 ; W. 199
Moore S. 168 ; T. 101
Moorhouse (More-) G. 106 ; T. P. 222 ; W. 47
Morewood A. 185 ; J. 185
Morgan J. J. 162 ; W. L. G. 159
Morrison H. S. 224
Morton Bishop 115, 202 ; C. 175 ; F. A. 175
Mounson R. 37, 204
Mowbray J. 38, 118
Moxon (Mogson) J. 92, 204 ; P. 95, 99, 204
Murgatroyd R. 154 ; T. 137, 155, 169

Naylor (Nai-, -er) C. 40, 45, 76, 78–81, 88-9, 181, 188 ; E. 168 ; G. 42 ; J. 104, 177, 202 ; M. E. 148, 217 ; M. J. 28, 114, 146-8, 201 ; W. 104, 188
Nettleton C. E. 220
Nevile (-ill) C. 101, 172 ; F. 100, 132 ; G. 95, 99, 169, 213 ; J. 99 ; S. 100 ; T. 170
Nevinson W. 102, 168
Newby (-ie) J. 47, 170, 213 ; H. 213
Newcastle Duke of 139
Newstead R. 51, 168
Norcliffe C. B. 153
Norfolk R. 89, 99, 100
North R. 169
Norton E 170. 214 ; T. 95, 99, 102

Oates J. 168 ; T. 102 ; W. 101, 168
O'Donohoe J. P. 175 ; M. 175
O'Dwyer A. 217
Oldroyd R. 37
Oley B. 122, 202 ; D. 92, 95, 99, 126
Ouldfield 178, 180
Oxley G. 103

Paley J. 154
Parkin E. 224
Patten (-on) R. 47 ; T. 41
Paul L. 181 ; S. 181, 189
Paulden G. 45–7 ; W. 27, 95, 98

Payne T. C. P. 174
Peacock M. 151 ; M. H. 114, 151
Pearson F. W. 197 ; G. 221 ; R. 190 ; W. 197
Pease T. 92, 99, 125–6
Pegge (Peck) 9 ; S. 169, 210
Pell D. 204 ; W. 204
Perkins A. 155 ; J. 155 ; T. 170, 211
Peterson A. 103, 171, 216 ; A. T. T. 217 ; H. 103.
Phear Dr. 125
Phillimore R. P. 162
Phillips W. 159
Pickersgill J. 185–6
Pighills R. 41–2
Pilkington L. 100–1 ; T. 45
Pilley F. G. 224
Pilling E. 159
Pindar N. 205 ; W. 175, 205
Pitt F. 82, 101, 134, 168
Place W. 222
Pocklington J. 170, 213 ; R. 170, 212
Pollard (-de) R. 8, 9, 42, 97 ; S. 182, 190 ; W. 7, 9, 41, 78–9, 98
Pope W. H. 220
Poppleton W. 218
Popplewell E. 190 ; J. 190
Potter J. 52, 89, 99, 129, 130, 175, 208 ; T. 208
Powell (Poile) R. 46 ; W. E. 162
Preston T. 170
Price C. P. 162
Primrose Dr. 136
Proud M. 112
Pullan (-ein, -on) B. 182 ; J. 30, 83, 105, 219

Quenedy D. 159, 171

Radcliffe (Rat-) G. 92, 99, 126, 205 ; J. 99, 127, 129, 175, 205, 208 ; R. 121
Ramsden J. 170, 175, 215
Randall R. B. 221
Rawlin (-ing) F. 156 ; T. 121
Rawsoun J. 47
Rayner J. 194 ; R. 104
Rayney F. 206 ; H. 206
Read R. 168
Readhead O. 23
Reddall D. 156, 172
Redshaw G. 100
Reid L. T. 196 ; T. 196

INDEX OF PERSONS.

Reynolds H. W. 115 ; R. 106
Rheinhardt G. B. 217 ; J. 218
Rhodes (Rodes, Roo-, Roa-), A. 122 ; J. W. 193 ; W. 20, 44, 75-6, 87
Richardson E. 171, 191 ; J. 40 ; S. 101, 168 ; W. 43
Rickaby J. 102-3, 170, 215
Riddlesden W. 47
Ridsdale E. 102-3 ; G. 103 ; J. 102-3
Riley (Ry-) J. 178, 180 ; S. 170
Rishworth T. 104
Robarts E. 45
Robertson T. 4
Robinson E. 205 ; F. 43 ; H. 169, 211 ; J. 80, 89, 99, 126, 189, 190, 205 ; M. 23 ; T. 7, 8, 20, 34, 40, 75-6, 78, 87, 97, 144, 171, 190, 205
Robson R. 43
Rogers C. 143 ; E. 145 ; J. 143 ; T. 28, 143-6, 148, 191
Rooe J. 89, 94, 99
Roundall R. 170, 175, 215
Routh G. 170, 213
Rowley W. 221
Ruecastle J. 181 ; W. 181, 186, 189
Russell W. A. 163

Sacheverel W. 169, 210
Sager J. 168
Sandars G. 105
Sanderson T. J. 150, 160, 183, 195, 200 ; T. K. 407
Saunders R. 114, 121
Savile (-il, -el, -ell, -ille, Say-) A. 45 ; C. 168 ; D. 9 ; E. 7, 46 ; F. 46 ; G. 7, 8, 9, 19, 20, 34-6, 49, 87, 97, 117 ; H. 8 ; J. 8, 36, 49, 50, 87-8, 93-4, 97-8, 117 ; J. S. 221 ; Mr. 46 ; P. Y. 31, 84, 105 ; R. 34, 45 ; S. 37 ; T. 27 ; W. 8, 9, 20, 34, 36, 45, 54, 75-6, 78, 87, 97, 121, 167, 221
Scatcherd (Sk-) A. 43, 75-6, 78-9, 87, 97
Schorey J. B. 199 ; T. 199
Scoley T. 39
Scott G. H. 196 ; H. C. 196 ; J. 81, 100, 132, 168, 175, 189, 220 ; T. 82, 100, 132, 134, 181
Scrooby J. 168
Secker T. 219
Senior G. 207 ; J. 207, 217 ; T. 47, 122, 207, 219 ; W. 223

Serjeantson W. 102
Seton I. 211 ; J. 211
Sewell (Su-) H. 20, 36
Seymour E. 170
Shackleton W. 156
Sharp (-pe) H. 23 ; J. 132, 171, 194 ; S. 83-4, 90, 104, 147, 191-2 ; W. 192
Shaw A. 209 ; G. 189 ; J. 112 ; S. 209 ; T. H. 183, 195, 237 ; W. 189, 209
Shelmendine W. 154
Shelton T. 100, 132
Shepherd (-ard) E. 218 ; H. 214 ; J. 171, 189, 190 ; S. 168, 189
Shepley M. 168 ; W. 41
Shillito M. 168
Shutlworth R. 89
Siddall J. 47
Sill D. 101, 134, 209, 211 ; E. 211 ; J. 51, 82, 101-2, 134 ; T. 80, 100-1, 168, 209
Sim (Sym) C. 40 ; O. C. 157
Simpson C. H. 220 ; J. 171, 215 ; J. P. 30, 83-4, 105
Sisson J. L. 156, 192, 200 ; R. S. 218
Skelton J. 159, 169, 171, 182, 190
Slack S. B. 162
Slinger T. 207
Smalfoot R. 41
Smallpage D. 103 ; J. 112, 143 ; S. 171, 190, 216
Smith (-yth, -ythe) C. 34 ; Dr. 178 ; F. 222 ; J. 81, 100-4, 132, 168 ; J. G. 105 ; J. H. 104-5 ; K. 181 ; R. 42, 101, 168 ; T. 70, 215 ; W. 41, 46
Smithson C. O. 221 ; J. 104 ; R. 104
Snape R. 156
Snowden (-aw-) E. 39 ; R. 156, 199 ; W. 104, 156
Somaster (-estar) F. 89, 100 ; T. 46, 79, 95, 98
Sonyer (-ior) T. 44, 46, 122
Spink (-e) A. 154 ; C. P. 223 ; J. 101 : S. 133 ; W. 82, 101, 134, 168
Spivy (-ye) E. 40 ; G. 34, 36, 40, 47, 76, 98
Spong W. 221
Spooner J. 168
Stable J. 42
Standish F. 215 ; T. 215
Stansfield J. 88, 98
Stapleton W. 126

Statter A. W. 221 ; W. 217 ; W. A. 27, 221
Staveley M. 213
Stead J. W. 222
Steer C. 102 ; W. 103
Steingass F. 161
Stephenson C. 199 ; D. 219 ; J. 199
Stevens T. 160
Stewart W. 31, 107, 147, 149 ; W. H. 106-7, 220
Stocks (-es) J. 46 ; S. 30
Stollard J. S. 161, 172
Storie (-y, -ye) J. 50-1, 79, 88, 95, 98, 124, 185, 203
Strafford Earl 202
Straton N. D. J. 106
Straubenzee C. S. van 103
Streete Mr. 166
Stringer R. 154, 189
Strong F. W. 162
Sunderland J. 37, 50 ; S. 182, 191
Swift (-e) R. 44, 47
Swire R. 170, 213 ; S. 175, 213-4
Sykes G. W. 175, 196 ; J. 131 ; R. 175

Tate J. 191 ; W. 191
Tavora Marquis 105
Taylor (Tailer) F. 47 ; H. M. 150, 194 ; J. 28-9, 30, 83-4, 114, 149, 150, 194-5, 237 ; J. H. 150, 194-5 ; J. W. 193 ; R. 79, 89 ; R. V. 153 ; T. 106, 208, 220 ; W. 208 ; W. W. 150, 195, 199
Teale J. 104
Tenison Archb. 208
Terry J. N. 219
Tew E. 83-4, 105 ; P. 106
Thomas W. 83-4, 104
Thompson (Thomson, Tomson) A. 215 ; B. 133-4 ; J. 47 ; R. 89, 175, 205 ; S. 168, 210 ; T. 47 ; W. 134, 210
Thornes J. 47
Thornton G. H. 223 ; J. 175, 197 ; R. 100-1 ; T. 101, 172
Thorold R. 170
Thorpe H. 102
Tidswell B. 182, 190 ; R. 182
Tilletson S. 121
Tilson J. 101, 168
Tomline M. 170, 212
Tomlinson E. 30, 83-4, 105 ; R. 183 ; W. 170, 212 ; W. H. B. 106

(254)

INDEX OF PERSONS.

Tootal Mr. 159; T. 105
Tossell J. G. 163, 172
Tottenham J. 103; L. A. 102-3
Tottie J. 47
Townend W. 222
Trollope A. 170, 212; T. A. 212
Tucker R. 170, 215
Turner W. 100, 135
Tyndall G. 20

Ubank Mr. 168
Usher S. 168
Uvedale A. 170, 212

Varley Mr. 186
Vernon W. 98
Vialls G. 32, 221

Waddington J. 168
Wade R. 157; T. 157; W. 189
Wadsworth, W. M. 195
Wainwright J. 218
Wakefield R. 4
Walker C. H. H. 175, 197; C. J. 175; G. 207, 209; H. 104, 112, 223; H. M. 184, 224; H. S. 223; J. 47, 168; J. W. 144; J. Y. 184; O. 206; T. 95, 99, 182, 184, 209; W. 83, 101, 112, 170, 182, 190; W. H. 184; W. J. 120
Waller (Waler) W. 92-3, 98
Wandesford C. 170
Warberton T. 168
Ward G. H. 220
Warriner R. 46
Washbourn J. A. R. 158: W. 158

Wastell J. 208; L. 208
Waterall J. 159
Waterhouse D. 188; H. 41; J. 92, 95, 99, 188; R. 41, 78, 98
Watkinson B. 81-2, 100, 132, 134, 168; E. 10, 40, 75, 87, 92, 95, 97, 99; H. 7, 8, 10, 40, 97; J. 81-2, 100, 132, 134, 168; Mr. 46; R. 33
Watson B. 106-7; J. 219; R. 101
Webster J. 170, 212; T. 212
Wells R. 170, 211 : T. 211
Wentworth G. 169, 210; J. 206; M. 101, 206; P. 102; T. 203; W. 203
Westerman G. H. 105
Westmorland J. 194
Wharton G. 39, 75, 98
Wheatley E. 168; F. 101; M. 168; T. 100-1
Whisson S. 172
Whitaker (-s) E. 36; J. 122. 177, 202
White F. 100; R. 189; T. 189
Whitham S. 107
Whitley J. 203; M. 203
Wice H. 195; J. H. 106-8, 195
Widrington T. 94
Wighton W. 170, 213
Wilberforce Archd. 150
Wilbie J. 153
Wilbore J. 40; L. 203; R. 203
Wilcock (-e) J. 153; Mr. 50; R. 43, 227
Wilkinson C. 218; J. E. 196; Mr. 156; Wm. 161
William Rufus 2
William III. 206

Wilsford R. 170, 213
Wilson A. 136, 168; B. 102, 114, 129, 135-8, 154, 168, 190; C. 92, 95, 99, 126, 204; E. 136; H. 155-6, 171; J. 92, 99, 126, 136, 181, 189; L. 39, 47, 88, 95, 98; R. 50, 99; T. 81-2, 100, 134, 138, 181, 189, 190; W. 136, 221
Wingfield M. 50-1, 185
Winter G. 203; R. 203
Winterbourne L. 205; M. 205
Witton (Wytton) R. 7, 75, 80-1, 95, 100-1, 132, 134, 168
Woffenden J. 47
Wolff H. D. 219
Wood (-e) A. à 9, 48-9; C. 168; E. 3, 4; F. H. 221; J. C. 158, M. 216; Mr. 159; T. 153; W. 216; W. D. 220; W. S. 192
Woodcock T. 193; V. W. 221; W. 169
Woodrove Mrs. 46
Woodward R. F. 158
Woollen J. 52, 189, 209
Wormald H. 84, 105
Worsfold J. N. 175; W. B. 175
Worsoppe E. 204; R. 205
Wray J. 181
Wright B. 181, 190; T. G. 105, 151; W. 181; W. H. 221

Young J. W. 161

Zouch C. 103, 158, 168, 211, 214; H. 102, 211; S. 102, T. 102-3, 129, 133, 135-8, 140-1, 148, 214, 240

(255)

ERRATA.

p. 9, l. 6, for Hasleden *read* Haselden.
p. 34, l. 6, for ten pounds *read* five pounds.
p. 48, l. 22, for £10 *read* £5.
p. 71, l. 33, for monthe *read* tenthe.
p. 170, l. 12, for Uredale *read* Uvedale.
p. 175, l. 29, for John *read* Joseph.
p. 181, l. 19, *read* see p. 155.

LIST OF SUBSCRIBERS.

Alderson, Rev. W. H., M.A., St. Bees, Cumberland.
Ashton, J. W., B.A., The Rectory, Fakenham, Norfolk.
Atkinson, Geo. James, Town Clerk of Liverpool.

Bailey, Geo., Marygate, York.
Banks, Wm., 46, Grey Street, Hull.
Boase, Rev. C. W., M.A., Exeter College, Oxford.
Beaumont, H., 38, Bond Street, Wakefield.
Benington, Henry, Wentworth Terrace, Wakefield.
Beverley, H. A., Walton House, Wakefield.
Bittleston, Rev. Edwin, M.A., South Stainley Vicarage, Ripley, Leeds.
Book Society, Wakefield (H. Benington).
Bradbury, W. H., 10, Bouverie Street, E.C.
Brear, Haydn, 76, Northgate, Wakefield.
Briggs, Wm., 4, South Parade, Wakefield.
Brown, Mrs. Henry, Westfield Terrace, Wakefield.
Bruce, Samuel, LL.B., St. John's House, Wakefield.
Bullock, Rev. R. G. P., M.A., St. Luke's Vicarage, Leeds.
Bullock, Rev. R., M.A., Denton Vicarage, Ben Rhydding, Leeds.

Calverley, Edmund, Oulton Hall, Leeds.
Cardwell, Jas., Bread Street, Wakefield.
Carter, Rev. J. H., M.A., Weaste Parsonage, Manchester.
Carter, H. M., Outwood Hall, Wakefield.
Carter, W. F., B.A., 33, Waterloo Street, Birmingham.
Cave, Rev. F. A. Cave Browne, M.A., Longridge Vicarage, Preston.
Chadwick, S. J., Lyndhurst, Dewsbury.
Charlesworth, John, Wakefield.
Childe, H. S., St. John's Villa, Wakefield.
Christie, Rev. G. J. B., B.A., Kirby Hill, Boroughbridge, Yorks.
Church Institution, Wakefield.
Clapham, Col. W. W., Crumpsall House, Manchester.
Clare College Library, Cambridge (Rev. H. W. Fulford, M.A., Librarian).
Clark, Robert, L.R.C.P., 78, Church Street, Lancaster.
Collins, F., M.D., Fulford, York.
Connor, T. H., Doncaster.

LIST OF SUBSCRIBERS.

Cradock, Percy S., Westfield House, Wakefield.
Crawley, Edward W., Acorn Villas, Ilkley.
Crouch, John Peachy, Doncaster.

Dawson, H. A., Redville, St. John's, Wakefield.
Denison, S., 32, Clarendon Road, Leeds.
Dickons, J. N., 12, Oak Villas, Manningham, Bradford.
Dixon, W. Vibart, Wakefield.
Dodgson, J., Leeds.
Dunn, Rev. T., M.A., Burton Vicarage, Neston, Cheshire.

Edleston, Rev. J., LL.D., Gainford Vicarage, near Darlington.

Farrah, John, Low Harrogate.
Farrer, John, Oulton, near Leeds.
Fennell, C. W., Westgate, Wakefield.
Fennell, Wm., Westgate, Wakefield.
Fernandes, J. L., Tavora House, Grange-over-Sands.

Galloway, F. C., Castle View, Biskey Howe Terrace, Bowness-on-Windermere.
Gerrard, J., Wakefield.
Greaves, J. O., St. John's, Wakefield.
Green, Sir. Edward, Bart., M.P., Nunthorpe Hall, York.
Green, H. G. E., St. John's, Wakefield.
Green, Hugo, St. John's, Wakefield.

Hainsworth, L., 120, Bowling Old Lane, Bradford.
Hall, G. and J., Wakefield.
Hall, Miss, Sandal Grange, near Wakefield.
Hardcastle, Mrs., The Towers, Bond Street, Wakefield.
Hardy, J. N., 1, St. John's Terrace, Wakefield.
Haslegrave, J., Stanley Hall, Wakefield.
Higgin, Geo., In the Ray, Maidenhead, Berks.
Holdsworth, Richard, Castle Lodge, Sandal.
Holdsworth, T. H., Sandal Hall.
Holmes, Rev. R. E., B.A., 4, Laygate Terrace, South Shields.
Howard, Dr. Altofts, Normanton.
Hudson, C. J., 4, Wentworth Terrace, Wakefield.

Ince, Rev. H. G., M.A., The Vicarage, Stanley.

LIST OF SUBSCRIBERS.

Jackson, Richard, Commercial Street, Leeds.
Johnson, R. T., B.A., 73, Albert Road, Southport

Kendell, D.B., M.B., Thornhill House, Walton.
Kershaw, J. B., M.A., The Grammar School, Wakefield.
Kingswell, W. H., Wakefield.

Latimer, Thomas, Woodlands Cottage, Sandal.
Leeds Library (F. E. Yates, Librarian).
Linfield, Rev. R. P., M.A., Elton, Bury, Lanc.
Lupton, Rev. J. H., M.A., 7, Earl's Terrace, Kensington Road, W.

Mackie, Col. E. A., Manor House, Heath, Wakefield.
Mackie, Miss E. G., St. John's, Wakefield. 2 Copies.
Magrath, Rev. J. R., D.D., Provost's Lodgings, Queen's College, Oxford.
Marshall, C. H., Silcoates House, near Wakefield.
Marks, J. C., St. John's, Wakefield.
Marks, W. W., The Embankment, Bedford.
Mason, Chas. Maurice, Idle, Bradford.
Mason, Henry, St. John's, Wakefield.
Miall, L. C., Professor, 5, Montpellier Terrace, Leeds
Milthorp, Francis, Fern Bank, St. John's, Wakefield.

New Book Club, Wakefield (J. F. Ianson).
Norcliffe, Rev. Chas. Best, M.A., Langton Hall, Malton, Yorks.

Oxley, Henry, 12, Bond Street, Wakefield.

Peacock, G. H., M.A., Christ's College, Brecon.
Peacock, M., Newton Park, Leeds.
Pearson, Geo., The Glen, Harrogate.
Perkin, F. K., Lansdowne Terrace, Wakefield.
Pickard, Wm., Registry House, Wakefield.
Pilley, F. G., Downing College, Cambridge.
Plews, Harry, 3, Westfield Park, Wakefield.
Powell, F. S., M.P., Horton Old Hall, Bradford.

Randall, Joseph, Bank Chambers, George Street, Sheffield.
Rayner, Joseph, M.A., New Sharlston, near Wakefield.
Roberts, A. H., 35, Virginia Road, Leeds.

LIST OF SUBSCRIBERS.

Roberts, C. C.. Snowhill Lodge, Wakefield.
Roberts, Geo., Lofthouse, Wakefield.
Rowley, Walter, F.S.A., Alder Hill, Meanwood, Leeds.

St. Paul's School Library, Hammersmith Road, W.
Sanderson, M. E., Wakefield.
Sanderson, T. K., Wakefield.
Sanderson, Rev. T. J., M.A., Brington Rectory, Huntingdon.
Scott, J., Almshouse Lane, Wakefield.
Scott, Rev. R. F., M.A., St. John's College, Cambridge.
Senior, Rev. Joseph, LL.D., 14, Trafalgar Square, Scarboro'.
Sharp, Rev. Canon. M.A., The Vicarage, Horbury.
Shaw, Rev. T. H., M.A., Everton Vicarage, near Sandy, Beds.
Skidmore, Chas., Stipendiary Magistrate, Bradford.
Smith, Mrs. Martha, Spring Bank House, Sandal.
Statter, A. W., Croft House, Rotherham.
Statter, W. A., Thornhill House, Wakefield.
Statter, W., Snapethorpe Hall, near Wakefield.
Stead, J. W. 23, Park Row, Leeds.
Stephenson, D., Eastmoor, Wakefield.
Stephenson, Simeon, Westfield Grove, Wakefield.
Stewart, Martin, Esq., M.A., F.G.S., Edgar House, Chester.
Stewart, W. H., Milnthorp House, Sandal.
Stollard, J. S., M.A., 12, Westfield Grove, Wakefield.
Straton, The Ven. Archdeacon, M.A., The Vicarage, Wakefield.
Stuart, J. Erskine, High Street, Heckmondwike.
Sutcliffe, John W., Goxhill, near Seaton, Hull.
Sykes, G. W., B.A., Red Hill, Castleford.
Sykes, John, M.D., F.S.A., Doncaster.
Sykes, Percival, 23, Broad Street, Ludlow, Salop.

Taylor, H. M., M.A., Trinity College, Cambridge.
Taylor, Rev. R. V., B.A., Melbecks Vicarage, near Richmond.
Taylor, Thomas, The Towers, Wakefield.
Taylor, W. W., M.A., 10, King Street, Oxford.
Tew, Percy, M.A., Heath Hall, Wakefield.
Tew, T. W., Carleton Grange, Pontefract. 2 Copies.
Tomlinson, W. H. B., Cliffe Field, Wakefield.
Tweedale, John, F.R.I., B.A., 12, South Parade, Leeds.

University College Library, Oxford (R. W. Macan).

LIST OF SUBSCRIBERS.

Vialls, Geo., 13, Grange Park, Ealing, W.

Wakefield, The Right Rev. the Lord Bishop of, Overthorpe, Dewsbury.
Wadsworth, Mrs. C. S., Belgravia Towers, St. John's, Wakefield.
Walker, Rev. H. Milnes, B.A., St. Peter's, Bishop Wearmouth, Sunderland.
Walker, J. W., F.S.A., Boyncliff, Wakefield.
Walker, W , Laurel Bank, Sandal.
Walley, Rev. S. C., B.A., Kirkthorpe Vicarage, near Wakefield.
Watson, B., Westgate, Wakefield.
Watson, Wm., The Gables, Wakefield.
Webster, Geo., 70, Westgate, Wakefield.
Whitehead, J W., St. John's Parade, Wakefield.
Whitehead, Joseph, York House, York Street, Wakefield.
Whiteley, Wm., Westbourne Grove, W.
Wice, J. H., St. John's, Wakefield.
Wood, B., Free Library, Bradford.
Wood, Rev. W. S., D.D., Higham Vicarage, Rochester.
Woodhead, Joseph, Longdenholme, Huddersfield.
Wright, T. G., M.D., Northgate, Wakefield.

www.ingramcontent.com/pod-product-compliance
Lightning Source LLC
Chambersburg PA
CBHW032055220426
43664CB00008B/1006